# Rethinking
### the Gospel Sources

# Rethinking
## the Gospel Sources

## From Proto-Mark to Mark

**DELBERT BURKETT**

T&T CLARK INTERNATIONAL
*A Continuum imprint*
NEW YORK • LONDON

T & T Clark International, Madison Square Park, 15 East 26th Street, New York, NY 10010

T & T Clark International, The Tower Building, 11 York Road, London SE1 7NX

T & T Clark International is a Continuum imprint.

Cover design: Thomas Costanzo

*Library of Congress Cataloging-in-Publication Data*

Burkett, Delbert Royce.
    Rethinking the Gospel sources : from proto-Mark to Mark / Delbert Burkett.
        p. cm.
    Includes bibliographical references.
    ISBN 0-567-02540-3 (hardcover) — ISBN 0-567-02550-0 (pbk.)
    1. Synoptic problem. 2. Bible. N.T. Gospels—Criticism, interpretation, etc. I. Title.
BS2555.52.B87 2004
226'.066—dc22

                                                                    2004003687


*Printed in the United States of America*


04 05 06 07 08 09     10 9 8 7 6 5 4 3 2 1

# *Contents*

# *Preface*

THIS BOOK IS THE FIRST of a projected three-volume study of the sources of the canonical Gospels. This first volume presents a new theory concerning the sources of Mark with its parallels in Matthew and/or Luke.

Except where indicated, I have used the Greek text common to the twenty-seventh edition of Nestle/Aland and the fourth edition of the United Bible Societies edition. If a different Greek text were used, a few of the details of my case might need to be modified, but none of the major points or conclusions. Where appeal to the Greek has not been necessary, I have used my own fairly literal English translation.

I am grateful to Louisiana State University for a sabbatical during the fall semester of 2002 that helped me to complete this work. I am also grateful to Professors William O. Walker Jr., Christopher Tuckett, and David Peabody for reading all or part of the manuscript and offering helpful suggestions.

# Abbreviations

| | |
|---|---|
| BETL | Bibliotheca ephemeridum theologicarum lovaniensium |
| CBQ | *Catholic Biblical Quarterly* |
| ETL | *Ephemerides theologicae lovanienses* |
| EuroJTh | *European Journal of Theology* |
| ICC | International Critical Commentary |
| JBL | *Journal of Biblical Literature* |
| JSNT | *Journal for the Study of the New Testament* |
| JSNTSup | Journal for the Study of the New Testament Supplement Series |
| NovT | *Novum Testamentum* |
| NTS | *New Testament Studies* |
| RB | *Revue biblique* |
| SBLMS | Society of Biblical Literature Monograph Series |
| SNTSMS | Society for New Testament Studies Monograph Series |
| TZ | *Theologische Zeitschrift* |
| WUNT | Wissenschaftliche Untersuchungen zum Neuen Testament |
| ZTK | *Zeitschrift für Theologie und Kirche* |

# CHAPTER 1

# *Introduction to the Problem*

THE SYNOPTIC PROBLEM remains one of the central unresolved issues in the study of the Gospels. Some sort of literary relationship exists between the three Synoptic Gospels, Matthew, Mark, and Luke. Since these gospels share many of the same stories and sayings in much the same order with much the same wording, they must in some way depend on each other or on the same written sources. But the exact nature of such dependence remains in dispute.

The simplest theories make one of these gospels the first and the other two dependent upon it. Thus there are theories of Matthean priority, Markan priority, and Lukan priority. Through the twentieth century down to the present, most scholars have advocated Markan priority, the view that Mark wrote first and that Matthew and Luke copied from Mark. The predominant theory advocating Markan priority has been the two-document hypothesis. This theory affirms that Matthew and Luke drew material from both Mark and a source or sources, now lost, designated "Q." In an expanded form of the theory, Matthew also used other material designated "M," while Luke used other material designated "L." First proposed by German scholars in the nineteenth century,[1] this theory received its classic statement for English-speaking scholars in the work of B. H. Streeter.[2] Streeter's work remains the standard

---

1. For the German origins of the two-document hypothesis, see Werner Georg Kümmel, *The New Testament: The History of the Investigation of Its Problems* (Nashville: Abingdon, 1972), 74–84, 146–55; William R. Farmer, *The Synoptic Problem: A Critical Analysis* (New York: Macmillan, 1964; repr. Dillsboro, NC: Western North Carolina Press, 1976), 1–47; Hajo Uden Meijboom, *A History and Critique of the Origin of the Marcan Hypothesis 1835–1866: A Contemporary Report Rediscovered* (trans. and ed. John J. Kiwiet; New Gospel Studies 8; Macon, GA: Mercer University Press, 1993). Hans-Herbert Stoldt gives a more polemical account in *History and Criticism of the Marcan Hypothesis* (Macon, GA: Mercer University Press; Edinburgh: T & T Clark, 1980), 1–131. See also David Laird Dungan, *A History of the Synoptic Problem: The Canon, the Text, the Composition, and the Interpretation of the Gospels* (New York: Doubleday, 1999).

2. Burnett Hillman Streeter, *The Four Gospels: A Study of Origins* (rev. ed.; London: Macmillan, 1930).

defense of this most widely held theory, though other significant defenses of it have followed.[3]

While the classical two-document hypothesis has predominated, it has never been able to shake off the criticism raised by the "minor agreements" of Matthew and Luke against Mark. These consist of places where Matthew and Luke supposedly follow Mark yet agree with each other against Mark. The two-document hypothesis explains these by appeal to variant readings in the manuscripts or independent redaction by Matthew and Luke. Scholars who find these explanations unconvincing have proposed several other theories that try to provide a more plausible explanation while retaining Markan priority. One such theory, now known as the "three-source hypothesis," starts with the two-document hypothesis but modifies it by supposing that Luke knew Matthew as well as Q and Mark. W. C. Allen held essentially this view, though he did not use the designation "Q."[4] More recent proponents include Robert H. Gundry[5] and Ron Price.[6] Another theory of Markan priority, pro-

3. E.g., Joseph A. Fitzmyer, "The Priority of Mark and the 'Q' Source in Luke," in *Jesus and Man's Hope* (ed. D. G. Miller; 2 vols.; Pittsburgh: Pittsburgh Theological Seminary, 1970), 1:131–70; repr. in Joseph A. Fitzmyer, *To Advance the Gospel: New Testament Studies* (New York: Crossroad, 1981), 3–40; Werner Georg Kümmel, *Introduction to the New Testament* (rev. ed.; Nashville: Abingdon, 1975), 38–80; Frans Neirynck, "Synoptic Problem," in *The Interpreter's Dictionary of the Bible, Supplement* (ed. Keith Krim; Nashville: Abingdon, 1976), 845a–48b; repr. in *The Two-Source Hypothesis: A Critical Appraisal* (ed. Arthur J. Bellinzoni Jr.; Macon, GA: Mercer University Press, 1985), 85–93; G. M. Styler, "The Priority of Mark," in C. F. D. Moule, *The Birth of the New Testament* (3rd ed.; San Francisco: Harper & Row, 1982), 285–316; Christopher M. Tuckett, *The Revival of the Griesbach Hypothesis: An Analysis and Appraisal* (SNTSMS 44; Cambridge/New York: Cambridge University Press, 1983); idem, "Synoptic Problem," in *The Anchor Bible Dictionary* (ed. D. N. Freedman; New York: Doubleday, 1992), 6.263–70; Peter M. Head, *Christology and the Synoptic Problem: An Argument for Markan Priority* (SNTSMS 94; Cambridge: Cambridge University Press, 1997); Robert H. Stein, *Studying the Synoptic Gospels: Origin and Interpretation* (2nd ed.; Grand Rapids: Baker, 2001); Scot McKnight, "A Generation Who Knew Not Streeter: The Case for Markan Priority," in *Rethinking the Synoptic Problem* (ed. David Alan Black and David R. Beck; Grand Rapids: Baker Academic, 2001), 65–95; Mark Goodacre, "Setting in Place the Cornerstone: The Priority of Mark," in idem, *The Case Against Q: Studies in Markan Priority and the Synoptic Problem* (Harrisburg, PA: Trinity Press International, 2002), 19–45.

4. Willougby C. Allen, *A Critical and Exegetical Commentary on the Gospel According to Matthew* (ICC; New York: Scribner's, 1907), xiii–lxii.

5. Robert H. Gundry, *Matthew: A Commentary on His Literary and Theological Art* (Grand Rapids: Eerdmans, 1982), 4–5; idem, "Matthean Foreign Bodies in Agreements of Luke with Matthew against Mark: Evidence that Luke Used Matthew," in *The Four Gospels 1992* (ed. F. van Segbroeck et al.; 3 vols.; BETL 100; Leuven: Leuven University Press, 1992), 1466–95. Neirynck and Gundry spar over one of Gundry's examples: Frans Neirynck, "Luke 10:25–28: A Foreign Body in Luke?" in *Crossing the Boundaries: Essays in Biblical Interpretation in Honour of Michael D. Goulder* (ed. S. E. Porter et al.; Biblical Interpretation Series 8; Leiden: Brill, 1994), 149–65; Robert H. Gundry, "A Rejoinder on Matthean Foreign Bodies in Luke 10:25–28," *ETL* 71 (1995): 139–50.

6. Ron Price, "A Three Source Theory for the Synoptic Problem," *Journal of Biblical Studies* 1:4 (2001). Online: http://journalofbiblicalstudies.org.

posed by A. M. Farrer, dispenses with Q, arguing that Luke used Matthew as well as Mark.[7] Michael Goulder[8] and Mark Goodacre[9] in particular have championed this view. It has been criticized, among other reasons, for requiring of Luke an implausible editorial procedure.[10] Yet another theory of Markan priority also dispenses with Q, but proposes that Matthew came last and used both Mark and Luke. Ronald Huggins has advocated this view, calling it the theory of "Matthean posteriority."[11]

While all these theories assume Markan priority, challenges to that assumption have not been lacking. The most significant have come from those who advocate Matthean priority. B. C. Butler defended the Augustinian hypothesis, according to which Matthew wrote first, followed by Mark, who abridged Matthew's gospel, while Luke followed last, drawing from both Matthew and Mark.[12] Another influential defense of Matthean priority was mounted by William R. Farmer, who revived the Griesbach hypothesis.[13] Also known as the two-gospel hypothesis, this theory proposes that Matthew was written first, and then Luke. Most proponents of this theory take the view that Luke used Matthew. All maintain that Mark came last as an abridgment and

---

7. A. M. Farrer, "On Dispensing with Q," in *Studies in the Gospels: Essays in Memory of R. H. Lightfoot* (ed. D. E. Nineham; Oxford: Blackwell, 1955), 55–88; repr. in Bellinzoni, *The Two-Source Hypothesis*, 321–56.

8. Michael D. Goulder, *Midrash and Lection in Matthew* (London: SPCK, 1974); idem, "On Putting Q to the Test," *NTS* 24 (1978): 218–34; idem, "The Order of a Crank," in *Synoptic Studies: The Amplesworth Conferences of 1982 and 1983* (ed. C. M. Tuckett; JSNTSS 7; Sheffield: JSOT Press, 1984), 111–30; idem, *Luke: A New Paradigm* (2 vols.; JSNTSS 20; Sheffield: Sheffield Academic Press, 1989); idem, "Is Q a Juggernaut?" *JBL* 115 (1996): 667–81.

9. Mark Goodacre, *Goulder and the Gospels: An Examination of a New Paradigm* (Sheffield: Sheffield Academic Press, 1996); idem, "Fatigue in the Synoptics," *NTS* 44 (1998): 45–58; idem, *The Synoptic Problem: A Way through the Maze* (London/New York: Sheffield Academic Press, 2001); idem, *The Case Against Q*.

10. Christopher M. Tuckett, "On the Relationship between Matthew and Luke," *NTS* 30 (1984): 130–42; idem, "The Existence of Q," in *The Gospel behind the Gospels: Current Studies in Q* (ed. Ronald A. Piper; Leiden: Brill, 1995), 31–45; David R. Catchpole, "Did Q Exist?" in idem, *The Quest for Q* (Edinburgh: T & T Clark, 1993), 1–59; John S. Kloppenborg Verbin, "Goulder and the New Paradigm: A Critical Appreciation of Michael Goulder on the Synoptic Problem," in Christopher A. Rollston, ed., *The Gospels According to Michael Goulder* (Harrisburg: Trinity Press International, 2002), 29–60; Robert A. Derrenbacker Jr., "Greco-Roman Writing Practices and Luke's Gospel: Revisiting 'The Order of a Crank,'" in Rollston, *Gospels According to Michael Goulder*, 61–83.

11. Ronald V. Huggins, "Matthean Posteriority: A Preliminary Proposal," *NovT* 34 (1992): 1–22; repr. in *The Synoptic Problem and Q: Selected Studies from Novum Testamentum* (ed. David E. Orton; Leiden: Brill, 1999), 204–25.

12. Basil Christopher Butler, *The Originality of St Matthew: A Critique of the Two-Document Hypothesis* (Cambridge: Cambridge University Press, 1951). A similar view is taken by John Wenham, *Redating Matthew, Mark & Luke: A Fresh Assault on the Synoptic Problem* (London: Hodder & Stoughton, 1991; Downers Grove, IL: InterVarsity Press, 1992).

13. Farmer, *Synoptic Problem*.

combination of Matthew and Luke. This theory has been discussed extensively by both proponents[14] and critics.[15]

The combined assault of Butler and Farmer showed the weakness of some of the traditional arguments for the two-document hypothesis, and it is fair to say that this theory does not have as strong a hold on scholarship as it did before. Nevertheless, while the Augustinian and Griesbach hypotheses have their advocates, most scholars continue to regard any theory of Matthean priority as implausible. These theories have not convincingly explained why anyone would abridge Matthew (or Matthew and Luke) into such a gospel as Mark. If Matthew already existed, why would anyone create Mark, since Matthew contains almost all of Mark's material plus a great deal more? Nor have they plausibly explained the passages where either Mark or Luke seems to preserve an earlier form of the tradition than Matthew. In addition, they require strange editorial behavior on the part of Mark and/or Luke.

Lukan priority has attracted fewer advocates than either Markan or Matthean priority.[16] Most of these belong to the "Jerusalem School of Synoptic Research," which follows the theory of Robert L. Lindsey.[17] Lindsey does not use the term "Q," but he posits a pre-Synoptic source that we could call Q1, and a revision of Q1 that we might call Q2. In Lindsey's view, Luke

---

14. E.g., William R. Farmer, "Modern Developments of Griesbach's Hypothesis," *NTS* 23 (1976/77): 275–95; George Wesley Buchanan, "Has the Griesbach Hypothesis Been Falsified?" *JBL* 93 (1974): 550–72; Bernard Orchard, *Matthew, Luke & Mark* (2nd ed.; Manchester: Koinonia Press, 1977); William R. Farmer, ed., *New Synoptic Studies: The Cambridge Gospel Conference and Beyond* (Macon, GA: Mercer University Press, 1983); various papers in Tuckett, *Synoptic Studies*; various papers in *The Interrelations of the Gospels* (ed. David L. Dungan; BETL 95; Leuven: Leuven University Press, 1990); David L. Dungan, "Two-Gospel Hypothesis," in *The Anchor Bible Dictionary* (ed. David Noel Freedman; 6 vols.; Garden City, NY: Doubleday, 1992), 6:671–79; Allan J. McNicol, ed., with David L. Dungan and David B. Peabody, *Beyond the Q Impasse—Luke's Use of Matthew: A Demonstration by the Research Team of the International Institute for Gospel Studies* (Preface by William R. Farmer; Valley Forge, PA: Trinity Press International, 1996); William R. Farmer, "The Case for the Two-Gospel Hypothesis," in Black and Beck, *Rethinking the Synoptic Problem*, 97–135; David B. Peabody, ed., with Lamar Cope and Allan J. McNicol, *One Gospel from Two: Mark's Use of Matthew and Luke* (Harrisburg, PA: Trinity Press International, 2002).

15. E.g., Fitzmyer, "Priority of Mark"; Charles H. Talbert and Edgar V. McKnight, "Can the Griesbach Hypothesis Be Falsified?" *JBL* 91 (1972): 338–68; Christopher Tuckett, "The Griesbach Hypothesis in the 19th Century," *JSNT* 3 (1979): 29–60; idem, *Revival of the Griesbach Hypothesis*; Styler, "Priority of Mark," 293–98, 304–12; Sherman E. Johnson, *The Griesbach Hypothesis and Redaction Criticism* (SBLMS 41; Atlanta: Scholars Press, 1991); Mark Goodacre, "*Beyond the Q Impasse* or Down a Blind Alley?" *JSNT* 76 (1999): 33–52.

16. William Lockton, "The Origin of the Gospels," *Church Quarterly Review* 94 (1922): 216–39.

17. Robert L. Lindsey, "A Modified Two-Document Theory of the Synoptic Dependence and Interdependence," *NovT* 6 (1963): 239–63; repr. in *Synoptic Problem and Q*, 7–31; idem, "A New Approach to the Synoptic Gospels," *Mishkan* 17–18 (1992–93): 87–106.

wrote first, drawing from both Q1 and Q2. Luke was used by Mark, Mark was used by Matthew, and both Mark and Matthew used Q1 as well. Such a theory fails to explain plausibly why Mark omitted from Luke not only a great deal of material, but also stylistic features that occur frequently in Luke.

A survey of the debate makes one thing abundantly clear. Each of these theories of mutual dependence has problems, whether one starts with Mark, Matthew, or Luke. Such problems have led some scholars to conclude that none of the simpler theories work.[18] Neither Mark nor Matthew nor Luke served as the source for the other two, but all depended on a set of earlier sources now lost. The relations between the Synoptic Gospels are more complex than the simpler theories have assumed. While these more complex theories have gained no substantial support, they do take seriously the difficulties entailed by simpler solutions and seek to find a way forward.

In my own study of the problem, I too have concluded that the simpler theories do not work. No one Synoptic served as a source for either of the other two. All theories of Markan priority, Matthean priority, and Lukan priority thus start from a wrong premise. I base this conclusion in part upon the history of the discussion and in part on new data that will be presented in this book. This data calls into question all theories of mutual dependence and suggests instead that all three Synoptics drew on a set of earlier written sources that have been lost.

In presenting a new theory based on this data, I will be in dialogue most often with the theory of Markan priority. I use the term "Markan priority" in a strict sense to mean the view that our canonical Mark was the first Synoptic Gospel and was used as a source by both Matthew and Luke. Markan priority in this sense characterizes several theories of Synoptic relations, most notably the two-document hypothesis, the three-source hypothesis, and Farrer's theory. By this strict definition, theories of an Ur-Markus or Proto-Mark would not advocate Markan priority, but priority of a pre-Markan gospel. My own theory in fact includes a Proto-Mark, though it differs from any previous theory of Proto-Mark.

In this study I am concerned primarily with the material in Mark with its parallels in Matthew and/or Luke. Hence the subtitle of my study designates its limits: "from Proto-Mark to Mark." With respect to the "double tradition" found in Matthew and Luke, I do not challenge the validity of the Q hypothesis. My own theory includes something that could be called Q, though I will not develop this aspect of the theory in the present work. While my theory includes the hypothesis of Q, as well as M and L, it goes beyond the scope of the present study to delineate the contents of these sources or to discuss how they have been incorporated into Matthew and Luke.

Chapters 2 through 6 present new data that leads to five major con-

---

18. See Chapter 7.

clusions. 1) The Gospel of Mark did not serve as a source for either Matthew or Luke. 2) The Gospel of Matthew did not serve as a source for either Mark or Luke. 3) Matthew did not use Mark, nor did Mark use Matthew, but both used the same three sources. 4) Luke did not use Mark, nor did Mark use Luke, but both used the same sources. 5) Mark often conflated two or more sources that were also used by Matthew and Luke respectively. Chapter 7 uses these five major conclusions as criteria to evaluate current theories of Synoptic relations. Since no current theory meets all five criteria, I present a new multi-source theory that does. This theory proposes that a primitive gospel (Proto-Mark) underwent two revisions (Proto-Mark A and Proto-Mark B). Matthew knew Proto-Mark A, Luke knew Proto-Mark B, while Mark knew and conflated both. In addition, several smaller sources also contributed material. Chapters 8 to 11 discuss all these sources in greater detail. Finally, Chapter 12 gives examples of how this theory would account for the composition of Mark.

**CHAPTER 2**

# *Markan Redaction Absent from Matthew and Luke*

THE TWO-DOCUMENT HYPOTHESIS, like other theories of Markan priority, affirms that Matthew and Luke copied Mark. One persistent problem for this hypothesis has been posed by the minor agreements of Matthew and Luke against Mark. These include agreements of wording, order, inclusion, and omission. While these agreements have received frequent attention, the agreements of omission in particular have not been fully appreciated in previous studies. These provide the strongest evidence against the view that Matthew and Luke drew directly from Mark. They call into question not only the two-document hypothesis but also any other theory of Markan priority, such as Farrer's theory. A new examination of the minor agreements, focusing on the agreements of omission, will indicate strongly that Matthew and Luke did not use Mark.

## Minor Agreements: The State of the Question

Critics of the two-document hypothesis find its Achilles' heel in the minor agreements of Matthew and Luke against Mark in the triple tradition. In this theory Matthew and Luke supposedly copied Mark independently, yet in numerous places they agree with each other against Mark. It is customary to categorize such agreements as "major" or "minor." The two-document hypothesis explains the major agreements by noting that Mark and Q sometimes preserved the same story or saying. The major agreements then would be places where Matthew and Luke abandoned Mark to follow a parallel tradition in Q. The minor agreements, where no parallel tradition from Q is in evidence, have been more problematic for the theory. Streeter gave two explanations for these agreements: 1) some arose as Matthew and Luke independently made the same improvements to Mark's text; 2) in other cases, copyists altered the texts of the gospels, creating agreements between Matthew and Luke that did not exist in the original manuscripts.[1] Subsequent proponents

---

1. Streeter, *Four Gospels*, 293–331.

of the two-document hypothesis continue to give these same two explanations.[2] In evaluating these explanations, we must consider three different aspects of the question: the nature of individual agreements, the number of agreements, and the concentration of agreements within a single context.

1. The first aspect was investigated by Frans Neirynck and associates, who compiled a comprehensive list of the minor agreements and categorized them according to type.[3] Certain types of agreements could be explained by supposing that Matthew and Luke independently made the same revision to Mark's text. These include instances where Matthew and Luke have δέ instead of Mark's καί or an aorist tense instead of Mark's imperfect or a different order of words. Other agreements, however, are not easily explained in this way, and in these cases, proponents of the two-document hypothesis must argue that the text is corrupt. For example, in both Matthew 26:68 and Luke 22:64, Jesus' persecutors ask him τίς ἐστιν ὁ παίσας σε, a sentence that is lacking in Mark 14:65. Critics of the two-document hypothesis regard this agreement as significant, Michael Goulder calling it "particularly acute."[4] Proponents of the two-document hypothesis argue that the extra words did not originally appear in Matthew but were added later from Luke by a scribe.[5] This explanation faces the difficulty that all known manuscripts of Matthew include the words.

Another significant agreement occurs at the end of Peter's denial. Matthew and Luke, but not Mark, describe Peter's remorse with the words καὶ ἐξελθὼν ἔξω ἔκλαυσεν πικρῶς (Matt 26:75; Luke 22:62; cf. Mark 14:72 καὶ ἐπιβαλὼν ἔκλαιεν). To get rid of this agreement, proponents of Markan priority are forced to accept the variant reading of 0171 and certain Old Latin manuscripts, in which Luke 22:62 is absent. However, on text-critical grounds there is no reason to doubt that Luke 22:62 belonged to the original text. Its omission from these few witnesses is easily explained as an instance of haplography: a scribe's eye skipped from ΤΡΙΣΚΑΙ at the beginning of the verse to ΠΙΚΡΩΣΚΑΙ at the end, so that he omitted everything in between.[6] The only reason for a modern scholar to omit this verse from Luke would be to save the two-document hypothesis.

---

2. E.g., S. McLoughlin, "Les accords mineurs Mt-Lc contre Mc et le problème synoptique," in *De Jésus aux évangiles: tradition et rédaction dans les évangiles synoptiques* (ed. I. de la Potterie; Gembloux: Duculot, 1967), 17–40.

3. Frans Neirynck, ed., with Theo Hansen and Frans van Segbroeck, *The Minor Agreements of Matthew and Luke Against Mark with a Cumulative List* (BETL 37; Leuven: Leuven University Press, 1974).

4. Goulder, "Is Q a Juggernaut?" 670; cf. idem, *Luke*, 6–11.

5. E.g., Streeter, *Four Gospels*, 325–28; Frans Neirynck, "ΤΙΣ ΕΣΤΙΝ Ο ΠΑΙΣΑΣ ΣΕ: Mt 26,68/Lk 22,64 (diff Mk 14,65)," *ETL* 63 (1987): 5–47; Tuckett, "Synoptic Problem," 267.

6. Edward W. Burrows, "The Use of Textual Theories to Explain Agreements of Matthew and Luke against Mark," in *Studies in New Testament Language and Text* (ed. J. K. Elliott; Leiden: Brill, 1976), 99n. 29.

In these and in a number of other instances, proponents of the two-document hypothesis must appeal to textual variants that have little or no support in the manuscripts. Streeter examined a number of minor agreements in
the editions of Hort and Tischendorf and explained thirty-four of these by
appeal to textual corruption, adding that he would explain others in the same
way.[7] However, as William Farmer pointed out, textual critics have had ample
opportunity since Streeter's time to examine the changes to the text that he
suggested, yet few of these changes (I count six) have been adopted into new
critical editions of the New Testament. Furthermore, appeal to textual variants could be used to increase the minor agreements as easily as to decrease
them.[8] In most cases, therefore, Streeter's appeal to textual corruption looks
like an expedient to save a theory rather than a judicious attempt to determine the original text.

2. A second aspect of the question is the number of such agreements. One
can allow for an occasional chance agreement of two editors revising the same
document independently, but if it happens too often, one begins to suspect
that something more than coincidence was at work. Proponents of the two-
document hypothesis do not find the number of minor agreements a stum-
bling block. Critics of the theory, however, find the number more
troublesome. Andreas Ennulat finds and examines about a thousand such
agreements.[9] E. P. Sanders gives the same number and judges that these are
too numerous to attribute to coincidence and similar editorial policies of
Matthew and Luke.[10] While judgments differ, only one study with which I am
familiar has tried to put the question on an objective basis. Richard Vinson's
study attempts to determine statistically whether the number of minor agreements is sufficient cause to reject the two-document hypothesis.[11] Vinson
expressed the number of minor agreements as a percentage of the number of
words in Mark. He then determined similar percentages in two analogous
cases: an experiment performed at Duke University in which ten graduate
students independently edited a common source, and the quotations of classical Greek sources by early Christian apologists. From comparing these three
rates, Vinson calculated that the chances that Matthew and Luke could have
produced their rate of minor agreements by independently editing Mark are

---

7. Streeter, *Four Gospels*, 306–31.
8. Farmer, *Synoptic Problem*, 146–47.
9. Andreas Ennulat, *Die "Minor Agreements": Untersuchungen zu einer offenen Frage des synoptischen Problems* (WUNT 2.62; Tübingen: Mohr, 1994), 417.
10. E. P. Sanders and Margaret Davies, *Studying the Synoptic Gospels* (London: SCM; Philadelphia: Trinity Press International, 1989), 73.
11. Richard Bolling Vinson, "The Significance of the Minor Agreements as an Argument Against the Two-Document Hypothesis" (Ph.D. diss., Duke University, 1984). Vinson's study was criticized by Timothy A. Friedrichsen, "The Minor Agreements of Matthew and Luke against Mark: Critical Observations on R. B. Vinson's Statistical Analysis," *ETL* 65 (1989):

less than one in two thousand. This statistical examination of the minor agreements thus concludes that they do pose a significant problem for the two-document hypothesis.

A more informal test cited by Ulrich Luz points in the same direction. Luz had the first version of his commentary on Matthew checked by coworkers, two of whom made abbreviations and improvements in a considerable number of passages. The number of places where they improved the text independently in the same way averaged about one per page. Luz concludes that the theory of independent editing "is basically possible but in view of the large number of the minor agreements is not sufficient as an explanation."[12]

3. The third aspect of the question is the concentration of minor agreements. If the agreements are scattered and separated, it would be more plausible to explain them as coincidence than if they are concentrated in a single context. Certain passages do in fact show a high concentration of such agreements and are not generally thought to have a Q overlap. One of these is the miracle story in which Jesus calms a storm (Mark 4:35–41).[13] Table 2.1 shows the Matthew/Luke agreements in this narrative.

Table 2.1
Matthew/Luke agreements in Mark 4:35–41 parr

| Matthew | Mark | Luke |
|---|---|---|
| — | 4:35 when evening came | — |
| 8:23 he got into the boat | 4:36 they took him along as he was in the boat | 8:22 he got into the boat |
| — | 4:36 and other boats were with him | — |
| 8:23 his disciples followed him | | 8:22 along with his disciples |
| 8:24 in the sea | | 8:23 into the lake |
| — | 4:38 and he was in the stern on the pillow | — |
| 8:25 they approached him | | 8:24 they approached him |

395–408. However, most of Friedrichsen's objections had already been anticipated and addressed by Vinson.

12. Ulrich Luz, *Matthew 1–7: A Continental Commentary* (Minneapolis: Fortress, 1989), 48n. 62.

13. Albert Fuchs in particular has emphasized the minor agreements in this passage in support of his theory of a Deutero-Mark, e.g., in "Die 'Seesturmperikope' Mk 4,35–41 parr im Wandel der urkirchlichen Verkündigung," in *Minor Agreements: Symposium Göttingen 1991* (ed. Georg Strecker; Göttingen: Vandenhoeck & Ruprecht, 1993), 65–92.

| Matthew | Mark | Luke |
|---|---|---|
| 8:25 saying | 4:38 and say to him | 8:24 saying |
| — | 4:38 do you not care that | — |
| — | 4:39 "Quiet, be still." | — |
| — | 4:39 the wind | — |
| — | 4:41 a great fear | — |
| 8:27 the men were amazed | | 8:25 they were amazed |

Here Matthew and Luke have not only the same omissions from Mark, but also the same additions to Mark. The individual agreements are significant, and the total number is even more so. However we explain these agreements, the high concentration of them in a single story makes it difficult to think that Matthew and Luke got the story from Mark.

The same is true for the beginning of the mission instructions (Mark 6:7–13 parr). Both the triple tradition and the double tradition preserve a set of these instructions. Luke has kept the two sets distinct, in Luke 9:1–6 and 10:1–12 respectively, while Matthew has conflated the two sets in Matthew 10:1–15. We should not be surprised to find that Luke agrees with Matthew against Mark in the double tradition version (Luke 10:1–12), but if Matthew and Luke copied the triple tradition from Mark, we would not expect to find that Luke agrees significantly with Matthew against Mark in the triple tradition version (Luke 9:1–6). Yet this is precisely what we do find, as Table 2.2 shows.

Table 2.2
Matthew/Luke agreements in Mark 6:7 parr

| Matthew 10:1, 7–8 | Mark 6:7 | Luke 9:1–2 |
|---|---|---|
| 10:1c and to heal every disease | | 9:1c and to heal diseases |
| 10:7 preach saying that the kingdom of heaven is at hand | | 9:2b to preach the kingdom of God |
| 8 Heal the sick | | and heal the sick |

Matthew and Luke clearly did not copy this material from Mark, since Mark does not have it. It cannot be explained as independent editing by Matthew and Luke, since the amount of agreement against Mark here is too great. Nor can it be explained as parallel material from Q, since Luke keeps the double tradition version distinct from the triple tradition version. The two-document hypothesis has no plausible explanation for this agreement.

A similar difficulty pertains to a passage in the passion narrative. In the two verses of Jesus' interrogation before the Sanhedrin (Mark 14:61–62), Luke and Matthew show five agreements in wording against Mark (Table 2.3).

Table 2.3

**Minor agreements in Mark 14:61–62**

| Matthew 26:63–64 | Mark 14:61–62 | Luke 22:67–70 |
|---|---|---|
| that you tell us if you are the Christ | you are the Christ? | tell us if you are the Christ |
| Son of God | Son of the Blessed One | Son of God |
| you (s.) said | | you (pl.) say |
| from now on | | from the present time |
| sitting at the right hand | at the right hand sitting | sitting at the right hand |

In both Luke and Matthew, his interrogators address him with an imperative ("tell us if you are the Christ") rather than a question ("you are the Christ?") as in Mark; both Luke and Matthew have "Son of God" instead of Mark's "Son of the Blessed One"; in both Luke and Matthew, Jesus answers indirectly ("you say that I am" or "you said it"), whereas in Mark he answers directly ("I am"); in both Luke and Matthew, Jesus precedes his prediction with a temporal expression (ἀπ' ἄρτι, ἀπὸ τοῦ νῦν) that does not occur in Mark; both Luke and Matthew put "sitting" before "at the right hand," while Mark has the reverse order. Conceivably Luke and Matthew could have independently revised the unusual expression "Blessed One" to the more common "God," and they could have independently conformed "at the right hand sitting" to the order of LXX Psalm 110:1. The remaining agreements, however, are more difficult to explain as the result of independent editing, and the number of such agreements makes the theory of independent editing even more implausible. It is difficult to accept the view that Matthew and Luke were independently editing Mark at this point.

While the minor agreements have been widely discussed, scholars continue to make different judgments concerning their significance. In the view of some, among whom I number myself, the evidence presented thus far suffices to raise serious doubts about the two-document hypothesis. Other scholars, however, disagree. If the question is to be resolved—admittedly a big "if"—then we need some new perspective that will tip the balance in favor of one view or the other. In the rest of this chapter I will attempt to present such a new perspective, one that I think tips the balance not only against the two-document hypothesis, but against any theory of Markan priority.

## Benign Features of Mark Absent
## from Matthew and Luke

One might classify the minor agreements in various ways, but one way would be to distinguish among agreements of wording, order, inclusion, and omission. The agreements of omission have received the least attention but in my view provide the strongest evidence against the theory that Matthew and Luke drew directly from Mark. Proponents of Markan priority explain these as instances where Matthew and Luke both omitted the same Markan material as they abbreviated Mark. According to Streeter, "it would have been quite impossible for two persons to abbreviate practically every paragraph in the whole of Mark without concurring in a very large number of their omissions."[14] Without further investigating the nature of these presumed omissions, he dismissed them in a single paragraph under the heading "Irrelevant Agreements."[15] Subsequent Markan prioritists have often adopted a divide-and-conquer strategy toward these omissions. By looking at each separately, one is generally able to come up with some conjecture as to why both Matthew and Luke would have omitted it.[16]

Streeter's summary dismissal of these so-called omissions does not do justice to the problem that they pose for Markan priority; nor does the divide-and-conquer method. These omissions include recurring features of Mark that are completely absent from both Matthew and Luke. Entire themes and stylistic features that occur repeatedly in Mark are lacking in the other two Synoptics. What needs explaining, then, is not the omission of individual words or sentences, but the omission of entire themes and recurring features of Mark's style.

It is true that Markan prioritists have sought to explain some of these stylistic features. Streeter, for example, mentioned Mark's fondness for the historic present, καί instead of δέ, parataxis instead of subordination, occasional omission of the subject, φέρειν in place of ἄγειν, and "after three days" instead of "on the third day."[17] He explained these as unidiomatic features of Mark's Greek style that would naturally have been corrected by Matthew and Luke independently. Other recurring features of Mark have been found not stylistically but ideologically objectionable, such as Mark's preference for say-

---

14. Streeter, *Four Gospels*, 295.

15. S. McLoughlin follows suit in dismissing these "negative agreements" as "insignificant" ("Les Accords Mineurs," 19).

16. This approach is taken, for example, by Stein (*Studying the Synoptic Gospels*, 128), and Tuckett ("Synoptic Problem," 266).

17. Streeter, *Four Gospels*, 296–99.

ing that Jesus healed "many" instead of "all," and his references to the "hardness" of the disciples' hearts. According to Markan prioritists, since these features of Mark would have posed difficulties for the early church, both Matthew and Luke had reason to omit them.[18]

For the sake of argument, let us assume that Streeter and others are correct in identifying these particular features of Mark as the more original form of the tradition, as objectionable features that have been revised away identically by Matthew and Luke. This assumption would neither establish Markan priority nor eliminate the problem posed for that theory by the agreements of omission. First, it would not establish Markan priority because we could have the same sort of revision if all three Synoptics depended upon a source that preceded any of the three. Matthew and Luke could have independently removed these objectionable features from the pre-Synoptic source while Mark retained them. Thus, the presence of the more primitive reading in Mark would not prove that Matthew and Luke copied from Mark. Second, identifying a few stylistic features of Mark as objectionable would not eliminate the problem, because the great majority of the Markan features lacking in Matthew and Luke are not objectionable either grammatically or ideologically. The supposedly objectionable features constitute only a small part of the missing Markan features. Most of these Markan features are benign, that is, neither stylistically nor ideologically objectionable. It is on these benign features of Mark's style that I wish to focus here. These recurring features are difficult to explain as common omissions of Matthew and Luke, but are more easily understood as instances of Markan redaction unknown to Matthew and Luke. A list of these features would include over fifty items. Some occur only twice; others occur as many as twenty-seven times. Almost all are totally absent from Matthew and Luke. I will discuss some of the more significant items and simply list others.

1. Table 2.4 shows a significant trait of Mark's style: his distinctive uses of the word πολύς. In all of the tables that follow, a line (—) indicates that Matthew or Luke has material parallel to Mark but not the relevant Markan feature. A blank space indicates that Matthew or Luke has no material parallel to Mark.

In all, Mark uses the word πολύς fifty-eight times. Of these instances, forty-four have no equivalent in Matthew and forty-nine have no equivalent in Luke. According to the theory of Markan priority, then, Matthew eliminated the word or the material in which it occurred 76 percent of the time, while Luke eliminated it 84 percent of the time.[19]

---

18. Allen, *Matthew*, xxxi–xxxiv, xxxvii–xxxix; John C. Hawkins, *Horae Synopticae: Contributions to the Study of the Synoptic Problem* (2nd ed.; Oxford: Clarendon Press, 1909; repr. Grand Rapids: Baker, 1968), 117–25; Stein, *Studying the Synoptic Gospels*, 67–73.

19. These percentages are high, even compared to what the normal practice of Matthew

## Table 2.4
## Distinctive Markan uses of πολύς

A. πολύς, in the story of Jairus' daughter (Mark 5:21-43 parr)

| Mark | Matthew | Luke |
| --- | --- | --- |
| 5:21 πολύς | 9:18 — | 8:40 — |
| 5:23 πολλά | 9:18 — | 8:41 — |
| 5:24 πολύς | 9:19 — | 8:42 — |
| 5:26 πολλά | | 8:43 — |
| 5:26 πολλῶν | | 8:43 — |
| 5:38 πολλά | 9:23 — | 8:52 — |
| 5:43 πολλά | | 8:56 — |

B. πολύς, neuter accusative used adverbially

| | | |
| --- | --- | --- |
| 1:45 πολλά | 9:31 — | 5:15 — |
| 3:12 πολλά | 12:16 — | 4:41 — |
| 5:10 πολλά | | 8:31 — |
| 5:23 πολλά | 9:18 — | 8:41 — |
| 5:38 πολλά | 9:23 — | 8:52 — |
| 5:43 πολλά | | 8:56 — |
| 6:20 πολλά | | |
| 9:26 πολλά | 17:18 — | |
| 12:27 πολύ | 22:32 — | 20:38 — |
| 15:3 πολλά | 27:12 — | 23:10 — |

C. πολλοί, subject or predicate, referring to a crowd with Jesus

| | | |
| --- | --- | --- |
| 2:2 πολλοί | | |
| 2:15b πολλοί | | |
| 6:2 πολλοί | 13:54 αὐτούς | 4:22 πάντες |
| 6:31 πολλοί | | |
| 6:33 πολλοί | 14:13 οἱ ὄχλοι | 9:11 οἱ ὄχλοι |
| 9:26b πολλούς | | |
| 10:48a πολλοί | 20:31 ὁ ὄχλος | 18:39 οἱ προάγοντες |
| 11:8 πολλοί | 21:8 ὁ ὄχλος | 19:36 verb ending: they |

and Luke would be, given the theory of Markan priority. On that theory, Matthew chose not to retain the exact wording of Mark 60% of the time, while Luke chose not to retain it 74% of the time (figures derived from Stein, *Studying the Synoptic Gospels*, 127).

D. πολύς + ἄλλος

| 7:4 ἄλλα πολλά | | |
|---|---|---|
| 12:5 πολλοὺς ἄλλους | 21:36 — | |
| 15:41 ἄλλαι πολλαί | | |

E. πολύς + τοιοῦτος

| 4:33 τοιαύταις πολλαῖς | 13:34 — | |
|---|---|---|
| 7:13 τοιαῦτα πολλά | | |

But these statistics do not tell the full story. When we look at certain specific uses of πολύς in Mark, the percentage that is absent from Matthew and Luke climbs to 100 percent. In one case, several instances of πολύς are concentrated in a single Markan story, the story of Jairus's daughter (Table 2.4A). Here Mark uses some form of the word πολύς seven times, in the senses "large," "much," "many," and "greatly." In the same story, neither Matthew nor Luke uses the word at all. Even if we take into account Matthew's shorter version of this story, it is difficult to explain how πολύς would disappear from the story a total of fourteen times, seven in Matthew and seven in Luke.

Furthermore, several distinctive ways of using the word in Mark are also totally absent from Matthew and Luke. For example, Mark uses the word in an adverbial sense ten times: once the singular πολύ and nine times the plural πολλά (Table 2.4B).[20] None of these ten instances appear in either Matthew or Luke, even though both have parallels to most of the Markan passages where they occur. The problem for the theory of Markan priority is to explain why Matthew and Luke would both completely omit this usage from Mark. Was it objectionable stylistically? Apparently not, since it is normal usage both in classical Greek and elsewhere in the New Testament. Luke himself uses the singular πολύ twice in non-Markan contexts (Luke 7:47; Acts 18:27), and other New Testament authors use it five times (2 Cor 8:4; Heb 12:9, 25; James 5:16; Rev 5:4). Similarly, the plural πολλά is used four times by Paul (Rom 16:6, 12; 1 Cor 16:12, 19) and once by the author of James (James 3:2). Matthew too may use it once where Mark does not, although the text there is uncertain (Matt 9:14). In any case, it is a benign feature of Mark's style.

If, then, Matthew and Luke had no reason to omit it intentionally, did they eliminate it unintentionally in the process of omitting some Markan passages and rewriting others? This seems unlikely. On the theory of Markan priority, the adverbial usage had twenty opportunities to survive the editorial

---

20. Hawkins lists adverbial πολλά as a word characteristic of Mark's gospel, citing these nine instances; in all other cases in Mark he takes πολλά as an adjective (Hawkins, *Horae Synopticae*, 13, 35). The only other possible instances of adverbial πολλά in Mark would be three occurrences of the expression πολλὰ παθεῖν (Mark 5:26; 8:31; 9:12). Here, however, πολλά is better understood as the direct object of πάσχειν, as in *Iliad* 23.607 and *Odyssey* 5.223.

process, ten in Matthew and ten in Luke. The fact that it does not appear at all suggests that Matthew and Luke simply did not know it.

We find the same phenomenon when we examine other distinctive uses of πολύς in Mark. Mark uses πολλοί eight times as subject or predicate to refer to a crowd of people with Jesus (Table 2.4C). This usage does not occur in either Matthew or Luke. Finally, Mark uses πολύς three times in the expression "many other" (Table 2.4D) and twice in the expression "many such" (Table 2.4E). In no case do the other evangelists have either expression. There is nothing objectionable about these expressions. In fact, in non-Markan contexts, both Matthew and Luke do use πολύς in a similar expression.[21]

Taken all together, these distinctive uses of πολύς occur in Mark twenty-seven times. On the theory of Markan priority, Matthew and Luke dropped all twenty-seven occurrences. Put another way, taking Matthew and Luke together, there were fifty-four chances for at least one occurrence of one of these uses to make it through the redactional process. Yet not a single one survived. The theory of Markan priority, whether in the two-document hypothesis or in some other form, such as Farrer's theory, would have us believe either that Matthew and Luke shared an aversion to these common expressions of size and degree or that the editorial process resulted in the coincidental elimination of this word to a highly improbable degree.

Is there then some other explanation? The most obvious explanation is that the instances of the expression that occur uniquely in Mark did not occur in the material that Matthew and Luke shared with Mark. By some channel yet to be determined, all three evangelists received some of the same material. Mark redacted this in his own distinctive style, impressing on it his predilection for adverbial πολλά and other uses of πολύς. Since this Markan redaction did not occur in the material received by Matthew and Luke, they did not know it.

2. A second significant trait of Mark's style is his use of the word πάλιν ("again" or "back"). David Peabody has called attention to a distinctive use of this word in Mark.[22] In fifteen instances, Mark uses πάλιν in narrative to indicate the repetition of an action that occurred in a previous pericope. As Table 2.5 shows, none of these occurs in Matthew or Luke.

Mark often uses the word πάλιν to indicate the repetition of some prior action, as when a crowd gathers "again" or Jesus goes "back" into Jerusalem. The prior action that is repeated occurs sometimes in the same pericope and sometimes in a previous pericope. In the latter case, the word serves as a technique to link one pericope with another. This use of πάλιν to link different pericopes occurs fifteen times in Mark. It is thus a frequent feature of the gospel's narrative style.

---

21. ἕτεροι πολλοί (Matt 15:30; Luke 3:18; 8:3; 22:65).

22. David Barrett Peabody, *Mark as Composer* (New Gospel Studies 1; Macon, GA: Mercer University Press, 1987), 115–47.

Table 2.5
A distinctive Markan use of πάλιν

| Mark | Matthew | Luke |
|---|---|---|
| 2:1 (refers back to 1:21) | 9:1 — | 5:17 — |
| 2:13 (refers back to 1:16) | | 5:27 — |
| 3:1 (refers back to 1:21) | 12:9 — | 6:6 — |
| 3:20 (refers back to 2:1–2) | | |
| 4:1 (refers back to 2:13) | 13:1 — | 8:4 — |
| 5:21 (refers back to 4:35) | 9:1, 18 — | 8:40 — |
| 7:14 (refers back to 3:20, 23) | 15:10 — | |
| 7:31 (refers back to 7:24) | 15:29 — | |
| 8:1 (refers back to 6:34–36) | 15:32 — | |
| 8:13 (refers back to 8:10) | 16:4b — | |
| 10:1b (refers back to 2:13; 3:7–8; 4:1) | 19:2a — | |
| 10:1c (refers back to 2:13; 4:1) | 19:2b — | |
| 10:10 (refers back to 4:10; 7:17; 9:28) | | |
| 10:32 (refers back to 3:13–15; 6:7; 9:35) | 20:17 — | 18:31 — |
| 11:27 (refers back to 11:15) | | |

Significantly, not a single one of these fifteen instances occurs in either Matthew or Luke.[23] The complete absence of this usage from Matthew and Luke poses the same problem for Markan priority that we saw earlier with πολύς: if Matthew and Luke were copying Mark, then why does this frequent Markan usage not appear in either of their gospels? They had no reason to intentionally omit it, since it is neither ungrammatical nor ideologically objectionable. It is a benign feature of Mark's style. Did they then eliminate it unintentionally in the process of omitting some Markan passages and revising others? This again seems unlikely when we consider that the word had thirty opportunities to survive the editorial process, fifteen in Matthew and fifteen in Luke. The fact that it does not appear at all calls into question the view that Matthew and Luke were copying Mark. It suggests instead that Matthew and Luke did not know this usage: it did not occur in the version or versions of the material that they used. In other words, they did not use Mark.

3. Table 2.6 shows a third stylistic feature of Mark that leads to the same conclusion: the use of ἴδε.

_____

23. Of the remaining thirteen instances of πάλιν in Mark, Matthew has five and Luke has one.

### Table 2.6
### Mark's use of ἴδε

| Mark | Matthew | Luke |
|---|---|---|
| 2:24 ἴδε | 12:2 ἰδού | 6:2 — |
| 3:34 ἴδε | 12:49 ἰδού | 8:21 — |
| 11:21 ἴδε | 21:20 — | |
| 13:1 ἴδε | 24:1 — | 21:5 — |
| 13:21 ἴδε | 24:23 ἰδού | 17:23 ἰδού |
| 13:21 ἴδε | 24:23 — | 17:23 ἰδού |
| 15:4 ἴδε | 27:13 — | |
| 15:35 ἴδε | 27:47 — | |
| 16:6 ἴδε | 28:6 ἴδετε | |

Mark employs the particle ἴδε nine times, not one of which occurs in the parallels in Matthew or Luke. Did Matthew and Luke have an aversion to this particle? Certainly not Matthew, who uses it elsewhere (Matt 25:20, 22, 25; Matt 26:65//Mark 14:64). The theory of Markan priority is stuck with the strange conclusion that Matthew used this particle elsewhere, but avoided it wherever he found it in Mark. More plausibly, the particle belongs to a layer of redaction in Mark that was unknown to Matthew or Luke. Mark, with a predilection for the word, added it to the material that he shared with Matthew and Luke, sometimes substituting it for ἰδού and sometimes inserting it anew into the tradition.

4. Table 2.7 illustrates one of the most interesting pieces of evidence against Markan priority: the distribution of φημί in the Synoptics.

### Table 2.7
### φημί in the Synoptics

A. φημί in Mark (6)

| Matthew | Mark | Luke |
|---|---|---|
| 17:10 εἶπεν | 9:12 ἔφη | |
| | 9:38 ἔφη | 9:49 εἶπεν |
| 19:20 λέγει | 10:20 ἔφη | 18:21 εἶπεν |
| 19:28 εἶπεν | 10:29 ἔφη | 18:29 εἶπεν |
| 22:29 εἶπεν | 12:24 ἔφη | 20:34 εἶπεν |
| 26:33 εἶπεν | 14:29 ἔφη | 22:33 εἶπεν |

B. φημί in Matthew (16)

| Matthew | Mark | Luke |
|---|---|---|
| 4:7 ἔφη | | 4:12 εἶπεν |
| 8:8 ἔφη | | 7:6 λέγων |
| 13:28 ἔφη | | |
| 13:29 φησιν | | |
| 14:8 φησίν | 6:25 λέγουσα | |
| 17:26 ἔφη | | |
| 19:21 ἔφη | 10:21 εἶπεν | 18:22 εἶπεν |
| 21:27 ἔφη | 11:33 λέγει | 20:8 εἶπεν |
| 22:37 ἔφη | 12:29 ἀπεκρίθη | 10:26 εἶπεν |
| 25:21 ἔφη | | 19:17 εἶπεν |
| 25:23 ἔφη | | 19:19 εἶπεν |
| 26:34 ἔφη | 14:30 λέγει | 22:34 εἶπεν |
| 26:61 ἔφη | 14:58 λέγοντος | |
| 27:11 ἔφη | 15:2 λέγει | 23:3 ἔφη |
| 27:23 ἔφη | 15:14 ἔλεγεν | 23:22 εἶπεν |
| 27:65 ἔφη | | |

C. φημί in Luke (8)

| Matthew | Mark | Luke |
|---|---|---|
| | | 7:40 φησίν |
| | | 7:44 ἔφη |
| | | 15:17 ἔφη |
| 26:71 λέγει | 14:69 ἤρξατο λέγειν | 22:58 ἔφη |
| 26:72 ἠρνήσατο | 14:70 ἠρνεῖτο | 22:58 ἔφη |
| 26:64 λέγει | 14:62 εἶπεν | 22:70 ἔφη |
| 27:11 ἔφη | 15:2 λέγει | 23:3 ἔφη |
| | | 23:40 ἔφη |

As indicated in Table 2.7A, Mark uses the word ἔφη, "he said," six times. Matthew and Luke each have an equivalent expression in five of the six cases, a combined total of ten equivalents. Yet they never once use Mark's ἔφη. Nine times they have εἶπεν, and once Matthew has λέγει. The theory of Markan priority would be almost compelled to affirm that Matthew and Luke both had an aversion to the word ἔφη. Yet we know this not to be the case. In other contexts, Matthew uses ἔφη or another form of φημί sixteen times (Table 2.7B), while Luke uses it eight times in his gospel (Table 2.7C) and twenty-five times in Acts. Here, given the theory of Markan priority, we have a strange phenomenon indeed. Both Matthew and Luke use ἔφη more frequently than Mark does, yet whenever they encounter it in Mark, they both studiously avoid it. If nothing else, this phenomenon should make proponents of Markan priority a bit uncomfortable.

But proponents of Matthean or Lukan priority would be no better off. If we look at the use of φημί throughout the Synoptic tradition, as shown in Table 2.7, we notice a very striking fact. Though the word occurs a total of thirty times, only once do two evangelists have it in the same passage (Matt 27:11//Luke 23:3). Apart from this one exception, the word is used by only one evangelist at a time. This distribution of the word would be difficult to account for in any theory that affirmed direct dependence of one Synoptic on another, since regardless of which gospel we identified as the first, we would have to say that the dependent evangelists felt free to use φημί anywhere except where they found it in their source.

Another explanation seems more plausible. If all three Synoptics were dependent upon a common source or common sources that preceded any of the three, we could suppose that this earlier material did not make much use of the word φημί. The evangelists themselves, however, did use the word as they redacted the material. Since they worked independently, their uses of the word did not coincide. Hence, the term almost always appears in only a single gospel at a time. Thus the distribution of φημί speaks against any theory of direct dependence among the Synoptics, including the theory of Markan priority.

5. Some unique Markan expressions occur only twice, yet these too add their weight to the cumulative testimony against Markan priority. One example is Mark's use of the participle ἐναγκαλισάμενος (Table 2.8).

### Table 2.8
### ἐναγκαλισάμενος in Mark

| Mark | Matthew | Luke |
|---|---|---|
| 9:36 Jesus takes a child in his arms (ἐναγκαλισάμενος) | 18:2 — | 9:47 — |
| 10:16 Jesus takes children in his arms (ἐναγκαλισάμενος) | 19:15 — | |

All three Synoptics share two stories in which Jesus teaches the disciples to accept children (Mark 9:33–37; 10:13–16). In both stories, Mark has Jesus take the children in his arms, both times with the participle ἐναγκαλισά-μενος (Mark 9:36; 10:16). Matthew and Luke lack this description. It is difficult to imagine why both evangelists would have omitted this detail had they known it. It is not difficult, however, to explain why Mark would have added it. By having Jesus embrace the children, Mark has made the scene more touching and has graphically illustrated the attitude that Jesus' teaching advocates.

6. The Markan expressions that we have examined are completely absent from the parallels in Matthew and Luke. In addition, numerous Markan expressions occur only rarely in the parallels. An example is Mark's use of the imperfect of εἰμί plus a participle (Table 2.9).

### Table 2.9
### Imperfect of εἰμί plus a participle in Mark

| Mark | Matthew | Luke |
|---|---|---|
| 1:6 ἦν ἐνδεδυμένος | 3:4 εἶχεν τὸ ἔνδυμα αὐτοῦ | |
| 1:13 ἦν πειραζόμενος | 4:1 πειρασθῆναι | 4:2 πειραζόμενος |
| 1:22 ἦν διδάσκων | 7:29 ἦν διδάσκων | 4:32 — |
| 1:33 ἦν ἐπισυνηγμένη | | |
| 2:6 ἦσαν καθήμενοι καὶ διαλογιζόμενοι | 9:3 — | 5:17 ἦσαν καθήμενοι 5:21 ἤρξαντο διαλογίζεσθαι |
| 2:18 ἦσαν νηστεύοντες | | |
| 4:38 ἦν καθεύδων | | 8:23 ἀφύπνωσεν |
| 5:5 ἦν κράζων καὶ κατακόπτων | | |
| 5:11 ἦν βοσκομένη | 8:30 ἦν βοσκομένη | 8:32 ἦν βοσκομένη |
| 6:52 ἦν πεπωρωμένη | | |
| 9:4 ἦσαν συλλαλοῦντες | 17:3 συλλαλοῦντες | 9:30 συνελάλουν |
| 10:22 ἦν ἔχων | 19:22 ἦν ἔχων | 18:23 ἦν πλούσιος |
| 10:32 ἦσαν ἀναβαίνοντες | 20:17 ἀναβαίνων | 19:28 ἀναβαίνων |
| 10:32 ἦν προάγων | | 19:28 ἐπορεύετο ἔμπροσθεν |
| 14:4 ἦσαν ἀγανακτοῦντες | 26:8 ἠγανάκτησαν | |
| 14:40 ἦσαν καταβαρυνόμενοι | 26:43 ἦσαν βεβαρημένοι | |
| 14:49 ἤμην διδάσκων | 26:55 ἐκαθεζόμην διδάσκων | 22:53 ὄντος μου |

| Mark | Matthew | Luke |
|------|---------|------|
| 14:54 ἦν συγκαθήμενος | 26:58 ἐκάθητο | 22:55 ἐκάθητο |
| 15:7 ἦν δεδεμένος | 27:16 εἶχον δέσμιον | |
| 15:26 ἦν ἐπιγεγραμμένη | 27:37 γεγραμμένην | 23:38 — |
| 15:40 ἦσαν θεωροῦσαι | 27:55 ἦσαν θεωροῦσαι | 23:49 — |
| 15:43 ἦν προσδεχόμενος | 27:57 ἐμαθητεύθη | 23:51 προσεδέχετο |
| 15:46 ἦν λελατομημένον | 27:60 ἐλατόμησεν | 23:53 λαξευτῷ |

Mark uses this construction twenty-three times. Matthew has parallel material in seventeen instances but uses the construction in only five of these. Luke has parallel material in fifteen instances, but uses the construction in only two of these. While Matthew and Luke lack most of the Markan instances, each uses the construction outside of the parallels to Mark: Matthew three times (Matt 9:36; 24:38; 27:61) and Luke over forty times in his gospel and almost forty times in Acts.

This construction is one cited by C. H. Turner in his "Notes on Marcan Usage" in which he championed the two-document hypothesis.[24] The weakness of Turner's study is that he simply presupposes the theory that he wishes to defend. With respect to the construction under discussion, Turner simply assumes Mark's priority. He recognizes that Luke "is not averse" to this construction elsewhere in his gospel, but concludes that "he prunes it away drastically from his Marcan material."[25] To say that Luke is not averse to this construction is an understatement. It is a characteristic feature of Luke's style that he employs about eighty times in his two-volume work. Turner does not explain why Luke would act so strangely as to use this characteristic construction freely throughout both volumes of his work but to "prune" it almost every time he found it in Mark. Why would he feel free to use it everywhere except where he found it in Mark? Despite Turner's assumption, the two-document hypothesis cannot plausibly explain the absence of this feature of Mark's style from the parallels in Luke.

Could some other theory of Markan priority, such as Farrer's theory, succeed where the two-document hypothesis fails? A proponent of Farrer's theory might argue that Luke lacks the construction in parallels to Mark because at these points Luke was following Matthew, who had already eliminated most instances of the construction from the Markan material. A glance at Table 2.9, however, shows the inadequacy of this explanation. In only two of the twenty-three instances could it be argued that Luke followed Matthew (Luke 19:28; 22:55). In every other instance, Luke diverges from Matthew.

24. J. K. Elliott, ed., *The Language and Style of the Gospel of Mark: An Edition of C. H. Turner's "Notes on Marcan Usage" Together with Other Comparable Studies* (Leiden: Brill, 1993), 1–146.

25. Elliott, *Language and Style*, 92.

Thus the absence of this Markan construction from the parallels, especially in Luke, poses a problem for any theory of Markan priority. It is more reasonable to conclude that Mark shared a source or sources with Matthew and Luke and that this earlier material occasionally used the imperfect of εἰμί with a participle. While these instances of the construction were retained, each by one or more of the Synoptic evangelists, Mark and Luke frequently, and Matthew infrequently, added further instances. Such a theory would explain why Mark and Luke both frequently have the construction, but only rarely in parallel passages. Most instances of the construction in Mark would belong to a layer of Markan redaction that was unknown to Matthew or Luke.

7. The unique material in Mark includes not only characteristic expressions, such as those we have examined, but also characteristic motifs that involve more than one expression. Table 2.10 sets out one example: terms in Mark that put Jesus or his disciples at the center of a circle. Mark contains thirteen such instances, of which Matthew has none and Luke has only two.

### Table 2.10
### Mark's "circular" language

A. περιβλέπομαι

| Mark | Matthew | Luke |
|------|---------|------|
| 3:5 Jesus looks around | 12:13 — | 6:10 Jesus looks around |
| 3:34 Jesus looks around | 12:49 — | 8:21 — |
| 5:32 Jesus looks around | 9:22 — | 8:46 — |
| 9:8 disciples look around | 17:8 — | 9:36 — |
| 10:23 Jesus looks around | 19:23 — | 18:24 — |
| 11:11 Jesus looks around | | |

B. περί in a local sense

| | | |
|---|---|---|
| 3:32 crowd "around" Jesus | 12:47 — | 8:19 — |
| 3:34 those "around" Jesus | 12:49 — | 8:21 — |
| 4:10 those "around" Jesus | 13:10 — | 8:9 — |
| 9:14 crowd "around" disciples | 17:14 — | 9:37 — |

C. κύκλῳ

| | | |
|---|---|---|
| 3:34 "in a circle" around Jesus | 12:49 — | 8:21 — |
| 6:6 villages "round about" | 9:35 — | |
| 6:36 villages "round about" | 14:15 — | 9:12 villages "round about" |

As the table shows, Mark liked terms that put Jesus or his disciples at the center of a circle. Six times he uses the verb περιβλέπομαι, "look around." Four of these times it is Jesus who looks around at a group of people surrounding him (Mark 3:5; 3:34; 5:32; 10:23); once he looks around when he enters the Temple (11:11); and once it is the disciples who look around (9:8). Four other times Mark uses the preposition περί in its local sense, three times to refer to those "around" Jesus (3:32; 3:34; 4:10), and once in reference to a crowd "around" the disciples (9:14). Three times he uses the adverbial noun κύκλῳ, once to depict people sitting around Jesus "in a circle" (3:34), and twice of towns and villages "round about" Jesus' location (6:6; 6:36).

To these thirteen Markan instances of "circular" terms, Matthew has no equivalents whatsoever and Luke has only two (Mark 3:5//Luke 6:10; Mark 6:36//Luke 9:12), even though both evangelists share with Mark almost all of the passages in which these terms occur. On the theory of Markan priority, we would have to say that Matthew omitted all thirteen instances of circular terminology while Luke omitted eleven of the thirteen. Did then Matthew and Luke share some aversion to circles? If this seems less than credible, the alternative is to suppose that Matthew and Luke used a version of the material in which the bulk of this language did not appear. This circular language appears for the most part to be Markan redaction that Matthew and Luke did not know.

In two instances, Luke does use either περιβλέπομαι or κύκλῳ in a parallel to Mark. In these instances, it appears that the material shared by Mark and Luke already contained these expressions.[26] Since neither word is strange or unusual, we should not be surprised if both words occurred in the material prior to Mark. Mark apparently took over these two terms from the shared source, and, from his predilection for such expressions, added eleven other instances of circular language that did not occur in the earlier material.

8. Table 2.11 sets out another redactional motif in Mark: an emphasis on Jesus' teaching.[27] Mark uses either διδάσκειν or διδαχή twenty-one times in portraying Jesus, and once his disciples, in the act of teaching.[28] Nine of these instances occur in three characteristic Markan phrases: "he began to teach," "he taught them," and "in his teaching." All of these characteristic phrases are

---

26. We will subsequently find that Mark and Luke shared a source that I call Proto-Mark B. The two expressions common to Mark and Luke would have come from this source.

27. Helmut Koester points out this emphasis in "History and Development of Mark's Gospel (From Mark to Secret Mark and 'Canonical' Mark)," in *Colloquy on New Testament Studies: A Time for Reappraisal and Fresh Approaches* (ed. Bruce Corley; Macon, GA: Mercer University Press, 1983), 44–47.

28. I leave out of consideration Mark 7:7//Matt 15:9, because the verb has a subject other than Jesus or his disciples and therefore reflects a different theme.

Table 2.11
Jesus teaches in Mark (διδάσκειν and διδαχή)

| Mark | Matthew | Luke |
|---|---|---|
| 1:21 ἐδίδασκεν | 5:2 ἐδίδασκεν | 4:31 διδάσκων |
| 1:22a διδαχῇ | 7:28 διδαχῇ | 4:32a διδαχῇ |
| 1:22b διδάσκων | 7:29 διδάσκων | 4:32b — |
| 1:27 διδαχή | | 4:36 — |
| 6:6 διδάσκων | 9:35 διδάσκων | 8:1 — |
| 6:30 ἐδίδαξαν | 14:12b — | 9:10a — |
| 9:31 ἐδίδασκεν | 17:22 — | 9:43b — |
| 11:17 ἐδίδασκεν | 21:13 — | 19:46 — |
| 11:18 διδαχῇ | | 19:47 διδάσκων |
| 12:14 διδάσκεις | 22:16 διδάσκεις | 20:21 διδάσκεις |
| 12:35 διδάσκων | 22:42 — | 20:41 — |
| 14:49 διδάσκων | 26:55 διδάσκων | 22:53 — |

| Mark | Matthew | Luke |
|---|---|---|
| 4:1 ἤρξατο διδάσκειν | 13:1 — | 8:4 — |
| 6:2 ἤρξατο διδάσκειν | 13:54 ἐδίδασκεν αὐτούς | 4:16 — |
| 6:34 ἤρξατο διδάσκειν | 14:14 — | 9:11 — |
| 8:31 ἤρξατο διδάσκειν | 16:21 ἤρξατο δεικνύειν | 9:22 — |

| Mark | Matthew | Luke |
|---|---|---|
| 2:13 ἐδίδασκεν αὐτούς | 9:9 — | 5:27 — |
| 4:2a ἐδίδασκεν αὐτούς | 13:3a — | 8:4 — (but cf. 5:3) |
| 10:1 ἐδίδασκεν αὐτούς | 19:2 — | |

| Mark | Matthew | Luke |
|---|---|---|
| 4:2b ἐν τῇ διδαχῇ αὐτοῦ | 13:3b — | 8:4 — |
| 12:38 ἐν τῇ διδαχῇ αὐτου | 23:2 — | 20:45 — |

missing from the parallels in Matthew and Luke, as are five of Mark's remaining references to teaching (Mark 1:27; 6:30; 9:31; 11:17; 12:35).[29]

Thus fully two-thirds of Mark's references to Jesus' teaching are absent from Matthew and Luke. On the theory of Markan priority, we would have to assume that Matthew and Luke both tended to eliminate the theme of Jesus' teaching where they found it in Mark, especially where Mark used certain

---

29. Mark's extra references appear in summary statements of Jesus' activity (1:27; 2:13; 6:2; 6:30; 6:34; 10:1), as introductions to individual sayings (8:31; 9:31; 11:17; 12:35; 12:38), and in the introduction to the parable discourse (4:1; 4:2a; 4:2b). To introduce the parable discourse, Mark uses each of his three characteristic phrases once.

characteristic phrases. Why they would both do so, however, would be a difficult question to answer. It is easier to explain this phenomenon as the redactional activity of one editor, Mark, than as the activity of two editors, both deciding to omit the theme. More plausibly, therefore, Mark found references to Jesus' teaching in his sources and augmented this theme by adding further references. In making these additional references, he repeatedly used certain characteristic modes of expression. Matthew and Luke, then, did not use Mark, but shared with Mark some source or sources that did not have these redactional additions.

9. Not only do Matthew and Luke lack stylistic features of Mark, they lack entire themes. Table 2.12 shows seven passages unique to Mark that share such a theme: Jesus' great popularity and his consequent lack of privacy.

### Table 2.12
### Jesus' popularity in Mark

| Mark | Matthew | Luke |
|---|---|---|
| 1:33 "And the whole city was gathered at the door." | 8:16 — | 4:40 — |
| 1:45 A healed man "began to proclaim it πολλά . . . so that [Jesus] could no longer enter a city openly." | 9:31 — | 5:15 — |
| 2:1-2 "it was heard that he was at home. And so many were gathered that there was no longer room even at the door." | 9:10 — | 5:17 — |
| 3:20 "And the crowd came together again so that they could not even eat bread." | | |
| 6:31 "And he said to them, 'Come by yourselves to a deserted spot and rest a while.' For many were coming and going, and they did not even have time to eat." | 14:12–13 — | 9:10 — |
| 7:24 "Going into a house he did not want anyone to know, but he could not hide." | 15:21 — | |
| 9:30–31a "they were going through Galilee and he did not want anyone to know. For he was teaching his disciples." | 17:22 — | 9:43 — |

In these passages, Mark depicted Jesus as a man mobbed by crowds, a man who had difficulty living a normal life and who sometimes had to seek privacy. All seven instances of this theme are missing from both Matthew and Luke. These passages are related not only thematically but also stylistically, to each other and to other unique material in Mark. Two of the passages use a form of συνάγω with the phrase πρὸς τὴν θύραν to describe a crowd gathered at Jesus' door (1:33; 2:2). Three use the construction ὥστε μή or μηκέτι with an infinitive to describe something that Jesus' popularity made difficult to do (1:45; 2:2; 3:20). Three of the passages state that Jesus' popularity curtailed some normal activity, either his ability to enter a city openly (1:45) or his opportunity to eat (3:20; 6:31). Two describe thwarted attempts of Jesus to escape the crowd (6:31; 7:24).[30] Two use the phrase οὐκ (or οὐδένα) ἤθελεν with a form of γινώσκειν to state that Jesus wanted no one to know his whereabouts (7:24; 9:30).[31] One uses adverbial πολλά (1:45), which we identified earlier as a distinctive Markan use of πολύς (Table 2.4B). Two use πολλοί referring to a crowd with Jesus (2:2; 6:31), another Markan use of πολύς (Table 2.4C). One uses πάλιν to describe repetition of an action mentioned in an earlier pericope (3:20), another feature that we have identified as Markan redaction (Table 2.5). One has Jesus teaching the disciples in a passion prediction (9:31a), as occurs also elsewhere in Mark 8:31, both times being instances of the Markan motif of Jesus' teaching (Table 2.11).

The theory of Markan priority cannot reasonably explain why Matthew and Luke would omit these related passages. If they had Mark before them, it is not plausible to think that either, much less both, just happened to omit all seven occurrences of this theme. Nor is it likely that both noticed the theme and made a conscious decision to eliminate it wherever it occurred. It is a benign theme, not one likely to offend the sensibilities of either evangelist, much less both. This "popularity versus privacy" theme in Mark thus provides the strongest possible evidence of Markan redaction unknown to Matthew and Luke: it involves multiple passages that are thematically and stylistically related, it is benign, and it is completely absent from both Matthew and Luke. The most obvious explanation is that Mark added this theme to material that he shared with Matthew and Luke. It did not occur in the version of the material that Matthew and Luke were using.

10. So far, we have been examining individual stylistic and thematic features of Mark. We must also consider an instance where several Markan features occur together in a single passage, most of which is absent from Matthew and Luke. Such a passage is Mark 9:14–16, the introduction to an exorcism story in which Jesus frees a possessed boy. As Table 2.13 shows, Mark's introduction is considerably longer than those of Matthew and Luke and contains numerous terms that occur uniquely or almost uniquely in Mark.

---

30. In the first instance, Jesus goes to a deserted place to be alone with his disciples, but the crowd follows him there. In the second, Jesus tries to hide in a house in Tyre, but a woman with a need finds him.

31. These passages involve Jesus' desire to conceal his whereabouts to avoid the press of the crowd, and they occur only in Mark. This motif differs from the motifs of secrecy that have parallels in all three of the Synoptics. These include prohibitions against revealing Jesus' identity (Mark 1:24–25, 34; 3:10–12; 8:30; 9:9), prohibitions against telling about a miracle (Mark 1:43–45; 5:43; 7:36; 8:26), and characterization of the parables as secrets (Mark 4:10–12, 22, 33–34).

## Table 2.13
### Markan vocabulary in Mark 9:14–16

A. Mark 9:14–16 and parallels. Markan vocabulary is in italics.

| Matt 17:14 | Mark 9:14–16 | Luke 9:37 |
|---|---|---|
| As they came to the crowd, | And coming to the disciples, he saw a large crowd *around them* (περὶ αὐτούς) and scribes *arguing* (συζητοῦντας) with them. And *immediately* (εὐθὺς) when all the crowd saw him, *they were astounded* (ἐξεθαμβήθησαν). And *running forward* (προστρέχοντες) *they greeted* (ἠσπάζοντο) him. And *he asked* (ἐπηρώτησεν) them, "Why *are you arguing* (συζητεῖτε) with them?" | A large crowd met him. |

B. Italicized terms absent from parallels

| Mark | Matthew | Luke |
|---|---|---|
| 1:27 θαμβέομαι | | 4:36 θάμβος |
| 9:15 ἐκθαμβέομαι | | |
| 10:24 θαμβέομαι | | |
| 10:32 θαμβέομαι | | |
| 14:33 ἐκθαμβέομαι | 26:37 — | |
| 16:5 ἐκθαμβέομαι | 28:4 — | 24:5 — |
| 16:6 θαμβέομαι | 28:5 — | 24:5 — |

| | | |
|---|---|---|
| 1:27 συζητέω | | 4:36 — |
| 8:11 συζητέω | 16:1 — | |
| 9:10 συζητέω | | 9:36 — |
| 9:14 συζητέω | | |
| 9:16 συζητέω | | |
| 12:28 συζητέω | 22:34–35 — | 10:25 — |

| | | |
|---|---|---|
| 6:33 συντρέχω | 14:13 — | 9:11 — |
| 6:55 περιτρέχω | 14:35 — | |
| 9:15 προστρέχω | | |
| 9:25 ἐπισυντρέχω | | |
| 10:17 προστρέχω | 19:16 — | 18:18 — |

| Mark | Matthew | Luke |
|---|---|---|
| 3:32 περί around Jesus | 12:47 — | 8:19 — |
| 3:34 περί around Jesus | 12:49 — | 8:21 — |
| 4:10 περί around Jesus | 13:10 — | 8:9 — |
| 9:14 περί around disciples | 17:14 — | 9:37 — |

| | | |
|---|---|---|
| 9:15 ἀσπάζομαι | | |
| 15:18 ἀσπάζομαι | 27:29 — | |

C. Italicized terms usually absent from parallels

| | Mark | Matthew | Luke |
|---|---|---|---|
| εὐθύς | 41 | 5 | 0 |
| ἐπερωτάω | 25 | 7 | 9 |

The extra material in Mark's version of the introduction has a high con-centration of Markan vocabulary: (ἐκ)θαμβέομαι, συζητέω, τρέχω in com-pounds, περί of people around Jesus or the disciples (cf. Table 2.9B above), ἀσπάζομαι (both + αὐτόν), εὐθύς, and ἐπερωτάω.[32] As shown in Table 2.13B, five of these seven terms appear more than once in Mark but never in the parallels to Mark in Matthew and Luke. If we follow Streeter, the theory of Markan priority affirms that Matthew and Luke eliminated these five words from the exorcism story in abbreviating Mark's introduction. They omitted the words when they omitted the bulk of this passage. This explana-tion is not implausible if we look at this passage alone. However, the theory must also affirm that Matthew and Luke also eliminated these words every-where else they occur in Mark, by either omitting the material in which they occur or revising it. That *is* implausible. We have no reason to think that either Matthew or Luke so disliked these words that they would single them out intentionally for omission. In non-Markan contexts, Luke uses συζητέω (Luke 22:23; 24:15), προστρέχω (Acts 8:30), and ἀσπάζομαι (Luke 1:40; 10:4), while Matthew uses ἀσπάζομαι (Matt 5:47; 10:12). Nor is it likely that every occurrence of every word would disappear unintentionally in the process of editing. Taken together, the five terms occur in Mark twenty-four times. That means that they had forty-eight opportunities to survive the redactional process: twenty-four times in Matthew and twenty-four times in Luke. The probability that these words would be eliminated by chance all forty-eight times is practically nil.

---

32. Hawkins lists εὐθύς as a word that is characteristic of Mark's gospel (*Horae Synopticae*, 12–13). While he does not include ἐπερωτάω in his list, he later notes that it deserves consider-ation as being characteristic of Mark (p. 14).

Only one explanation makes sense of the data: Matthew and Luke did not abbreviate the introduction to the exorcism story—Mark expanded it. The high concentration of Markan vocabulary in such a brief compass suggests that Mark's extra material in this passage comes from Mark's own hand rather than from prior tradition. Mark composed this material and used the same language in other places, where he also revised and expanded the material that he received. This redactional level in Mark was not known to Matthew and Luke. They used not Mark but Mark's source or sources, which did not include Mark's redactional additions.

11. The introduction that we have just examined is followed in all three gospels by the exorcism story itself (Mark 9:17–27).[33] Since Mark's account of this exorcism is over twice as long as either of the others, this story provides what the theory of Markan priority would have to regard as a major agreement of omission by Matthew and Luke. Unlike the omissions discussed above, this is not the omission of a recurring feature of Mark. Yet it too provides evidence for a layer of Markan redaction unknown to Matthew and Luke.

The reason for Mark's verbosity is that he has combined two different stories or two different versions of the same story. This fact has been recognized by numerous scholars. Bultmann, for example, pointed to inconsistencies and repetitions in Mark's story as evidence that two distinct versions have been combined. 1) Verses 14–19 focus on the unbelief of the disciples, while in vv. 21ff. it is the father's unbelief that is the point. 2) The illness is described twice in vv. 18 and 21ff. 3) The crowd is already present in v. 14 yet in v. 25 comes on the scene for the first time. 4) The reaction of the demon occurs twice, in v. 20 and v. 26. Without being too precise, Bultmann finds that "the first story occupies roughly vv. 14–20 and the second vv. 21–27."[34] Other scholars, with variations, have agreed.[35]

For two reasons it appears that Matthew and Luke did not know Mark's conflated version of the story.[36] First, as we saw above, the introduction to the

---

33. Mark and Matthew have attached to the story an addendum, in which Jesus uses the event to teach his disciples (Matt 17:19–20; Mark 9:28–29). Form-critically, the miracle story is complete by itself, so the addendum is probably a later addition. Here we will be concerned only with the miracle story proper.

34. Rudolf Bultmann, *The History of the Synoptic Tradition* (rev. ed; New York: Harper & Row, 1968), 211.

35. Vincent Taylor, *The Gospel According to St. Mark* (London: Macmillan, 1952), 395–96; H. J. Held, "Matthew as Interpreter of the Miracle Stories," in G. Bornkamm, G. Barth, and H. J. Held, *Tradition and Interpretation in Matthew* (London: SCM, 1963), 187; Reginald Fuller, *Interpreting the Miracles* (London: SCM, 1963), 34; D. E. Nineham, *The Gospel of St Mark* (Harmondsworth: Penguin, 1963), 242, 246–47; Eduard Schweizer, *The Good News According to Mark* (Atlanta: John Knox, 1970), 187; Paul J. Achtemeier, "Miracles and the Historical Jesus: A Study of Mark 9:14-29," *CBQ* 37 (1975): 471–91, esp. 475–82.

36. This view is taken by Johannes Weiss, *Die älteste Evangelium* (Göttingen: Vandenhoeck & Ruprecht, 1903), 249–50; Wilhelm Bussmann, *Zur Geschichtsquelle* (Vol. 1 of *Synoptische Studien*; Halle: Weisenhause, 1925), 81–83; Koester, "History and Development of Mark's

story contains a high concentration of recurring Markan vocabulary that never appears in the parallels to Mark in Matthew or Luke (Table 2.13). This led us to conclude that this passage came from Mark's own hand and was unknown to either Matthew or Luke.

Second, if Matthew and Luke had copied Mark's account, we would expect their versions to show evidence of both stories combined in Mark. In fact, however, Matthew and Luke appear to have known only one of the stories. This becomes clear from Table 2.14. The first two columns show the versions of Matthew and Luke, respectively. In the third column (marked Version A), I have placed the Markan material that has a parallel in Matthew and/or Luke. In the final column (marked Version B), I have placed the Markan material that has no parallel in either Matthew or Luke, i.e., the material that Matthew and Luke supposedly agreed to omit. The result is that each Markan column presents an internally consistent version of the exorcism, lacking some material at the beginning.

Table 2.14

**Two stories conflated in Mark 9:17–27**

| Matt 17:14b–18 | Luke 9:38–42 | Mark 9:17–27 Version A | Mark 9:17–27 Version B |
|---|---|---|---|
| 14b a man came up to him . . . 15 saying, "Lord, | 38 And behold a man from the crowd cried out, saying, "Teacher, | 17a And a man from the crowd replied to him, "Teacher, | |
| pity my son | I beg you, look upon my son . . . | 17b I brought my son to you, | |
| | | | who has an unspeaking spirit, |
| because he is moonstruck and suffers terribly. | 39 And behold a spirit seizes him . . . and it convulses him with foam | 18a And wherever it seizes him, it tears him and he foams at the mouth | |
| | | | 18b and he gnashes his teeth and dries up." |

Gospel," 50–52; Harold Riley, *The Making of Mark: An Exploration* (Macon, GA: Mercer University Press, 1989), 105–8.

| Matt 17:14b–18 | Luke 9:38–42 | Mark 9:17–27 Version A | Mark 9:17–27 Version B |
|---|---|---|---|
| For often it throws him into the fire and often into the water. | | 22a And often it has thrown him into fire or into water to destroy him. | |
| 16 And I brought him to your disciples, but they were not able to heal him." | 40 And I requested your disciples to cast it out, but they were not able." | 18c And I asked your disciples to cast it out, but they could not." | |
| 17 Replying, Jesus said, "O faithless and perverse generation, how long must I be with you? How long must I endure you? Bring him here to me." | 41 Replying, Jesus said, "O faithless and perverse generation, how long must I be with you and endure you? Bring your son over here." | 19 Replying to them, he says, "O faithless generation, how long must I be with you? How long must I endure you? Bring him to me." | |
| | 42 While he was still coming, the demon tore at him and convulsed him. | 20 So they brought him to him. Upon seeing him, the spirit immediately convulsed him. Falling on the ground, he rolled around foaming at the mouth. | |
| | | | 21 And he asked his father, "How long a time since this happened to him?" He said, "Since child-hood. |
| | | | 22b But if you can do any-thing, help us, having compas-sion for us." |

| Matt 17:14b–18 | Luke 9:38–42 | Mark 9:17–27 Version A | Mark 9:17–27 Version B |
|---|---|---|---|
| | | | 23 Jesus said to him, "If you can? All things are possible to one who believes." 24 Immediately the father of the child cried out and said, "I believe! Help my unbelief!" 25a Jesus, seeing that a crowd was running up, |
| 18 And Jesus rebuked him, | But Jesus rebuked the unclean spirit | 25b He rebuked the unclean spirit, | |
| | | | 25c (said) to him, "You unspeaking and mute spirit, I command you, come out of him and never enter him again." 26a Crying out and convulsing severely, |
| and the demon came out of him. | | it came out. | |
| And the child was healed from that hour. | and cured the child. | | |
| | | | 26b he became as if dead, so that many said that he had died. 27 But |

| Matt 17:14b–18 | Luke 9:38–42 | Mark 9:17–27 Version A | Mark 9:17–27 Version B |
|---|---|---|---|
| | | | Jesus, grasping his hand, raised him and he stood up. |

By separating the story in this way, we see that each Markan column, apart from the beginning, presents a relatively complete story on its own. In each, a father brings his possessed son to Jesus and Jesus casts out the demon. Furthermore, the story in each column is internally consistent, since the inconsistent features of the conflated version are distributed between the two columns, as shown in Table 2.15.

**Table 2.15**

**Inconsistencies in the conflated story**

| Version A | Version B |
|---|---|
| The crowd arrives before Jesus and the father converse (Matt; Luke; Mark 9:14a). | The crowd arrives after Jesus and the father converse (Mark 9:25a). |
| The demon is an "unclean spirit" that tries to destroy the boy (Matt; Luke; Mark 9:22a, 25b). | The demon is an "unspeaking and mute spirit" that prevents the boy from talking (Mark 9:17b, 25c). |
| The spirit convulses the boy and throws him on the ground before Jesus speaks to it (Luke; Mark 9:20). | The spirit convulses the boy after Jesus speaks to it (Mark 9:26). |
| The story revolves around the disciples' lack of faith (Matt; Luke; Mark 9:18c–19). | The story revolves around the father's faith or lack of faith (Mark 9:22b–24). |

Separating the material into columns also brings to light a few features of the two versions that are not inconsistencies as such, but simply differences in the two accounts (Table 2.16).

Thus the material shared by Mark with Matthew and Luke presents a relatively complete, internally consistent story; while the material unique to Mark also presents a relatively complete, internally consistent story. This fact suggests that Mark has conflated two stories, one of which also appears in Matthew and Luke (Version A), and one of which appears only in Mark (Version B).

Table 2.16
Other differences between Version A and Version B

| Version A | Version B |
| --- | --- |
| Jesus rebukes the spirit (Matthew; Luke; Mark 9:25b). | Jesus commands the spirit to come out of the boy in direct discourse (Mark 9:25c). |
| The child is healed or cured (Matthew; Luke; omitted by Mark). | The child falls down as dead and Jesus raises him (Mark 9:26b–27). |

How consistent are these results with theories of Markan priority? The problem is to explain how Matthew and Luke, while copying from Mark, both came to completely omit Version B. One would have to explain not simply the omission of isolated words and sentences, but the omission of an entire story embedded within another. To explain this omission, Farrer's theory would have to affirm that Matthew exercised the skills of a modern source critic. He first had to identify in Mark's conflated account all of the elements of Version B before excising them from the story. Luke then chose to follow Matthew rather than Mark. The two-document hypothesis would require us to believe that Matthew and Luke independently exercised source-critical skills and came up with the same results in distinguishing Version A from Version B. They then independently agreed on which version to omit and which to include. Either theory of Markan priority asks too much of us. A more reasonable explanation is that Matthew and Luke knew only Version A. While all three evangelists knew Version A, only Mark knew Version B as well. He received Version A from the source or sources that he shared with Matthew and Luke, and he combined this with Version B, which he obtained from some other source. Since Matthew and Luke did not know Mark, they did not know either Version B or the conflated account found in Mark.

Version B shows a few characteristics of Mark's style, such as εὐθύς (9:24) and τρέχω in a compound (9:25a). Is it possible then that Mark created this material as a supplement to Version A rather than finding it in a preexisting form?[37] Either alternative would pose the same problem for Markan priority, since in either case one would have to explain how Matthew and Luke managed to identify and omit Mark's additions to the story. It seems doubtful, however, that one can attribute the B version to Mark, though he may well have overlaid it with elements of his own style. If Mark created this material to supplement Version A, we would expect it to be more consistent with Version A and we would not expect it to constitute an entire story by itself.

---

37. Such is the position taken by Peabody, Cope, and McNicol, *One Gospel from Two*, 202–6.

The character of Mark's extra material (Version B) thus suggests that it came from a pre-Markan story similar to, but not fully consistent with, Version A.

12. Finally, in addition to those features discussed above, Table 2.17 lists without discussion other recurring features of Mark. These occur in Markan material with no parallel as well as material with a parallel in Matthew and/or Luke. For the most part, these features of Mark do not occur at all in the parallels in Matthew or Luke. Only in the first three examples (εἰσπορεύομαι, ἀναστάς, πρωΐ) does either Matthew or Luke have the stylistic feature in one or more parallels to Mark. In these three cases, it appears that the feature occasionally occurred already in the sources shared by the evangelists. Mark, however, shows a predilection for these features, adding additional instances in his redaction. In the remaining instances, the Markan feature does not occur at all in the parallels in Matthew and Luke. The great majority of these stylistic features are benign, and many occur in Matthew or Luke elsewhere than the Markan parallels. Joined with the features already discussed, those listed in Table 2.17 add confirmation that Mark includes a layer of redaction that was unknown to Matthew or Luke.

### Table 2.17
### Further distinctive features of Mark

A. Features that occur four or more times

εἰσπορεύομαι. Used elsewhere in Luke-Acts eight times.

| Mark | Matthew | Luke |
|---|---|---|
| 1:21 εἰσπορεύονται | 4:13 ἐλθὼν κατῴκησεν | 4:31 κατῆλθεν |
| 4:19 εἰσπορευόμεναι | 13:22 — | 8:14 πορευόμενοι |
| 5:40 εἰσπορεύεται | 9:25 εἰσελθών | 8:54 — |
| 6:56 εἰσεπορεύετο | | |
| 7:15 εἰσπορευόμενον | 15:11 εἰσερχόμενον | |
| 7:18 εἰσπορευόμενον | 15:17 εἰσπορευόμενον | |
| 7:19 εἰσπορεύεται | | |
| 11:2 εἰσπορευόμενοι | 21:2 — | 19:30 εἰσπορευόμενοι |

ἀναστάς. Used elsewhere in Luke ten times.

| Mark | Matthew | Luke |
|---|---|---|
| 1:35 ἀναστάς | | 4:42 — |
| 2:14 ἀναστάς | 9:9 ἀναστάς | 5:28 ἀναστάς |

| Mark | Matthew | Luke |
|---|---|---|
| 7:24 ἀναστάς | 15:21 ἐξελθών | |
| 10:1 ἀναστάς | 19:1 — | |
| 14:57 ἀναστάντες | 26:60 προσελθόντες | |
| 14:60 ἀναστάς | 26:62 ἀναστάς | |
| 16:9 ἀναστάς | | |

πρωί. Used elsewhere by Matthew (Matt 16:3; 20:1).

| | | |
|---|---|---|
| 1:35 πρωί | | 4:42 — |
| 11:20 πρωί | 21:18 πρωί | |
| 13:35 πρωί | | |
| 15:1 πρωί | 27:1 πρωία | |
| 16:2 πρωί | 28:1 — | 24:1 — |
| 16:9 πρωί | | |

διαστέλλομαι. Used elsewhere by Matthew (Matt 16:20) and Luke (Acts 15:24).

| | | |
|---|---|---|
| 5:43 διαστέλλομαι | | 8:56 — |
| 7:36 διαστέλλομαι | | |
| 7:36 διαστέλλομαι | | |
| 8:15 διαστέλλομαι | 16:6 — | |
| 9:9 διαστέλλομαι | 17:9 ἐντέλλομαι | |

εἰμί in genitive absolute. Used elsewhere by Luke (Luke 14:32; 22:53).

| | | |
|---|---|---|
| 8:1 ὄντος | | |
| 11:11 οὔσης | 21:17 — | |
| 14:3 ὄντος | 26:6 — | |
| 14:66 ὄντος | 26:69 — | 22:55 — |

κηρύσσειν + δαιμόνια ἐκβάλλειν

| | | |
|---|---|---|
| 1:39 κηρύσσειν + δαιμόνια ἐκβάλλειν | | 4:44 κηρύσσειν |
| 3:14–15 κηρύσσειν + δαιμόνια ἐκβάλλειν | 10:1 πνεύματα ἐκβάλλειν | 6:13 — |
| 6:12–13 κηρύσσειν + δαιμόνια ἐκβάλλειν | | 9:6 — |
| 16:15–17 κηρύσσειν + δαιμόνια ἐκβάλλειν | | |

λίαν. Used elsewhere by Matthew (Matt 2:16; 4:8; 8:28; 27:14) and Luke (Luke 23:8).

| Mark | Matthew | Luke |
|---|---|---|
| 1:35 λίαν | | 4:42 — |
| 6:51 λίαν | 14:33 — | |
| 9:3 λίαν | 17:2 — | 9:29 — |
| 16:2 λίαν | 28:1 — | 24:1 — |

B. Features that occur three times in Mark but never in the parallel in Matthew or Luke.

- ἄρρωστοι: Mark 6:5, 13; 16:18. Elsewhere Matt 14:14.
- μάστιξ: Mark 3:10; 5:29; 5:34. Elsewhere Luke 7:21; Acts 22:24.
- μεθερμηνεύομαι: Mark 5:41; 15:22; 15:34. Elsewhere Matt 1:23; Acts 4:36; 13:8.
- μετὰ τρεῖς ἡμέρας + ἀνίστημι: Mark 8:31; 9:31; 10:34.
- ὁ βαπτίζων as epithet of John: Mark 1:4; 6:14, 24.
- ὅταν + ἀνίστημι: Mark 9:9; 12:23, 25.
- ὅταν + indicative: Mark 3:11; 11:19, 25 (all in clauses with no parallel in Matthew or Luke).
- ὅτι interrogative: Mark 2:16; 9:11, 28 (also Mark 2:7 v. l.; 8:12 v. l.; 14:60 v. l.).
- ὅτι οὕτως: Mark 2:8, 12; 15:39.
- πωρόω and πώρωσις used of the heart: Mark 3:5; 6:52; 8:17.
- -χου as adverbial ending: Mark 1:28 and 16:20 (πανταχοῦ); 1:38 (ἀλλαχοῦ). Elsewhere Luke 9:6 (πανταχοῦ).
- Duplication used distributively: Mark 6:7 (δύο δύο); 6:39 (συμπόσια συμπόσια); 6:40 (πρασιαὶ πρασιαί).
- Expression of mental or emotional activity within Jesus: Mark 2:8 and 8:12 (τῷ πνεύματι αὐτοῦ); 5:30 (ἐν ἑαυτῷ).

C. Features that occur twice in Mark but never in the parallel in Matthew or Luke.

- ἄνθρωπος ἐν πνεύματι ἀκαθάρτῳ: Mark 1:23; 5:2.
- ἀπὸ τοῦ ὄχλου in the sense "away from the crowd": Mark 7:17, 33.
- [δια]γενομένου σαββάτου: Mark 6:2; 16:1.
- ζητοῦσίν σε: Mark 1:37; 3:32.
- ἡδέως αὐτοῦ ἤκουεν: Mark 6:20; 12:37.
- θυγάτριον: Mark 5:23; 7:25.
- κάθημαι or καθίζω κατέναντι: Mark 12:41; 13:3.

- καθίσας: Mark 9:35; 12:41. Elsewhere Matt 5:1; 13:48; Luke-Acts (8 times).
- καὶ [ἕνεκεν] τοῦ εὐαγγελίου following ἕνεκεν ἐμοῦ: Mark 8:35; 10:29.
- μέγας of fear or amazement: Mark 4:41; 5:42. Elsewhere Luke 2:9; 8:37.
- νεανίσκος περιβεβλημένος: Mark 14:51; 16:5.
- οἱ δὲ ἐσιώπων: Mark 3:4; 9:34.
- ου[κ] ἤδει[σαν] τί ἀποκριθῇ [ἀποκριθῶσιν]: Mark 9:6; 14:40.
- πίπτειν ἐπὶ τῆς γῆς: Mark 9:20; 14:35. Elsewhere πίπτειν ἐπὶ τὴν γῆν, Matt 10:29; 13:8; Acts 9:4.
- πρὸς τὴν θάλασσαν: Mark 3:7; 4:1.
- πτύσας as method of healing: Mark 7:33; 8:23.
- στήκω: Mark 3:31; 11:25.
- [ὑπερ]περισσῶς ἐξεπλήσσοντο: Mark 7:37; 10:26.
- Command to spirit in direct discourse: Mark 5:8; 9:25.

For many of the items that I have discussed or listed I am indebted to David Peabody's compilation of recurring literary features of Mark.[38] From Peabody's collection I have extracted primarily those features that are absent from the parallels in Matthew and Luke. In a subsequent work, Peabody and his colleagues in the International Institute for Renewal of Gospel Studies present an argument similar to the one that I have made here.[39] They point to evidence for a "Markan Overlay," by which they mean "a network of repeated words, phrases, grammatical constructions, themes, literary structures, and theological motifs" that are characteristic of Mark but generally absent from the parallels in Matthew and Luke. As proponents of the Griesbach hypothesis, they include in this overlay what they see as "repeated and consistent Markan alterations of the texts of Matthew or Luke or some combination of Markan supplements and modifications."[40] Since I see insuperable difficulties with the Griesbach hypothesis, I cannot follow these scholars to their ultimate conclusion. We do agree, however, that the Gospel of Mark contains an overlay of Markan redaction that is absent from the parallels in Matthew and Luke, that this Markan redaction was unknown to Matthew and Luke, and that the presence of such redaction in Mark poses a serious problem for any theory of Markan priority.

## Conclusion

The theory of Markan priority affirms that both Matthew and Luke used canonical Mark as their main source. The evidence presented above poses a

---

38. Peabody, *Mark as Composer*, 31–113.
39. Peabody, Cope, and McNicol, *One Gospel from Two*, 35–45, 383–91.
40. Ibid., 35.

real problem for any form of that theory, whether it be Farrer's theory, the two-document hypothesis, or the three-source theory. Mark is replete with recurring expressions, motifs, and themes that are totally or almost totally absent from Matthew and Luke. Since the great majority of these are benign, it is difficult to explain why either evangelist would omit them. It is more difficult to explain why both would. Since these features are numerous, individually and as a group, it is also difficult to see how Matthew and Luke could have unintentionally omitted them all in the process of revision.

According to Farrer's theory, Matthew would have been the first to omit all of these Markan features. Either he omitted them intentionally, or their omission was the unintended consequence of other revisions that he made. Since the great majority of these are benign, it is difficult to explain why Matthew would omit them intentionally, especially since he uses some of them in contexts other than in parallels to Mark. Since these features are numerous, individually and as a group, it is also difficult to see how Matthew could have unintentionally omitted them all in the process of revision. According to this theory, Luke came last, drawing on both Mark and Matthew. Either Luke intentionally made the same omissions from Mark as Matthew, or he unintentionally made these omissions by always following Matthew at those places where Matthew omitted the stylistic features of Mark in question. Neither explanation of Luke's procedure is plausible. Since the great majority of the stylistic features are benign, it is difficult to explain why Luke would omit them intentionally, especially since he uses some of them in contexts other than in parallels to Mark. Since these features are numerous, individually and as a group, it is also improbable that Luke would always just happen to be following Matthew at those places where Matthew made these omissions from Mark. Farrer's theory thus has no plausible explanation for the editorial procedure of either Matthew or Luke with respect to these features of Mark's style. It also fails to explain how Matthew, presumably followed by Luke, could have identified and omitted Version B from the conflated exorcism stories in Mark 9:14–27.

The two-document hypothesis fares no better in explaining the absence of this Markan material from Matthew and Luke. According to this theory, Matthew and Luke independently omitted the recurring stylistic features in question. Since it is difficult to explain why either evangelist would intentionally omit them, it is more difficult to explain why both would do so independently. It is also difficult to see how Matthew and Luke could have unintentionally omitted so many recurring features of Mark's style independently in the process of revision. Likewise, it is difficult to explain how Matthew and Luke independently identified and omitted Version B from the conflated exorcism stories in Mark 9:14–27.

The three-source hypothesis starts with the two-document hypothesis and adds the view found in Farrer's theory that Luke also knew Matthew. It therefore faces the same objections as both the two-document hypothesis and Farrer's theory. Thus, no theory of Markan priority adequately explains the "agreements of omission" of Matthew and Luke against Mark.

If the stylistic features that we have identified occurred uniquely in Matthew or uniquely in Luke, they would be readily identified by Markan prioritists as redactional additions of one evangelist that were unknown to the other two. To be consistent, we must identify them as such when they appear uniquely in Mark. These distinctive, recurring features of Mark show that this gospel includes a whole layer of Markan redaction that was unknown to Matthew and Luke. Mark's conflation of the exorcism stories in Mark 9:17–27 points in the same direction. The conclusion seems inevitable that Matthew and Luke did not use as a source the Mark that we now know. In some way yet to be discussed, all three evangelists drew on a common source or set of sources. The evangelist responsible for Mark revised those sources in his own unique way, just as the other evangelists did. In so doing, he added whole stories and overlaid the tradition with a layer of his own stylistic and thematic peculiarities. We can state our main conclusion thus:

*The Gospel of Mark did not serve as a source for either Matthew or Luke.*

# Chapter 3

# *Matthean Redaction Absent from Mark and Luke*

THE MAIN ALTERNATIVE to Markan priority has always been Matthean priority, the view that Matthew's gospel came first and was used as a source by both Mark and Luke. Once we reject Markan priority, as we did in Chapter 2, must we then fall back on Matthean priority, as espoused by either the Griesbach or the Augustinian hypothesis? As Paul would say, μὴ γένοιτο (Rom 6:2, etc.). The same argument that we raised against Markan priority in Chapter 2 applies equally well to Matthean priority. The Gospel of Matthew has recurring features of style that are completely or almost completely absent from both Mark and Luke. Entire themes and stylistic features that occur repeatedly in Matthew are lacking in the other two Synoptics. What needs explaining, then, is not the omission of individual words or sentences, but the omission of entire themes and recurring features of Matthew's style. Since the great majority of these are benign, i.e., not objectionable either grammatically or ideologically, they are difficult to explain as omissions by either Mark or Luke, more difficult to explain as omissions by both. They are easily explained, however, as a level of redaction in Matthew unknown to either Mark or Luke. Their absence from Mark and Luke indicates that neither gospel depended on Matthew. Here I will discuss some of the more significant items and simply list others.

## Distinctive Features of Matthew

1. Matthew favors above all the word "then" (τότε), using it ninety times in his gospel. Mark has a parallel to Matthew in forty-four of these ninety cases, but uses τότε in only five of the forty-four. Similarly, Luke has a parallel in forty cases, but uses τότε in only seven of them. Given the theory of Matthean priority, it is hard to explain why Mark and Luke both omitted the term so often. It is a benign term, not objectionable either stylistically or ideologically. Luke at any rate had no aversion to it, since he used it twenty-one times in Acts and another eight times in his gospel where Matthew does not

have it. Why then would he eliminate it thirty-three of forty times from the material that he drew from Matthew? Why would Mark similarly eliminate it thirty-nine of forty-four times from the material that he drew from Matthew?

Is it possible that Mark and Luke had a common aversion not to the word itself but to its overuse? That is not likely. The word occurs in Matthew about three times per chapter on the average. That frequency for such a common word would not attract attention to itself unless one were specifically looking for the word. The general absence of this word from the parallels in Mark and Luke suggests instead that neither used Matthew. Let us suppose then that all three evangelists used the same or similar sources for the triple tradition and that Matthew and Luke used Q as well. In the triple tradition, all three found τότε four times (Mark 2:20; 3:27; 13:14; 13:26), and all retained it each time, except that Luke substituted a parallel from Q for the second passage. Similarly, Matthew and Luke found τότε four times in Q (Luke 6:42; 11:24; 11:26; 14:21) and both retained it each time. Mark added one more instance of τότε to these and Luke added eight, whether from other sources or redaction, but Matthew far outdid the others by adding eighty-two instances of τότε beyond the eight that he shared with Mark and/or Luke. These eighty-two instances unique to Matthew thus make sense only as Matthean redaction unknown to Mark or Luke.

2. Matthew also relies heavily on the word προσέρχομαι. He uses it fifty-one or fifty-two times, as shown in Table 3.1. A line ( — ) indicates that Mark or Luke has a parallel to Matthew, but does not have the relevant Matthean feature. A blank space indicates that Mark or Luke has no parallel to Matthew.

Table 3.1
**προσέρχομαι in Matthew**

| Matthew | Mark | Luke |
|---|---|---|
| 4:3 προσελθών | | 4:3 — |
| 4:11 προσῆλθον | 1:13 — | |
| 5:1 προσῆλθαν αὐτῷ | 3:13 ἀπῆλθον πρὸς αὐτόν | 6:13 — |
| 8:2 προσελθών | 1:40 ἔρχεται πρὸς αὐτόν | 5:12 — |
| 8:5 προσῆλθεν αὐτῷ | | 7:2 — |
| 8:19 προσελθών | | 9:57 — |
| 8:25 προσελθόντες | 4:38 — | 8:24 προσελθόντες |
| 9:14 προσέρχονται αὐτῷ | 2:18 ἔρχονται | 5:33 — |
| 9:18 v. l. προσελθών | 5:22 ἔρχεται | 8:41 ἦλθεν |
| 9:20 προσελθοῦσα | 5:27 ἐλθοῦσα | 8:44 προσελθοῦσα |

| Matthew | Mark | Luke |
|---|---|---|
| 9:28 προσῆλθον αὐτῷ | cf. 10:50 ἦλθεν πρός | cf. 18:40 ἐγγίσαντος αὐτοῦ |
| 13:10 προσελθόντες | 4:10 — | 8:9 — |
| 13:27 προσελθόντες | | |
| 13:36 προσῆλθον αὐτῷ | | |
| 14:12 προσελθόντες | 6:29 ἦλθον | |
| 14:15 προσῆλθον αὐτῷ | 6:35 προσελθόντες αὐτῷ | 9:12 προσελθόντες |
| 15:1 προσέρχονται τῷ Ἰησοῦ | 7:1 συνάγονται πρὸς αὐτόν | |
| 15:12 προσελθόντες | 7:17 — | |
| 15:23 προσελθόντες | | |
| 15:30 προσῆλθον αὐτῷ | 7:32 — | |
| 16:1 προσελθόντες | 8:11 ἐξῆλθον | |
| 17:7 προσῆλθεν | | |
| 17:14 προσῆλθεν αὐτῷ | 9:17 — | 9:38 — |
| 17:19 προσελθόντες τῷ Ἰησοῦ | 9:28 — | |
| 17:24 προσῆλθον | | |
| 18:1 προσῆλθον τῷ Ἰησοῦ | 9:33 — | 9:46 — |
| 18:21 προσελθών | | |
| 19:3 προσῆλθον αὐτῷ | 10:2 προσελθόντες | |
| 19:16 προσελθὼν αὐτῷ | 10:17 προσδραμών | 18:18 — |
| 20:20 προσῆλθεν αὐτῷ | 10:35 προσπορεύονται αὐτῷ | |
| 21:14 προσῆλθον αὐτῷ | | |
| 21:23 προσῆλθον αὐτῷ | 11:27 ἔρχονται πρὸς αὐτόν | 20:1 ἐπέστησαν |
| 21:28 προσελθὼν τῷ πρώτῳ | | |
| 21:30 προσελθὼν τῷ ἑτέρῳ | | |
| 22:23 προσῆλθον αὐτῷ | 12:18 ἔρχονται πρὸς αὐτόν | 20:27 προσελθόντες |
| 24:1 προσῆλθον | 13:1 — | 21:5 — |
| 24:3 προσῆλθον αὐτῷ | 13:3 — | 21:7 — |
| 25:20 προσελθών | | 19:16 παρεγένετο |
| 25:22 προσελθών | | 19:18 ἦλθεν |

| Matthew | Mark | Luke |
|---|---|---|
| 25:24 προσελθών | | 19:20 ἦλθεν |
| 26:7 προσῆλθεν αὐτῷ | 14:3 ἦλθεν | |
| 26:17 προσῆλθον τῷ Ἰησοῦ | 14:12 — | 22:9 — |
| 26:49 προσελθὼν τῷ Ἰησοῦ | 14:45 προσελθὼν αὐτῷ | 22:47 ἤγγισεν τῷ Ἰησοῦ |
| 26:50 προσελθόντες | 14:46 — | |
| 26:60 προσελθόντων | 14:56 — | |
| 26:60 προσελθόντες | 14:57 — | |
| 26:69 προσῆλθεν αὐτῷ | 14:66 ἔρχεται | 22:56 — |
| 26:73 προσελθόντες | 14:70 — | 22:59 — |
| 27:58 προσελθὼν τῷ Πιλάτῳ | 15:43 εἰσῆλθεν πρὸς τὸν Πιλᾶτον | 23:52 προσελθὼν τῷ Πιλάτῳ |
| 28:2 προσελθών | | |
| 28:9 προσελθοῦσαι | | |
| 28:18 προσελθών | | |

Matthew's preference for this word has no echo in either Mark or Luke. Mark has thirty-four parallels to Matthew's fifty-two passages, but only three instances of the word in these. Luke has twenty-seven parallels with only five instances of the word. Did either Mark or Luke have an aversion to this term? No, since outside of the Matthean parallels Mark uses it twice, while Luke uses it five times elsewhere in the gospel and ten times in Acts. The relative paucity of the term in Mark and Luke is hard to explain given the theory of Matthean priority. It makes sense, however, if neither Mark nor Luke used Matthew. All three evangelists found the term as many as seven times in their sources for the triple tradition. Mark retained the term in three of these; Luke retained it in five; while Matthew kept it in all seven and added it another forty-five times, whether from sources or redaction. Since the term never appears in Luke's version of Q, Matthean redaction probably accounts for the five times that it appears in Matthew's Q material. Matthew's extra forty-five instances of the term are thus much easier to explain as Matthean additions than as omissions from Matthew made by Luke and Mark.

It therefore seems strange that proponents of the Griesbach hypothesis have fixed on one instance of this term in Luke as evidence that Luke knew Matthew. Their argument is this: Matthew uses προσέρχομαι twenty-five times with the dative, a construction that occurs nowhere else in the New Testament except for three parallel passages in Mark and Luke. The construction is therefore a characteristic Matthean grammatical construction. Since it occurs in Luke 23:52, where Matthew and Luke are in sequential parallel and have the same wording for nine consecutive words, then Luke must have copied this verse directly from Matthew.[1] This argument has several flaws, but we need mention only one. It is not the case that προσέρχομαι with the dative "occurs nowhere else in the New Testament" except in the gospels of Matthew, Mark, and Luke. It occurs elsewhere a total of thirteen times in four different writers, one of whom is Luke himself in Acts.[2] Thus the use of the dative with the verb is no more Matthean than Lukan. The dative is the normal case that any Greek writer would use to express the goal of the action in this verb. The presence of such a construction in Luke says nothing about its source. Even if the argument were based on accurate facts, it focuses on a single instance of προσέρχομαι that Luke supposedly took from Matthew, thus ignoring the forty-five other instances of the term in Matthew that would have to disappear from Luke (and Mark) by the same theory.

3. Matthew uses the verb φημί sixteen times (see Table 2.7). In only one instance does the word appear in a parallel in Mark or Luke (Matt 27:11//Luke 23:3). Thus, on the theory of Matthean priority, Mark and Luke together must have omitted the word or the material in which it occurred thirty-one times: sixteen in Mark and fifteen in Luke. Yet this conclusion seems hardly likely, since both evangelists readily use the term elsewhere. They seem to object to it only where they supposedly found it in Matthew. As we discussed previously in relation to Table 2.7, only once do two evangelists have this word in the same passage. This distribution of this word speaks against any theory of direct dependence among the Synoptics, including the theory of Matthean priority. It suggests instead that all three Synoptic evangelists relied on an earlier source or sources that rarely used φημί. Each of the evangelists added the word to the earlier material, but since they did so independently, they did not add it in the same places. Matthew found the word once in earlier material shared with Luke (Matt 27:11//Luke 23:3) and added it fifteen more times. Since Mark and Luke did not use Matthew, they did not know these fifteen redactional additions.

4. Thirteen times Matthew uses the participle λεγόμενος to indicate what a person or place was "called" (Table 3.2). Only once does Matthew's participle appear in a parallel (Mark 15:7). Given the theory of Matthean priority, both Mark and Luke must have studiously avoided this construction whenever Matthew used it. In twenty-five of the twenty-six times that it might have occurred in their works combined, they either replaced it or omitted the

---

1. McNicol, *Beyond the Q Impasse*, 24.
2. John 12:21; Acts 8:29; 9:1; 10:28; 18:2; 22:26; 23:14; 1 Tim 6:3; Heb 4:16; 7:25; 11:6; 12:18, 22.

Table 3.2
λεγόμενος in Matthew

| Matthew | Mark | Luke |
|---|---|---|
| 1:16 Ἰησοῦς ὁ λεγόμενος χριστός | | |
| 2:23 πόλιν λεγομένην Ναζαρέτ | | |
| 4:18 Σίμωνα τὸν λεγόμενον Πέτρον | 1:16 Σίμωνα | |
| 9:9 ἄνθρωπον . . . Μαθθαῖον λεγόμενον | 2:14 Λευὶν τὸν τοῦ | 5:27 τελώνην ὀνόματι Ἀλφαίου          Λευίν |
| 10:2 Σίμων ὁ λεγόμενος Πέτρος | 3:16 ἐπέθηκεν ὄνομα τῷ Σίμωνι Πέτρον | 6:14 Σίμωνα ὃν καὶ ὠνόμασεν Πέτρον |
| 26:3 τοῦ ἀρχιερέως τοῦ λεγομένου Καϊάφα | | |
| 26:14 ὁ λεγόμενος Ἰούδας Ἰσκαριώτη | 14:10 Ἰούδας Ἰσκαριώθ | 22:3 Ἰούδαν τὸν καλού-μενον Ἰσκαριώτην |
| 26:36 χωρίον λεγόμενον Γεθσημανί | 14:32 χωρίον οὗ τὸ ὄνομα Γεθσημανί | 22:40 τοῦ τόπου |
| 27:16 δέσμιον . . . λεγόμενον (Ἰησοῦν) Βαραββᾶν | 15:7 ὁ λεγόμενος Βαραββᾶς | |
| 27:17 Ἰησοῦν τὸν λεγόμενον χριστόν | 15:9 τὸν βασιλέα τῶν Ἰουδαίων | |
| 27:22 Ἰησοῦν τὸν λεγόμενον χριστόν | 15:12 [ὃν λέγετε] τὸν βασιλέα τῶν Ἰουδαίων | 23:20 τὸν Ἰησοῦν |
| 27:33 τόπον λεγόμενον Γολγοθᾶ | 15:22 τὸν Γολγοθᾶν τόπον | |
| 27:33 Κρανίου Τόπος λεγόμενος | 15:22 ὅ ἐστιν μεθερμηνευόμενον Κρανίου Τόπον | 23:33 τὸν τόπον τὸν καλούμενον Κρανίον |

material in which it occurred. It would be difficult, however, to find an expla-nation for such a procedure. The construction was neither ungrammatical nor even uncommon. Elsewhere Luke uses it four times (Luke 22:1; 22:47; Acts 3:2; 6:9). John uses it nine times, and it occurs six more times in the rest of the New Testament. If Mark and Luke were following Matthew, they had no reason to omit this construction so consistently. More likely, therefore, Matthew found it once in earlier material that he shared with Mark and used it frequently in his redaction. Mark and Luke did not know these redactional additions because they did not have Matthew as a source.

   5. Twelve times Matthew uses the term ἐκεῖθεν (Table 3.3).

Table 3.3
ἐκεῖθεν in Matthew

| Matthew | Mark | Luke |
|---|---|---|
| 4:21 ἐκεῖθεν | 1:19 — | 5:10 — |
| 5:26 ἐκεῖθεν | | 12:59 ἐκεῖθεν |
| 9:9 ἐκεῖθεν | 2:14 — | 5:27 — |
| 9:27 ἐκεῖθεν | | |
| 11:1 ἐκεῖθεν | | |
| 12:9 ἐκεῖθεν | 3:1 — | 6:6 — |
| 12:15 ἐκεῖθεν | 3:7 — | 6:17 — |
| 13:53 ἐκεῖθεν | 6:1 ἐκεῖθεν | 4:16 — |
| 14:13 ἐκεῖθεν | 6:32 — | 9:10 — |
| 15:21 ἐκεῖθεν | 7:24 ἐκεῖθεν | |
| 15:29 ἐκεῖθεν | 7:31 — | |
| 19:15 ἐκεῖθεν | 10:16 — | |

Mark has ἐκεῖθεν in a parallel to Matthew only twice, Luke only once. These shared uses of the term are not difficult to understand, since ἐκεῖθεν was a word that any Greek author might use. What is difficult to understand is why Mark and Luke have it so infrequently in parallels to Matthew if they were using Matthew. Both authors used the term elsewhere. Mark used it three times outside of these parallels to Matthew, while Luke used it twice elsewhere in his gospel and four times in Acts. It is only when they supposedly found it in Matthew that they seem reluctant to use it. More plausibly, the term occurred a few times in sources that preceded the evangelists and Matthew added to the number in his redaction. Mark and Luke knew the term from the earlier sources but did not know Matthew's redactional additions.

   6. Matthew also likes the word ἀναχωρέω ("withdraw"), using it five times in material unique to his gospel and five times elsewhere (Table 3.4). This appears to be another example of a word that Matthew found occasionally in the sources of the triple tradition (Matt 12:15//Mark 3:7; possibly Matt 14:13//Luke 9:10) and found useful in redacting other parts of his material. It is easier to explain its presence in Matthew by this theory than to explain its absence from Mark and Luke given the theory of Matthean priority.

Table 3.4
ἀναχωρέω in Matthew

| Matthew | Mark | Luke |
|---|---|---|
| 2:12 ἀνεχώρησαν | | |
| 2:13 ἀναχωρησάντων | | |
| 2:14 ἀνεχώρησεν | | |
| 2:22 ἀνεχώρησεν | | |
| 4:12 ἀνεχώρησεν | 1:14 ἦλθεν | 4:14 ὑπέστρεψεν |
| 9:24 ἀναχωρεῖτε | 5:39 — | 8:52 — |
| 12:15 ἀνεχώρησεν | 3:7 ἀνεχώρησεν | 6:17 — |
| 14:13 ἀνεχώρησεν | 6:32 ἀπῆλθον | 9:10 ὑπεχώρησεν |
| 15:21 ἀνεχώρησεν | 7:24 ἀπῆλθεν | |
| 27:5 ἀνεχώρησεν | | |

7. Matthew consistently uses the verb προσκυνέω in describing the homage that people express toward Jesus (Table 3.5).

Table 3.5
προσκυνέω with Jesus as object in Matthew

| Matthew | Mark | Luke |
|---|---|---|
| 2:2 προσκυνῆσαι | | |
| 2:8 προσκυνήσω | | |
| 2:11 προσεκύνησαν | | |
| 8:2 προσεκύνει | 1:40 [γονυπετῶν] | 5:12 πεσὼν ἐπὶ πρόσωπον |
| 9:18 προσεκύνει | 5:22 πίπτει πρὸς τοὺς πόδας | 8:41 πεσὼν παρὰ τοὺς πόδας |
| 14:33 προσεκύνησαν | 6:51 — | |
| 15:25 προσεκύνει | 7:25 προσέπεσεν πρὸς τοὺς πόδας | |
| 20:20 προσκυνοῦσα | 10:35 — | |
| 28:9 προσεκύνησαν | | |
| 28:17 προσεκύνησαν | | |

Both Matthew and Luke use προσκυνέω in the story of Jesus' temptation to affirm that one should worship God but not Satan (Matt 4:9, 10; Luke 4:7, 8). Matthew consistently uses the same word to describe homage directed toward

Jesus and once of homage from a slave to a master (Matt 18:26). Except in the temptation story, neither Mark nor Luke ever uses this word in parallels to Matthew. Given the theory of Matthean priority, it might appear that Mark and Luke were reluctant to direct "worship" toward Jesus. However, that would be an erroneous conclusion, since elsewhere both use the word with Jesus as object (Mark 5:6; Luke 24:52; cf. Mark 15:19). They only lack it when it appears in Matthew. More likely, therefore, Mark and Luke simply did not know Matthew's use of the term.

8. Six times Matthew uses the term μεταβαίνω, three times with ἐκεῖθεν (Table 3.6).

Table 3.6
μεταβαίνω in Matthew

| Matthew | Mark | Luke |
|---|---|---|
| 8:34 μεταβῇ | 5:17 ἀπελθεῖν | 8:37 ἀπελθεῖν |
| 11:1 μετέβη ἐκεῖθεν | | |
| 12:9 μεταβὰς ἐκεῖθεν | 3:1 — | 6:6 — |
| 15:29 μεταβὰς ἐκεῖθεν | 7:31 ἐξελθών | |
| 17:20 μετάβα | | 17:6 ἐκριζώθητι |
| 17:20 μεταβήσεται | | 17:6 ὑπήκουσεν |

Both Mark and Luke had the opportunity to use Matthew's μεταβαίνω several times if they were following Matthew, yet neither took advantage of it. Luke's failure to use the word is particularly striking, since in Acts 18:7 he writes μεταβὰς ἐκεῖθεν, the phrase in Matthew 12:9 that Luke supposedly omitted in Luke 6:6. Again, it seems unlikely that either Mark or Luke was using Matthew.

9. Only Matthew among the evangelists uses the term παρουσία (Table 3.7).

Table 3.7
παρουσία in Matthew

| Matthew | Mark | Luke |
|---|---|---|
| 24:3 παρουσίας | 13:4 — | 21:7 — |
| 24:27 παρουσία | | 17:24 — |
| 24:37 παρουσία | | 17:26 — |
| 24:39 παρουσία | | 17:30 — |

Luke had four opportunities to use the term παρουσία in material that he supposedly took from Matthew, yet not once did he do so. This seems strange, since the term was not uncommon in early Christian circles. Paul and the authors of James, 2 Peter, and 1 John all use it in the same technical sense as Matthew to refer to the coming of Jesus. Did Luke have an aversion to the term? Mark must have had it as well then, since he also avoids it in the one parallel he has with Matthew's passages. More likely, neither Mark nor Luke knew Matthew's version of this material.

10. Not only words, but also certain grammatical constructions recur in Matthew, such as a genitive absolute followed by ἰδού or καὶ ἰδού (Table 3.8).

Table 3.8
Genitive absolute plus (καὶ) ἰδού in Matthew

| Matthew | Mark | Luke |
|---|---|---|
| 1:20 ταῦτα δὲ αὐτοῦ ἐνθυμηθέντος ἰδού | | |
| 2:1 τοῦ δὲ Ἰησοῦ γεννηθέντος . . . , ἰδού | | |
| 2:13 ἀναχωρησάντων δὲ αὐτῶν ἰδού | | |
| 2:19 τελευτήσαντος δὲ τοῦ | Ἡρῴδου ἰδού | |
| 9:10 αὐτοῦ ἀνακει- μένου . . . , καὶ ἰδού | 2:15 κατακεῖσθαι αὐτὸν . . . , καί | 5:29 —, καί |
| 9:18 ταῦτα αὐτοῦ λαλοῦντος αὐτοῖς, ἰδού | 5:22 καί | 8:41 καὶ ἰδού |
| 9:32 αὐτῶν δὲ ἐξερχο- μένων ἰδού | | 11:14 καί |
| 12:46 ἔτι αὐτοῦ λαλοῦντος τοῖς ὄχλοις ἰδού | 3:31 καί | 8:19 δέ |
| 17:5 ἔτι αὐτοῦ λαλοῦντος ἰδού | 9:7 καὶ ἐγένετο | 9:34 ταῦτα δὲ αὐτοῦ λέγοντος ἐγένετο |
| 26:47 καὶ ἔτι αὐτοῦ λαλοῦντος ἰδού | 14:43 καὶ εὐθὺς ἔτι αὐτοῦ λαλοῦντος | 22:47 ἔτι αὐτοῦ λαλοῦντος ἰδού |
| 28:11 πορευομένων δὲ αὐτῶν ἰδού | | |

This construction occurs five times in material unique to Matthew and six times in material with a parallel in Mark or Luke. Only once does it occur in one of these parallels, at Luke 22:47. Proponents of the Griesbach hypothesis have taken this one instance as evidence that Luke used Matthew, since here a unique literary characteristic of Matthew appears in Luke.[3] However, to call this a "unique" characteristic of Matthew overstates the case, since it occurs elsewhere in Acts 1:10 (πορευομένου αὐτοῦ, καὶ ἰδού). Though Matthew liked the construction, he did not invent it, and it may occasionally have occurred in the sources common to the evangelists. Its presence in Luke 22:47 does not show that Luke got it from Matthew. On the contrary, when we stop focusing on a single passage, the whole picture presented by Table 3.8 suggests just the opposite. Luke 22:47 and Acts 1:10 show that Luke had no aversion to the construction. Why then, given the theory that Luke used Matthew, did he almost always eliminate it when he found it in Matthew? Why, given the theory that Mark used Matthew, did Mark always eliminate it? The almost complete absence of the construction from both Mark and Luke suggests that they were not using Matthew, but a source or sources that contained at most only one instance of this grammatical construction. Matthew used the same source or sources, but added further instances of the construction in his redaction.

11. In some cases, Matthean redaction consists of a recurring phrase rather than a recurring word or grammatical construction. After describing certain events, Matthew often quotes a passage from scripture, introducing it with a special formula, such as "This took place to fulfill what was spoken by the prophet" (1:22–23; 2:15; 2:17–18; 2:23; 4:13–16; 8:17; 12:15–21; 13:35; 21:4–5; 26:56; 27:9–10; cf. 2:5–6). These "fulfillment quotations" with their recurring phrase reflect the theme that Jesus fulfilled prophetic scriptures. Though characteristic of Matthew, they are completely absent from Mark and Luke. It might be possible to come up with some reason why both Luke and Mark did not choose to include these passages. However, it would require some ingenuity, since both seemed to like the idea that Jesus fulfilled scripture. It seems more likely that they did not include these passages because they did not use Matthew. These passages belong to a layer of redaction that Matthew superimposed on the sources that he shared with the other evangelists.

12. Another recurring phrase in Matthew is "to heal every disease and every sickness" (Table 3.9). Luke 9:1 shows that the idea of healing diseases was not unknown to Luke. However, Matthew's precise phrase never appears elsewhere, even when both Mark and Luke have parallels to Matthew. Most likely, then, Matthew's unique phrase represents his own development and was unknown to the other evangelists.

---

3. McNicol, *Beyond the Q Impasse*, 23–24.

Table 3.9
"to heal every disease and every sickness"

| Matthew | Mark | Luke |
|---|---|---|
| 4:23d θεραπεύων πᾶσαν νόσον καὶ πᾶσαν μαλακίαν | | |
| 9:35 θεραπεύων πᾶσαν νόσον καὶ πᾶσαν μαλακίαν | 6:6b — | 8:1 — |
| 10:1 θεραπεύειν πᾶσαν νόσον καὶ πᾶσαν μαλακίαν | 6:7 — | 9:1 νόσους θεραπεύειν |

13. A similar development probably explains the phrase that ends each of Matthew's discourses (Table 3.10).

Table 3.10
Formula at end of discourses in Matthew

| Matthew | Mark | Luke |
|---|---|---|
| 7:28 καὶ ἐγένετο ὅτε ἐτέλεσεν ὁ Ἰησοῦς τοὺς λόγους τούτους | | 7:1 ἐπειδὴ ἐπλήρωσεν πάντα τὰ ῥήματα αὐτοῦ εἰς τὰς ἀκοὰς τοῦ λαοῦ |
| 11:1 καὶ ἐγένετο ὅτε ἐτέλεσεν ὁ Ἰησοῦς διατάσσων | after 6:11 — | after 9:5 — after 10:16 — |
| 13:53 καὶ ἐγένετο ὅτε ἐτέλεσεν ὁ Ἰησοῦς τὰς παραβολὰς ταύτας | after 4:34 — | after 8:18 — |
| 19:1 καὶ ἐγένετο ὅτε ἐτέλεσεν ὁ Ἰησοῦς τοὺς λόγους τούτους | after 9:50 — | |
| 26:1 καὶ ἐγένετο ὅτε ἐτέλεσεν ὁ Ἰησοῦς πάντας τοὺς λόγους τούτους | after 13:36 — | after 21:36 — |

While Matthew has the same recurring phrase at the end of each discourse, Luke has a similar phrase at the end of the first discourse only, while Mark has no such phrase at all. Proponents of both the Griesbach hypothesis and Farrer's theory take Luke's phrase in Luke 7:1 as evidence that Luke knew Matthew.[4] According to these theories, Matthew came first and created a formula that he placed at the end of each of his five discourses. Luke followed

---

4. McNicol, *Beyond the Q Impasse*, 21–22; Goulder, *Luke*, 12, 376; Goodacre, *Synoptic Problem*, 153.

Matthew in placing a similar phrase after his own Sermon on the Plain. The question that both theories must answer is why Luke did not put the same phrase at the end of his other discourses. If Luke liked Matthew's phrase well enough to include it after his first discourse, why did he omit it after his missionary discourses (Luke 9:1–5; 10:1–20), parable discourse (Luke 8:4–18), and eschatological discourse (Luke 21:5–36)? The Griesbach hypothesis must answer the further question of why Mark did not use the phrase at all. Why did Mark consistently omit it after each of his discourses? By focusing on the one parallel to Matthew in Luke 7:1, the argument ignores all the other parallels, in which neither Luke nor Mark shows knowledge of Matthew's phrase.

An alternative explanation starts from the Q hypothesis. Matthew and Luke found the phrase in question at the end of the Q sermon, which Matthew expanded into the Sermon on the Mount and Luke into the Sermon on the Plain. Whether Matthew or Luke preserved the more original wording, or whether they both revised it, would have to be argued. In any case, Matthew apparently took this formula as a model for ending a discourse and ended his four other discourses in the same way. From this perspective, Luke used the phrase in only one place because that is the only place that he found it in his sources. Mark, with no access to Q or Matthew or Luke, never knew it.

14. As another feature of his redactional technique, Matthew has a propensity to make insertions or interpolations into his sources, either from another source or by his own hand. The fact that neither Mark nor Luke has these interpolations shows that they did not use Matthew but a form of the material prior to Matthew's redaction. In one instance, Matthew makes very nearly the same interpolation twice, as shown in Table 3.11.

Table 3.11
"I desire mercy" in Matthew

| Matthew | Mark | Luke |
|---|---|---|
| 9:13a But go and learn what this means: "I desire mercy and not sacrifice." | 2:17 — | 5:32 — |
| 12:7 But if you had known what this means—"I desire mercy and not sacrifice"—you would not have condemned the innocent. | 2:26 — | 6:4 — |

The first interpolation occurs in the controversy story on eating with sinners. The conclusion of that story compares the sick and the well on the one hand, with sinners and righteous people on the other. Matthew's insertion interrupts that conclusion, coming between the two parts of the comparison. On that basis alone, we would suspect that Matthew's extra statement in 9:13a is a secondary addition to the story. That suspicion is confirmed when we find the same theme—"I desire mercy and not sacrifice"—in Matthew's controversy story about plucking grain on the Sabbath. In both cases Mark and Luke lack Matthew's theme. This theme is one that would be readily acceptable to Mark and Luke, both writing for Gentile Christian audiences with no attachment to the Jewish sacrificial system. It would certainly appeal to any author who would include the parable of the good Samaritan (Luke 10:29–37). It is difficult to believe therefore that either Mark or Luke, much less both, would omit this theme twice had they known it. The agreement of Mark and Luke against Matthew shows clearly in this case that Mark and Luke preserve an earlier form of the material, into which Matthew has twice inserted the same theme. The absence of the theme twice from both Mark and Luke makes sense only if neither Mark nor Luke used Matthew.

In the story of Jesus' baptism, we find another Matthean interpolation. Matthew has John confess that he is unworthy to baptize Jesus (Matt 3:14–15). This confession is best explained as a secondary apologetic motif that Matthew added to the story to prevent Jesus from appearing subordinate to John. Neither Mark nor Luke has it. Thus both have a more primitive version of the story than Matthew. Proponents of Farrer's theory have to argue that Luke omitted Matthew's interpolation. Proponents of Matthean priority have to argue that both Luke and Mark omitted it. Such an argument is necessitated by the theory, but not suggested by the material itself. Attention to the passage, apart from prior theoretical constraints, indicates that Matthew preserves a form of the story that is secondary to those of Mark and Luke. That conclusion leads to the further conclusion that neither Mark nor Luke was following Matthew.

I have discussed only these three examples of interpolations, since they most clearly illustrate the secondary character of Matthew's additions. However, once we see that Matthew used interpolation in redacting earlier material, it is not difficult to find other examples (e.g., Matt 11:12–15; 12:5–6; 12:11–12a; 14:28–31; 16:17–19; 19:28b). In each case, Matthew inserts extra material into the middle of other material that is complete without it. Both Mark and Luke consistently preserve more original forms of the material without Matthew's interpolations. This fact makes clear that they did not use Matthew as a source.

15. A number of other words and phrases occur in Matthew two or more times, but never in a parallel passage in Mark or Luke.[5] I will simply list these.

---

5. Many of these were drawn from Dennis Gordon Tevis, "An Analysis of Words and Phrases Characteristic of the Gospel of Matthew" (Ph.D. diss., Southern Methodist University, 1983).

Added to the features already discussed, these confirm the conclusion that
Matthew includes a layer of redaction that was unknown to Mark or Luke.

- ἄλλην παραβολήν: 13:24; 13:31; 13:33; 21:33
- ἀνομία: 7:23; 13:41; 23:28; 24:12
- ἀπὸ τῆς ὥρας ἐκείνης (9:22; 15:28; 17:18) or ἐν τῇ ὥρᾳ ἐκείνῃ (8:13) to
  indicate immediate healing
- βασιλεία αὐτοῦ, referring to Son of Man: 13:41; 16:28
- γενηθήτω + σοι or ὑμῖν (8:13; 9:29; 15:28); + τὸ θέλημά σου (6:10; 26:42)
- διασαφέω: 13:36; 18:31
- διασάφησον (φράσον) ἡμῖν τὴν παραβολήν: 13:36; 15:15
- δικαιοσύνη: 3:15; 5:6; 5:10; 5:20; 6:1; 6:33; 21:32
- διστάζω: 14:31; 28:17
- δυνάμεις πολλάς: 7:22; 13:58
- ἐθνικός: 5:47; 6:7; 18:17
- εἰς τὴν ἁγίαν πόλιν: 4:5; 27:53
- εἰς τὴν γέενναν τοῦ πυρός (5:22; 18:9) and εἰς τὴν κάμινον τοῦ πυρός
  (13:42; 13:50) and εἰς τὸ πῦρ τὸ αἰώνιον (18:8; 25:41)
- ἐκβάλλειν εἰς τὸ σκότος τὸ ἐξώτερον: 8:12; 22:13; 25:30
- ἐν ἡμέρᾳ κρίσεως: 10:15; 11:22; 11:24; 12:36
- ἐν τῇ βασιλείᾳ τοῦ πατρὸς αὐτῶν (μου): 13:43; 26:29
- ἐλθὼν κατῴκησεν εἰς + place name: 2:23; 4:13
- ἐνθυμέομαι (1:20; 9:4) and ἐνθυμήσεις (9:4; 12:25)
- ἐξέρχομαι εἰς ὑπάντησιν: 8:34; 25:1
- ἐσείσθη(ησαν): 21:10; 27:51; 28:4
- ἑταῖρε: 20:13; 22:12; 26:50
- ἡ μήτηρ τῶν υἱῶν Ζεβεδαίου: 20:20; 27:56
- ἠγέρθη ἀπὸ τῶν νεκρῶν: 14:2; 27:64; 28:7
- καὶ ἀνοίξας τὸ στόμα αὐτου: 5:2; 17:27
- καὶ ἰδοὺ σεισμὸς μέγας ἐγένετο: 8:24; 28:2
- καὶ περισσευθήσεται: 13:12; 25:29
- κατ᾽ ὄναρ: 1:20; 2:12; 2:13; 2:19; 2:22; 27:19
- κουστωδία: 27:65; 27:66; 28:11
- κύριε σῶσον: 8:25; 14:30
- (ἐκ)λάμπειν: 5:15; 5:16; 13:43; 17:2; + ὡς ὁ ἥλιος (13:43; 17:2)
- λέγειν ναί in response to a question: 9:28; 13:51; 17:25; 21:16
- μαθητεύω: 13:52; 27:57; 28:19
- μέχρι (ἕως) τῆς σήμερον: 11:23; 27:8; 28:15
- ὃ ἐὰν δήσῃς ἐπὶ τῆς γῆς ἔσται δεδεμένον ἐν τοῖς οὐρανοῖς: 16:19; 18:18
- ὁ πατὴρ ὑμῶν (μου) ὁ οὐράνιος: 5:48; 6:14; 6:26; 6:32; 15:13; 18:35; 23:9
- ὁ υἱὸς τοῦ ἀνθρώπου καθίζειν ἐπὶ θρόνου δόξης αὐτοῦ: 19:28; 25:31
- ὁδηγοὶ τυφλοί: 15:14; 23:16; 23:24
- οἱ ἀρχιερεῖς καὶ οἱ Φαρισαῖοι: 21:45; 27:62

- οἱ δώδεκα μαθηταὶ αὐτοῦ: 10:1; 11:1
- οἱ μαθηταὶ ποιεῖν ὡς (καθὼς) συνέταξεν αὐτοῖς ὁ Ἰησοῦς: (1:24); 21:6; 26:19
- οἱ υἱοὶ τῆς βασιλείας: 8:12; 13:38
- οἱ Φαρισαῖοι καὶ Σαδδουκαῖοι: 3:7; 16:1; 16:6; 16:11; 16:12; (22:34)
- πορεύεσθε μᾶλλον πρός: 10:6; 25:9
- πρὸς τό + infinitive: 5:28; 6:1; 13:30; 23:5; 26:12
- σεληνιάζομαι: 4:24; 17:15
- συναίρειν λόγον μετά: 18:23, 24; 25:19
- συντέλεια τοῦ αἰῶνος: 13:39; 13:40; 13:49; 24:3; 28:20
- σφόδρα: 2:10; 17:6; 17:23; 18:31; 19:25; 26:22; 27:54; + λυπεῖσθαι (17:23; 18:31; 26:22); + ἐφοβήθησαν (17:6; 27:54)
- τὰ πρόβατα τὰ ἀπολωλότα οἴκου Ἰσραήλ: 10:6; 15:24
- τί ὑμῖν (σοι) δοκεῖ: 17:25; 18:12; 21:28; 22:42; 26:66
- τίς ἐστιν (ἔσται) ἐξ ὑμῶν ἄνθρωπος: 7:9; 12:11
- τότε συνῆκαν ὅτι εἶπεν: 16:12; 17:13

## Conclusion

These examples should suffice to make the point. The Gospel of Matthew includes a layer of redaction that was unknown to either Mark or Luke. These words, phrases, themes, grammatical constructions, and redactional techniques characteristic of Matthew hardly ever show up in Mark or Luke. These are pervasive features of Matthew's style, neither grammatically nor ideologically objectionable. Their absence from Mark and Luke is therefore difficult to explain if either used Matthew, more so if both did. It is not sufficient to take a divide-and-conquer strategy and try to explain their absence on a passage-by-passage basis. What needs explaining is not the absence of individual passages or particular instances of particular words, but the absence of recurring characteristics of Matthew's style.

According to both the Griesbach hypothesis and Farrer's theory, either Luke intentionally omitted all of these Matthean features, or their omission was the unintended consequence of other revisions that he made. Since the great majority of these features are benign, it is difficult to explain why Luke would omit them intentionally, especially since he uses some of them in contexts other than in parallels to Mark. Since these features are numerous, individually and as a group, it is also difficult to see how Luke could have unintentionally omitted them all in the process of revision. The Griesbach hypothesis would further affirm that Mark came last, drawing on both Matthew and Luke. Either Mark intentionally made the same omissions from Matthew as Luke, or he unintentionally made these omissions by always following Luke at those places where Luke omitted the stylistic features of

Matthew in question. Neither explanation of Mark's procedure is plausible. Since the great majority of the stylistic features are benign, it is difficult to explain why Mark would omit them intentionally, especially since he uses some of them in contexts other than in parallels to Matthew. Since these features are numerous, individually and as a group, it is also improbable that Mark would always just happen to be following Luke at those places where Luke made these omissions from Matthew. The Griesbach hypothesis thus has no plausible explanation for the editorial procedure of either Luke or Mark with respect to these features of Matthew's style. The same is true for the Augustinian hypothesis, which simply puts Mark before Luke in the order of transmission.

The simplest explanation is that neither Mark nor Luke knew these stylistic traits of Matthew. The source used by these evangelists was not Matthew, but some earlier form of the material that lacked Matthew's redactional additions. To the conclusion reached in Chapter 2 we can now add a second:

> *The Gospel of Matthew did not serve as a source*
> *for either Mark or Luke.*

# Chapter 4

# *Sources Common to Mark and Matthew*

PROPONENTS OF MATTHEAN PRIORITY will have no trouble accepting the critique of Markan priority in Chapter 1. Likewise, proponents of Markan priority will agree with the critique of Matthean priority in Chapter 2. The catch is that the argument in each chapter is precisely the same. The same type of data suggests that both Mark and Matthew include a level of redaction that the other two Synoptic evangelists did not know. One cannot accept the argument of one chapter without accepting the argument of the other. Thus both Markan and Matthean prioritists are partly correct. Markan prioritists rightly reject Matthean priority, while Matthean prioritists rightly reject Markan priority.

After rejecting both Markan priority and Matthean priority, we might be expected to take the logical next step and dispose of Lukan priority in the same way. I doubt that it would be difficult to do. We could look through lists of Lukan stylistic characteristics and find those that are unique to Luke. We would be sure to include the "new-character narrative," a unique feature of Luke's style pointed out by Patrick Dickerson.[1] We could then argue that Luke contains a level of redaction unknown to either Mark or Matthew and conclude that Luke did not serve as a source for either Mark or Matthew. We could, but we will not. Hardly anyone argues for Lukan priority, so, with apologies to those who do, I will turn instead to the constructive portion of this study. If neither Mark nor Matthew nor (presumably) Luke served as the source for the other two gospels, then what source or sources did they use? The present chapter begins the attempt to find a plausible answer to that question. We will start by examining the relationship between Mark and Matthew, comparing them with respect to the order of their common material.

Arguments from order have played a fundamental role in the debate over Synoptic relations.[2] The relative order of pericopes in the triple tradition has

---

1. Patrick L. Dickerson, "The New Character Narrative in Luke-Acts and the Synoptic Problem," *JBL* 116 (1997): 291–312.

2. See especially Christopher M. Tuckett, "The Argument from Order and the Synoptic Problem," *TZ* 36 (1980): 338–54; David J. Neville, *Arguments from Order in Synoptic Source Criticism: A History and Critique* (Macon, GA: Mercer University Press, 1994).

seemed to support more than one interpretation. To proponents of Markan priority, it suggests that Matthew and Luke generally followed Mark's order. To proponents of the Griesbach hypothesis, it suggests that Mark generally followed the common order of Matthew and Luke. Both groups agree that the phenomenon of order is significant and that in some sense the Gospel of Mark represents "the middle term" in the arrangement of the material. That is, Mark and Matthew often agree in order, as do Mark and Luke, while Matthew and Luke do not usually agree against Mark. I will therefore take as my starting point the order of Mark relative to Matthew and Luke. I will compare Mark's order with Matthew's in the present chapter and Mark's order with Luke's in Chapter 5.

In the material that Mark and Matthew have in common, we find instances of both common order and divergence in order. We must find a plausible explanation for both. Several theories might explain the common order, but the divergences have presented more of a problem. To illustrate this latter point, I will take the theory of Markan priority as my primary dialogue partner in the present chapter. This most common theory explains the divergences in order by hypothesizing that Matthew generally followed the order of Mark but sometimes moved material from its original order in Mark. I will first show that this theory does not adequately account for the divergences. Then I will present evidence for an alternative explanation: that Mark and Matthew shared more than one source, which they combined independently.

## Divergent Order as Explained by Markan Priority

The theory of Markan priority accounts for the common order of Mark and Matthew by postulating that Matthew copied Mark, generally following Mark's order. Divergences from that order occurred when Matthew rearranged Mark's material. This theory has a degree of merit, since there is good reason to think that Matthew did sometimes rearrange his sources. However, while some divergences in order can be attributed to Matthew's rearrangements of material, not all of the divergences are so easily explained. For example, the theory of Markan priority has difficulty explaining Matthew 7:28–9:34 as Matthew's rearrangement of Mark. Table 4.1 shows the order of Mark compared with that of Matthew in this section.

The first two columns of Table 4.1 set out the contents of the section in Matthew's order. The third column gives the corresponding material in Mark. As the table shows, when Matthew's material is listed in sequential order, the corresponding material in Mark is out of sequence. Markan prioritists argue that this is so because Matthew rearranged Mark's material into a new sequence. The problem with this view is that no one has ever plausibly

Table 4.1
Matthew 7:28–9:34 with parallel in Mark

|                        | Matthew 7:28–9:34 | Mark            |
|------------------------|-------------------|-----------------|
| Jesus finished         | 7:28a             |                 |
| People astonished      | 7:28b–29          | 1:22            |
| Demon in synagogue     |                   | 1:23–28         |
| Jesus heals a leper    | 8:1–4             | 1:40–42, 44     |
| A centurion's servant  | 8:5–13            |                 |
| At Peter's house       | 8:14–15           | 1:29–31         |
| Healing at evening     | 8:16              | 1:32, 34        |
| Scripture fulfilled    | 8:17              |                 |
| A preaching tour       |                   | 1:35–39         |
| Jesus crosses the sea  | 8:18              | 4:35            |
| Would-be followers     | 8:19–22           |                 |
| Jesus calms a storm    | 8:23–27           | 4:36–41         |
| Gerasene demoniac      | 8:28–34           | 5:1–20          |
| A paralytic            | 9:1–8             | 2:1–12          |
| Eating with sinners    | 9:9–13            | 2:13–17         |
| Question about fasting | 9:14–17           | 2:18–22         |
| Plucking grain         |                   | 2:23–28         |
| Withered hand          |                   | 3:1–6           |
| Jairus's daughter      | 9:18–26           | 5:21–43         |
| Two blind men          | 9:27–30a          |                 |
| They spread the news   | 9:30b–31          | 1:43–44a, 45a   |
| Mute demoniac          | 9:32–34           |                 |

explained why Matthew would rearrange this material. The usual explanation is that following the Sermon on the Mount, which illustrated Jesus' teaching, Matthew wanted to compile a section illustrating Jesus' miracles. Thus, in Matthew 7:28–9:34, Matthew drew together a series of miracle stories, omitting or postponing whatever material in Mark's sequence did not fit this aim. This position was stated in detail by W. C. Allen,[3] whose work received the approval of Streeter,[4] and it has continued to appear in standard presentations of the theory of Markan priority.[5] However, even a cursory examination

---

3. Allen, *Matthew*, xv–xvii.
4. Streeter, *Four Gospels*, 161n. 2, 274n. 1.
5. E.g., Kümmel, *Introduction*, 59; Styler, "Priority of Mark," 313.

of Table 4.1 casts doubt on this theory. The traditional explanation does not account for Matthew's treatment of either miracle or non-miracle material in this section. If Matthew's aim here was to illustrate Jesus' miracles, then why did he omit some material that fit this aim and include other material that did not?

1. If Matthew were following Mark with the aim of illustrating Jesus' miracles, then his treatment of Mark's miracle material is odd. First, it is strange that he would omit the miracle story in Mark 1:23–28. Allen admits that it is difficult to explain why Matthew would omit this story, but he attempts to do so anyway.[6] Second, why would Matthew take Mark's story of the leper out of its Markan sequence, place most of it (Mark 1:40–42, 44) closer to the beginning of this section, and join the rest (Mark 1:43–44a, 45a) to a non-Markan story near the end of the section? Finally, why would he take Mark's sequence of three miracle stories (Mark 4:35–5:43), precisely the type of sequence that he was allegedly aiming for, and separate the third story from the other two by three controversy stories (Mark 2:1–22), two of which have nothing to do with miracles?

2. Likewise, if Matthew's aim was to illustrate Jesus' miracles, then his treatment of non-miracle material is inconsistent at best. First, Allen claims that Matthew omitted Mark 1:35–39 because it "would be out of place in a series of miracles."[7] But that explanation is hardly convincing given the three other pericopes that Matthew includes that are also out of place in such a series (Matt 8:19–22; 9:9–13; 9:14–17). Allen does not even attempt to explain why Matthew would include this non-miracle material. Second, according to Allen, Matthew postponed the two controversy stories in Mark 2:23–3:6—one would suppose because they contained no miracle.[8] But in fact, the second of these does relate a miracle (Mark 3:1–6). Why in that case postpone it? Why not postpone instead the other two controversy stories that do lack a miracle (Mark 2:13–22//Matt 9:9–17)? Kümmel's answer to this question is interesting: "the two controversy sayings in Mt 9:9–17 are out of place in a cycle of miracles and can be accounted for only on the ground that this is where they occur in Mk."[9] This, of course, is no answer at all, since if Matthew moved the other controversy stories from their position in Mark, he could have moved these as well. Here Matthew does just the opposite of what the theory requires of him: he postpones a controversy story that relates a miracle, but keeps two controversy stories with no miracle.

---

6. Allen, *Matthew*, xv–xvi.
7. Ibid., xvi.
8. Ibid., xvi.
9. Kümmel, *Introduction*, 60.

The theory that Matthew aimed to present a collection of miracle stories is belied by the observations just made. Some proponents of Markan priority have recognized this fact, among them Christopher Tuckett. Tuckett acknowledges that the traditional explanation is "too simplistic" and provides a different explanation that he hopes will make the theory of Markan priority more credible here.[10] While the traditional theory gave a single explanation for all of Matthew's supposed changes to Mark's order in this section, Tuckett gives a different explanation for each of them.

1. According to Tuckett, Matthew moved the story of the leper from its place in Mark 1:40–45 to an earlier position so that it would be the first miracle story following the Sermon on the Mount (Matt 8:1–4). He did this because the story shows Jesus maintaining a positive attitude toward the Old Testament, as does the Sermon on the Mount, for which Matthew 5:17 serves as a kind of "title." This explanation marks an advance over the traditional view, since it at least has the merit of plausibility. It fails to explain, however, why Matthew would break the leper story in two, putting part of it earlier (Matt 8:1–4; Mark 1:40–42, 44) and part of it later (Matt 9:30b–31; Mark 1:43–44a, 45a).

2. According to Tuckett, Matthew moved the story of the woman with a hemorrhage (with the associated story of Jairus's daughter) from its place in Mark 5:21–43 to an earlier position at Matthew 9:18–25 because it expresses the theme of the "faith" needed by those who respond to Jesus, the same theme found in the following story of the two blind men (Matt 9:27–31) and possibly in the next story of the deaf-dumb demoniac (Matt 9:32–34). This explanation faces a number of serious objections. First, while the stories of the woman and the blind men mention faith, the story of the demoniac does not. Thus the explanation would work only for the first two stories. Second, why put these two stories here? According to Tuckett, the second story, concerning the two blind men, was created by Matthew as a duplicate of Mark's story of blind Bartimaeus. As a creation of Matthew, it had no prior position in the order of the gospel material. The first story, however, did have a position in the order of Mark. Why not, then, leave the first story where it was in Mark and put the free-floating story of the blind men with it? What was there about the location of Matthew 9:18ff. that drew both of these stories to it? Third, if Matthew intended to create a section on faith, he certainly could have done a better job. As mentioned, the third story in this series does not mention faith, but three other miracle stories in Matthew do (Matt 8:10, 13;

---

10. C. M. Tuckett, "Arguments from Order: Definition and Evaluation," in *Synoptic Studies: The Ampleforth Conferences of 1982 and 1983* (ed. C. M. Tuckett; JSNTSS 7; Sheffield: JSOT Press, 1984), 197–219, esp. 207–11.

9:2; 15:28). If the theme of faith did not draw these stories to Matthew 9:18ff., then why should we think that it drew the story of the woman with a hemorrhage from Mark 5:21–43?

3. According to Tuckett, Matthew moved the two miracle stories in Mark 4:35–5:20 to an earlier position to make them part of a subsection (Matt 8:18–9:17) centered on the theme of "discipleship." It is true that one can find the theme of discipleship, in the sense of following Jesus, at the beginning of this material (Matt 8:19–22). However, if it shows up after that, it is certainly not to the forefront. The main point of the story in which Jesus calms a storm is not discipleship, but lies in the question "What sort of man is this?" (Matt 8:27). The story of the Gadarene demoniac ends with Jesus being asked to leave the region (Matt 8:34), but, contra Tuckett, does not focus on the fate of his disciples. In the healing of the paralytic one might find an implicit reference to the disciples in the "men" who have authority to forgive sins, but it is not developed. In the next story Jesus eats with sinners, and in the final story he makes a pronouncement about fasting. One could infer that in these stories Jesus sets an example for his disciples, but that idea never comes out explicitly. Jesus' disciples are usually present in these stories, at least implicitly, but it is a stretch to say that discipleship constitutes the central theme. In a few places that theme might be coaxed out of the stories with a little imaginative help, but if Matthew really intended to center this section on discipleship, would he not have made it a little more obvious?

In short, Tuckett's explanation, while superior in some ways to the traditional one, still fails to convince. Of course it remains possible that some Markan prioritist at some time in the future might come up with a convincing explanation of Matthew's divergences from Mark's order in this section. All that we can say with certainty is that no one to date has done so. But unless or until that happens, we may suspect that the attempt to do so rests on a fundamental misconception: namely, the mistaken view that Matthew copied Mark.

## An Alternative Explanation: Shared Sources

The problem that remains, then, is to account for the fact that Mark and Matthew frequently have a common order but at other times diverge in order. As we have seen, the view that Matthew copied Mark does not adequately explain the divergences. Would the opposite view, that Mark copied Matthew, provide a better alternative? In fact, the Griesbach hypothesis, which affirms that Mark copied both Matthew and Luke, has less trouble explaining the divergences, since Mark's divergences from Matthew could usually be explained as places where Mark was following Luke. However, the Griesbach hypothesis must be rejected, since, among other reasons, the results of Chapter 3 ruled out the view that Mark copied Matthew.

If neither Matthew copied Mark nor Mark copied Matthew, then only one alternative remains: both copied the same source or sources. If they shared only a single source, we would not expect to find a great deal of divergence in the order of their shared material. What we actually do find is that these gospels diverge in order not infrequently. In some cases it is likely that the divergent order arose as one evangelist altered the original order of a single shared source. Other divergences, however, suggest that the evangelists had more than one source in common that they independently combined. To identify such sources, I have looked for sequences of material that have the same order in Matthew as in Mark. The material in Matthew, when viewed as a single sequence, shows marked divergences from the order of Mark. However, when we divide Matthew's material into three distinct sequences, each sequence has the same order as the corresponding material in Mark. These three sequences are shown in Table 4.2. The first two columns of Table 4.2 list the material in Mark in Mark's order. The next three columns show that the corresponding material in Matthew falls into three distinct sequences, which I have designated Sequence A, Sequence B, and Sequence C, respectively. The last column of the table, designated by a question mark, lists material in Matthew that I initially leave aside for separate discussion since it either does not fit into one of the three sequences or might fit into more than one.

Table 4.2
Sequences common to Mark and Matthew

|  | Mark | Matthew (Seq. A) | Matthew (Seq. B) | Matthew (Seq. C) | Matthew (?) |
|---|---|---|---|---|---|
| **John and Jesus** |  |  |  |  |  |
| Beginning of gospel | 1:1 |  |  |  |  |
| Written in Isaiah | 1:2a | 3:3a |  |  |  |
| I send my messenger | 1:2b |  |  |  |  |
| Isaiah 40:3 | 1:3 | 3:3b |  |  |  |
| John in wilderness | 1:4a |  |  |  | 3:1b |
| Preaching baptism | 1:4b |  |  |  |  |
| All go to John | 1:5a | 3:5a |  |  |  |
| Baptism for sins | 1:5b | 3:6 |  |  |  |
| John's lifestyle | 1:6 |  |  |  | 3:4 |
| One more powerful | 1:7–8 | 3:11 |  |  |  |
| Jesus' baptism | 1:9–11 | 3:13, 16b–17 |  |  |  |
| Jesus' temptation | 1:12-13 | 4:1–2, 11b |  |  |  |

| | Mark | Matthew (Seq. A) | Matthew (Seq. B) | Matthew (Seq. C) | Matthew (?) |
|---|---|---|---|---|---|
| **Jesus in Galilee** | | | | | |
| John arrested | 1:14a | 4:12a | | | |
| To Galilee | 1:14b | 4:12b | | 4:23a | |
| Preaching the kingdom | 1:14c–15 | 4:17 | | 4:23c | |
| Jesus calls fishermen | 1:16–20 | 4:18–22 | | | |
| To Capernaum | 1:21a | | 4:13b | | |
| Jesus teaches | 1:21b | 5:2 | | | |
| People astonished | 1:22 | 7:28b–29 | | | |
| Demon in synagogue | 1:23–27 | | | | |
| Report goes out | 1:28 | | | 4:24a | |
| At Peter's house | 1:29–31 | 8:14–15 | | | |
| They bring the ill | 1:32 | 8:16a | | 4:24b | |
| Whole city gathers | 1:33 | | | | |
| Jesus heals many | 1:34a | 8:16b | | 4:24c | |
| Prohibition to demons | 1:34b | | | | |
| A preaching tour | 1:35–39 | | | | |
| Jesus heals a leper | 1:40–42 | | 8:2–3 | | |
| Jesus indignant | 1:43 | | | | 9:30b |
| Let no one know | 1:44a | | 8:4a | | 9:30c |
| Go to the priest | 1:44b | | 8:4b | | |
| They spread the news | 1:45a | | | | 9:31 |
| Jesus in wilderness | 1:45b | | | | |
| **Controversy stories** | | | | | |
| Lame man healed | 2:1–12 | 9:1b–8 | | | |
| Eating with sinners | 2:13–17 | 9:9–12, 13b | | | |
| About fasting | 2:18–20 | 9:14–15 | | | |
| Old and new | 2:21–22 | 9:16–17 | | | |
| Plucking grain | 2:23–28 | 12:1–4, 8 | | | |
| Withered hand | 3:1–6 | 12:9–10, 12b–14 | | | |
| **Ministry to a crowd** | | | | | |
| Jesus withdraws | 3:7a | 12:15a | | | |
| To the sea | 3:7b | | | | |
| A crowd follows | 3:7c | 12:15b | | 4:25a | |
| From Galilee | 3:7d | | | 4:25b | |
| Judea and Jerusalem | 3:7e–8a | | | 4:25c | |
| Idumaea | 3:86 | | | | |

|  | Mark | Matthew (Seq. A) | Matthew (Seq. B) | Matthew (Seq. C) | Matthew (?) |
|---|---|---|---|---|---|
| Across the Jordan | 3:8c |  |  | 4:25d |  |
| Tyre and Sidon | 3:8d |  |  |  |  |
| Hearing they come | 3:8e |  |  |  |  |
| A boat for escape | 3:9 |  |  |  |  |
| Jesus heals many | 3:10a | 12:15c |  |  |  |
| They touch him | 3:10b |  |  |  |  |
| Demons know him | 3:11 |  |  |  |  |
| Prohibition to demons | 3:12 | 12:16 |  |  |  |
| **Jesus chooses 12** |  |  |  |  |  |
| On the mount | 3:13a |  |  | 5:1b |  |
| Jesus chooses 12 | 3:13b–19 |  |  |  | 10:1–4 |
| Jesus at home | 3:20a |  |  |  |  |
| A crowd gathers | 3:20b |  |  | 8:1b |  |
| Not able to eat | 3:20c |  |  |  |  |
| Jesus beside himself | 3:21 |  |  |  |  |
| **Beelzebul debate** |  |  |  |  |  |
| By Beelzebul | 3:22 | 12:24 |  | 9:34 |  |
| Satan divided | 3:23–26 | 12:25–26 |  |  |  |
| Binding the strong | 3:27 | 12:29 |  |  |  |
| Unforgivable sin | 3:28–29 | 12:31 |  |  |  |
| Because they said | 3:30 |  |  |  |  |
| Jesus' true family | 3:31–35 | 12:46–50 |  |  |  |
| **Parable discourse** |  |  |  |  |  |
| Ministry from boat | 4:1–2 | 13:1–3a |  |  |  |
| Parable of sower | 4:3–9 | 13:3b–9 |  |  |  |
| Reason for parables | 4:10–12 | 13:10–11, 13 |  |  |  |
| Sower explained | 4:13–20 | 13:18–23 |  |  |  |
| Several sayings | 4:21–24 |  |  |  |  |
| Have and have not | 4:25 |  |  |  | 13:12 |
| Growing seed | 4:26–29 |  |  |  |  |
| The mustard seed | 4:30–32 | 13:31–32 |  |  |  |
| Use of parables | 4:33–34 | 13:34–35 |  |  |  |
| **Miracle stories** |  |  |  |  |  |
| Let's cross the sea | 4:35 |  | 8:18b |  |  |
| Leaving the crowd | 4:36a | 13:36a |  |  |  |
| Jesus calms a storm | 4:36b–41 |  | 8:23–27 |  |  |

| | Mark | Matthew (Seq. A) | Matthew (Seq. B) | Matthew (Seq. C) | Matthew (?) |
|---|---|---|---|---|---|
| Gerasene demoniac | 5:1–17 | | 8:28–34 | | |
| Jesus gets in boat | 5:18a | | 9:1a | | |
| Would-be follower | 5:18b–20 | | | | |
| Jesus crosses sea | 5:21a | | 9:1a | | |
| A crowd gathers | 5:21b | | | | |
| Jairus's daughter | 5:22–43 | | 9:18–26 | | |
| **Further ministry** | | | | | |
| Jesus at hometown | 6:1–6a | 13:53b–58 | | | |
| Cities and villages | 6:6b | | | 9:35 | |
| **Mission instructions** | | | | | |
| He summons the 12 | 6:7a | | 10:1a | | |
| Sent two by two | 6:7b | | | | |
| Power over spirits | 6:7c | | 10:1b | | |
| What not to take | 6:8–9 | | 10:9–10a | | |
| Stay in one house | 6:10 | | 10:11 | | |
| If not received | 6:11 | | 10:14 | | |
| The 12 go forth | 6:12–13 | | | | |
| Opinions about Jesus | 6:14–16 | 14:1–2 | | | |
| John's imprisonment | 6:17 | 14:3 | | | |
| John's death | 6:18–29 | 14:4–12a | | | |
| The 12 return | 6:30 | 14:12b | | | |
| **Further ministry** | | | | | |
| To a deserted spot | 6:31–33 | 14:13 | | | |
| Jesus' compassion | 6:34a | 14:14a | | 9:36 | |
| Jesus ministers | 6:34b | 14:14b | | | |
| Jesus feeds 5,000 | 6:35–44 | 14:15–21 | | | |
| Jesus walks on water | 6:45–52 | 14:22–27, 32–33 | | | |
| In Gennesaret | 6:53–56 | 14:34–36 | | | |
| On hand washing | 7:1–23 | 15:1–20 | | | |
| A Gentile woman | 7:24–30 | 15:21–28 | | | |
| To Sea of Galilee | 7:31 | 15:29a | | | |
| Deaf mute healed | 7:32–36 | | | | |
| The crowd amazed | 7:37 | 15:31 | | | |
| Jesus feeds 4,000 | 8:1–10 | 15:32–39 | | | |
| Pharisees seek sign | 8:11–13 | 16:1, 4 | | | |
| No bread | 8:14–21 | 16:5–12 | | | |

| | Mark | Matthew (Seq. A) | Matthew (Seq. B) | Matthew (Seq. C) | Matthew (?) |
|---|---|---|---|---|---|
| Blind man at Bethsaida | 8:22–26 | | | | |
| Peter's confession | 8:27–30 | 16:13–16, 20 | | | |
| **Going to Jerusalem** | | | | | |
| 1st passion prediction | 8:31 | 16:21 | | | |
| Jesus rebukes Peter | 8:32–33 | 16:22–23 | | | |
| Passion discourse | 8:34–9:1 | 16:24–28 | | | |
| Transfiguration | 9:2–10 | 17:1–9 | | | |
| Coming of Elijah | 9:11–13 | 17:10–13 | | | |
| Demonized boy | 9:14–27 | 17:14–18 | | | |
| On failed exorcisms | 9:28–29 | 17:19–20 | | | |
| 2nd passion prediction | 9:30–32 | 17:22–23 | | | |
| At Capernaum in house | 9:33ab | 17:24a, 25b | | | |
| On greatness | 9:33c–35 | 18:1, 4 | | | |
| On little ones | 9:36–37 | 18:2, 5 | | | |
| Strange exorcist | 9:38–40 | | | | |
| A cup of water | 9:41 | | | | 10:42 |
| Offending little ones | 9:42 | 18:6 | | | |
| Offensive member | 9:43–47 | 18:8–9 | | | |
| Several sayings | 9:48–50 | | | | |
| **In Judea** | | | | | |
| Jesus goes to Judea | 10:1 | 19:1b–2 | | | |
| On divorce | 10:2–12 | 19:3–9 | | | |
| Jesus and children | 10:13–14 | 19:13–14 | | | |
| Receive as a child | 10:15 | | | | 18:3 |
| Laying on hands | 10:16 | 19:15a | | | |
| Rich young man | 10:17–22 | 19:16–22 | | | |
| Riches and rewards | 10:23–31 | 19:23–30 | | | |
| 3rd passion prediction | 10:32–34 | 20:17–19 | | | |
| Brothers seek honor | 10:35–40 | 20:20–23 | | | |
| On greatness | 10:41–45 | 20:24–28 | | | |
| Blind man at Jericho | 10:46–52 | 20:29–34 | | | |
| **In Jerusalem** | | | | | |
| Triumphal entry | 11:1–10 | 21:1–9 | | | |
| Jesus enters Jerusalem | 11:11a | | | | |
| Out to Bethany | 11:11b | | | | 21:17 |
| Jesus curses fig tree | 11:12–14 | | | | 21:18–19a |

| | Mark | Matthew (Seq. A) | Matthew (Seq. B) | Matthew (Seq. C) | Matthew (?) |
|---|---|---|---|---|---|
| Jesus enters Jerusalem | 11:15a | 21:10a | | | |
| Jesus cleanses Temple | 11:15b–17 | 21:12–13 | | | |
| Priests and scribes | 11:18 | | | | |
| Jesus leaves city | 11:19 | | | | |
| Fig tree withers | 11:20–21 | | | | 21:19b–20 |
| Moving mountains | 11:22–24 | | | | 21:21–22 |
| To be forgiven | 11:25–[26] | | | | 6:14–15 |
| Back to Jerusalem | 11:27a | | | | |
| Question of authority | 11:27b–33 | 21:23–27 | | | |
| Parable of tenants | 12:1–12a | 21:33–46a | | | |
| They leave Jesus | 12:12b | | | | 22:22b |
| Tribute to Caesar | 12:13–17 | 22:16–22a | | | |
| On resurrection | 12:18–27 | 22:23–32 | | | |
| Great commandment | 12:28–31 | 22:35–40 | | | |
| Not far from kingdom | 12:32–34a | | | | |
| No one dared | 12:34b | | | | 22:46b |
| Christ and David | 12:35–37a | 22:41–45 | | | |
| Against scribes | 12:37b–40 | 23:1, 6–7a, [14] | | | |
| Widow's offering | 12:41–44 | | | | |
| **Eschatology** | | | | | |
| Temple prediction | 13:1–2 | 24:1–2 | | | |
| Signs of the end | 13:3–8 | 24:3–8 | | | |
| Watch out | 13:9a | | | | |
| Handed over | 13:9b | 24:9a | | | |
| Before rulers | 13:9c | | | | |
| First the gospel | 13:10 | | | | 24:14 |
| Spirit speaks, betrayed | 13:11–12a | | | | |
| Killed, hated, endure | 13:12b–13 | 24:9bc, 13 | | | |
| Desolating sacrilege | 13:14–19 | 24:15–21 | | | |
| Before the end | 13:20–23 | 24:22–25 | | | |
| The end | 13:24–32 | 24:29, 30b–36 | | | |
| Stay awake | 13:33–34 | 25:13–14 | | | |
| Stay awake | 13:35 | | | | 24:42 |
| **Passion narrative** | | | | | |
| Jewish leaders plot | 14:1–2 | 26:2a, 3–5 | | | |

|                       | Mark       | Matthew (Seq. A) | Matthew (Seq. B) | Matthew (Seq. C) | Matthew (?) |
|-----------------------|------------|------------------|------------------|------------------|-------------|
| Anointing at Bethany  | 14:3–9     | 26:6–13          |                  |                  |             |
| Judas makes a deal    | 14:10–11   | 26:14–16         |                  |                  |             |
| Passover prepared     | 14:12–17   | 26:17–20         |                  |                  |             |
| Betrayal predicted    | 14:18–21   | 26:21–25         |                  |                  |             |
| Last supper           | 14:22–25   | 26:26–29         |                  |                  |             |
| Mount of Olives       | 14:26–31   | 26:30–35         |                  |                  |             |
| Gethsemane            | 14:32–42   | 26:36–46         |                  |                  |             |
| Jesus' arrest         | 14:43–50   | 26:47–56         |                  |                  |             |
| Youth flees naked     | 14:51–52   |                  |                  |                  |             |
| Denial and trial      | 14:53–72   | 26:57–75         |                  |                  |             |
| Before Pilate         | 15:1–20a   | 27:1–31a         |                  |                  |             |
| Jesus' crucifixion    | 15:20b–41  | 27:31b–56        |                  |                  |             |
| Jesus' burial         | 15:42–47   | 27:57–61         |                  |                  |             |
| The empty tomb        | 16:1–8     | 28:1–8           |                  |                  |             |
| **Jesus' resurrection** |          |                  |                  |                  |             |
| Mary sees Jesus       | 16:9       | 28:9             |                  |                  |             |
| Report disbelieved    | 16:10–11   |                  |                  |                  |             |
| Appearance to two     | 16:12–13   |                  |                  |                  |             |
| Appearance to 11      | 16:14      | 28:17            |                  |                  |             |
| Charge to disciples   | 16:15–16   | 28:19            |                  |                  |             |
| Preaching with signs  | 16:17–20   |                  |                  |                  |             |

Each sequence in Matthew has the same order as the corresponding material in Mark. Sequence A includes the bulk of the material that Matthew shares with Mark. Sequence B consists of elements that do not fit into A, while Sequence C consists of elements that do not fit into the order of either of the first two sequences. While the material in each Matthean sequence has the same order as in Mark, the sequences cannot be combined to create one larger sequence that has the same order as Mark. To see this, imagine moving the elements of Sequence B to the left into the column of Sequence A. There they would be out of sequence with the rest of the material in that column. However, when we give these elements their own column, as we have done, they form a second sequence of material with the same order in Matthew as in Mark. The same is true if we imagine moving the elements of Sequence C to the left into the column of either Sequence A or Sequence B. In either column, they would be out of sequence with the rest of the material in that column. However, when we give these elements their own column, as we have done, they form a third sequence of material with the same order in Matthew as in Mark.

Thus, the material shared by Mark and Matthew falls into three sequences that have the same order in Matthew as in Mark. As far as I am aware, no one has previously noticed this phenomenon. This arrangement seems odd given the theory that Matthew copied from Mark. In that theory, one would have to suppose that the first Matthean column represents material that Matthew kept in the same position as Mark, while the second and third would be material that he moved from Mark's sequence. Presumably, Matthew had a free hand to move Mark's material wherever he chose, so long as it fit his supposed redactional purpose. Nevertheless, one would have to suppose that when Matthew moved material from Mark, even when he moved it several chapters away, he usually kept the transferred material in the same order that it had in Mark. From the transferred material he thus created two other sequences of material with the same order in Matthew as in Mark. While this explanation is perhaps conceivable, it makes Matthew's supposed redactional procedure rather strange.

Perhaps a different theory would more plausibly account for the data. These three Matthean sequences, while surprising if formed by Matthew's rearrangement of Mark, are precisely what we would expect to find if Mark and Matthew shared three distinct sources and combined them independently. This theory explains, first, why both gospels include the same material: because they used the same sources. Second, this theory explains why the material in each source has the same order in Mark and Matthew when viewed separately: because both evangelists generally followed the order of the sources. Third, it explains why Mark and Matthew sometimes diverge in order when the material in each is viewed as a whole: because the evangelists, working independently, did not insert material from one source in the same place with respect to the material from the other sources.

It seems probable therefore that each Matthean sequence represents a distinct source that Matthew shared with Mark. Mark and Matthew had these three sources in common and combined them independently, usually following the order of their sources. It is this general adherence to the order of their sources that allows us to distinguish these sources, as I have done in Table 4.2. When we list the material in Mark's order, it is Matthew's divergences from that order that show at what points he has switched to a different source. One could also adopt the reverse procedure, listing the same material in Matthew's order and using Mark's divergences as a key to identifying the different sources. The table produced by that procedure would have one Matthean column and three Markan sequences, each with the same order in Mark as in Matthew. I emphasize this fact lest my use of Mark's order in Table 4.2 leave the impression that Mark's order is somehow fundamental. The procedure is completely reversible. What is significant is neither Mark's order nor Matthew's order, but the fact that each gospel has the same three sequences of material, though combined differently. In Table 4.2, the sequences in Matthew are easy to distinguish because they appear in separate columns. The sequences in Mark, since they are combined in a single column, can only be distinguished by comparing each Markan passage with its parallel in Matthew to see which sequence it belongs to.

## Material of Uncertain Sequence

The last column of Table 4.2, designated with a question mark, contains Matthean material that I have initially left out of the three sequences. While none of this material fits into Sequence A, most of it would fit into either Sequence B or Sequence C (Matt 3:1b; 3:4; 10:42; 18:3; 21:17–22; 22:22b; 22:46b; 24:14; 24:42). A few other items fit into none of the sequences (Matt 9:30b–31; 10:1–4; 13:12; 6:14–15). We must therefore use criteria other than order to identify the sources from which this material came.

1. *Matthew 3:1b, 4.* The first two passages (Matt 3:1b, 34) both relate to John the Baptist. With respect to order, they would fit into either Sequence B or Sequence C. We can infer therefore that either source B or source C began with material concerning John. The following considerations suggest that this was source C. The C material that we have so far identified twice refers to preaching the "gospel" or *evangelion* (Matt 4:23; 9:35). Since the same term occurs in Mark 1:1, this verse too probably came from C, though it has been omitted by Matthew. Since the phrase "the beginning of the gospel" in Mark 1:1 probably refers to the preaching of John the Baptist, it is likely that the C source began with material concerning John. I will therefore tentatively assign Matthew 3:1b and 3:4 to Sequence C in Table 4.2.

2. *Matthew 9:30b–31.* The next passage in the "uncertain" column (Matt 9:30b–31) in its present location does not fit into any of the three sequences. The reason seems to be that either Mark or Matthew disturbed the sequence by moving this material from its original position in one of the sources. Mark's version of this material occurs in the story in which Jesus heals a leper (Mark 1:43–44a, 45a). This material, marked by the terms ἐμβριμησάμενος, ἐξελθών, and διαφημίζειν, has no parallel in the leper story in either Matthew (Matt 8:2–4) or Luke (Luke 5:12–16). This agreement of Matthew and Luke against Mark could indicate that this material did not originally belong to the leper story but has been inserted into it from elsewhere by Mark. Matthew's version of this material (Matt 9:30b–31) occurs at the end of the story in which Jesus heals two blind men (Matt 9:27–30a). If this is its original position, then Mark must have known the story of the two blind men (from B?), omitted most of it, but moved these elements to conflate with the leper story. The alternative is to suppose that these elements originally stood in the leper story (from B). While Mark retained them there, Matthew moved

them to the story of the two blind men. Either possibility is conceivable, and I cannot say which is more likely. I will therefore leave the question unresolved.

3. *Matthew 10:1–4.*The next passage in the "uncertain" column, Jesus' choice of the Twelve (Matt 10:1–4), fits into none of the three sequences, again probably because either Mark or Matthew moved this material from its original position in one of the sources. Mark locates this passage in the context of Jesus' ascent to a mountain: Jesus ascends the mountain (Mark 3:13a), chooses the Twelve (Mark 3:13b–19), and (implicitly after descending) encounters a crowd (Mark 3:20a). Since the first and last elements in this series belong in Sequence C, it seems likely that the middle term, Jesus' choice of the Twelve, belongs to the same sequence. Matthew, however, has another event occur between Jesus' ascent to the mountain and his descent (Matt 5:1b; 8:1), namely, the Sermon on the Mount, while he locates Jesus' choice of the Twelve elsewhere, at the beginning of his missionary discourse (Matt 10:1–4). We can allow Luke to cast the deciding vote, and he sides with Mark. Luke agrees with Mark that between ascending and descending the mountain, Jesus chose the Twelve (Mark 3:13–19; Luke 6:12–16). And, as we shall see in Chapter 5, Luke has this in a sequence that can be identified as that of C. Matthew's divergence from the common order of Mark and Luke is therefore best attributed to Matthean redaction. Matthew apparently moved the names of the Twelve from their original position in C in order to augment his missionary discourse. Thus we can assign Matt 10:1–4 to Sequence C in Table 4.2.

4. *Matthew 13:12.* The next passage, the saying "Have and have not" (Matt 13:12//Mark 4:25), fits into none of the three sequences, probably because Matthew moved it from its original order. Both Mark and Matthew place this saying in the parable discourse, which belongs to Sequence A. Its position in Matthew, however, appears to be secondary, since it interrupts the explanation of Jesus' reason for speaking in parables (Matt 13:10–11, 13). Since Luke agrees with Mark, Mark apparently retained the original order of the saying from Sequence A, while Matthew rearranged it.

5. *Matthew 10:42; 18:3.* With respect to order, Matthew 10:42 (Mark 9:41) and Matthew 18:3 (Mark 10:15) could fit into either Sequence B (following Matt 10:14) or Sequence C (following Matt 9:36). With respect to content, they more likely belong with Matthew 10:14 in Sequence B. All three verses share the idea of receiving the messengers or message of Jesus, two of them employing the same verb (δέξηται):

And whatever place does not receive (δέξηται) you or listen to you, as you go out of there, shake off the dust under your feet as a testimony to them. (Mark 6:11; cf. Matt 10:14)

For whoever gives you a cup of cold water to drink in the name that you are of Christ, amen I tell you, he will not lose his reward. (Mark 9:41; cf. Matt 10:42)

Amen I tell you, whoever does not receive (δέξηται) the kingdom of God as a child will not enter it. (Mark 10:15; cf. Matt 18:3)

I will therefore tentatively assign Matthew 10:42 and 18:3 to Sequence B in Table 4.2.

6. *Matthew 21:17–22; 6:14–15.* With respect to order, the story in which Jesus curses a fig tree (Matt 21:17–22) could fit into either Sequence B or Sequence C. Since the story takes place near Jerusalem, it probably came from a source that had a passion narrative. In Chapter 5 we will find evidence to suggest that C may have included a passion narrative. I will therefore tentatively assign the cursing of the fig tree to Sequence C in Table 4.2.

Along with the material on the fig tree, Mark includes an exhortation to forgive in order to be forgiven (Mark 11:25–[26]), a saying that Matthew puts in the Sermon on the Mount (Matt 6:14–15). Matthew probably moved this material to augment the sermon, while Mark preserved it in its original order in C.

7. *Matthew 22:22b; 22:46b.* With respect to order, Matthew 22:22b and 22:46b could fit into either Sequence B or Sequence C. Their content, however, suggests that they most likely belong in Sequence A. The first relates that Jesus' opponents left him; the second, that they no longer dared to question him. Such references to Jesus' opponents connect these verses with the controversy stories in Sequence A. These verses have a different position in Matthew than in Mark, and the easiest explanation for this difference is that Matthew rearranged them. In Matthew 22:22b, the evangelist apparently felt it was premature to have Jesus' opponents leave after the parable of the tenants (as in Mark), so he postponed their departure until after they had questioned Jesus on tribute to Caesar. A similar motivation can be discerned for his postponement of 22:46b, which states that no one dared ask Jesus any further questions. Matthew apparently felt that it was premature to place this before Jesus' question about David's son (as in Mark), and so postponed it to the end of that discussion.

8. *Matthew 24:14, 42.* The last two items in the "uncertain" column, Matt 24:14 and 24:42, both have an eschatological tone. Both therefore probably came from the same source, which, as we can infer from their order, would be either Sequence B or Sequence C. Since Matthew 24:14 refers to "preaching

the gospel," a motif that we previously saw in C, we can assign these passages to Sequence C.

## Sources Common to Mark and Matthew

Table 4.2 has served its purpose as our initial attempt to compare the order of Matthew with that of Mark. We now need a revision of that table to incorporate the conclusions that have emerged from our discussion of it. Table 4.3 below incorporates three types of revisions.

1. First, we can now speak of sources instead of "sequences." Our comparison of Mark and Matthew revealed three distinct sequences of material, each of which has the same order in Matthew as in Mark, but which cannot be combined to form a larger sequence with the same order in both gospels. In moving from comparison to interpretation, I argued that these sequences are best understood as the remnants of three sources that Mark and Matthew shared but combined differently.

The first source identified in Table 4.2 includes the bulk of the material common to Matthew and Mark. Since it extends into the passion and resurrection narratives, it constitutes a complete passion gospel. As it includes the greater part of Mark—and no material from Q, M, or L—it could be considered an earlier version of Mark, a Proto-Mark. Since in Chapter 5 we will encounter a second version of Proto-Mark, I distinguish this version shared by Matthew and Mark by designating it Proto-Mark A (PMA). In using the terminology "Mark" and "Proto-Mark," I do not mean to imply that the same evangelist composed both gospels. I mean only that Mark developed from Proto-Mark.

In addition to Proto-Mark A, we have identified two other sources, both considerably shorter than Proto-Mark A. For lack of a better name, I will continue to designate the second source with the letter "B," meaning the B source or the B material. Likewise, I will continue to designate the third source with the letter "C."

2. As our second type of revision, we can now incorporate the "uncertain" column of Table 4.2 into our three sources. I left these items aside in Table 4.2 because they could not be assigned to one of our sequences on the basis of order alone. Using other criteria, however, we subsequently assigned most of these items, with more or less probability, to one or another of our sources. A few of these items did not fit into any of the three sequences, probably because either Mark or Matthew disturbed the sequence by moving the material from its original place in one of the sources. Thus, while the main divergences in order between Mark and Matthew arose because they inde-

pendently combined the same sources, other divergences arose as they redacted those sources, rearranging the material. In Table 4.3 I have indicated such rearrangements by references in small type preceded by an arrow (e.g., →13:12). While I place the reference at the place in the source where it probably stood originally, the arrow points to the place where the evangelist moved the material.

3. Third, we can now consider possible omissions of the sources. In using their sources, Mark and Matthew probably not only rearranged material but also omitted some of it. Therefore, some material from these sources may have been preserved by Mark alone or by Matthew alone. It may not be possible in every instance to identify such material. The procedure that I adopted in Table 4.2 was to list material in Matthew only if it has a parallel in Mark. That gave the assured minimum content of their shared sources. In Table 4.3 I have gone a step further by indicating a few places where I suspect that one evangelist or the other has omitted material from the source. A line ( — ) indicates these conjectured omissions. Subsequently I give my reasons for making these conjectures. It would be possible to add other instances besides those that I have given and to question those instances that I have added. We can never have the same certainty concerning these conjectures as for the material that both gospels include.

By incorporating these revisions into Table 4.2, we get Table 4.3.

Table 4.3
**Sources common to Mark and Matthew**

|                      | Mark   | Matthew (PMA) | Matthew (B) | Matthew (C) |
|----------------------|--------|---------------|-------------|-------------|
| **John and Jesus**   |        |               |             |             |
| Beginning of gospel  | 1:1    |               |             | —           |
| Written in Isaiah    | 1:2a   | 3:3a          |             |             |
| I send my messenger  | 1:2b   |               |             | —           |
| Isaiah 40:3          | 1:3    | 3:3b          |             |             |
| John in wilderness   | 1:4a   |               |             | 3:1b        |
| Preaching baptism    | 1:4b   |               |             |             |
| Kingdom at hand      | —      |               |             | 3:2         |
| All go to John       | 1:5a   | 3:5a          |             |             |
| Baptism for sins     | 1:5b   | 3:6           |             |             |
| John's lifestyle     | 1:6    |               |             | 3:4         |
| One more powerful    | 1:7–8  | 3:11          |             |             |

|  | Mark | Matthew (PMA) | Matthew (B) | Matthew (C) |
|---|---|---|---|---|
| Jesus' baptism | 1:9–11 | 3:13, 16b–17 |  |  |
| Jesus' temptation | 1:12–13 | 4:1–2, 11b |  |  |
| **Jesus in Galilee** |  |  |  |  |
| John arrested | 1:14a | 4:12a |  |  |
| To Galilee | 1:14b | 4:12b |  | 4:23a |
| Teaching in synagogues | — |  |  | 4:23b |
| Preaching the kingdom | 1:14c–15 | 4:17 |  | 4:23c |
| Jesus calls fishermen | 1:16–20 | 4:18–22 |  |  |
| To Capernaum | 1:21a |  | 4:13b |  |
| Jesus teaches | 1:21b | 5:2 |  |  |
| People astonished | 1:22 | 7:28b–29 |  |  |
| Demon in synagogue | 1:23–27 | — |  |  |
| Report goes out | 1:28 | — |  | 4:24a |
| At Peter's house | 1:29–31 | 8:14–15 |  |  |
| They bring the ill | 1:32 | 8:16a |  | 4:24b |
| Whole city gathers | 1:33 |  |  |  |
| Jesus heals many | 1:34a | 8:16b |  | 4:24c |
| Prohibition to demons | 1:34b | — |  |  |
| A preaching tour | 1:35–39 |  |  |  |
| Jesus heals a leper | 1:40–45 |  | 8:2–4 |  |
| **Controversy stories** |  |  |  |  |
| Lame man healed | 2:1–12 | 9:1b–8 |  |  |
| Eating with sinners | 2:13–17 | 9:9–12, 13b |  |  |
| About fasting | 2:18–20 | 9:14–15 |  |  |
| Old and new | 2:21–22 | 9:16–17 |  |  |
| Plucking grain | 2:23–28 | 12:1–4, 8 |  |  |
| Withered hand | 3:1–6 | 12:9–10, 12b–14 |  |  |
| **Ministry to a crowd** |  |  |  |  |
| Jesus withdraws | 3:7a | 12:15a |  |  |
| To the sea | 3:7b |  |  |  |
| A crowd follows | 3:7c | 12:15b |  | 4:25a |
| From Galilee | 3:7d |  |  | 4:25b |
| Judea and Jerusalem | 3:7e–8a |  |  | 4:25c |
| Idumaea | 3:8b |  |  |  |
| Across the Jordan | 3:8c |  |  | 4:25d |
| Tyre and Sidon | 3:8d |  |  |  |

|  | Mark | Matthew (PMA) | Matthew (B) | Matthew (C) |
|---|---|---|---|---|
| Hearing they come | 3:8e | | | |
| A boat for escape | 3:9 | | | |
| Jesus heals many | 3:10a | 12:15c | | |
| They touch him | 3:10b | | | |
| Demons know him | 3:11 | — | | |
| Prohibition to demons | 3:12 | 12:16 | | |
| **Jesus chooses 12** | | | | |
| On the mount | 3:13a | | | 5:1b |
| Jesus chooses 12 | 3:13b–19 | | | →10:1-4 |
| Down the mount | — | | | 8:1a |
| Jesus at home | 3:20a | | | |
| A crowd gathers | 3:20b | | | 8:1b |
| Not able to eat | 3:20c | | | |
| Jesus beside himself | 3:21 | | | |
| **Beelzebul debate** | | | | |
| A mute demoniac | — | 12:22–23 | | 9:32–33 |
| By Beelzebul | 3:22 | 12:24 | | 9:34 |
| Satan divided | 3:23–26 | 12:25–26 | | |
| Binding the strong | 3:27 | 12:29 | | |
| Unforgivable sin | 3:28–29 | 12:31 | | |
| Because they said | 3:30 | | | |
| Jesus' true family | 3:31–35 | 12:46–50 | | |
| **Parable discourse** | | | | |
| Ministry from boat | 4:1–2 | 13:1–3a | | |
| Parable of sower | 4:3–9 | 13:3b–9 | | |
| Reason for parables | 4:10–12 | 13:10–11, 13 | | |
| Sower explained | 4:13–20 | 13:18–23 | | |
| Several sayings | 4:21–24 | | | |
| Have and have not | 4:25 | →13:12 | | |
| Growing seed | 4:26–29 | — | | |
| The mustard seed | 4:30–32 | 13:31–32 | | |
| The leaven | — | 13:33 | | |
| Use of parables | 4:33–34 | 13:34–35 | | |
| **Miracle stories** | | | | |
| Let's cross the sea | 4:35 | | 8:18b | |
| Leaving the crowd | 4:36a | 13:36a | | |

| | Mark | Matthew (PMA) | Matthew (B) | Matthew (C) |
|---|---|---|---|---|
| Jesus calms a storm | 4:36b–41 | | 8:23–27 | |
| Gerasene demoniac | 5:1–17 | | 8:28–34 | |
| Jesus gets in boat | 5:18a | | 9:1a | |
| Would-be follower | 5:18b–20 | | | |
| Jesus crosses sea | 5:21a | | 9:1a | |
| A crowd gathers | 5:21b | | | |
| Jairus's daughter | 5:22–43 | | 9:18–26 | |
| **Further ministry** | | | | |
| Jesus at hometown | 6:1–6a | 13:53b–58 | | |
| Cities and villages | 6:6b | | | 9:35 |
| **Mission instructions** | | | | |
| He summons the 12 | 6:7a | | 10:1a | |
| Sent two by two | 6:7b | | | |
| Power over spirits | 6:7c | | 10:1b | |
| What not to take | 6:8–9 | | 10:9–10a | |
| Stay in one house | 6:10 | | 10:11 | |
| If not received | 6:11 | | 10:14 | |
| The 12 go forth | 6:12–13 | — | | |
| Opinions about Jesus | 6:14–16 | 14:1–2 | | |
| John's imprisonment | 6:17 | 14:3 | | |
| John's death | 6:18–29 | 14:4–12a | | |
| The 12 return | 6:30 | 14:12b | | |
| **Further ministry** | | | | |
| To a deserted spot | 6:31–33 | 14:13 | | |
| Jesus' compassion | 6:34a | 14:14a | | 9:36 |
| Jesus ministers | 6:34b | 14:14b | | |
| Jesus feeds 5,000 | 6:35–44 | 14:15–21 | | |
| Jesus walks on water | 6:45–52 | 14:22–27, 32–33 | | |
| In Gennesaret | 6:53–56 | 14:34–36 | | |
| On hand washing | 7:1–23 | 15:1–20 | | |
| A Gentile woman | 7:24–30 | 15:21–28 | | |
| To Sea of Galilee | 7:31 | 15:29a | | |
| Various healings | — | 15:29b–30 | | |
| Deaf mute healed | 7:32–36 | | | |
| The crowd amazed | 7:37 | 15:31 | | |
| Jesus feeds 4,000 | 8:1–10 | 15:32–39 | | |

|  | Mark | Matthew (PMA) | Matthew (B) | Matthew (C) |
|---|---|---|---|---|
| Pharisees seek sign | 8:11–13 | 16:1, 4 | | |
| No bread | 8:14–21 | 16:5–12 | | |
| Blind man at Bethsaida | 8:22–26 | | | |
| Peter's confession | 8:27–30 | 16:13–16, 20 | | |
| **Going to Jerusalem** | | | | |
| 1st passion prediction | 8:31 | 16:21 | | |
| Jesus rebukes Peter | 8:32–33 | 16:22–23 | | |
| Passion discourse | 8:34–9:1 | 16:24–28 | | |
| Transfiguration | 9:2–10 | 17:1–9 | | |
| Coming of Elijah | 9:11–13 | 17:10–13 | | |
| Demonized boy | 9:14–27 | 17:14–18 | | |
| On failed exorcisms | 9:28–29 | 17:19–20 | | |
| 2nd passion prediction | 9:30–32 | 17:22–23 | | |
| At Capernaum in house | 9:33ab | 17:24a, 25b | | |
| On greatness | 9:33c–35 | 18:1, 4 | | |
| On little ones | 9:36–37 | 18:2, 5 | | |
| Strange exorcist | 9:38–40 | | | |
| A cup of water | 9:41 | | 10:42 | |
| Offending little ones | 9:42 | 18:6 | | |
| Offensive member | 9:43–47 | 18:8–9 | | |
| Several sayings | 9:48–50 | | | |
| **In Judea** | | | | |
| Jesus goes to Judea | 10:1 | 19:1b–2 | | |
| On divorce | 10:2–12 | 19:3–9 | | |
| Jesus and children | 10:13–14 | 19:13–14 | | |
| Receive as a child | 10:15 | | 18:3 | |
| Laying on hands | 10:16 | 19:15a | | |
| Rich young man | 10:17–22 | 19:16–22 | | |
| Riches and rewards | 10:23–31 | 19:23–30 | | |
| 3rd passion prediction | 10:32–34 | 20:17–19 | | |
| Brothers seek honor | 10:35–40 | 20:20–23 | | |
| On greatness | 10:41–45 | 20:24–28 | | |
| Blind man at Jericho | 10:46–52 | 20:29–34 | | |
| **In Jerusalem** | | | | |
| Triumphal entry | 11:1–10 | 21:1–9 | | |
| Jesus enters Jerusalem | 11:11a | | | — |
| Out to Bethany | 11:11b | | | 21:17 |

| | Mark | Matthew (PMA) | Matthew (B) | Matthew (C) |
|---|---|---|---|---|
| Jesus curses fig tree | 11:12–14 | | | 21:18–19a |
| Jesus enters Jerusalem | 11:15a | 21:10a | | |
| Jesus cleanses Temple | 11:15b–17 | 21:12–13 | | |
| Priests and scribes | 11:18 | | | |
| Jesus leaves city | 11:19 | | | |
| Fig tree withers | 11:20–21 | | | 21:19b–20 |
| Moving mountains | 11:22–24 | | | 21:21–22 |
| To be forgiven | 11:25[–26] | | | →6:14–15 |
| Back to Jerusalem | 11:27a | | | |
| Question of authority | 11:27b–33 | 21:23–27 | | |
| Parable of tenants | 12:1–12a | 21:33–46a | | |
| They leave Jesus | 12:12b | →22:22b | | |
| Tribute to Caesar | 12:13–17 | 22:16–22a | | |
| On resurrection | 12:18–27 | 22:23–32 | | |
| Great commandment | 12:28–31 | 22:35–40 | | |
| Not far from kingdom | 12:32–34a | | | |
| No one dared | 12:34b | 22:46b | | |
| Christ and David | 12:35–37a | 22:41–45 | | |
| Against scribes | 12:37b–40 | 23:1, 6–7a, [14] | | |
| Widow's offering | 12:41–44 | | | |
| **Eschatology** | | | | |
| Temple prediction | 13:1–2 | 24:1–2 | | |
| Signs of the end | 13:3–8 | 24:3–8 | | |
| Watch out | 13:9a | — | | |
| Handed over | 13:9b | 24:9a | | |
| Before rulers | 13:9c | — | | |
| First the gospel | 13:10 | | | 24:14 |
| Spirit speaks, betrayed | 13:11–12a | — | | |
| Killed, hated, endure | 13:12b–13 | 24:9bc, 13 | | |
| Desolating sacrilege | 13:14–19 | 24:15–21 | | |
| Before the end | 13:20–23 | 24:22–25 | | |
| The end | 13:24–32 | 24:29, 30b–36 | | |
| Stay awake | 13:33–34 | 25:13–14 | | |
| Stay awake | 13:35 | | | 24:42 |
| **Passion narrative** | | | | |
| Jewish leaders plot | 14:1–2 | 26:2a, 3–5 | | |
| Anointing at Bethany | 14:3–9 | 26:6–13 | | |

|                         | Mark      | Matthew (PMA) | Matthew (B) | Matthew (C) |
|-------------------------|-----------|---------------|-------------|-------------|
| Judas makes a deal      | 14:10–11  | 26:14–16      |             |             |
| Passover prepared       | 14:12–17  | 26:17–20      |             |             |
| Betrayal predicted      | 14:18–21  | 26:21–25      |             |             |
| Last supper             | 14:22–25  | 26:26–29      |             |             |
| Mount of Olives         | 14:26–31  | 26:30–35      |             |             |
| Gethsemane              | 14:32–42  | 26:36–46      |             |             |
| Jesus' arrest           | 14:43–50  | 26:47–56      |             |             |
| Youth flees naked       | 14:51–52  |               |             |             |
| Denial and trial        | 14:53–72  | 26:57–75      |             |             |
| Before Pilate           | 15:1–20a  | 27:1–31a      |             |             |
| Jesus' crucifixion      | 15:20b–41 | 27:31b–56     |             |             |
| Jesus' burial           | 15:42–47  | 27:57–61      |             |             |
| The empty tomb          | 16:1–8    | 28:1–8        |             |             |
| **Jesus' resurrection** |           |               |             |             |
| Mary sees Jesus         | 16:9      | 28:9          |             |             |
| See me in Galilee       | —         | 28:10         |             |             |
| Report disbelieved      | 16:10–11  |               |             |             |
| Appearance to two       | 16:12–13  |               |             |             |
| Eleven go to Galilee    | —         | 28:16         |             |             |
| Appearance to 11        | 16:14     | 28:17         |             |             |
| Charge to disciples     | 16:15–16  | 28:19         |             |             |
| Preaching with signs    | 16:17–20  |               |             |             |

## Proto-Mark A

Most of the material that Matthew shares with Mark came from the source that I have designated "Proto-Mark A," as shown in the middle column of Table 4.3. In Chapter 5 I will identify a related gospel shared by Mark and Luke that I will designate "Proto-Mark B," and in Chapter 8 I will conjecture that Proto-Mark A and Proto-Mark B are independent revisions of a yet earlier gospel that I will call simply "Proto-Mark." For now I simply indicate the passages that either Matthew or Mark probably omitted from Proto-Mark A.

Matthew probably omitted several passages from Proto-Mark A. I have indicated these in Table 4.3 with a line ( — ).

1. In three instances Matthew lacks material concerning demons that Mark includes (Mark 1:23–28; 1:34b; 3:11). In these passages the demons tes-

tify to the identity of Jesus, and all three testimonies occur in Mark in the context of material from Proto-Mark A. If these passages originally stood in Proto-Mark A, it is not hard to explain why Matthew might have omitted them. He may have felt reluctant to rely on the testimony of evil spirits, especially given the accusation that Jesus was in collusion with their boss (Matt 9:34; 12:24). Most likely, therefore, Matthew omitted these passages from Proto-Mark A, from which Mark took them.

2. Matthew also lacks the parable of the growing seed, which Mark includes in the parable discourse from Proto-Mark A (Mark 4:26–29). If this parable too stood in Proto-Mark A, Matthew omitted it, putting in its place the parable of the weeds (Matt 13:24–30).

3. In Mark, after Jesus gives mission instructions to the Twelve, they go forth to preach (Mark 6:12–13) and subsequently report back to Jesus (Mark 6:30). Matthew has no parallel to the departure of the disciples, but does have a parallel to their subsequent return when they report to Jesus (Matt 14:12b). Matthew has linked this report to the preceding story about John the Baptist so that it appears to be a report about John's death. However, the parallel in Mark shows that it was originally a report about the apostles' mission. This report stands in the sequence of Proto-Mark A, and if Proto-Mark A included the disciples' return, it must also have included their departure. It appears then that both the departure and return stood in Proto-Mark A. Matthew omitted the former but kept the latter, turning it into a report about John.

Mark links the departure of the disciples (Mark 6:12–13) to a preceding set of mission instructions (Mark 6:7–11). If the departure stood in Proto-Mark A and was omitted at that point by Matthew, was the same true for the mission instructions, or did Proto-Mark A lack the instructions and merely say that Jesus sent out the disciples to preach? I have not resolved that question to my own satisfaction, but since I have found no evidence that mission instructions did stand in Proto-Mark A, I have not included them in my reconstruction of that gospel.

4. Matthew also lacks much of the material on persecution from the eschatological discourse in Proto-Mark A (Mark 13:9ac, 11–12a). He probably omitted this because he had previously included the Q version of this material (Matt 10:17–22).

Mark too apparently omitted a few items from Proto-Mark A.

1. Mark lacks the parable of the leaven, which Matthew includes following the parable of the mustard seed (Matt 13:33; cf. Luke 13:20–21). If the parable of the leaven did not originally stand in the parable discourse (from Proto-Mark A), then Matthew must have added it, presumably from Q. If it

did originally stand in the parable discourse, then Mark omitted it, perhaps because he felt that the idea of corruption associated with leaven made it a poor metaphor for the kingdom of God (cf. Mark 8:15 parr; 1 Cor 5:6–8; Gal 5:9). I have tentatively adopted the latter explanation.

2. Where Matthew has a summary of various healings (Matt 15:29b–30), Mark has the healing of a deaf mute (Mark 7:32–36). Without claiming certainty, I consider it likely that the summary in Matthew came from Proto-Mark A and was omitted by Mark in favor of the story of the deaf mute.

3. Two passages of Proto-Mark A that have been preserved in both Mark and Matthew predict that the disciples will see the risen Jesus in Galilee (Mark 14:28//Matt 26:32; Mark 16:7//Matt 28:7). Matthew includes a further such prediction and an account of the disciples going to Galilee (Matt 28:10; 28:16). Since these additional items in Matthew continue the theme introduced in Proto-Mark A, it is likely that they also came from Proto-Mark A, though no parallel has been preserved in Mark. It appears then that Proto-Mark A included three predictions of an appearance in Galilee as well as the disciples' journey there. Matthew preserved all of these items, while Mark included only the first two, omitting the third prediction and the disciples' trip.

## The B Material

The fourth column of Table 4.3 shows a second source common to Mark and Matthew. I have designated this with the letter "B." The first part of this material consists of miracle stories: Jesus heals a leper, calms a storm, casts demons into pigs, heals a woman, and raises a young girl. The second part consists of mission instructions that Jesus delivers to his disciples.

Mark and Matthew differ on where they put this material with respect to Proto-Mark A. For example, Matthew puts the leper story (Matt 8:2–4) before the healing at Peter's house from Proto-Mark A (Matt 8:14–15; Mark 1:29–31), while Mark puts it after (Mark 1:40–45). Likewise, while Mark has the remaining miracle stories after the parable discourse from Proto-Mark A (Mark 4:1–34; Matt 13:1–35), Matthew has them before. Thus, while these stories occur in the same order in both Mark and Matthew, they do not occur in the same position with respect to the Proto-Mark A material. This common order but different position is precisely what we would expect if Mark and Matthew independently combined the B material with Proto-Mark A. Both evangelists generally followed the order of the sources but inserted the B material at different points in the sequence of Proto-Mark A. I will discuss the B material further in Chapter 10.

# The C Material

The last column of Table 4.3 shows a third source common to Mark and Matthew, one that I have designated with the letter "C." The central part of the material in this column, from Matthew 4:23 through 9:36, does not fit into the sequence of either Proto-Mark A or the B material. It constitutes a third distinct sequence of material that Mark and Matthew have in different positions with respect to their other two shared sources. For example, Matthew has kept intact the summary of Jesus' ministry in Matt 4:23–25, while Mark has spread this material over several chapters, from Mark 1:14b to 3:8c. This feature of the C material suggests that it came from a third source distinct from either Proto-Mark A or the B material. Mark and Matthew both knew this source but combined it differently with their other sources.

The C material shows a certain fondness for the motif of "preaching the gospel," as shown in Table 4.4.

### Table 4.4
### "Preaching the gospel" in C

| Matthew | Mark |
|---|---|
| 4:23 And he went about in the whole of Galilee, teaching in their synagogues and *preaching the gospel* of the kingdom ... | 1:14 ... *preaching the gospel* of God ... |
| 9:35 And Jesus went about all the cities and villages teaching in their synagogues and *preaching the gospel* of the kingdom ... | 6:6b And he went about the villages round about teaching. |
| 24:14 And *this gospel* of the kingdom *will be preached* in the whole world ... | 13:10 And first *the gospel must be preached* to all the nations. |

The first two passages in Table 4.4 have affinities not only in using the expression "preaching the gospel" but also in giving similar summaries of Jesus' ministry.[11]

---

11. It is common in synopses to parallel Matthew 4:23 with Mark 1:39 instead of Mark 1:14 as I have done here. However, Matthew 4:23 speaks of "*teaching* in their synagogues," unlike Mark 1:39, which speaks of "*preaching* in their synagogues." Furthermore, Matthew 4:23 refers to "preaching the gospel (*evangelion*)," a phrase absent from Mark 1:39 but present in Mark 1:14.

Matthew probably omitted some of the C material. I have indicated some of these omissions in Table 4.3. 1) Mark 1:1, omitted by Matthew, may be the beginning of C, since it refers to the "gospel," a typical motif of this source. 2) Mark 1:2b, also omitted by Matthew, may be the next element of this source, since, as a quotation of Malachi 3:1, it intrudes into the quotation from Isaiah in Proto-Mark A. As the continuation of Mark 1:1, it links John the Baptist with the beginning of the gospel, and, like the following C passage (Mark 1:6; Matt 3:4), it implicitly identifies John as Elijah (cf. Mal 3:1; 4:5). 3) Mark has two statements that Jesus entered Jerusalem, one apparently from C (Mark 11:11a) and one from Proto-Mark A (Mark 11:15a). Matthew omitted the C version, keeping only the Proto-Mark A version (Matt 21:10a).

Mark also probably omitted C material. 1) Mark lacks several bits of material that Matthew has in the context of other C material (Matt 3:2; 4:23b; 9:32–33). In these cases, Mark probably omitted material from C that Matthew preserved. 2) Both Mark and Matthew relate that Jesus ascended a mountain (Mark 3:13a; Matt 5:1b), but only Matthew says that he came down (Matt 8:1a). Since Luke also has a version of this material in which Jesus comes down (Luke 6:17a), the descent probably stood in the story originally and was omitted by Mark.

The C material had some relation to Proto-Mark A, as shown by the fact that these sources occasionally overlap. In these instances, Matthew sometimes has two versions of the same material, one in the sequence of Proto-Mark A and one in the sequence of C. These doublets are excerpted from Table 4.3 above and presented as Table 4.5.

Table 4.5
Doublets of PMA and C in Matthew

|                        | Mark      | Matthew (PMA) | Matthew (C) |
|------------------------|-----------|---------------|-------------|
| To Galilee             | 1:14b     | 4:12b         | 4:23a       |
| Preaching the kingdom  | 1:14c–15  | 4:17          | 4:23c       |
| They bring the ill     | 1:32      | 8:16a         | 4:24b       |
| Jesus heals many       | 1:34a     | 8:16b         | 4:24c       |
| A crowd follows        | 3:7c      | 12:15b        | 4:25a       |
| By Beelzebul           | 3:22      | 12:24         | 9:34        |
| Jesus' compassion      | 6:34a     | 14:14a        | 9:36        |

This material in C occurs in the same order as the corresponding material in Proto-Mark A. In these instances, Matthew included the overlapping material from both sources, thus creating doublets. The fact that Mark has material from both sources but no doublets where they overlap indicates that in the overlapping passages he either omitted one version or conflated the two. In any case, the presence of such doublets in Matthew confirms our initial conclusion that C and Proto-Mark A constituted two distinct sources. I will discuss C more fully in Chapter 11.

## Application of the Theory to Matthew 7:28–9:34

The data that we have presented suggests that Mark and Matthew shared three sources: Proto-Mark A and two less extensive sources, B and C. The evangelists combined these sources independently so that the material from B and C does not occur in the same position with respect to Proto-Mark A in the two gospels. Yet because each evangelist usually followed the order of the sources, we can identify these as three distinct sequences of material that usually have the same order in Matthew as in Mark. This common order was interrupted occasionally as one evangelist or the other rearranged or omitted material from one of the sources.

Having set forth this hypothesis, we can now return to the question with which we began this chapter: how to account for the differences in order of the material that Matthew shares with Mark in Matthew 7:28–9:34. As we saw above, Markan prioritists have unconvincingly tried to explain these divergences in order as Matthean rearrangements of Mark. Our hypothesis permits a more plausible explanation: Matthew used the same sources as Mark but combined them differently. Table 4.6 shows the sources used by Matthew in this section, according to our theory.

Table 4.6

Matthew's sources in Matthew 7:28–9:34

|  | Matthew | Mark (PMA) | Mark (B) | Mark (C) | Luke (Q) |
|---|---|---|---|---|---|
| Jesus finished | 7:28a |  |  |  | 7:1a |
| People astonished | 7:28b–29 | 1:22 |  |  |  |
| Down the mount | 8:1a |  |  | — |  |
| A crowd gathers | 8:1b |  |  | 3:20b |  |
| Jesus heals a leper | 8:2–4 |  | 1:40–45 |  |  |
| Centurion's slave | 8:5–10, 13 |  |  |  | 7:1b–10 |
| At Peter's house | 8:14–15 | 1:29b–31 |  |  |  |
| Healing the ill | 8:16 | 1:32, 34 |  |  |  |

|                      | Matthew | Mark (PMA) | Mark (B)    | Mark (C) | Luke (Q) |
|----------------------|---------|------------|-------------|----------|----------|
| Scripture            | 8:17    |            |             |          |          |
| Let's cross the sea  | 8:18    |            | 4:35        |          |          |
| Would-be followers   | 8:19–22 |            |             |          | 9:57–60  |
| Jesus calms a storm  | 8:23–27 |            | 4:36b–41    |          |          |
| Gerasene demoniac    | 8:28–34 |            | 5:1–17      |          |          |
| Crossing the sea     | 9:1a    |            | 5:18a, 21a  |          |          |
| To his own town      | 9:1b    | 2:1a       |             |          |          |
| Lame man healed      | 9:2–8   | 2:3–12     |             |          |          |
| Eating with sinners  | 9:9–13  | 2:14–17    |             |          |          |
| About fasting        | 9:14–15 | 2:18–20    |             |          |          |
| Old and new          | 9:16–17 | 2:21–22    |             |          |          |
| Jairus's daughter    | 9:18–26 |            | 5:22–43     |          |          |
| Two blind men        | 9:27–31 |            |             |          |          |
| Mute demoniac        | 9:32–33 |            |             | —        |          |
| By Beelzebul         | 9:34    |            |             | 3:22     |          |

The first two columns of Table 4.6 present the material in the order in which it occurs in Matthew. The next three columns demonstrate how the corresponding material in Mark consists of three distinct sequences. The material in each of these columns has the same order in Mark as in Matthew. These columns represent the three sources that Mark shared with Matthew: Proto-Mark A, B, and C, respectively. The last column in the table shows material that Luke shared with Matthew, i.e., Q. For convenience I refer to Q as a single source, though the material generally assigned to Q may actually come from more than one source. Thus in this section Matthew combined four sources: three shared with Mark and one shared with Luke.

Matthew's sources at this point included several miracle stories but also some non-miracle material. The B source narrated a series of miracle stories (Matt 8:2–4; 8:23–9:1a; 9:18–26), while C related an exorcism (Matt 9:32–34). Proto-Mark A related the healings at Peter's house and afterward (Matt 8:14–16) but then turned to a series of controversy stories (Matt 9:1b–17). Q provided both a miracle story (Matt 8:5–10, 13) and the non-miracle pericope on would-be followers (Matt 8:19–22). It is clear that Matthew's aim here was not to create a sequence of miracle stories, since he includes the non-miracle material and breaks up the sequence of miracles in B (seen in Mark 4:35–5:43) with the controversy stories from Proto-Mark A (seen in Mark 2:1–22). His procedure was simply to follow the order of his sources, alternately taking material from one then another. His reasons for shifting from one source to another at any particular point may not be recoverable. The data presented here does not enable us to determine whether one individual combined all four sources at one time or whether the combination occurred in stages. It simply shows the final outcome of the process. While the present study is concerned primarily with the formation of Mark, this example shows how our hypothesis can also be applied to explain the formation of Matthew.

## Conclusion

When two gospels have the same material in a different order, it is certainly possible that the material came from a single source and that one evangelist or both altered the original order. However, it is equally possible that the evangelists had more than one source in common and independently combined these sources. In either case they would have the same material in a different order. While the theory of Markan priority relies solely on the first of these possibilities to account for divergences in order, I have suggested that both are necessary to adequately explain the data. If rearrangement of the material were the sole explanation, then we would not expect to find the rearranged material in the same order in each gospel. If this observation is correct, then the divergences in order in the material shared by Mark and Matthew had two causes. First, not all of the common material came from the same source. Mark and Matthew shared three distinct sources that they independently combined. Thus they have not only the same material, but also the same three sequences of material, combined differently in each gospel. Second, the evangelists sometimes omitted or rearranged the material. Thus, even material that came from the same source sometimes wound up in a different position in Mark than in Matthew.

If this explanation is correct, then it rules out all theories that make Mark the source of Matthew, or Matthew the source of Mark. Neither Mark nor Matthew relied upon the other, but both drew from the same sources. A colleague whose judgment I respect suggested that I amend that statement to read "the same *or similar* sources." To some extent I agree with this qualification, since I do not imagine that Mark and Matthew worked from identical manuscripts. Their manuscripts of Proto-Mark A, for example, may have differed through alterations made by previous scribes. It is even possible that Matthew used a form of Proto-Mark A that had already been combined with Q or M. However, even though Mark and Matthew may have received Proto-Mark A in different forms, there must have existed at some point an autograph copy of Proto-Mark A that contained, minimally, the material in

Sequence A (Table 4.2), material that Mark and Matthew now have in the same order. It is in this sense that I affirm that Mark and Matthew used the same source. The same considerations apply to B and C as well. With this proviso, we can state our conclusion thus:

> *Matthew did not use Mark, nor did Mark use Matthew,*
> *but both used the same three sources.*

# Chapter 5

# *Sources Common to Mark and Luke*

OUR NEXT STEP is to compare the order of Mark and Luke. When we do so, we obtain results similar to those obtained in Chapter 4 in comparing Mark and Matthew. The material in Luke, when viewed as a single sequence, shows marked divergences from the order of Mark. However, when we divide Luke's material into three distinct sequences, each sequence has the same order as the corresponding material in Mark. These three sequences are shown in Table 5.1. The first two columns of the table list the material in Mark in Mark's order. The next three columns show that the corresponding material in Luke falls into three distinct sequences, which I have designated Sequence 1, Sequence 2, and Sequence 3, respectively. The last column of the table, designated by a question mark, lists material in Luke that I initially leave aside for separate discussion, since, for the most part, it does not fit into any of the three sequences.

Table 5.1
Sequences common to Mark and Luke

|  | Mark | Luke (Seq. 1) | Luke (Seq. 2) | Luke (Seq. 3) | Luke (?) |
|---|---|---|---|---|---|
| **John and Jesus** |  |  |  |  |  |
| Beginning of gospel | 1:1 |  |  |  |  |
| Written in Isaiah | 1:2a |  |  |  | 3:4a |
| My messenger | 1:2b |  |  |  |  |
| Isaiah 40:3 | 1:3 |  |  |  | 3:4b |
| John in wilderness | 1:4a | 3:2b |  |  |  |
| Preaching baptism | 1:4b | 3:3b |  |  |  |
| John's baptism | 1:5 |  |  |  |  |
| John's lifestyle | 1:6 |  |  |  |  |
| One more powerful | 1:7–8 | 3:16 |  |  |  |

| | Mark | Luke (Seq. 1) | Luke (Seq. 2) | Luke (Seq. 3) | Luke (?) |
|---|---|---|---|---|---|
| Jesus' baptism | 1:9–11 | 3:21b–22 | | | |
| Jesus' temptation | 1:12–13 | 4:1–2 | | | |
| **Jesus in Galilee** | | | | | |
| John arrested | 1:14a | | | | |
| To Galilee | 1:14b | 4:14a | | | |
| Preaching the kingdom | 1:14c–15 | | | | |
| Jesus calls fishermen | 1:16–20 | | | | 5:2, 10–11 |
| Teaching in Capernaum | 1:21–22 | 4:31–32 | | | |
| Demon in synagogue | 1:23–27 | 4:33–36 | | | |
| Report goes out | 1:28 | 4:37 | | 4:14b | |
| At Peter's house | 1:29–31 | 4:38–39 | | | |
| Healing the ill | 1:32, 34 | 4:40–41 | | | |
| A preaching tour | 1:35–39 | 4:42–44 | | | |
| Jesus heals a leper | 1:40–42, 44 | 5:12–14 | | | |
| The word spreads | 1:45 | 5:15–16 | | | |
| **Controversy stories** | | | | | |
| Lame man healed | 2:1–12 | 5:18–26 | | | |
| Eating with sinners | 2:13–17 | 5:27–32 | | | |
| About fasting | 2:18–20 | 5:33–35 | | | |
| Old and new | 2:21–22 | 5:36–38 | | | |
| Plucking grain | 2:23–28 | 6:1–5 | | | |
| Withered hand | 3:1–6 | 6:6–11 | | | |
| **Ministry to a crowd** | | | Parables | | |
| With his disciples | 3:7a | 6:17b | | | |
| To the sea | 3:7b | | 5:1b | | |
| A crowd follows | 3:7c | 6:17c | | (5:17b) | |
| From Galilee | 3:7d | | | 5:17c | |
| Judea and Jerusalem | 3:7e–8a | 6:17d | | 5:17d | |
| Idumaea | 3:8b | | | | |
| Across the Jordan | 3:8c | | | | |
| Tyre and Sidon | 3:8d | 6:17e | | | |
| Hearing, they came | 3:8e | 6:18a | 5:1a | | |
| A boat for escape | 3:9 | | 5:3 | | |
| Jesus heals many | 3:10a | 6:18b, 19b | | 5:17e | |
| They touch him | 3:10b | 6:19a | | | |
| Jesus and demons | 3:11–12 | | | | 4:41bc |

| | Mark | Luke (Seq. 1) | Luke (Seq. 2) | Luke (Seq. 3) | Luke (?) |
|---|---|---|---|---|---|
| **Jesus chooses 12** | | | | | |
| On the mount | 3:13a | | | 6:12a | |
| Jesus chooses 12 | 3:13b–19 | | | 6:13–16 | |
| A crowd gathers | 3:20b | | | 6:17b | |
| Jesus beside himself | 3:21 | | | | |
| **Miscellaneous** | | | | | |
| Beelzebul debate | 3:22–27 | | | | |
| Unforgivable sin | 3:28–29 | | | | |
| Because they said | 3:30 | | | | 11:18b |
| Jesus' true family | 3:31–35 | 8:19–21 | | | |
| **Parable discourse** | | | | | |
| Ministry from boat | 4:1–2 | | | | |
| Parable of sower | 4:3–9 | | 8:4–8 | | |
| Reason for parables | 4:10–12 | | 8:9–10 | | |
| Sower explained | 4:13–20 | | 8:11–15 | | |
| Lamp on lampstand | 4:21 | | 8:16 | | |
| Nothing hidden | 4:22 | | 8:17 | | |
| Ears to hear | 4:23 | | | | |
| How you hear | 4:24a | | 8:18a | | |
| Measure you give | 4:24b | | | | |
| Added to you | 4:24c | | | | |
| Have and have not | 4:25 | | 8:18b | | |
| Growing seed | 4:26–29 | | | | |
| The mustard seed | 4:30–32 | | 13:18–19 | | |
| Use of parables | 4:33–34 | | | | |
| **Miracle stories** | | | | | |
| Jesus calms a storm | 4:35–41 | 8:22–25 | | | |
| Gerasene demoniac | 5:1–17 | 8:26–37a | | | |
| Would-be follower | 5:18–20 | 8:37b–39 | | | |
| Jairus's daughter | 5:21–43 | 8:40–56 | | | |
| **Further ministry** | | | | | |
| Jesus at hometown | 6:1–6a | | | | 4:16,22,24 |
| Cities and villages | 6:6b | | | 8:1 | |
| **Mission instructions** | | | | | |
| He summons the 12 | 6:7a | 9:1a | | | |
| Sent two by two | 6:7b | | | | |

|                          | Mark     | Luke (Seq. 1) | Luke (Seq. 2) | Luke (Seq. 3) | Luke (?) |
|--------------------------|----------|---------------|---------------|---------------|----------|
| Power over spirits       | 6:7c     | 9:1b          |               |               |          |
| What not to take         | 6:8–9    | 9:3           |               |               |          |
| Stay in one house        | 6:10     | 9:4           |               |               |          |
| If not received          | 6:11     | 9:5           |               |               |          |
| The 12 go forth          | 6:12-13  | 9:6           |               |               |          |
| **Further ministry**     |          |               |               |               |          |
| Opinions about Jesus     | 6:14–16  | 9:7–9         |               |               |          |
| John's imprisonment      | 6:17     |               |               |               | 3:19–20  |
| John's death             | 6:18–29  |               |               |               |          |
| The 12 return            | 6:30     | 9:10a         |               |               |          |
| Ministry to crowd        | 6:31–34  | 9:10b–11      |               |               |          |
| Jesus feeds 5,000        | 6:35–44  | 9:12–17       |               |               |          |
| Jesus walks on water     | 6:45–52  |               |               |               |          |
| In Gennesaret            | 6:53–56  |               |               |               |          |
| On hand washing          | 7:1–23   |               |               |               |          |
| A Gentile woman          | 7:24–30  |               |               |               |          |
| Deaf mute healed         | 7:31–37  |               |               |               |          |
| Jesus feeds 4,000        | 8:1–10   |               |               |               |          |
| Pharisees seek sign      | 8:11–13  |               |               |               |          |
| No bread                 | 8:14–21  |               |               |               |          |
| Blind man at Bethsaida   | 8:22–26  |               |               |               |          |
| Peter's confession       | 8:27–30  | 9:18–21       |               |               |          |
| **Going to Jerusalem**   |          |               |               |               |          |
| 1st passion prediction   | 8:31     | 9:22          |               |               |          |
| Jesus rebukes Peter      | 8:32–33  |               |               |               |          |
| Passion discourse        | 8:34–9:1 | 9:23–27       |               |               |          |
| Transfiguration          | 9:2–10   | 9:28–36       |               |               |          |
| Coming of Elijah         | 9:11–13  |               |               |               |          |
| Demonized boy            | 9:14–27  | 9:37–43a      |               |               |          |
| On failed exorcisms      | 9:28–29  |               |               |               |          |
| 2nd passion prediction   | 9:30–32  | 9:43b–45      |               |               |          |
| At Capernaum in house    | 9:33ab   |               |               |               |          |
| On greatness             | 9:33c–35 | 9:46, 48c     |               |               |          |
| On little ones           | 9:36–37  | 9:47–48ab     |               |               |          |
| Unknown exorcist         | 9:38–40  | 9:49–50       |               |               |          |
| A cup of water           | 9:41     |               |               |               |          |

| | Mark | Luke (Seq. 1) | Luke (Seq. 2) | Luke (Seq. 3) | Luke (?) |
|---|---|---|---|---|---|
| On offenses | 9:42–48 | | | | |
| Salted with fire | 9:49 | | | | |
| Spoiled salt | 9:50a | 14:34 | | | |
| Salt and peace | 9:50b | | | | |
| **In Judea** | | | | | |
| Jesus goes to Judea | 10:1 | | | | |
| Teaching on divorce | 10:2–9 | | | | |
| Ruling on divorce | 10:11–12 | 16:18 | | | |
| Jesus and children | 10:13–16 | 18:15–17 | | | |
| Rich young man | 10:17–22 | 18:18–23 | | | |
| Riches and rewards | 10:23–31 | 18:24–30 | | | |
| Up to Jerusalem | 10:32a | | | 19:28 | |
| 3rd passion prediction | 10:32b–34 | 18:31–33 | | | |
| Brothers seek honor | 10:35–40 | | | | |
| On greatness | 10:41–45 | | | | 22:24–27 |
| Blind man at Jericho | 10:46–52 | 18:35–43 | | | |
| **In Jerusalem** | | | | | |
| Triumphal entry | 11:1–10 | 19:29–38 | | | |
| Cursing a fig tree | 11:11–15a | | | | |
| Jesus cleanses Temple | 11:15b–17 | 19:45–46 | | | |
| Priests and scribes | 11:18 | 19:47–48 | | | |
| Cursing a fig tree | 11:19–27a | | | | |
| Question of authority | 11:27b–33 | 20:1–8 | | | |
| Parable of tenants | 12:1–12 | 20:9–17, 19 | | | |
| Tribute to Caesar | 12:13–17 | 20:20–26 | | | |
| On resurrection | 12:18–27a | 20:27–38 | | | |
| Jesus answers well | 12:28a | 20:39 | | | |
| Great commandment | 12:28b–31 | | | | |
| Not far from kingdom | 12:32–34a | | | | |
| No one dared | 12:34b | 20:40 | | | |
| Christ and David | 12:35–37a | 20:41–44 | | | |
| Against scribes | 12:37b–40 | 20:45–47 | | | |
| Widow's offering | 12:41–44 | 21:1–4 | | | |
| **Eschatology** | | | | | |
| Temple prediction | 13:1–2 | 21:5–6 | | | |
| Signs of the end | 13:3–8 | 21:7–11 | | | |

| | Mark | Luke (Seq. 1) | Luke (Seq. 2) | Luke (Seq. 3) | Luke (?) |
|---|---|---|---|---|---|
| On persecution | 13:9–13 | 21:12–19 | | | |
| Desolating sacrilege | 13:14–19 | 21:20–24 | | | |
| Before the end | 13:20–23 | | | | |
| The end | 13:24–31 | 21:25–33 | | | |
| The unknown time | 13:32–35 | | | | |
| **Passover** | | | **Supper** | | |
| Jewish leaders plot | 14:1–2 | 22:1–2 | | | |
| Anointing at Bethany | 14:3–9 | | | | 7:36–38 |
| Judas makes a deal | 14:10–11 | 22:3–6 | | | |
| Passover prepared | 14:12–17 | 22:7–14 | | | |
| Betrayal predicted | 14:18–21 | 22:21–23 | | | |
| Lord's Supper sayings | 14:22–24 | | 22:19–20 | | |
| Passover sayings | 14:25 | | | 22:15–18 | |
| To Mount of Olives | 14:26 | | | 22:39a | |
| All will scatter | 14:27 | | | | |
| See you in Galilee | 14:28 | | | | |
| Denial predicted | 14:29–30 | 22:33–34 | | | |
| Fidelity affirmed | 14:31 | | | | |
| To Gethsemane | 14:32a | 22:40a | | | |
| Jesus grieves | 14:32b–34a | | | | |
| Jesus prays | 14:35–38a | 22:40b–46 | | | |
| Jesus prays again | 14:39–41a | | | | |
| The hour arrives | 14:41c–42 | | | | |
| **Jesus' arrest** | | | | | |
| Judas and crowd | 14:43a | 22:47a | | | |
| Swords and spears | 14:43b | | | | |
| Kiss as sign | 14:44 | | | | |
| Judas kisses Jesus | 14:45 | 22:47b | | | |
| They seize Jesus | 14:46 | | | | |
| Slave's ear cut off | 14:47 | 22:50 | | | |
| As against a thief | 14:48 | 22:52 | | | |
| I taught in Temple | 14:49a | 22:53a | | | |
| Scriptures fulfilled | 14:49b | | | | |
| Disciples flee | 14:50 | | | | |
| Youth flees naked | 14:51–52 | | | | |
| **Denial and trial** | | | **Trial** | | |
| To the high priest | 14:53a | 22:54a | | | |

| | Mark | Luke (Seq. 1) | Luke (Seq. 2) | Luke (Seq. 3) | Luke (?) |
|---|---|---|---|---|---|
| Council assembles | 14:53b | | 22:66 | | |
| Peter follows | 14:54a | 22:54b | | | |
| Court of high priest | 14:54b | | | | |
| Sitting with servants | 14:54c | 22:55 | | | |
| False witnesses | 14:55–61a | | | | |
| Sanhedrin's question | 14:61b–64 | | 22:67–71 | | |
| Jesus is mocked | 14:65 | | | 22:63–65 | |
| Peter denies Jesus | 14:66–72 | 22:56–62 | | | |
| **Before Pilate** | | | | | |
| In the morning | 15:1a | 22:66a | | | |
| Council decides | 15:1b | | | | |
| Jesus led to Pilate | 15:1c | 23:1b | | | |
| You King of Jews? | 15:2 | 23:3 | | | |
| Jesus stays silent | 15:3–5 | 23:9–10 | | | |
| Barabbas or Jesus | 15:6–7 | 23:[17], 19 | | | |
| Barabbas or Jesus | 15:8–11 | | | | |
| Barabbas or Jesus | 15:12–15 | 23:18–25 | | | |
| Pilate flogs Jesus | 15:15c | | | | |
| Hail, King of Jews | 15:16-20a | | | | |
| **Jesus' crucifixion** | | | | | |
| They lead him out | 15:20b | 23:26a | | | |
| Simon carries cross | 15:21 | 23:26b | | | |
| Arrival at Golgotha | 15:22 | 23:33a | | | |
| Wine with myrrh | 15:23 | | | | |
| They crucify him | 15:24a | 23:33b | | | |
| Garments divided | 15:24b | 23:34b | | | |
| The third hour | 15:25 | | | | |
| Epigraph/charge | 15:26 | 23:38 | | | |
| Bandits crucified | 15:27 | | | 23:33c | |
| People watch | | | | 23:35a | |
| Passersby mock | 15:29–30 | | | | |
| The rulers mock | 15:31–32a | | | 23:35b | |
| The soldiers mock | | | | 23:36–37 | |
| The bandits mock | 15:32b | | | 23:39 | |
| Darkness over land | 15:33 | 23:44 | | 23:45a | |
| Jesus forsaken | 15:34–35 | | | | |
| Jesus given vinegar | 15:36a | | | | |

|  | Mark | Luke (Seq. 1) | Luke (Seq. 2) | Luke (Seq. 3) | Luke (?) |
|---|---|---|---|---|---|
| Will Elijah come | 15:36b | | | | |
| With a loud voice | 15:37a | 23:46a | | | |
| Receive my spirit | | | 23:46b | | |
| Jesus expires | 15:37b | 23:46c | | | |
| Temple veil torn | 15:38 | | | 23:45b | |
| Centurion confesses | 15:39 | 23:47 | | | |
| The women watch | 15:40–41a | 23:49 | | | |
| And many others | 15:41b | | | | 8:3 |
| **Burial and tomb** | | | | | |
| Jesus' burial | 15:42–46 | 23:50–54 | | | |
| The women watch | 15:47 | 23:55 | | | |
| The empty tomb | 16:1–8 | 23:56–24:9 | | | |
| **Jesus' resurrection** | | | | | |
| Appearance to Mary | 16:9a | | | | |
| Mary's seven demons | 16:9b | | | | 8:2b |
| Report disbelieved | 16:10–11 | 24:10b–11 | | | |
| Appearance to two | 16:12–13 | 24:13–33, 35 | | | |
| Appearance to 11 | 16:14 | 24:36 | | | |
| Charge to preach | 16:15 | 24:47a | | | |
| Charge to baptize | 16:16 | | | | |
| Signs to follow | 16:17–18 | | | | |
| Jesus taken up | 16:19 | 24:51 | | | |
| Disciples preach | 16:20 | | | | |

Each sequence in Luke has the same order as the corresponding material in Mark. Yet the sequences cannot be combined to create one larger sequence that has the same order as Mark. Sequence 1 includes most of the material that Luke shares with Mark. Sequence 2 contains items that do not fit into Sequence 1, while Sequence 3 contains elements that do not fit into the order of either of the first two sequences.

These Lukan sequences are precisely what we would expect to find if Mark and Luke shared several distinct sources and combined them independently. Therefore, each Lukan sequence probably represents a distinct source that Luke shared with Mark. The two evangelists used the same sources and usually followed the order of each source. Their gospels diverge in order when viewed as a whole, because the evangelists combined their sources independently and did not insert material from one source in the same place with respect to the material from the other sources.

The largest sequence, Sequence 1, probably came from a single major source known to both Mark and Luke. Since it extends into the passion and resurrection narratives, it constitutes a complete passion gospel. As it includes the greater part of Mark—and no material from Q, M, or L—it could be considered an earlier version of Mark, a Proto-Mark. This source overlaps to a great degree with Proto-Mark A, the major source shared by Mark and Matthew that we delineated in Chapter 4. Yet it differs as well, lacking some of the material in Proto-Mark A and including other material that Proto-Mark A lacks. It thus appears to be a distinct version of the same source represented by Proto-Mark A. I have therefore designated it Proto-Mark B (PMB). If our conclusions thus far are correct, then Matthew knew Proto-Mark A, Luke knew Proto-Mark B, while Mark knew both.

## Material of Uncertain Sequence

The last column of Table 5.1, designated with a question mark, contains Lukan material that I have initially left out of the three sequences. Most of these items fit into none of the sequences, presumably because either Mark or Luke moved them from their original position in one or another of the sources. We must therefore use criteria other than order to identify the sources from which this material came.

1. *Luke 3:4a, 3:4b.* With respect to order, the first two items in the uncertain column, Luke 3:4a and 3:4b, might fit into either Sequence 2 or Sequence 3. Other factors, however, suggest that they belong to Sequence 1. Together they constitute a quotation of Isaiah 40:3. In our analysis in Chapter 4, this quotation stood in the sequence of Proto-Mark A (see Table 4.3). We would therefore assume a priori that the parallel in Luke should stand in Proto-Mark B, i.e., Sequence 1. If that is the case, however, then why does Luke 3:4 not fit into the order of Sequence 1? The answer would be that either Mark or Luke disturbed the sequence by moving this material from its original order in the source. While Mark has this quotation (Mark 1:2a, 3) before the appearance of John the Baptist (Mark 1:4a; Luke 3:2b), Luke has it after (Luke 3:4). Since Luke's order is supported by Matthew (Matt 3:1b–3), it is likely that Mark moved the quotation closer to the beginning of his gospel in order to combine it with the quotation of Malachi 3:1 from C (Mark 1:2b). If this is correct, then Luke preserves the original order of Sequence 1, in which John's appearance (Luke 3:2b, 3b) preceded the quotation of Isaiah 40:3 (Luke 3:4).

2. *Luke 5:2, 10–11.* The rest of the passages in the uncertain column do not fit into any of the three sequences. The reason again seems to be that

either Mark or Luke disturbed the sequences by moving these passages from their original positions in the sources. In each case, therefore, I will try to determine which evangelist moved it and in which sequence (or source) it originally stood. In the first instance (Luke 5:2, 10–11), Luke seems to have the stronger motive for rearranging the material. While Mark includes the whole story in which Jesus calls four disciples (Mark 1:16–20), Luke has only elements of it (Luke 5:2, 10–11), which he has conflated with another story about a miraculous catch of fish (Luke 5:4–9). It would appear that Luke moved the elements of the call story from their original position in their source to the position that this latter story occupied in his gospel. But from which sequence (or source) did he move them? Logically, the call story, which introduces Peter, seems to prepare for the later story in which Jesus visits Peter's house (Mark 1:29–31; Luke 4:38–39). The fact that both these stories stand in Proto-Mark A supports the conclusion that they belong to the same sequence. We can assume therefore that also in Luke the former story came from the same sequence as the latter, in this case Sequence 1 (i.e., Proto-Mark B).

3. *Luke 4:41bc.* In Luke 4:41bc (Mark 3:11–12), the demons recognize Jesus and he orders them not to make him known. While Mark has this material as part of a summary in Sequence 1 (Mark 3:7–12; Luke 6:17–19), Luke includes it in an earlier story, also in Sequence 1 (Mark 1:32–34; Luke 4:40–41). Since Matthew, at least partially, supports Mark's placement of the prohibition (Matt 12:16//Mark 3:12), it appears that Luke moved this material from its original position in Sequence 1 to the earlier story. His reason for doing so, however, remains obscure.

4. *Luke 11:18b.* The next passage (Luke 11:18b) forms part of the Beelzebul controversy. Proto-Mark A, followed by Mark and Matthew, knew a short version of this controversy (Mark 3:22–30; Matt 12:24–31), while Q included a longer version. Matthew conflated the two versions in the position where the story occurred in Proto-Mark A (Matt 12:22–31), while Luke presumably kept the order of Q (Luke 11:14–23). While most of Luke's version can be attributed to Q, Luke 11:18b has no parallel in Matthew, but does have a parallel in Mark:

Because you say that I cast out the demons by Beelzebul. (Luke 11:18b)

Because they said, "He has an unclean spirit." (Mark 3:30)

The absence of this sentence from Matthew's gospel suggests that it did not occur in either of his sources, Proto-Mark A or Q, but came from a source shared by Mark and Luke. That source may have been Proto-Mark B (Sequence 1), if Proto-Mark B included a version of the Beelzebul controversy parallel to that in Proto-Mark A. If so, Luke kept only one element of the Proto-Mark B version (Luke 11:18b), moving it from its original place in that source to conflate it with the Q version.

5. *Luke 4:16, 22, 24.* All three evangelists relate the story in which Jesus visits his hometown. Mark and Matthew have this story in the sequence of Proto-Mark A near the middle of Jesus' ministry (Mark 6:1–6a; Matt 13:53b–58), while Luke places it earlier as the inaugural event of Jesus' ministry. Luke's order appears to be secondary, arising from his intention to create an inaugural sermon for Jesus. Only three verses of Luke's version (Luke 4:16, 22, 24) have a parallel in the Proto-Mark A version, and we may suspect that these came from a version of the story in Proto-Mark B parallel to that in Proto-Mark A. If so, Luke moved these from their original position in Proto-Mark B (Sequence 1).

6. *Luke 3:19–20.* Mark and Matthew have the account of John's imprisonment in the sequence of Proto-Mark A (Mark 6:17; Matt 14:3), while Luke's parallel comes earlier in the narrative (Luke 3:19–20). The awkwardness of Luke's order, in which John is imprisoned before he baptizes Jesus, shows its secondary character. Luke probably found John's imprisonment in Proto-Mark B (Sequence 1) parallel to the Proto-Mark A version. If so, Luke moved it, joining it with earlier material about John, apparently in order to complete the story of John before beginning the story of Jesus.

7. *Luke 22:24–27.* In the sequence of Proto-Mark A, Mark and Matthew have a story in which Jesus teaches the disciples that greatness lies in serving (Mark 10:41–45; Matt 20:24–28). Luke has a less developed version of this story, which he places in the context of the Last Supper (Luke 22:24–27). It is possible that Luke found his version in Proto-Mark B parallel to that in Proto-Mark A. However, since the two versions differ significantly, it is also possible that Luke's version came from some other source known only to Luke. I leave the question undecided.

8. *Luke 7:36–38.* In the sequence of Proto-Mark A, Mark and Matthew share a story in which a woman anoints Jesus (Mark 14:3–9; Matt 26:6–13). Luke has a related, but quite different story earlier in the narrative (Luke 7:36–50), of which only a few verses (Luke 7:36–38) resemble those of the Proto-Mark A version. I suspect that these verses came from a version of the story in Proto-Mark B (Sequence 1) parallel to that in Proto-Mark A, and that Luke moved them from their original position to conflate them with the related story.

9. *Luke 8:2b, 3*. The pericope on Jesus' female supporters occurs as a unity only in Luke 8:2–3, but the evidence suggests that Mark also knew it. In this passage, Luke mentions certain women who ministered to Jesus: Mary Magdalene, Joanna, Susanna, and many others. Mark lacks this material where it occurs in Luke but shows knowledge of it later. A passage from Proto-Mark A names other women who followed Jesus from Galilee (Matt 27:55–56; Mark 15:40–41b; cf. Luke 23:49). To this passage Mark adds "and many other (women) who had come up with him to Jerusalem" (Mark 15:41b). In mentioning these ἄλλαι πολλαί, Mark may be referring to Joanna, Susanna, and the ἕτεραι πολλαί of Luke 8:3. Apparently Proto-Mark B, preserved in Luke 8:3, gave one version of the women's names, while Proto-Mark A gave another later in the narrative. Mark kept the Proto-Mark A version in its place but augmented it with the "many others" of Proto-Mark B. A second Markan parallel to Luke 8:2–3 appears in the longer ending of Mark. Mark 16:9b identifies Mary Magdalene as a woman out of whom Jesus had cast seven demons, the same description given in Luke 8:2. If the longer ending came from a later hand than that of Mark, then this later author probably drew the phrase from Luke 8:2. If the longer ending came from Mark, then Mark took the phrase from the same source as Luke, i.e., Proto-Mark B, and moved it from its original position in that source.

## Sources Common to Mark and Luke

At this point we are ready to revise Table 5.1 to incorporate the conclusions that have emerged from our discussion of it. Table 5.2 below incorporates three types of revisions.

1. First, we can now speak of sources instead of "sequences." To some extent we have already taken this step by identifying Sequence 1 as the source "Proto-Mark B" (PMB). However, we still need designations for Sequences 2 and 3. Sequence 2 in Table 5.1 consists of material that does not fit into the sequence of Proto-Mark B. It does, however, appear in the sequence of Proto-Mark A that we delineated in Table 4.3. Since it occurs in the "A" version of Proto-Mark, but not the "B" version, I will designate it as "A" material. Sequence 3 in Table 5.1 consists of material that does not fit into the order of either Proto-Mark B or of the A material. Since some of it corresponds to material that we previously designated as "C" (cf. Table 4.3), it appears to belong to the C source.

2. As our second type of revision, we can now incorporate the uncertain elements of Table 5.1 into our three sources. These could not be assigned to one of our sequences on the basis of order alone, but by using other criteria I

subsequently assigned most of them to one or another of our sources. All of these passages came to be out of sequence because one evangelist or the other rearranged them. As before, in Table 5.2 I indicate such rearrangements by small type with an arrow pointing to the place to which the evangelist moved the material (e.g., →4:41bc).

3. Third, we can now consider possible omissions of the sources. In using their sources, Mark and Luke probably not only rearranged material but also omitted some of it. In Table 5.2 I indicate a few places where I suspect that one evangelist or the other has omitted material from the source. I mark these conjectured omissions with a line ( — ) and subsequently give my reasons for making these conjectures.

By incorporating these revisions into Table 5.1, we get Table 5.2.

### Table 5.2
### Sources common to Mark and Luke

|  | Mark | Luke (PMB) | Luke (A) | Luke (C) |
|---|---|---|---|---|
| **John and Jesus** |  |  |  |  |
| Beginning of gospel | 1:1 |  |  |  |
| My messenger | 1:2b |  |  |  |
| John in wilderness | 1:4a | 3:2b |  |  |
| Preaching baptism | 1:4b | 3:3b |  |  |
| Written in Isaiah | →1:2a | 3:4a |  |  |
| Isaiah 40:3 | →1:3 | 3:4b |  |  |
| John's baptism | 1:5 |  |  |  |
| John's lifestyle | 1:6 |  |  |  |
| One more powerful | 1:7–8 | 3:16 |  |  |
| Jesus' baptism | 1:9–11 | 3:21b–22 |  |  |
| Jesus' temptation | 1:12–13 | 4:1–2 |  |  |
| **Jesus in Galilee** |  |  |  |  |
| John arrested | 1:14a |  |  |  |
| To Galilee | 1:14b | 4:14a |  |  |
| Teaching in synagogues | — |  |  | 4:15a |
| Preaching the kingdom | 1:14c–15 | — |  |  |
| Jesus calls fishermen | 1:16–20 | →5:2, 10–11 |  |  |
| Teaching in Capernaum | 1:21–22 | 4:31–32 |  |  |
| Demon in synagogue | 1:23–27 | 4:33–36 |  |  |
| Report goes out | 1:28 | 4:37 |  | 4:14b |

|  | Mark | Luke (PMB) | Luke (A) | Luke (C) |
|---|---|---|---|---|
| At Peter's house | 1:29–31 | 4:38–39 |  |  |
| Healing the ill | 1:32, 34 | 4:40–41 |  |  |
| A preaching tour | 1:35–39 | 4:42–44 |  |  |
| Jesus heals a leper | 1:40–42, 44 | 5:12–14 |  |  |
| The word spreads | 1:45 | 5:15–16 |  |  |
| **Controversy stories** |  |  |  |  |
| Lame man healed | 2:1–12 | 5:18–26 |  |  |
| Eating with sinners | 2:13–17 | 5:27–32 |  |  |
| About fasting | 2:18–20 | 5:33–35 |  |  |
| Old and new | 2:21–22 | 5:36–38 |  |  |
| Plucking grain | 2:23–28 | 6:1–5 |  |  |
| Withered hand | 3:1–6 | 6:6–11 |  |  |
| **Ministry to a crowd** |  |  | Parables |  |
| With his disciples | 3:7a | 6:17b |  |  |
| To the sea | 3:7b |  | 5:1b |  |
| A crowd follows | 3:7c | 6:17c |  | (5:17b) |
| From Galilee | 3:7d |  |  | 5:17c |
| Judea and Jerusalem | 3:7e–8a | 6:17d |  | 5:17d |
| Idumaea | 3:8b |  |  |  |
| Across the Jordan | 3:8c |  |  |  |
| Tyre and Sidon | 3:8d | 6:17e |  |  |
| Hearing, they came | 3:8e | 6:18a | 5:1a |  |
| A boat for escape | 3:9 |  | 5:3 |  |
| Jesus heals many | 3:10a | 6:18b, 19b |  | 5:17e |
| They touch him | 3:10b | 6:19a |  |  |
| Jesus and demons | 3:11–12 | →4:41bc |  |  |
| **Jesus chooses 12** |  |  |  |  |
| On the mount | 3:13a |  |  | 6:12a |
| Jesus chooses 12 | 3:13b–19 |  |  | 6:13–16 |
| Down the mount | — |  |  | 6:17a |
| A crowd gathers | 3:20b |  |  | 6:17b |
| Jesus beside himself | 3:21 |  |  |  |
| **Miscellaneous** |  |  |  |  |
| A mute demoniac | — | — |  |  |
| Beelzebul debate | 3:22–27 | — |  |  |
| Unforgivable sin | 3:28–29 | — |  |  |

|  | Mark | Luke (PMB) | Luke (A) | Luke (C) |
|---|---|---|---|---|
| Because they said | 3:30 | →11:18b | | |
| Certain women healed | — | 8:2a | | |
| Mary's seven demons | →16:9b | 8:2b | | |
| And many others | →15:41b | 8:3 | | |
| Jesus' true family | 3:31–35 | 8:19–21 | | |
| **Parable discourse** | | | | |
| Ministry from boat | 4:1–2 | | | |
| Parable of sower | 4:3–9 | | 8:4–8 | |
| Reason for parables | 4:10–12 | | 8:9–10 | |
| Sower explained | 4:13–20 | | 8:11–15 | |
| Lamp on lampstand | 4:21 | | 8:16 | |
| Nothing hidden | 4:22 | | 8:17 | |
| Ears to hear | 4:23 | | | |
| How you hear | 4:24a | | 8:18a | |
| Measure you give | 4:24b | | | |
| Added to you | 4:24c | | | |
| Have and have not | 4:25 | | 8:18b | |
| Growing seed | 4:26–29 | | | |
| The mustard seed | 4:30–32 | | 13:18–19 | |
| The leaven | — | | 13:20–21 | |
| Use of parables | 4:33–34 | | — | |
| **Miracle stories** | | | | |
| Jesus calms a storm | 4:35–41 | 8:22–25 | | |
| Gerasene demoniac | 5:1–17 | 8:26–37a | | |
| Would-be follower | 5:18–20 | 8:37b–39 | | |
| Jairus's daughter | 5:21–43 | 8:40–56 | | |
| **Further ministry** | | | | |
| Jesus at hometown | 6:1–6a | →4:16, 22, 24 | | |
| Cities and villages | 6:6b | | | 8:1 |
| **Mission instructions** | | | | |
| He summons the 12 | 6:7a | 9:1a | | |
| Sent two by two | 6:7b | | | |
| Power over spirits | 6:7c | 9:1b | | |
| What not to take | 6:8–9 | 9:3 | | |
| Stay in one house | 6:10 | 9:4 | | |
| If not received | 6:11 | 9:5 | | |

|  | Mark | Luke (PMB) | Luke (A) | Luke (C) |
|---|---|---|---|---|
| The 12 go forth | 6:12–13 | 9:6 |  |  |
| **Further ministry** |  |  |  |  |
| Opinions about Jesus | 6:14–16 | 9:7–9 |  |  |
| John's imprisonment | 6:17 | →3:19–20 |  |  |
| John's death | 6:18–29 |  |  |  |
| The 12 return | 6:30 | 9:10a |  |  |
| Ministry to crowd | 6:31–34 | 9:10b–11 |  |  |
| Jesus feeds 5,000 | 6:35–44 | 9:12–17 |  |  |
| Jesus walks on water | 6:45–52 |  |  |  |
| In Gennesaret | 6:53–56 |  |  |  |
| On hand washing | 7:1–23 |  |  |  |
| A Gentile woman | 7:24–30 |  |  |  |
| Deaf mute healed | 7:31–37 |  |  |  |
| Jesus feeds 4,000 | 8:1–10 |  |  |  |
| Pharisees seek sign | 8:11–13 |  |  |  |
| No bread | 8:14–21 |  |  |  |
| Blind man at Bethsaida | 8:22–26 |  |  |  |
| Peter's confession | 8:27–30 | 9:18–21 |  |  |
| **Going to Jerusalem** |  |  |  |  |
| 1st passion prediction | 8:31 | 9:22 |  |  |
| Jesus rebukes Peter | 8:32–33 |  |  |  |
| Passion discourse | 8:34–9:1 | 9:23–27 |  |  |
| Transfiguration | 9:2–10 | 9:28–36 |  |  |
| Coming of Elijah | 9:11–13 |  |  |  |
| Demonized boy | 9:14–27 | 9:37–43a |  |  |
| On failed exorcisms | 9:28–29 |  |  |  |
| 2nd passion prediction | 9:30–32 | 9:43b–45 |  |  |
| At Capernaum in house | 9:33ab |  |  |  |
| On greatness | 9:33c–35 | 9:46, 48c |  |  |
| On little ones | 9:36–37 | 9:47–48ab |  |  |
| Unknown exorcist | 9:38–40 | 9:49–50 |  |  |
| A cup of water | 9:41 |  |  |  |
| On offenses | 9:42–48 |  |  |  |
| Salted with fire | 9:49 |  |  |  |
| Spoiled salt | 9:50a | 14:34 |  |  |
| Salt and peace | 9:50b |  |  |  |

| | Mark | Luke (PMB) | Luke (A) | Luke (C) |
|---|---|---|---|---|
| **In Judea** | | | | |
| Jesus goes to Judea | 10:1 | | | |
| Teaching on divorce | 10:2–9 | | | |
| Ruling on divorce | 10:11–12 | 16:18 | | |
| Jesus and children | 10:13–16 | 18:15–17 | | |
| Rich young man | 10:17–22 | 18:18–23 | | |
| Riches and rewards | 10:23–31 | 18:24–30 | | |
| Up to Jerusalem | 10:32a | | | 19:28 |
| 3rd passion prediction | 10:32b–34 | 18:31–33 | | |
| Brothers seek honor | 10:35–40 | | | |
| On greatness | 10:41–45 | →22:24–27 | | |
| Blind man at Jericho | 10:46–52 | 18:35–43 | | |
| **In Jerusalem** | | | | |
| Triumphal entry | 11:1–10 | 19:29–38 | | |
| Cursing a fig tree | 11:11–15a | | | |
| Jesus cleanses Temple | 11:15b–17 | 19:45–46 | | |
| Priests and scribes | 11:18 | 19:47–48 | | |
| Cursing a fig tree | 11:19–27a | | | |
| Question of authority | 11:27b–33 | 20:1–8 | | |
| Parable of tenants | 12:1–12 | 20:9–17, 19 | | |
| Tribute to Caesar | 12:13–17 | 20:20–26 | | |
| On resurrection | 12:18–27a | 20:27–38 | | |
| Jesus answers well | 12:28a | 20:39 | | |
| Great commandment | 12:28b–31 | — | | |
| Not far from kingdom | 12:32–34a | | | |
| No one dared | 12:34b | 20:40 | | |
| Christ and David | 12:35–37a | 20:41–44 | | |
| Against scribes | 12:37b–40 | 20:45–47 | | |
| Widow's offering | 12:41–44 | 21:1–4 | | |
| **Eschatology** | | | | |
| Temple prediction | 13:1–2 | 21:5–6 | | |
| Signs of the end | 13:3–8 | 21:7–11 | | |
| On persecution | 13:9–13 | 21:12–19 | | |
| Desolating sacrilege | 13:14–19 | 21:20–24 | | |
| Before the end | 13:20–23 | | | |
| The end | 13:24–31 | 21:25–33 | | |

|                      | Mark      | Luke (PMB) | Luke (A) | Luke (C) |
|----------------------|-----------|------------|----------|----------|
| The unknown time     | 13:32–35  |            |          |          |
| **Passover**         |           |            | **Supper** |        |
| Jewish leaders plot  | 14:1–2    | 22:1–2     |          |          |
| Anointing at Bethany | 14:3–9    | →7:36–38   |          |          |
| Judas makes a deal   | 14:10–11  | 22:3–6     |          |          |
| Passover prepared    | 14:12–17  | 22:7–14    |          |          |
| Betrayal predicted   | 14:18–21  | 22:21–23   |          |          |
| Lord's Supper sayings| 14:22–24  |            | 22:19–20 |          |
| Passover sayings     | 14:25     |            |          | 22:15–18 |
| To Mount of Olives   | 14:26     |            |          | 22:39a   |
| All will scatter     | 14:27     |            |          |          |
| See you in Galilee   | 14:28     |            |          |          |
| Denial predicted     | 14:29–30  | 22:33–34   |          |          |
| Fidelity affirmed    | 14:31     |            |          |          |
| To Gethsemane        | 14:32a    | 22:40a     |          |          |
| Jesus grieves        | 14:32b–34a|            |          |          |
| Jesus prays          | 14:35–38a | 22:40b–46  |          |          |
| Jesus prays again    | 14:39–41a |            |          |          |
| The hour arrives     | 14:41c–42 |            |          |          |
| **Jesus' arrest**    |           |            |          |          |
| Judas and crowd      | 14:43a    | 22:47a     |          |          |
| Swords and spears    | 14:43b    |            |          |          |
| Kiss as sign         | 14:44     |            |          |          |
| Judas kisses Jesus   | 14:45     | 22:47b     |          |          |
| They seize Jesus     | 14:46     |            |          |          |
| Slave's ear cut off  | 14:47     | 22:50      |          |          |
| As against a thief   | 14:48     | 22:52      |          |          |
| I taught in Temple   | 14:49a    | 22:53a     |          |          |
| Scriptures fulfilled | 14:49b    |            |          |          |
| Disciples flee       | 14:50     |            |          |          |
| Youth flees naked    | 14:51–52  |            |          |          |
| **Denial and trial** |           |            | **Trial** |         |
| To the high priest   | 14:53a    | 22:54a     |          |          |
| Council assembles    | 14:53b    |            | 22:66    |          |
| Peter follows        | 14:54a    | 22:54b     |          |          |
| Court of high priest | 14:54b    |            |          |          |

| | Mark | Luke (PMB) | Luke (A) | Luke (C) |
|---|---|---|---|---|
| Sitting with servants | 14:54c | 22:55 | | |
| False witnesses | 14:55–61a | — | | |
| Sanhedrin's question | 14:61b–64 | | 22:67–71 | |
| Jesus is mocked | 14:65 | | | 22:63–65 |
| Peter denies Jesus | 14:66–72 | 22:56–62 | | |
| **Before Pilate** | | | | |
| In the morning | 15:1a | 22:66a | | |
| Council decides | 15:1b | | | |
| Jesus led to Pilate | 15:1c | 23:1b | | |
| You King of Jews? | 15:2 | 23:3 | | |
| Jesus stays silent | 15:3–5 | 23:9–10 | | |
| Barabbas or Jesus | 15:6–7 | 23:[17], 19 | | |
| Barabbas or Jesus | 15:8–11 | | | |
| Barabbas or Jesus | 15:12–15 | 23:18–25 | | |
| Pilate flogs Jesus | 15:15c | | | |
| Hail, King of Jews | 15:16–20a | | | |
| **Jesus' crucifixion** | | | | |
| They lead him out | 15:20b | 23:26a | | |
| Simon carries cross | 15:21 | 23:26b | | |
| Arrival at Golgotha | 15:22 | 23:33a | | |
| Wine with myrrh | 15:23 | | | |
| They crucify him | 15:24a | 23:33b | | |
| Garments divided | 15:24b | 23:34b | | |
| The third hour | 15:25 | | | |
| Epigraph/charge | 15:26 | 23:38 | | |
| Bandits crucified | 15:27 | | | 23:33c |
| People watch | | | | 23:35a |
| Passersby mock | 15:29–30 | | — | |
| The rulers mock | 15:31–32a | | | 23:35b |
| The soldiers mock | | | | 23:36–37 |
| The bandits mock | 15:32b | | | 23:39 |
| Darkness over land | 15:33 | 23:44 | | 23:45a |
| Jesus forsaken | 15:34–35 | | | |
| Jesus given vinegar | 15:36a | | | |
| Will Elijah come | 15:36b | | | |
| With a loud voice | 15:37a | 23:46a | | |

| | Mark | Luke (PMB) | Luke (A) | Luke (C) |
|---|---|---|---|---|
| Receive my spirit | | | 23:46b | |
| Jesus expires | 15:37b | 23:46c | | |
| Temple veil torn | 15:38 | | | 23:45b |
| Centurion confesses | 15:39 | 23:47 | | |
| The women watch | 15:40–41a | 23:49 | | |
| **Burial and tomb** | | | | |
| Jesus' burial | 15:42–46 | 23:50–54 | | |
| The women watch | 15:47 | 23:55 | | |
| The empty tomb | 16:1–8 | 23:56–24:9 | | |
| **Jesus' resurrection** | | | | |
| Names of women | cf. 16:9a | 24:10a | | |
| Report disbelieved | 16:10–11 | 24:10b–11 | | |
| Appearance to two | 16:12–13 | 24:13–33, 35 | | |
| Appearance to 11 | 16:14 | 24:36 | | |
| Charge to preach | 16:15 | 24:47a | | |
| Charge to baptize | 16:16 | | | |
| Signs to follow | 16:17–18 | | | |
| Jesus taken up | 16:19 | 24:51 | | |
| Disciples preach | 16:20 | | | |

# Proto-Mark B

The middle column of Table 5.2 lists the material that, on the basis of order and other criteria, we have identified as the main source common to Mark and Luke. Since this source contains much of the same material as Proto-Mark A, I have designated it "Proto-Mark B." I will explore the relationship between Proto-Mark A and Proto-Mark B more fully in Chapter 8, where I hypothesize that these two sources were independent revisions of a yet earlier gospel, Proto-Mark. Here I will simply discuss passages that either Mark or Luke may have omitted from Proto-Mark B. The following considerations suggest that Luke probably omitted at least three passages from it.

1. Though Luke has no parallel to Mark 1:14c–15, this material probably stood in Proto-Mark B, from which Luke omitted it. Part of this passage in Mark has a parallel in Matthew and can be traced to Proto-Mark A, but the rest occurs only in Mark (Table 5.3). Mark alone has the message "The time is fulfilled; believe in the gospel." While this could be Markan redaction, it seems more likely to be the Proto-Mark B parallel to the similar message in

Table 5.3

Mark 1:14c–15 parr

| Matthew 4:17 (PMA) | Mark 1:14c–15 (PMA) | Mark 1:14c–15 (PMB?) | Luke (PMB?) |
|---|---|---|---|
| 4:17 Jesus began to preach and say, | 1:14c preaching the gospel of God 15 and saying, | | |
| | | The time is fulfilled | — |
| Repent, for the kingdom of heaven has drawn near. | the kingdom of God has drawn near. Repent | | |
| | | believe in the gospel. | — |

Proto-Mark A: "Repent, for the kingdom of heaven has drawn near." Matthew knew only the Proto-Mark A version, while Mark knew both and conflated them. Luke would have known the Proto-Mark B version, but has not included it.

2. Luke has no parallel in the sequence of Proto-Mark B to Mark 3:27–29, part of the Beelzebul controversy. However, as we saw above in discussing Luke 11:18b, Luke probably knew a version of this material from Proto-Mark B, which he omitted in favor of the Q version (Luke 11:21–22; 12:10).

3. The pericope on the great commandment (Mark 12:28b–31) is part of a collection of controversy stories that stood together in Proto-Mark A (Matt 22:16–40; Mark 12:13–34). These all probably had a parallel in Proto-Mark B as well (Mark 12:13–34; Luke 20:20–40), but Luke lacks the Proto-Mark B version of the great commandment. He would have had a good reason to omit this, since he had included a parallel version from Q earlier in the narrative (Luke 10:25–28).

Mark too probably omitted a few items from Proto-Mark B. Since Proto-Mark A (Table 4.3) probably included an exorcism preceding the Beelzebul controversy (Mark 3:22–30), the parallel in Proto-Mark B may have included this exorcism as well. While Luke would have omitted the exorcism from Proto-Mark B in favor of the Q version, Mark apparently omitted the story altogether. Mark probably also found the parallel to Luke 8:2a in Proto-Mark B but omitted it when he rearranged the parallel to Luke 8:2b–3.

## The A Material

The fourth column in Table 5.2 shows three items that do not fit into the sequence of Proto-Mark B: a parable discourse, the words of institution of the Lord's Supper, and a narrative that includes Jesus' trial before the Sanhedrin and his death. These items occur in the same order in all three Synoptics, but Luke has them in a different position than Mark and Matthew with respect to the Proto-Markan material. In Mark and Matthew they occur in the sequence of Proto-Mark A. Since they stand in the "A" version of Proto-Mark but not in the "B" version, I have designated them collectively with the letter "A." These three items do not exhaust the A material but constitute the part that was known to Luke.

The best explanation for these items seems to be that each originally circulated separately. The parable discourse and the trial narrative would have circulated as written sources, while the words of institution of the Lord's Supper may have circulated as oral tradition. While the editor of Proto-Mark A added this A material to Proto-Mark, Luke independently added it to Proto-Mark B. The content of the material ensured that the two editors would put it in the same order, since the parables would naturally precede the Last Supper in the sequence of Jesus' ministry, while both would naturally precede Jesus' trial and death. Yet because the editors worked independently, they did not insert this material in the same places in their respective versions of the Proto-Markan material. Since Mark and Matthew both followed the order of Proto-Mark A, they have the A material in the same position in their gospels, in agreement against Luke.

The parable discourse began by relating how Jesus got into a boat to escape the crowd. After relating several parables, it concluded with a statement on Jesus' use of the parables. The editor of Proto-Mark A, followed by Mark and Matthew, kept this material together in a single context (Mark 4:1–34; Matt 13:1–35). Luke, however, in combining it with Proto-Mark B, split it into three parts: the introductory boat narrative (Luke 5:1, 3), the main body of the discourse (Luke 8:4–18), and the last two parables, the mustard seed and the leaven (Luke 13:18–21). This reconstruction assumes that the parables of the mustard seed and the leaven in Luke came from this discourse rather than from Q as proponents of Markan priority sometimes affirm. It further assumes that Mark omitted the parable of the leaven and that Luke omitted the conclusion of the discourse when he separated off the last two parables. We will see later that Mark probably knew two versions of the parable discourse: one from Proto-Mark A (shared with Matthew) and one that circulated separately (shared with Luke).

The narrative of Jesus' trial before the Sanhedrin has affinities with the account of Stephen's trial before the Sanhedrin in Acts (Acts 6:12–7:1; 7:55–60). Both probably developed from the same original narrative. The editor of Proto-Mark A incorporated this narrative into his gospel, which was followed by Mark and Matthew. Luke independently added the narrative to Proto-Mark B. In so doing he omitted two scenes that probably stood in the trial narrative: the false witnesses who accused Jesus of threatening to tear down the Temple (Mark 14:55–61a; Matt 26:59–63a) and the passersby who make the same accusation against Jesus on the cross (Mark 15:29–30; Matt 27:39–40). Since the first scene appears in Mark and Matthew as well as in the parallel narrative concerning Stephen's trial (Acts 6:13–14a), and since the second scene is related thematically to the first, it is likely that both constituted an original part of the source. I will discuss the A material more fully in Chapter 9.

## The C Material

The last column of Table 5.2 contains elements that do not fit into the sequence of either Proto-Mark B or the A material. Upon closer inspection, we notice that the elements in the first part of this column, through Luke 8:1, correspond to elements that we previously identified as "C" material. We can conclude therefore that Luke too knew the C source and drew at least these elements from it. We first encountered the C source when we found a sequence of material common to Mark and Matthew that did not fit into either Proto-Mark A or the B material (Table 4.2). Now we have found a similar sequence common to Mark and Luke that does not fit into either Proto-Mark B or the A material (Table 5.2). I combine these results here as Table 5.4.

Table 5.4
The C material

|  | Matthew (C) | Mark (C) | Luke (C) |
|---|---|---|---|
| **John the Baptist** |  |  |  |
| Beginning of gospel |  | 1:1 |  |
| I send my messenger |  | 1:2b |  |
| John in wilderness | 3:1b | 1:4a |  |
| Kingdom at hand | 3:2 |  |  |
| John's lifestyle | 3:4 | 1:6 |  |
| **Ministry in Galilee** |  |  |  |
| To Galilee | 4:23a | 1:14b |  |
| Teaching in synagogues | 4:23b |  | 4:15a |
| Preaching the kingdom | 4:23c | 1:14c–15 |  |

|  | Matthew (C) | Mark (C) | Luke (C) |
|---|---|---|---|
| Report goes out | 4:24a | 1:28 | 4:14b |
| They bring the ill | 4:24b | 1:32 | |
| Jesus heals many | 4:24c | 1:34a | |
| A crowd follows | 4:25a | 3:7c | (5:17b) |
| From Galilee | 4:25b | 3:7d | 5:17c |
| Judea and Jerusalem | 4:25c | 3:7e–8a | 5:17d |
| Across the Jordan | 4:25d | 3:8c | |
| Jesus heals many | | 3:10a | 5:17e |
| **Jesus chooses 12** | | | |
| On the mount | 5:1b | 3:13a | 6:12a |
| Jesus chooses 12 | →10:1–4 | 3:13b–19 | 6:13–16 |
| Down the mount | 8:1a | | 6:17a |
| A crowd gathers | 8:1b | 3:20b | 6:17b |
| **Beelzebul debate** | | | |
| A mute demoniac | 9:32–33 | | |
| By Beelzebul | 9:34 | 3:22 | |
| **Cities and villages** | 9:35 | 6:6b | 8:1 |
| **Jesus' compassion** | 9:36 | 6:34a | |
| **Up to Jerusalem** | | 10:32ab | 19:28 |
| **The fig tree** | | | |
| Jesus enters Jerusalem | | 11:11a | |
| Out to Bethany | 21:17 | 11:11b | |
| Jesus curses fig tree | 21:18–19a | 11:12–14 | |
| Fig tree withers | 21:19b–20 | 11:20–21 | |
| Moving mountains | 21:21–22 | 11:22–24 | |
| To be forgiven | →6:14–15 | 11:25[–26] | |
| **On the end-time** | | | |
| First the gospel | 24:14 | 13:10 | |
| Stay awake | 24:42 | 13:35a | |
| **Passion narrative** | | | |
| Passover sayings | | 14:25 | 22:15–18 |
| To Mount of Olives | | 14:26 | 22:39a |
| Jesus is mocked | | 14:65 | 22:63–65 |
| Bandits crucified | | 15:27 | 23:33c |
| People watch | | | 23:35a |
| The rulers mock | | 15:31–32a | 23:35b |
| The bandits mock | | 15:32c | 23:39 |

|                       | Matthew (C) | Mark (C) | Luke (C) |
|-----------------------|-------------|----------|----------|
| Darkness over land    |             | 15:33    | 23:45a   |
| Temple veil torn      |             | 15:38    | 23:45b   |

The elements of this material common to Mark and Matthew do not occur in the same position in these two gospels with respect to Proto-Mark A. Likewise, the elements of this material common to Mark and Luke do not occur in the same position in these two gospels with respect to Proto-Mark B. These facts suggest that each Synoptic evangelist used this source independently, each inserting elements from it at different places in the Proto-Markan sequence.

The sections of C designated "Ministry in Galilee," "Jesus chooses 12," and "Cities and villages" occur in all three Synoptics. This material thus forms the minimum assured content of C. Only Matthew and Luke have the two elements "Teaching in synagogues" (Matt 4:23b; Luke 4:15a) and "Down the mount" (Matt 8:1a; Luke 6:17a). Presumably Mark knew but omitted these elements. Only Mark and Matthew have the sections designated "John the Baptist," "Beelzebul debate," "Jesus' compassion," "The fig tree," and "On the end-time." Presumably Luke knew but omitted these sections.

The sections "Up to Jerusalem" and "Passion narrative" pose a special problem. In our comparison of Mark and Matthew (Table 4.2), these fell into the sequence of Proto-Mark A. However, in our comparison of Mark and Luke (Table 5.2), they fall into the sequence of C. Should we then assign these to A, to C, or to both? I will reserve an answer to this question for the fuller discussion of the C material in Chapter 11.

We saw in Chapter 4 that the C material to some extent overlapped with Proto-Mark A, so that Matthew sometimes included doublets of the overlapping material (Table 4.5). In a similar way, the C material overlapped with Proto-Mark B, so that Luke sometimes has two versions of the same material, one in the sequence of Proto-Mark B and one in the sequence of C. These doublets are excerpted from Table 5.2 above and presented as Table 5.5.

### Table 5.5
### Doublets of PMB and C in Luke

|                         | Mark    | Luke (PMB) | Luke (C) |
|-------------------------|---------|------------|----------|
| Report goes out         | 1:28    | 4:37       | 4:14b    |
| A crowd follows         | 3:7c    | 6:17c      | (5:17b)  |
| From Judea and Jerusalem | 3:7e–8a | 6:17d      | 5:17d    |
| Jesus heals many        | 3:10a   | 6:18b, 19b | 5:17e    |

The doublets from C occur in the same order as the corresponding material in Proto-Mark B. The presence of such doublets in Luke confirms our initial conclusion that C and Proto-Mark B constituted two distinct sources. Where they overlapped, Luke sometimes included both versions. Since Mark has material from both C and Proto-Mark B but no doublets where they overlap, we can infer that in each case he either omitted one of the doublets or conflated the two.

## Conclusion

From the preceding observations, a conclusion emerges that is similar to the one we reached with respect to Mark and Matthew. The divergences in order in the material shared by Mark and Luke had two causes. First, their common material came not from a single source but ultimately from several different sources. Both evangelists knew Proto-Mark B and the C source. Luke also knew several sources individually that Mark knew collectively from their inclusion in Proto-Mark A: a parable discourse, the words of institution of the Lord's Supper, and a narrative of Jesus' trial before the Sanhedrin. Thus, both gospels have the same sequences of material because both evangelists drew from the same sources. Yet these sources are combined in a different order in each gospel, because each evangelist worked independently of the other. Secondly, one evangelist or the other occasionally rearranged the material. Thus, even material that came from the same source sometimes wound up in a different position in Mark than in Luke.

If this explanation is correct, then it rules out all theories that make Mark the source of Luke, or Luke the source of Mark. We can state our conclusion thus:

> *Luke did not use Mark, nor did Mark use Luke,*
> *but both used the same sources.*

# Chapter 6

# *Conflation in Mark*

THE GRIESBACH HYPOTHESIS affirms that Mark combined or conflated Matthew and Luke. If our theory is correct, Mark did conflate his sources, but these were not Matthew and Luke. We have already seen one instance where Mark conflated two exorcism stories, one known to Matthew and Luke, the other unknown to them (Table 2.14). In this chapter I will give examples of two other types of conflation in Mark. 1) A test of dual expressions in Mark supports the conclusion that Mark frequently conflated two sources, one known to Matthew and one known to Luke. 2) An examination of Mark 3:7–12 supports the view that Mark occasionally conflated more than two sources that he shared with Matthew and Luke.

## Previous Scholarship on Conflation in Mark

Scholars with no allegiance to the priority of Mark have often argued for the presence of conflation in Mark.[1] E. P. Sanders, for example, has pointed out that "what is called conflation in Matthew [by the two-document hypothesis] occurs also, and much more frequently, in Mark."[2] The two-document hypothesis affirms that Matthew conflated two overlapping traditions, namely Mark and Q, in passages such as the Beelzebul controversy (Matt 12:22–30). This conclusion is based in part on the characteristics of Matthew's version. It appears to be the "middle term" between Mark and Luke, agreeing sometimes with one and sometimes with the other, while Mark and Luke have few agreements with each other against Matthew. Exactly the same characteristics, however, occur in Mark in much of the triple tradition: it appears to be the middle term between Matthew and Luke, agree-

---

1. Roland Mushat Frye, "The Synoptic Problems and Analogies in Other Literatures," in *The Relationships among the Gospels: An Interdisciplinary Dialogue* (ed. William O. Walker; San Antonio: Trinity University Press, 1978), 261–302; Pierson Parker, "The Posteriority of Mark," in *New Synoptic Studies: The Cambridge Gospel Conference and Beyond* (ed. William R. Farmer; Macon, GA: Mercer University Press, 1983), 67–142, esp. 104–109.

2. E. P. Sanders, "The Overlaps of Mark and Q and the Synoptic Problem," *NTS* 19 (1972/73): 462.

ing sometimes with one and sometimes with the other, while Matthew and Luke have few agreements with each other against Mark. If such characteristics count as conflation in Matthew, should they not also count as conflation in Mark?

Thomas Longstaff has made the most detailed study of conflation in Mark.[3] In the first part of his study, he examines three known instances of conflation: the Diatessaron of Tatian and the works of two medieval chroniclers, Benedict of Petersborough and Roger of Hovedon. From this examination he formulates a list of literary characteristics that result from conflation. In the second part of his study, he then examines six Markan pericopes and their parallels (Mark 1:29–31; 1:32–34; 3:1–6; 9:38–41; 11:15–19; 14:12–21). He finds in each passage the literary characteristics of conflation that were formulated in the first part of the study. The wording in each of these passages also shows a pattern of alternating agreement in which Mark agrees most closely first with one of the remaining Synoptics, then with the other, as, for example, in Mark 14:12–21:

| | |
|---|---|
| Mark 14:12a | Matthew |
| Mark 14:12b | Luke |
| Mark 14:12cff. | Matthew |
| Mark 14:13a | Luke |
| Mark 14:13b | Matthew |
| Mark 14:13c–16 | Luke |
| Mark 14:17–21 | Matthew |

Longstaff finds this alternation to be a significant embarrassment for the theory of Markan priority. Given the priority of Mark, Matthew and Luke must have acted quite strangely:

> It is somewhat as though each were free to re-write the Marcan account only in those details where the other had substantially preserved the content and language of that source. Such an explanation would be inconsistent with the view that Matthew and Luke are independent of one another. Furthermore, even if we suppose they knew one another, such an editorial method would be very difficult to understand and no examples of it are known.[4]

These results, in Longstaff's view, support the Griesbach hypothesis, according to which Mark conflated Matthew and Luke, following one then the other more closely.

---

3. Thomas R. W. Longstaff, *Evidence of Conflation in Mark? A Study in the Synoptic Problem* (Missoula, MT: Scholars Press, 1977).
4. Ibid., 138.

Longstaff's work has received mixed reviews. In criticizing it, Christopher Tuckett argued that the alternating agreement found by Longstaff is only "a matter of degree" and depends on "a subjective judgement."[5] Doubtless this may be true in a few instances, but in most of the cases examined by Longstaff it is clear when Mark is closer to Matthew and when it is closer to Luke. In Mark 14:12–21, for example, when Mark agrees more closely with Matthew or Luke, the other Synoptic generally either lacks the material in question or differs significantly. This alternating agreement is more than simply a subjective judgment on Longstaff's part. One might still, however, disagree on its significance. According to Tuckett and Joanna Dewey, Longstaff has shown only that Markan conflation in these passages is possible, not that this explanation is preferable to the theory of Markan priority.[6] William O. Walker Jr. gives a more positive evaluation. He concludes that if one were limited to two alternatives—either the two-document hypothesis or the Griesbach hypothesis—then Longstaff's work would strengthen the case for the latter over the former by making an impressive argument for the view that Mark conflated Matthew and Luke. Walker himself, however, would not like to see the options limited to just these two alternatives.[7]

My own approach is to view Longstaff's work in the light of the evidence that I have presented in Chapters 2 to 5. If, as I think, that evidence shows that no theory of Markan priority is viable, then the phenomena presented by Longstaff must be explained by some theory that does not involve Markan priority. That is, once we eliminate the theory of Markan priority on other grounds, it becomes probable that the phenomena illustrated by Longstaff do result from Markan conflation of material found in Matthew and Luke, respectively. However, this conclusion does not require us to accept Griesbach's view that Mark drew directly from Matthew and Luke. Longstaff's evidence would equally well support the view that Mark conflated not Matthew and Luke, but sources that he shared with Matthew and Luke, respectively. The latter view is more likely for two reasons: first, because unlike the Griesbach hypothesis it does not have to explain why Mark omitted so much of his sources; and second, because we have seen that in fact Mark did share sources with both Matthew and Luke.

## Dual Expressions as Conflation of Two Sources

Other evidence for conflation in Mark occurs in Mark's use of dual expressions. The presence of dual or duplicate expressions in Mark has played

---

5. Tuckett, *Revival of the Griesbach Hypothesis*, 49.

6. Ibid., 41–51; Joanna Dewey, "Order in the Synoptic Gospels: A Critique," *The Second Century* 6 (1987/88): 68–82.

7 William O. Walker Jr., "Order in the Synoptic Gospels: A Critique," *The Second Century* 6 (1987/88): 83–97.

an important role in some discussions of the Synoptic Problem.[8] Such expressions may be "duplicate," that is, equivalent in meaning and somewhat repetitious, or simply "dual," as when Mark has two imperatives or two temporal expressions in the same context. In many instances, the parallels in Matthew and Luke each have only one expression where Mark has two. The best-known example is Mark 1:32, shown in Table 6.1.

Table 6.1
Dual expressions in Mark 1:32

| Matthew 8:16 | Mark 1:32 | Luke 4:40 |
|---|---|---|
| When evening came | When evening came, | |
| | when the sun set | The sun having set |

Scholars who support the priority of Mark argue that Matthew and Luke independently simplified the redundancy of Mark's double expression. Proponents of the Griesbach hypothesis and other scholars argue for the reverse process: that Mark conflated two expressions in his sources, one known to Matthew and one known to Luke.

Previous attempts to decide between these two possibilities have not yielded conclusive results. Christopher Tuckett, for example, used Markan duplicate expressions in order to test the Griesbach hypothesis.[9] He gathered 213 examples from the lists compiled by Frans Neirynck, specifically from Neirynck's lists 10–13.[10] He classified these 213 duplicate expressions into ten groups (Matthew has one half while Luke the other; Matthew has one half while Luke has both halves; Matthew has one half while Luke has no parallel; etc.). He found only seventeen cases in which Matthew has one half while Luke has the other. He argued that these results were compatible with the theory of Markan priority: Matthew and Luke regularly omitted some of Mark's redundancy and "the number of times they do this by omitting different halves of the dual expression is not significantly high."[11] He concluded that he had found nothing to disprove the Griesbach hypothesis, but equally nothing to support it.

---

8. Hawkins, *Horae Synopticae*, 139–42; Frans Neirynck, *Duality in Mark: Contributions to the Study of the Markan Redaction* (BETL 31; Leuven University Press, 1972); idem, *Minor Agreements*, 287; idem, "Les expressions doubles chez Marc et le problème synoptique," *ETL* 59 (1983): 303–30; Tuckett, *Revival of the Griesbach Hypothesis*, 16–21; Parker, "Posteriority of Mark," 67–142, esp. 104–9; Philippe Rolland, "Marc, première harmonie évangélique?" *RB* 90 (1983): 23–79; idem, *Les premiers évangiles: un nouveau regard sur le problème synoptique* (Lectio Divina 116; Paris: Cerf, 1984), 109–22.

9. Tuckett, *Revival of the Griesbach Hypothesis*, 16–21.

10. Neirynck, *Duality in Mark*, 75–136, esp. 94–106.

11. Tuckett, *Revival of the Griesbach Hypothesis*, 20.

Since this test has yielded an inconclusive result, I propose to make another type of test of dual expressions in Mark. As I explain more fully in the Appendix, the categories of dual expressions compiled by Neirynck and used by Tuckett are somewhat ill defined. Perhaps a test based on a more clearly defined category of expressions would yield a more conclusive result. My own test is therefore based on Neirynck's most clearly defined category: dual temporal and local expressions. These can be defined as instances where Mark has two temporal or local expressions in the same context. There are fifty instances of these where we can compare the readings of all three gospels. These fall into the categories set out in Table 6.2.

### Table 6.2
### Dual temporal or local expressions in Mark

| Category | Matt has | Luke has | Dual expressions in Mark | No. of instances |
|---|---|---|---|---|
| 1. | both | both | 3:7c–8a; 5:1; 6:1–2; 13:11; 13:21 | 5 |
| 2. | both | one | 1:39; 4:5; 4:15ab; 4:16; 5:13; 6:35; 11:15; 13:29; 14:25; 16:1–2 | 10 |
| 3. | both | neither | 14:54 | 1 |
| 4. | one | both | 2:20; 4:15cd; 4:21; 5:14; 6:10b; 14:1a; 14:12; 14:49 | 8 |
| 5a. | one | other one | 1:12–13; 1:28; 1:32; 2:19bc; 3:8cd; 5:2–3; 5:12; 6:31–32; 10:27; 10:46; 11:2; 14:30; 15:42; 16:2 | 14 |
| 5b. | one | same one | 1:21ac; 12:23; 14:43 | 3 |
| 6. | one | neither | 2:1; 3:7b, 8b; 13:24 | 3 |
| 7. | neither | both | 5:11 | 1 |
| 8. | neither | one | 1:21b; 4:35; 10:30 | 3 |
| 9. | neither | neither | 4:38; 5:21 | 2 |

For the purpose of my test, I need instances in which Matthew and Luke each have one and only one half of Mark's dual expression. That limits our inquiry to those expressions in category 5, which includes seventeen of the fifty dual expressions. I have further divided this category into 5a (Matthew and Luke have different halves) and 5b (Matthew and Luke have the same half). These are set out more fully in Table 6.3.

## Table 6.3
## Dual temporal or local expressions, category 5

5a: Matthew and Luke have different halves

| Matt 4:1 (PMA) | Mark 1:12–13 | Luke 4:1 (PMB) |
|---|---|---|
| εἰς τὴν ἔρημον | εἰς τὴν ἔρημον | |
| | ἐν τῇ ἐρήμῳ | ἐν τῇ ἐρήμῳ |

| Matt 4:24a (C) | Mark 1:28 | Luke 4:37 (PMB) |
|---|---|---|
| | πανταχοῦ | εἰς πάντα τόπον |
| εἰς ὅλην | εἰς ὅλην | |
| | τὴν περίχωρον | τῆς περιχώρου |
| τὴν Συρίαν | τῆς Γαλιλαία | |

| Matt 8:16 (PMA) | Mark 1:32 | Luke 4:40 (PMB) |
|---|---|---|
| ὀψίας δὲ γενομένης | ὀψίας δὲ γενομένης | |
| | ὅτε ἔδυ ὁ ἥλιος | δύνοντος δὲ τοῦ ἡλίου |

| Matt 9:15 (PMA) | Mark 2:19bc | Luke 5:34 (PMB) |
|---|---|---|
| | ἐν ᾧ | ἐν ᾧ |
| ἐφ᾽ ὅσον | ὅσον χρόνον | |

| Matt 4:25 (C) | Mark 3:8cd | Luke 6:17 (PMB) |
|---|---|---|
| πέραν τοῦ Ἰορδάνου | πέραν τοῦ Ἰορδάνου | |
| | περὶ Τύρον καὶ Σιδῶνα | τῆς παραλίου Τύρου καὶ Σιδῶνος |

| Matt 8:28 (B) | Mark 5:2–3 | Luke 8:27 (PMB) |
|---|---|---|
| ἐκ τῶν μνημείων | ἐκ τῶν μνημείων | |
| | ἐν τοῖς μνήμασιν | ἐν τοῖς μνήμασιν |

| Matt 8:31 (B) | Mark 5:12 | Luke 8:32 (PMB) |
|---|---|---|
| εἰς τὴν ἀγέλην τῶν χοίρων | εἰς τοὺς χοίρους | |
| | εἰς αὐτοὺς | εἰς ἐκείνους |

| Matt 14:13 (PMA) | Mark 6:31–32 | Luke 9:10b (PMB) |
|---|---|---|
| | κατ᾽ ἰδίαν | κατ᾽ ἰδίαν |
| | εἰς ἔρημον τόπον | εἰς πόλιν καλουμένην Βηθσαϊδά |
| εἰς ἔρημον τόπον | εἰς ἔρημον τόπον | |
| κατ᾽ ἰδίαν | κατ᾽ ἰδίαν | |

| Matt 19:26 (PMA) | Mark 10:27 | Luke 18:26 (PMB) |
|---|---|---|
| παρὰ δὲ θεῷ | παρὰ θεῷ | |
| | παρὰ τῷ θεῷ | παρὰ τῷ θεῷ |

| Matt 20:29 (PMA) | Mark 10:46 | Luke 18:35 (PMB) |
|---|---|---|
| | εἰς Ἰεριχώ | εἰς Ἰεριχώ |
| ἀπὸ Ἰεριχώ | ἀπὸ Ἰεριχώ | |

| Matt 21:2 (PMA) | Mark 11:2 | Luke 19:30 (PMB) |
|---|---|---|
| εὐθέως | εὐθύς | |
| | εἰσπορευόμενοι εἰς αὐτήν | ἐν ᾗ εἰσπορευόμενοι |

| Matt 26:34 (PMA) | Mark 14:30 | Luke 22:34 (PMB) |
|---|---|---|
| | σήμερον | σήμερον |
| ἐν ταύτῃ τῇ νυκτί | ταύτῃ τῇ νυκτί | |

| Matt 27:57 (PMA) | Mark 15:42 | Luke 23:54 (PMB) |
|---|---|---|
| ὀψίας δὲ γενομένης | ὀψίας γενομένης | |
| | ἐπεὶ ἦν παρασκευή | ἡμέρα ἦν παρασκευῆς |

| Matt 28:1 (PMA) | Mark 16:2 | Luke 24:1 (PMB) |
|---|---|---|
| | λίαν πρωΐ | ὄρθρου βαθέως |
| τῇ ἐπιφωσκούσῃ | ἀνατείλαντος τοῦ ἡλίου | |

5b: Matthew and Luke have same half

| Matt 4:13 (B) | Mark 1:21 | Luke 4:31 (PMB) |
|---|---|---|
| εἰς Καφαρναούμ | εἰς Καφαρναούμ | εἰς Καφαρναούμ |
| | εἰς τὴν συναγωγήν | |

| Matt 22:28 (PMA) | Mark 12:23 | Luke 20:33 (PMB) |
|---|---|---|
| ἐν τῇ ἀναστάσει | ἐν τῇ ἀναστάσει | ἐν τῇ ἀναστάσει |
|  | [ὅταν ἀναστῶσιν] |  |

| Matt 26:47 (PMA) | Mark 14:43 | Luke 22:47 (PMB) |
|---|---|---|
|  | εὐθύς |  |
| ἔτι αὐτοῦ λαλοῦντος | ἔτι αὐτοῦ λαλοῦντος | ἔτι αὐτοῦ λαλοῦντος |

We now have seventeen dual temporal or local expressions in Mark, where in each case Matthew and Luke each have one and only one of Mark's two expressions. What is interesting is the fact that in fourteen instances (category 5a) Matthew and Luke disagree: Matthew has one of the Markan expressions, while Luke has the other. In only three instances (category 5b) do Matthew and Luke agree by having the same Markan expression. Is this distribution in category 5 probable given the theory of Markan priority? Let us ask that question first with respect to the two-document hypothesis and then with respect to other theories of Markan priority.

The classical two-document hypothesis affirms that Matthew and Luke independently copied from Mark. As they worked, their editorial preferences determined which of Mark's two dual expressions they chose. Is it probable that a set of two editors would have editorial preferences so different that they would choose different expressions in fourteen of these seventeen instances? That is, when each editor chose one and only one of Mark's two dual expressions, is it likely that they would so rarely choose the same expression? In answering this question, I make two assumptions. First, in the seventeen instances of editorial choice, only two outcomes are possible: either the editors agree in choosing the same expression or they disagree in choosing different expressions. Second, if we take any two editors at random and both work independently, with no intention to agree or disagree with the other, then neither of these outcomes is more probable than the other. Each is equally probable—that is, has a probability of one-half—in any particular instance. Note that we are not asking whether it is probable that the specific individuals Matthew and Luke would agree or disagree in any particular instance. Our question is rather the probability that any two editors chosen at random, whose editorial preferences we do not know in advance, would have editorial preferences so different that they would almost always disagree. Since the editors, along with their editorial preferences, are chosen at random, in any particular instance it is just as likely that they will agree as disagree.

If these assumptions are correct, we can find the probability that two editors would disagree to such an extent by using the formula for computing binomial probabilities. This formula applies when there is a series of independent "trials," and there are two possible outcomes of each trial.[12] In the present case, the series of trials consists of the seventeen instances in category 5, and the two possible outcomes are either agreement in choosing the same expression or disagreement in choosing different expressions. Applying this formula, we find that the probability that a pair of randomly chosen editors would choose different expressions in 14 or more of 17 instances is .0064.[13] Put more simply, there are 64 chances in 10,000 or 1 chance in 156 that the two editors would independently choose different expressions in 14 or more of the 17 instances.

What does this computation tell us? On the one hand, it does not completely rule out the possibility that Matthew and Luke edited Mark with this result. If we had 156 pairs of editors chosen at random and asked each pair to edit Mark independently by choosing one of Mark's expressions in each of these 17 instances, we could expect to find one pair of editors with editorial preferences so different that they would disagree in 14 or more instances. This result is therefore possible. On the other hand, with any single pair of editors it is highly improbable. The odds are 155 to 1 against it. In gambling, these odds would be termed a "long shot." The two-document hypothesis in this case is not a good bet.

Does the Farrer hypothesis or the three-source theory give a more probable explanation? According to these theories, Matthew copied from Mark, while Luke copied from both Mark and Matthew. In this case, Luke knew Matthew, and his choice of expressions was made with knowledge of Matthew's choice. With respect to the seventeen dual expressions under consideration, Luke nearly always omitted the one expression chosen by Matthew and chose the other expression in Mark that Matthew had not chosen. Why would Luke proceed in such a bizarre manner? One proponent of the Farrer hypothesis suggested in a private communication that Luke did not want to repeat what was already found in both of the other gospels: if Matthew chose one of Mark's expressions, Luke chose the other to avoid repetition. This suggestion, however, runs aground on the fact that Luke often does repeat what is found in both of the other gospels. For example, with respect to the other dual expressions in Mark, we need only to look at categories 4 and 5b to see this (Table 6.2). Here Matthew has only one of Mark's expressions, while Luke either chooses both expressions or chooses the same expression as Matthew.

---

12. Binomial probabilities are discussed in standard texts on probability and statistics: e.g., Ronald L. Iman and W. J. Conover, *A Modern Approach to Statistics* (New York: John Wiley & Sons, 1983), 131–41, 175–77; Davis Baird, *Inductive Logic: Probability and Statistics* (Englewood Cliffs, NJ: Prentice Hall, 1992), 234–61.

13. The problem could be restated as the probability of three or fewer agreements in seventeen trials. A standard table of the binomial distribution gives this value as .0064 (Iman and Conover, *A Modern Approach to Statistics*, 430).

Thus, instead of avoiding what is found in both gospels, Luke reproduces the same Markan expression as Matthew. Given the Farrer hypothesis, then, or the three-source hypothesis, the problem remains: Why does Luke nearly always have a different half than Matthew when each chooses one and only one of Mark's two expressions?

This little test of the dual expressions will probably not convince a committed proponent of Markan priority. It is always possible to find a way to discount statistics. One could argue, for example, that the sample is too small—only seventeen instances. If we had more instances, perhaps the odds against Markan priority would not be so great. Of course that argument is a double-edged sword. We could also suppose that the odds against it would be even greater. One might also challenge my assumption that in any particular trial, neither outcome—agreement or disagreement—is more probable than the other, but has a probability of one-half. This assumption presumes that neither half of the double expression is intrinsically more attractive than the other. If, however, one half or the other were somehow more attractive, then more editors would be inclined to agree in choosing it. In that case, the probability of agreement would be greater than one-half, while the probability of disagreement would be less than one-half. This objection has some validity. However, even if it were possible to factor it into our calculations, it would actually strengthen my argument rather than weaken it. It would make disagreement even less likely than we have supposed, so that the probability of two editors disagreeing as frequently as Matthew and Luke would be even less than our calculations indicate. Instead of being one chance in 156, it would be one chance in x, where x is greater than 156.

In any case, I do not present this test in isolation, but as part of a package that includes Chapters 2 to 5. If the evidence there indicates the implausibility of Markan priority, then our test of dual expressions simply confirms what we have concluded on other grounds. Beyond that, however, it does serve a further function. It points us in the direction of a different solution, one in which Mark conflated material found in Matthew and Luke, respectively.

A more reasonable explanation, then, takes account of our previous conclusion that Mark shared sources with both Matthew and Luke. When these sources overlapped, Mark conflated them. Since we have previously delineated these sources (Tables 4.3 and 5.2), we can identify the sources that Mark used in each of the seventeen instances of dual expressions, and these are shown in Table 6.3. In all seventeen instances, the expression that Mark shared with Luke came from Proto-Mark B. The expression that Mark shared with Matthew came most often from Proto-Mark A (12 times) but also from B (3 times) and C (2 times). Since Mark knew all of these sources—i.e., Proto-Mark A, Proto-Mark B, B, and C—in each case he knew both the source of Matthew's expression and the source of Luke's expression. In the fourteen instances where the sources differed, he drew on both, combining the single expressions into dual expressions. In the three remaining instances, where the sources had the same expression, Mark took this over and added a second expression. For example, at Mark 14:43, Mark found the phrase "while he was speaking" in both Proto-Mark A and Proto-Mark B. Preceding this he added "immediately" (εὐθύς), one of his favorite words, thereby creating a dual temporal expression. Mark 1:21 and 12:23 can be explained in a similar way. In this view, Mark created fourteen of the dual expressions by conflating his sources and the three others by making redactional additions.

## Conflation of More Than Two Sources

Most of the discussion of conflation in Mark has sought to determine whether or not the author of this gospel conflated two sources, identified as Matthew and Luke by proponents of the Griesbach hypothesis. Generally overlooked are those passages where it appears that Mark has conflated more than two sources. Here I will give one example. Mark 3:7–12 presents one of the most clear-cut instances of this type of conflation in Mark.[14] The following table shows the elements of this passage in Mark with their parallels in Matthew and Luke.

Table 6.4
Mark 3:7–12 and parallels

|  | Mark | Matt (C) | Luke (C) | Matt (PMA) | Luke (PMB) | Luke (Par) |
|---|---|---|---|---|---|---|
| Jesus withdrew | 3:7a |  |  | 12:15a |  |  |
| With his disciples | 3:7a |  |  |  | 6:17a |  |
| To the sea | 3:7b |  |  |  |  | 5:1b |
| A crowd followed | 3:7c | 4:25a | (5:17b) | 12:15b | 6:17cd |  |
| From Galilee | 3:7d | 4:25b | 5:17c |  |  |  |

---

14. M.-É. Boismard also argues that in Mark 3:7–11, Mark conflated and redacted the texts attested in Matthew and Luke. However, in the last verse of this pericope (Mark 3:12; par. Matt 12:16), he sees the reverse process: Matthew borrowed from the text attested by Mark (M.-É. Boismard, "Réponse aux deux autres hypothèses," in The Interrelations of the Gospels [ed. David L. Dungan; Leuven: Leuven University Press, 1990], 259–88, esp. 259–65). But Mark 3:12 cannot be distinguished from 3:7–11 in this way. The adverbial use of πολλά in 3:12 is a sign of Markan redaction, as we saw in Table 2.3B. Therefore Markan redaction unknown to Matthew or Luke extends to the entirety of Mark 3:7–12, consistent with the view that Mark found the whole pericope in his sources and redacted 3:12 along with the rest of it.

|  | Mark | Matt (C) | Luke (C) | Matt (PMA) | Luke (PMB) | Luke (Par) |
|---|---|---|---|---|---|---|
| Judea, Jerusalem | 3:7e-8a | 4:25d | 5:17d |  | 6:17e |  |
| From Idumea | 3:8b |  |  |  |  |  |
| Across Jordan | 3:8c | 4:25e | — |  |  |  |
| Tyre and Sidon | 3:8d |  |  |  | 6:17f |  |
| Hearing, they came | 3:8e |  |  |  | 6:18a | 5:1a |
| A boat for escape | 3:9 |  |  |  |  | 5:3ac |
| He healed many | 3:10a | — | 5:17e | 12:15c | 6:18c |  |
| They touch him | 3:10b |  |  |  | 6:19a |  |
| Demons know him | 3:11 |  |  | — | →4:41b |  |
| He enjoins secrecy | 3:12 |  |  | 12:16 | →4:41c |  |

To maintain the two-document hypothesis here, we would have to accept a rather implausible reconstruction. First, Matthew decided to break Mark's story into two parts. He left only the beginning and end of the story (Matt 12:15ab; 12:15c–16) in the same position as its Markan parallel. For some reason, he separated out the middle of Mark's story and placed it earlier in his gospel (at Matt 4:25). Second, by a strange coincidence, Luke independently decided to disperse Mark's story to an even greater degree. He kept 6:17–19 in the same place as Mark, and moved the other fragments to 4:41; 5:1, 3; and 5:17. It would be strange for one editor to act in this manner, but for both independently to act in this way with respect to the same Markan passage passes the bounds of credibility.

Would the Q hypothesis help here? Since only Matthew 12:15–16 and Luke 6:17–19 have the same place in Mark's outline as Mark's version, perhaps only these came from Mark, while Matthew 4:25 and Luke 5:17 came from Q. One problem with this idea is that in the material that would thus be assigned to Q, Matthew and Luke agree more closely with Mark than they do with each other. The phrase "from across the Jordan" occurs in Mark 3:8c and Matthew 4:25e but not in Luke, while a reference to Jesus' healing ministry occurs in Mark 3:10a and Luke 5:17e but not in Matthew. Another problem is that Matthew 12:15–16 and Luke 6:17–19, though both supposedly from Mark, have in common only three of Mark's 103 Greek words. Of the remaining 100 Markan words, Matthew and Luke somehow managed to include only those that the other evangelist omitted. A third problem is that even if we could trace these two passages to Mark and the other two to Q, that would still leave Luke 5:1, 3 unaccounted for.

Why would Matthew and Luke independently decide to atomize or in some cases duplicate the same story in Mark? Why would they both scatter different fragments of his story to other parts of their gospels? Apart from the few words in common, how could each so intuitively include only what the other omitted? The two-document hypothesis can answer none of these questions, even with the help of Q. In my judgment, the theory crashes completely on this text.

Farrer's theory, which assumes that Luke knew Matthew, provides no better explanation for this passage. First, it still has to explain why Matthew acted as he did. Second, it does not help to argue that Luke knew Matthew, since Luke did not follow Matthew in this passage. Most of the elements of Mark that he would have redistributed in this theory (Luke 4:41b; 5:1, 3; 5:17e) are not the same as those that Matthew would have moved (Matt 4:25), nor does he place them in the same context as Matthew. The most that could be said is that Luke saw how Matthew had atomized Mark's story and decided to go him one better. However, to say that and to say it convincingly are two different matters. Third, the theory that Luke knew Matthew must hold Luke responsible for the lack of overlap between Matthew 12:15–16 and Luke 6:17–19 with respect to their use of Mark. Luke must have decided to omit almost all of Mark that Matthew included while including all of Mark that Matthew omitted. Enough odd editorial behavior is already required of Luke by Farrer's hypothesis, and adding another type of the same to his repertoire does not help the theory.

On the other hand, the relation between the gospels in this passage can be explained simply if we put Mark at the end of the process rather than at the beginning. Mark knew several short passages about Jesus and crowds from the sources that he shared with Matthew and Luke: one from C (Matt 4:25//Luke 5:17), a parallel to C found in both Proto-Mark A (Matt 12:15–16) and Proto-Mark B (Luke 6:17–19; →4:41bc), and material from the parable discourse that he shared with Luke (Luke 5:1, 3). While Matthew and Luke kept these passages distinct, Mark conflated them into a single story, including parts of each, in order to produce a summary of Jesus' ministry to crowds. The text under consideration thus becomes explicable only if we abandon the view that Mark served as the source for Matthew and Luke and think of several shared sources that Mark conflated. I will return to this passage in Chapter 12 (Table 12.8) for a fuller discussion.

## Conclusion

The theory of Markan priority allows for conflation in Matthew, but not for the same phenomenon in Mark. The Griesbach hypothesis allows for conflation in Mark, but only if Mark is conflating Matthew and Luke. Both approaches are deficient. The data presented here suggests, contrary to the first theory, that Mark did conflate his sources. Contrary to the second theory, it suggests that these sources were not the gospels of Matthew and Luke, but sources that Mark shared with these gospels. Contrary to either theory, it suggests that Mark sometimes conflated more than two sources. We have seen previously that Mark shared three sources with Matthew and several sources with Luke. We also saw that these sources overlapped. Proto-Mark A overlapped extensively with Proto-Mark B, while the C material sometimes overlapped with both. Mark knew all three of these documents, yet he almost never created doublets where they overlap. When he found more than one version of the same material, he either omitted all but one version or, more frequently, conflated the different versions that he found. We can thus state the main conclusion of this chapter:

> *Mark often conflated two or more sources*
> *that were also used by Matthew and Luke respectively.*

# Chapter 7

# *Toward a New Theory*

SEVERAL CONCLUSIONS HAVE EMERGED from our study so far.

1. *The Gospel of Mark did not serve as a source for either Matthew or Luke.* Chapter 2 showed that Mark contains a significant layer of redaction absent from both Matthew and Luke—not only passages, but also recurring themes and characteristics of style. If neither Matthew nor Luke knew this layer of redaction in Mark, then Mark did not serve as a source for either.

2. *The Gospel of Matthew did not serve as a source for either Mark or Luke.* Chapter 3 showed that Matthean priority faces the same type of problem as Markan priority. Matthew contains a significant layer of redaction absent from both Mark and Luke—not only passages, but also recurring themes and characteristics of style. If neither Mark nor Luke knew this layer of redaction in Matthew, then Matthew did not serve as a source for either.

3. *Matthew did not use Mark, nor did Mark use Matthew, but both used the same three sources.* This conclusion resulted from our comparison of Mark and Matthew in Chapter 4. That comparison revealed three sequences of material that have the same order in Matthew as in Mark. These are best interpreted as sources that Mark and Matthew combined independently.

4. *Luke did not use Mark, nor did Mark use Luke, but both used the same sources.* This conclusion resulted from our comparison of Mark and Luke in Chapter 5. That comparison revealed several sequences of material that have the same order in Luke as in Mark. These are best interpreted as sources that Mark and Luke combined independently.

5. *Mark often conflated two or more sources that were also used by Matthew and Luke respectively.* This conclusion emerged from our study of Markan conflation in Chapter 6.

If these conclusions are valid, they must be affirmed by any plausible theory of Synoptic relations. These may not be the only propositions that such a theory must affirm, but they are those that emerge from the present study. In the rest of this chapter, therefore, I will use these five conclusions as criteria to evaluate current theories of Synoptic relations. I will not consider every such theory, but only those that are especially noteworthy or relevant. I will then set out a new theory in light of the criteria.

## Theories of Markan Priority

By definition, theories of Markan priority affirm that Mark served as the source for Matthew and Luke. All such theories are therefore ruled out by our first criterion. Of the five criteria, the two-document hypothesis satisfies only the second, in affirming that Luke did not use Matthew. Since the three-source hypothesis fails to satisfy even this criterion, affirming that Luke used Matthew as well as Q, it does not satisfy any of the criteria. Likewise, Farrer's hypothesis satisfies none of the five criteria.

## Theories of Matthean Priority

Among theories of Matthean priority, the Griesbach hypothesis affirms that Mark did not serve as a source for either Matthew or Luke, thus satisfying criterion 1. It also satisfies criterion 5 in finding conflation in Mark. It is ruled out, however, by criteria 2, 3, and 4, since it affirms that Luke used Matthew and that Mark drew directly from Matthew and Luke rather than from sources shared with Matthew and Luke. The Augustinian hypothesis satisfies none of the five criteria.

## Theory of Proto-Mark (Ur-Markus)

If the simpler theories do not satisfy the criteria, then perhaps more complex theories will. Early in the history of the Synoptic Problem, German scholars theorized that Matthew and Luke drew not from Mark but from an earlier edition of Mark, an "Ur-Markus" or "Proto-Mark." This view gave way to the simpler two-document hypothesis, but the problems with the latter have kept the earlier option alive.[1] If we modify the classical two-document hypothesis by adding a Proto-Mark, we have the following diagram:

---

1. E.g., Joseph A. Fitzmyer: "To my way of thinking, the possibility of Ur-Markus is still admissible" (Fitzmyer, "Priority of Mark" [1981], 16).

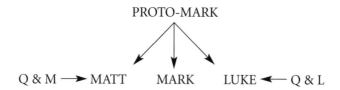

This theory satisfies the first criterion, since it is not canonical Mark but a pre-Markan gospel that serves as a source for Matthew and Luke. It thus allows Mark a stage of redaction unknown to Matthew or Luke. It can also account for the minor agreements as places where Matthew and Luke retained Proto-Mark while Mark revised it. The theory also satisfies the second criterion, since it does not make Luke dependent on Matthew. However, it does not satisfy criteria 3, 4, and 5, which call for multiple sources shared by Mark with Matthew and Luke, and conflation of those sources by Mark.

## Koester's Theory

Helmut Koester has proposed a Proto-Markan theory with several stages, as shown in the following diagram.[2]

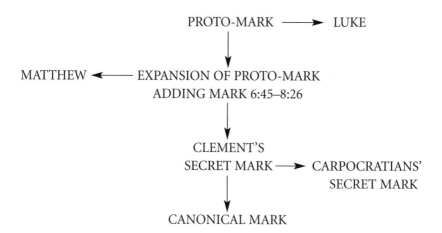

In this theory, Luke used Proto-Mark, while Matthew and Mark used subsequent expansions of Proto-Mark. Koester leaves room for the alternative view that Luke used a defective copy of the same version of Proto-Mark used by Matthew. Like the previous Proto-Mark theory, this one meets our first

2. Koester, "History and Development," 54–57.

criterion by making Matthew and Luke dependent not on canonical Mark but on earlier stages of Mark. It thus allows Mark a stage of redaction unknown to Matthew or Luke and could explain some of the minor agreements of Matthew and Luke as their common use of an earlier form of Mark that canonical Mark later revised. It is also noteworthy for recognizing several stages in the subsequent development of Proto-Mark. However, it does not provide for multiple sources common to Mark and each of the other Synoptics (criteria 3 and 4) or the evidence that canonical Mark has conflated earlier traditions known to Matthew and Luke respectively (criterion 5). Furthermore, the inclusion of "Secret Mark" in the lineage of Mark adds an extra degree of speculation, given the uncertainties surrounding that document.[3]

## Theory of Deutero-Mark

Other scholars have posited not a pre-Markan edition of Mark, but a post-Markan revision, a Deutero-Mark.[4] This theory currently has a number of adherents among German scholars.[5] According to this hypothesis, Matthew and Luke drew from the post-Markan edition as well as from Q. In a variation of this view, Albert Fuchs thinks that Q served as a source for Deutero-Mark as well as for Matthew and Luke. In its simplest form, this theory modifies the two-document hypothesis by adding a stage between Mark and the other Synoptics.

MARK

DEUTERO-MARK

MATT                    LUKE

---

3. Questions have been raised about the authenticity of the letter, attributed to Clement of Alexandria, that refers to Secret Mark. Furthermore the letter cites only two passages from Secret Mark, not enough to compare it in any detail with Mark.

4. For a brief survey of such theories from Sanday to Fuchs, see Neirynck, *Minor Agreements*, 20–24.

5. E.g., Albert Fuchs, *Sprachliche Untersuchungen zu Matthäus und Lukas: ein Beitrag zur Quellenkritik* (Analecta Biblica 49; Rome: Biblical Institute Press, 1971); Ulrich Luz, *Matthew 1–7*; Andreas Ennulat, *"Minor Agreements."*

The primary argument for positing a Deutero-Mark rather than a Proto-Mark has always been that the agreements of Matthew and Luke against Mark appear to be "improvements" over Mark. If so, it must have been an improved version of Mark subsequent to Mark, i.e., a Deutero-Mark, from which Matthew and Luke drew. For example, Ennulat argues that Deutero-Mark (followed by Matthew and Luke) improved on Mark by omitting Mark's frequently used εὐθύς or replacing it with εὐθέως.[6] This argument, however, is based on the fallacious assumption that redaction always results in improvement. It overlooks the possibility that a redacted work might be stylistically inferior to its prototype. Given the theory of Proto-Mark, we could assume that Mark wrote in a more colloquial style than the composer of Proto-Mark and rewrote the material of Proto-Mark in his own language. In that case, his revision might appear less polished than the original, from which the agreements of Matthew and Luke would have come. To reverse Ennulat's theory, we could assume that Proto-Mark (followed by Matthew and Luke) sometimes used εὐθέως, which Mark replaced and augmented with εὐθύς. What is clear is that Mark liked the word εὐθύς more than Matthew and Luke, but this fact in itself does not determine whether Mark's usage preceded or followed that seen in Matthew and Luke.

Proponents of Deutero-Mark also argue that the agreements of Matthew and Luke against Mark show certain theological tendencies, which they attribute to a post-Markan redaction used by Matthew and Luke. For example, Ennulat thinks that where Mark has Jesus and his disciples entering Simon's house (Mark 1:29), the composer of Deutero-Mark (followed by Matthew and Luke) had Jesus alone enter the house because he had a theological tendency to focus on the person of Jesus.[7] Again, however, we could just as easily explain the difference with a theory of Proto-Mark. Proto-Mark (followed by Matthew and Luke) had Jesus alone enter Simon's house. Mark, however, remembered that in an earlier story Jesus had called Andrew, James, and John along with Simon (Mark 1:16–20). What had happened to them in the meantime? Mark assumed that these disciples must have still been with Jesus and Simon in the later story and so added them. He did so not because of a theological tendency but in order to make the narrative more connected and coherent.

These two examples from Ennulat involve positive agreements of Matthew and Luke against Mark. In general, as I have shown, such positive agreements do not require a Deutero-Markan theory, but can be explained as well or better by a Proto-Markan theory. Furthermore, two features of the Synoptic tradition require a Proto-Mark rather than a Deutero-Mark. 1) As we saw in Chapter 2, Mark includes a layer of redaction that was unknown to Matthew and Luke. Since these redactional features are missing from both

6. Ennulat, *"Minor Agreements,"* 420.
7. Ibid., 422–23.

Matthew and Luke, proponents of Deutero-Mark would have to assume that Deutero-Mark did not include them either. The editor of Deutero-Mark either went through Mark intentionally omitting these features or he inadvertently revised them all out. If it is implausible to think that either Matthew or Luke omitted all these benign features of Mark's style, it is no more plausible to think that the editor of a Deutero-Mark did so. These benign features of Mark make sense only as a layer of redaction subsequent to the tradition used by Matthew and Luke. That is, Matthew and Luke drew on a form of the tradition that *preceded* Mark, a Proto-Markan tradition that existed before Mark redacted it. 2) As we saw in Chapters 4 and 5, the sequences common to Mark and Matthew along with those common to Mark and Luke are best explained as sources shared by Mark with these gospels. In other words, Matthew and Luke drew on Markan sources prior to Mark (Proto-Mark A and Proto-Mark B), rather than subsequent to Mark, as in the Deutero-Markan theory.

Of our five criteria, the theory of Deutero-Mark satisfies only criterion 2, since Matthew does not serve as a source for Luke. At first sight it also seems to satisfy criterion 1, since Matthew and Luke did not draw from canonical Mark but from Deutero-Mark. However, criterion 1 is based on the presence of redaction in Mark that was unknown to Matthew and Luke, and, as we have seen, the Deutero-Mark theory does not allow for this. Thus a theory of Deutero-Mark does not account for the evidence on which criterion 1 is based. Furthermore, this theory does not allow for the multiple sources shared by Mark with the other Synoptics (criteria 3 and 4) or the conflation of these sources by Mark (criterion 5).

## Boismard's Theory

Boismard's complex multi-source theory postulates four primitive sources (A, B, C, Q) as well as three intermediate gospels (intermediate Matthew, intermediate Mark, and Proto-Luke).[8] Both Rolland and Sanders provide diagrams of Boismard's theory, with some differences.[9] This theory meets the first of the criteria that we have established, since it does not make Matthew and Luke dependent on canonical Mark but on pre-Synoptic sources. It also satisfies the second and fifth, since it does not make Luke depend on Matthew and allows for conflation in Mark, in fact in more than

8. M.-É. Boismard with A. Lamouille and P. Sandevoir, *Tome II: Commentaire*, in *Synopse des quatre évangiles en français* (ed. P. Benoit and M.-É. Boismard; Paris: Cerf, 1972); cf. M.-É. Boismard, "The Two-Source Theory at an Impasse," *NTS* 26 (1979): 1–17. For evaluations of Boismard's theory, see Rolland, *Les premiers évangiles*, 232–44; E. P. Sanders and Margaret Davies, *Studying the Synoptic Gospels* (Philadelphia: Trinity Press International, 1989), 105–111.

9. Rolland, *Les premiers évangiles*, 233; idem, "A New Look at the Synoptic Question," *EuroJTh* 8 (1999): 135; Sanders and Davies, *Studying the Synoptic Gospels*, 105.

one way. However, it does not allow for criteria 3 and 4, the use of multiple sources common to Mark and the other Synoptics, at least not the specific sources that I delineated in Chapters 4 and 5. There are at least two other reasons for which it is unsatisfactory. First, it retains one of the fundamental weaknesses of the Griesbach hypothesis: since final Mark abridged earlier sources that already contained the Q material (intermediate Matthew and Proto-Luke), it is difficult to explain why such an abridgment as Mark was ever made. Second, when Boismard's theory and Rolland's theory (see below) are invoked to explain the same passage, Rolland's theory does so more efficiently. Rolland compares his own explanation of Synoptic relations in Mark 6:14–16 with that of Boismard.[10] Though I would not endorse all aspects of Rolland's discussion (especially his appeal to a primal Matthew in Hebrew), I consider his explanation of the passage more plausible than that of Boismard.

## Rolland's Theory

The theory of Philippe Rolland has received less attention than it deserves.[11] According to Rolland, a primitive gospel (C) contained the material common to all three Synoptics. This gospel underwent two independent revisions (AC and BC). Revision AC was used by Matthew, BC was used by Luke, while Mark conflated the two revisions. Matthew and Luke also used Q and their own special sources (M and L), while Mark added redactional elements (R) to his gospel. Rolland schematized his theory as follows:[12]

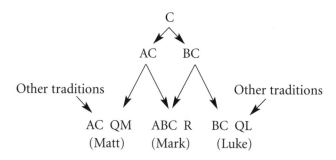

---

10. Philippe Rolland, "La question synoptique demande-t-elle une réponse compliquée?" *Biblica* 70 (1989): 217–23.

11. Philippe Rolland, "Les prédécesseurs de Marc: les sources présynoptiques de Mc, II, 18–22 et parallèles," *RB* 89 (1982): 370–405; idem, "Marc, première harmonie évangélique?"; idem, "Les évangiles des premières communautés chrétiennes," *RB* 90 (1983): 161–201; idem, *Les premiers évangiles*; idem, "L'arrière-fond sémitique des évangiles synoptiques," *ETL* 60 (1984): 358–62; idem, "Jésus connaissait leurs pensées," *ETL* 62 (1986): 118–21; idem, "Synoptique, Question," in *Dictionnaire encyclopédique de la Bible* (Maredsous, 1987), 1227–1231; idem, "La question synoptique demande-t-elle une réponse compliquée?"; idem, "A New Look at the Synoptic Question."

12. Rolland, *Les premiers évangiles*, 136.

This theory explains the material common to Matthew and Mark by their common reliance on revision AC; the material common to Luke and Mark by their common reliance on revision BC; and conflation in Mark by Mark's use of both AC and BC. It thus satisfies three of our criteria. It makes Matthew and Luke dependent not on canonical Mark but on the sources of Mark (criterion 1). It avoids making Luke dependent on Matthew (criterion 2). It also provides a reasonable explanation for the phenomenon of conflation in Mark without the drawbacks of the Griesbach hypothesis or the complexities of Boismard's theory (criterion 5).

Rolland's theory could be considered a modified form of the two-document hypothesis, since it postulates a Q source to account for the Matthew/Luke material and a second source, here a proto-gospel, to account for the triple tradition. The triple tradition, however, has undergone a more complex development than in the two-document hypothesis. Unlike the two-document hypothesis, Rolland's theory can account for the "minor agreements" of Matthew and Luke against Mark: some of these, at least, would have occurred where Mark made redactional changes to the tradition while Matthew and Luke retained an earlier form. Rolland's theory could also be considered a modified form of the Griesbach hypothesis, since it recognizes in Mark a conflation of two earlier sources attested respectively in Matthew and Luke. It can thus account for the type of evidence that I have presented in Chapter 6: evidence that Mark conflated and redacted earlier traditions known respectively to Matthew and Luke. Unlike the Griesbach hypothesis, however, it does not take the untenable position that Mark drew directly from Matthew and Luke. Rolland's theory thus retains the strongest aspects of both the two-document and the Griesbach hypotheses without their drawbacks.

In addition to the basic schema set out above, Rolland's theory includes other aspects, some of which I find more questionable. 1) Rolland characterizes the primitive gospel (C) as a Hebrew or Aramaic Matthew, identifying it with the "logia" attributed to Matthew by Papias. He designates it as "the Gospel of the Twelve," regarding it as a document that goes back to the early Jerusalem community led by the Twelve before the spread of Christianity outside of Palestine. 2) He designates the revision AC as a "Hellenistic Gospel," characterizing it as a Greek translation and expansion of C made in the Hellenistic Christian community at Antioch. 3) He designates the revision BC as a "Pauline Gospel," characterizing it as a Greek translation and expansion of C made among Pauline Christians in Ephesus or Philippi. 4) He designates Q as "the Gospel of the God-fearers," attributing a role in its formation to Philip the Evangelist in Caesarea. We need not accept these further refinements in agreeing with the basic schema.

This is the only theory other than Boismard's that meets as many as three of the criteria that we have established. It is the closest of any theory to the one that I propose. It would be nice if we could conclude the matter here. Unfortunately, it is necessary to complicate this theory somewhat to account for our second and third criteria, the need for more than one source common to Mark and Matthew and more than one source common to Mark and Luke. As far as it goes, however, I think that Rolland's theory is on the right track.

## A New Multi-Source Theory

Rolland does not use the term "Proto-Mark" in referring to his primitive gospel, though since it is an earlier form of the Markan tradition, it would be basically equivalent to what other scholars have designated by that term. Using that terminology, we can formulate a theory similar to his, in which Proto-Mark (in Greek) underwent two revisions (Proto-Mark A and Proto-Mark B), which served as sources for the Synoptic Gospels.

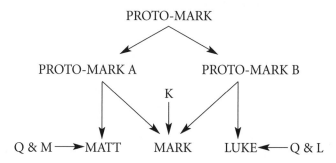

The greater part of the Synoptic tradition can be explained by this diagram. Proto-Mark A and Proto-Mark B were major sources that account for the bulk of the material common to Mark and Matthew on the one hand and Mark and Luke on the other. I identified these in Chapters 4 and 5 respectively. The letter K refers primarily to Mark's redaction but may also include a few items of material unique to Mark.

To complete this picture, we must also recognize the contribution of several smaller sources previously identified in Chapters 4 and 5. Rather than add these to the diagram, I will simply list them.

- The A material: a collection of material incorporated into Proto-Mark A, some of which also occurs in Luke in a different combination. The A material known to Luke includes a parable discourse, the words of institution of the Lord's Supper, and an account of Jesus' trial before the Sanhedrin. Mark knew this material from Proto-Mark A (shared with Matthew), but also knew some of it in a separate version (shared with Luke).
- The B material: a collection of material incorporated into Proto-Mark B, some of which also occurs in Matthew in a different combination. The B material known to Matthew consists of a series of miracle stories

and a set of mission instructions. Mark and Luke knew the B material from Proto-Mark B, but they also knew a separate version of the miracle stories and mission instructions, like that known to Matthew.
• The C material: a source used independently by each of the Synoptic evangelists. Some of this material overlapped with Proto-Mark A and Proto-Mark B.

This theory satisfies all five of the criteria that we have established. 1) Matthew and Luke did not use canonical Mark, but drew from Proto-Mark A and Proto-Mark B, respectively. 2) Neither Mark nor Luke used Matthew. The material common to Matthew and Luke came from one or more sources generally designated as Q. 3) Mark shared more than one source with Matthew: Proto-Mark A, elements of the B material, and C. 4) Mark also shared more than one source with Luke: Proto-Mark B, some of the A material, and C. 5) Conflation in Mark occurred as Mark combined his sources, some of which were known to Matthew and some to Luke.

In this theory, all three of the Synoptics, any two, or even any one may preserve the most original form of the tradition. For example, with respect to the Proto-Markan tradition, Matthew alone might preserve the most original form from Proto-Mark A if both Mark and Luke followed a revised form from Proto-Mark B. Likewise, Luke alone might preserve the most original form from Proto-Mark B if both Mark and Matthew followed a revised form from Proto-Mark A. Mark alone might preserve the most original form from either Proto-Mark A or Proto-Mark B if both Matthew and Luke revised the tradition.

In this theory, each Synoptic gospel includes a layer of redaction that was unknown to the other two. Chapters 2 and 3 identified some of this material in Mark and Matthew, respectively. Such redaction in Mark accounts for the negative minor agreements (agreements of omission) of Matthew and Luke against Mark: Mark sometimes added redactional touches to the sources, while Matthew and Luke lacked these because they knew the unredacted versions of the sources. The positive minor agreements have two causes: 1) in some instances Matthew and Luke may have independently revised the tradition in the same way, as theorized by the two-document hypothesis; 2) more often, however, such agreements arose when Matthew and Luke preserved the same earlier tradition while Mark revised it.

Previous chapters have presented the data and arguments for the criteria on which this theory is based. In subsequent chapters I will discuss more fully the various sources posited by this theory: the Proto-Markan tradition (Chapter 8), the A material (Chapter 9), the B material (Chapter 10), and the C material (Chapter 11).

# Chapter 8

# *Proto-Mark*

IN OUR THEORY, a primitive gospel, Proto-Mark, underwent two subsequent revisions, resulting in Proto-Mark A and Proto-Mark B. By starting with the two revisions, as we have previously delineated them, we can work back to the probable contents of Proto-Mark and draw some conclusions concerning its historical setting.

## Proto-Mark A and Proto-Mark B

If our theory is correct, Mark and Matthew shared a major source that I have designated as Proto-Mark A (Table 4.3). Mark and Luke shared a related source that I have designated as Proto-Mark B (Table 5.2). To permit easier comparison of these sources, I have set them side-by-side in Table 8.1.

Table 8.1
Contents of Proto-Mark A and Proto-Mark B

|  | Matthew (PMA) | Mark (PMA) | Mark (PMB) | Luke (PMB) |
|---|---|---|---|---|
| **John and Jesus** |  |  |  |  |
| John in wilderness | (3:1b) | 1:4a | 1:4a | (3:2b) |
| Preaching baptism | — | 1:4b | 1:4b | 3:3b |
| Written in Isaiah | 3:3a | →1:2a | →1:2a | 3:4a |
| Isaiah 40:3 | 3:3b | →1:3 | →1:3 | 3:4b |
| John's baptism | 3:5a, 6 | 1:5 |  |  |
| One more powerful | (3:11) | 1:7–8 | 1:7–8 | (3:16) |
| Jesus' baptism | 3:13, 16b–17 | 1:9–11 | 1:9–11 | 3:21b–22 |
| Jesus' temptation | 4:1–2 | 1:12–13a | 1:12–13a | 4:1–2 |
| Angels minister | 4:11b | 1:13c |  |  |
| **Jesus in Galilee** |  |  |  |  |
| John arrested | 4:12a | 1:14a |  |  |

143

|                          | Matthew (PMA) | Mark (PMA)    | Mark (PMB)    | Luke (PMB)     |
|--------------------------|---------------|---------------|---------------|----------------|
| To Galilee               | 4:12b         | 1:14b         | 1:14b         | 4:14a          |
| Preaching the kingdom    | 4:17          | 1:14c–15      | 1:14c–15      | —              |
| Jesus calls fishermen    | 4:18–22       | 1:16–20       | 1:16–20       | →5:2, 10–11    |
| To Capernaum             |               |               | 1:21a         | 4:31a          |
| Jesus teaches            | 5:2           | 1:21b         | 1:21b         | 4:31b          |
| People astonished        | 7:28b–29      | 1:22          | 1:22          | 4:32           |
| Demon in synagogue       | —             | 1:23–27       | 1:23–27       | 4:33–36        |
| Report goes out          | —             | 1:28          | 1:28          | 4:37           |
| At Peter's house         | 8:14–15       | 1:29–31       | 1:29–31       | 4:38–39        |
| Healing the ill          | 8:16          | 1:32, 34a–c   | 1:32, 34a–c   | 4:40–41a       |
| Prohibition to demons    | —             | 1:34d         | 1:34d         | 4:41c          |
| A preaching tour         |               |               | 1:35–39       | 4:42–44        |
| Jesus heals a leper      |               |               | 1:40–45       | 5:12–16        |
| **Controversy stories**  |               |               |               |                |
| To his own town          | 9:1b          | 2:1a          |               |                |
| Lame man healed          | 9:2–8         | 2:3–12        | 2:3–12        | 5:18–26        |
| Eating with sinners      | 9:9–12, 13b   | 2:14–17       | 2:14–17       | 5:27–32        |
| About fasting            | 9:14–15       | 2:18–20       | 2:18–20       | 5:33–35        |
| Old and new              | 9:16–17       | 2:21–22       | 2:21–22       | 5:36–38        |
| Plucking grain           | 12:1–4, 8     | 2:23–26, 28   | 2:23–26, 28   | 6:1–5          |
| Withered hand            | 12:9–10, 12b–14 | 3:1–6       | 3:1–6         | 6:6–11         |
| **Further ministry**     |               |               |               |                |
| Ministry to a crowd      | 12:15         | 3:7–10        | 3:7–10        | 6:17–19        |
| Demons know him          | —             | 3:11          | 3:11          | →4:41b         |
| Prohibition to demons    | 12:16         | 3:12          | 3:12          | →4:41c         |
| A mute demoniac          | 12:22–23      | —             | —             | —              |
| Beelzebul debate         | 12:24–29      | 3:22–27       | 3:22–27       | —              |
| Unforgivable sin         | 12:31         | 3:28–29       | 3:28–29       | —              |
| Because they said        |               |               | 3:30          | →11:18b        |
| Certain women healed     |               |               | —             | 8:2a           |
| Mary's seven demons      |               |               | →16:9b        | 8:2b           |
| And many others          |               |               | →15:41b       | 8:3            |
| Jesus' true family       | 12:46–50      | 3:31–35       | 3:31–35       | 8:19–21        |
| **Parable discourse**    |               |               |               |                |
| Ministry from a boat     | 13:1–3a       | 4:1–2         |               |                |
| Parable of sower         | 13:3b–9       | 4:3–9         |               |                |

|  | Matthew (PMA) | Mark (PMA) | Mark (PMB) | Luke (PMB) |
|---|---|---|---|---|
| Reason for parables | 13:10–11, 13 | 4:10–12 |  |  |
| Sower explained | 13:18–23 | 4:13–20 |  |  |
| Lamp on lampstand | — | 4:21 |  |  |
| The hidden revealed | — | 4:22 |  |  |
| How you hear | — | 4:24a |  |  |
| Have and have not | →13:12 | 4:25 |  |  |
| Man growing seed | — | 4:26–29 |  |  |
| The mustard seed | 13:31–32 | 4:30–32 |  |  |
| The leaven | 13:33 | — |  |  |
| Use of parables | 13:34–35 | 4:33–34 |  |  |
| **Miracle stories** |  |  |  |  |
| On that day |  |  | 4:35a | 8:22a |
| Leaving the crowd | 13:36a | 4:36a |  |  |
| Jesus calms a storm |  |  | 4:36b–41 | 8:22b–25 |
| Gerasene demoniac |  |  | 5:1–17 | 8:26–37a |
| Would-be follower |  |  | 5:18–20 | 8:37b–39 |
| Jairus's daughter |  |  | 5:21–43 | 8:40–56 |
| **Further ministry** |  |  |  |  |
| Jesus at hometown | 13:53b–58 | 6:1–6a | 6:1–6a | →4:16, 22, 24 |
| He summons the 12 |  |  | 6:7a | 9:1a |
| Power over spirits |  |  | 6:7c | 9:1b |
| What not to take |  |  | 6:8–9 | 9:3 |
| Stay in one house |  |  | 6:10 | 9:4 |
| If not received |  |  | 6:11 | 9:5 |
| The 12 go forth | — | 6:12–13 | 6:12–13 | 9:6 |
| Opinions about Jesus | 14:1–2 | 6:14–16 | 6:14–16 | 9:7–9 |
| John's imprisonment | 14:3 | 6:17 | 6:17 | →3:19–20 |
| John's death | 14:4–12a | 6:18–29 |  |  |
| The 12 return | 14:12b | 6:30 | 6:30 | 9:10a |
| To a deserted spot |  |  | 6:31a | 9:10b |
| To a deserted spot | 14:13a | 6:32 |  |  |
| A crowd follows | 14:13b | 6:33 | 6:33 | 9:11a |
| Jesus' compassion | 14:14a | 6:34a |  |  |
| Ministry to crowd | 14:14b | 6:34c | 6:34c | 9:11b |
| Jesus feeds 5,000 | 14:15–21 | 6:35–44 | 6:35–44 | 9:12–17 |

|                          | Matthew (PMA) | Mark (PMA) | Mark (PMB) | Luke (PMB) |
|--------------------------|---------------|------------|------------|------------|
| Jesus walks on water     | 14:22–33      | 6:45–52    |            |            |
| In Gennesaret            | 14:34–36      | 6:53–56    |            |            |
| On hand washing          | 15:1–20       | 7:1–23     |            |            |
| A Gentile woman          | 15:21–28      | 7:24–30    |            |            |
| To Sea of Galilee        | 15:29a        | 7:31       |            |            |
| Various healings         | 15:29b–30     | —          |            |            |
| The crowd amazed         | 15:31         | 7:37       |            |            |
| Jesus feeds 4,000        | 15:32–39      | 8:1–10     |            |            |
| Pharisees seek sign      | 16:1, 4       | 8:11–13    |            |            |
| No bread                 | 16:5–11a      | 8:14–21    |            |            |
| Peter's confession       | 16:13–16, 20  | 8:27–30    | 8:27–30    | 9:18–21    |
| **Going to Jerusalem**   |               |            |            |            |
| 1st passion prediction   | 16:21         | 8:31       | 8:31       | 9:22       |
| Jesus rebukes Peter      | 16:22–23      | 8:32–33    |            |            |
| Take up the cross        | 16:24         | 8:34       | 8:34       | 9:23       |
| Lose life to find it     | 16:25         | 8:35       | 8:35       | 9:24       |
| Gain world, lose life    | 16:26a        | 8:36       | 8:36       | 9:25       |
| The soul's worth         | 16:26b        | 8:37       |            |            |
| Ashamed of Jesus         |               |            | 8:38a      | 9:26a      |
| Son of Man in glory      | 16:27a        | 8:38b      | 8:38b      | 9:26b      |
| Some standing here       | 16:28         | 9:1        | 9:1        | 9:27       |
| Transfiguration          | 17:1–9        | 9:2–10     | 9:2–10     | 9:28–36    |
| Coming of Elijah         | 17:10–13      | 9:11–13    |            |            |
| Demonized boy            | 17:14–18      | 9:14–27    | 9:14–27    | 9:37–43a   |
| On failed exorcisms      | 17:19–20      | 9:28–29    |            |            |
| Going through Galilee     | 17:22a        | 9:30a      |            |            |
| 2nd passion prediction   | 17:22b–23     | 9:31       | 9:31       | 9:43b–44   |
| No understanding         |               |            | 9:32       | 9:45       |
| At Capernaum in house    | 17:24a, 25b   | 9:33ab     |            |            |
| On greatness             | 18:1, 4       | 9:33c–35   | 9:33c–35   | 9:46, 48c  |
| On little ones           | 18:2, 5       | 9:36–37    | 9:36–37    | 9:47–48b   |
| Unknown exorcist         |               |            | 9:38–40    | 9:49–50    |
| A cup of water           |               |            | 9:41       | —          |
| Offending little ones    | 18:6          | 9:42       |            |            |
| Offensive member         | 18:8–9        | 9:43–47    |            |            |
| Spoiled salt             |               |            | 9:50a      | 14:34      |

| | Matthew (PMA) | Mark (PMA) | Mark (PMB) | Luke (PMB) |
|---|---|---|---|---|
| **In Judea** | | | | |
| Jesus goes to Judea | 19:1b–2 | 10:1 | | |
| Teaching on divorce | 19:3–8 | 10:2–9 | | |
| Ruling on divorce | 19:9 | 10:11–12 | 10:11–12 | 16:18 |
| Jesus and children | 19:13–14 | 10:13–14 | 10:13–14 | 18:15–16 |
| Receive as a child | | | 10:15 | 18:17 |
| Laying on hands | 19:15a | 10:16b | | |
| Rich young man | 19:16–22 | 10:17–22 | 10:17–22 | 18:18–23 |
| Riches and rewards | 19:23–29 | 10:23–30 | 10:23–30 | 18:24–30 |
| Last shall be first | 19:30 | 10:31 | | |
| Up to Jerusalem | 20:17a | 10:32bc | | |
| 3rd passion prediction | 20:17b–19 | 10:32e–34 | 10:32e–34 | 18:31–33 |
| Brothers seek honor | 20:20–30 | 10:35–40 | | |
| Blind man at Jericho | 20:29–34 | 10:46–52 | 10:46–52 | 18:35–43 |
| **In Jerusalem** | | | | |
| Triumphal entry | 21:1–3, 6-9 | 11:1–10 | 11:1–10 | 19:29–38 |
| Jesus enters Jerusalem | 21:10a | 11:15a | | |
| Jesus cleanses Temple | 21:12–13 | 11:15b–17 | 11:15b–17 | 19:45–46 |
| Priests and scribes | | | 11:18 | 19:47–48 |
| Question of authority | 21:23–27 | 11:27b–33 | 11:27b–33 | 20:1–8 |
| Parable of tenants | 21:33–46a | 12:1–12a | 12:1–12b | 20:9–17, 19 |
| They leave Jesus | →22:22b | 12:12d | | |
| **Controversy stories** | | | | |
| Tribute to Caesar | 22:16–22a | 12:13–17 | 12:13–17 | 20:20–26 |
| On resurrection | 22:23–32 | 12:18–27a | 12:18–27a | 20:27–38 |
| Jesus answers well | | | 12:28a | 20:39 |
| Great commandment | 22:35–40 | 12:28b–31 | 12:28b–31 | — |
| No one dared | →22:46b | 12:34b | 12:34b | 20:40 |
| Christ and David | 22:41–45 | 12:35–37a | 12:35–37a | 20:41–44 |
| Against scribes | 23:1, 6–7a, 14 | 12:37b–40 | 12:37b–40 | 20:45–47 |
| Widow's offering | | | 12:41–44 | 21:1–4 |
| **Eschatology** | | | | |
| Temple prediction | 24:1–2 | 13:1–2 | 13:1–2 | 21:5–6 |
| Signs of the end | 24:3–8 | 13:3–8 | 13:3–8 | 21:7–11 |

|                        | Matthew (PMA) | Mark (PMA)     | Mark (PMB)     | Luke (PMB)       |
|------------------------|---------------|----------------|----------------|------------------|
| On persecution         | 24:9, 13      | 13:9bc, 11–13  | 13:9bc, 11–13  | 21:12–17, 19     |
| Desolating sacrilege   | 24:15–21      | 13:14–19       | 13:14–19       | 21:20–24         |
| Days shortened         | 24:22         | 13:20          |                |                  |
| Not here nor there     | 24:23         | 13:21          |                |                  |
| False Christs          | 24:24–25      | 13:22–23       |                |                  |
| Son of Man comes       | 24:29, 30b    | 13:24–26       | 13:24–26       | 21:25–27         |
| The elect gathered     | 24:31         | 13:27          |                |                  |
| Within a generation    | 24:32–35      | 13:28–31       | 13:28–31       | 21:29–33         |
| No one knows           | 24:36         | 13:32          |                |                  |
| Stay awake             | 25:13         | 13:33          |                |                  |
| Man on a journey       | 25:14         | 13:34          |                |                  |
| **Passover**           |               |                |                |                  |
| Jewish leaders plot    | 26:2a, 3–5    | 14:1–2         | 14:1–2         | 22:1–2           |
| Anointing at Bethany   | 26:6–13       | 14:3–9         | 14:3–9         | →7:36–38         |
| Judas makes a deal     | 26:14–16      | 14:10–11       | 14:10–11       | 22:3–6           |
| Passover prepared      | 26:17–20      | 14:12–17       | 14:12–17       | 22:7–14          |
| Betrayal predicted     | 26:21–25      | 14:18–21       | 14:18–21       | 22:21–23         |
| Last supper            | 26:26–29      | 14:22–25       |                |                  |
| To Mount of Olives     | 26:30         | 14:26          |                |                  |
| All will scatter       | 26:31         | 14:27          |                |                  |
| I will go to Galilee   | 26:32         | 14:28          |                |                  |
| Denial predicted       | 26:33–34      | 14:29–30       | 14:29–30       | 22:33–34         |
| Fidelity affirmed      | 26:35         | 14:31          |                |                  |
| To Gethsemane          | 26:36a        | 14:32a         | 14:32a         | 22:40a           |
| Jesus grieves          | 26:36b–38a    | 14:32b–34a     |                |                  |
| Jesus prays            | 26:38b–41     | 14:34b–38      | 14:35–38a      | 22:40b–46        |
| Jesus prays again      | 26:42–45a     | 14:39–41a      |                |                  |
| The hour arrives       | 26:45b–46     | 14:41c–42      |                |                  |
| **Jesus' arrest**      |               |                |                |                  |
| Judas and crowd        | 26:47a        | 14:43a         | 14:43a         | 22:47a           |
| Group with weapons     | 26:47b        | 14:43b         |                |                  |
| Kiss as signal         | 26:48         | 14:44          |                |                  |
| Judas kisses Jesus     | 26:49         | 14:45          | 14:45          | 22:47b           |
| They seize Jesus       | 26:50b        | 14:46          |                |                  |
| Slave's ear cut off    | 26:51         | 14:47          | 14:47          | 22:50            |
| As against a thief     | 26:55a        | 14:48          | 14:48          | 22:52            |

|  | Matthew (PMA) | Mark (PMA) | Mark (PMB) | Luke (PMB) |
|---|---|---|---|---|
| I taught in Temple | 26:55b | 14:49a | 14:49a | 22:53a |
| Scriptures fulfilled | 26:56a | 14:49b |  |  |
| The disciples flee | 26:56b | 14:50 |  |  |
| **Denial and trial** |  |  |  |  |
| Led to high priest | 26:57a | 14:53a | 14:53a | 22:54a |
| Council convenes | 26:57b | 14:53b |  |  |
| Peter follows | 26:58a | 14:54a | 14:54a | 22:54b |
| To priest's courtyard | 26:58b | 14:54b |  |  |
| Sitting with servants | 26:58c | 14:54c | 14:54c | 22:55 |
| False witnesses | 26:59–63a | 14:55–61a |  |  |
| Sanhedrin's question | 26:63b–66 | 14:61c–64 |  |  |
| Jesus is mocked | 26:67–68 | 14:65 |  |  |
| Peter denies Jesus | 26:69–75 | 14:66–72 | 14:66–72 | 22:56–62 |
| **Before Pilate** |  |  |  |  |
| In the morning | 27:1a | 15:1a | 15:1a | 22:66a |
| Council decides | 27:1b | 15:1b |  |  |
| They bind Jesus | 27:2a | 15:1c |  |  |
| Jesus led to Pilate | 27:2b | 15:1c | 15:1c | 23:1b |
| You King of Jews? | 27:11b | 15:2 | 15:2 | 23:3 |
| Jesus stays silent | 27:12–14 | 15:3–5 | 15:3–5 | 23:9–10 |
| Barabbas or Jesus | 27:15–16 | 15:6–7 | 15:6–7 | 23:[17], 19 |
| Barabbas or Jesus | 27:17–18, 20 | 15:8–11 |  |  |
| Barabbas or Jesus | 27:21–23, 26 | 15:12–15 | 15:12–15 | 23:18–25 |
| Pilate flogs Jesus | 27:26b | 15:15c |  |  |
| Hail, King of Jews | 27:27–31a | 15:16–20a |  |  |
| **Jesus' crucifixion** |  |  |  |  |
| They lead him out | 27:31b | 15:20b | 15:20b | 23:26a |
| To crucify him | 27:31c | 15:20c |  |  |
| Simon carries cross | 27:32 | 15:21 | 15:21 | 23:26b |
| Arrival at Golgotha | 27:33 | 15:22 | 15:22 | 23:33a |
| Wine with myrrh | 27:34 | 15:23 |  |  |
| They crucify him | 27:35a | 15:24a | 15:24a | 23:33b |
| Garments divided | 27:35b | 15:24b | 15:24b | 23:34b |
| Epigraph/charge | 27:37 | 15:26 | 15:26 | 23:38 |
| Bandits crucified | 27:38 | 15:27 |  |  |
| Passersby mock | 27:39–40 | 15:29–30 |  |  |
| Rulers mock | 27:41–42 | 15:31–32a |  |  |

|  | Matthew (PMA) | Mark (PMA) | Mark (PMB) | Luke (PMB) |
|---|---|---|---|---|
| Bandits mock | 27:44 | 15:32c | | |
| Darkness over land | 27:45 | 15:33 | 15:33 | 23:44 |
| Jesus forsaken | 27:46–47 | 15:34–35 | | |
| Jesus given vinegar | 27:48 | 15:36a | | |
| Will Elijah come | 27:49 | 15:36b | | |
| Jesus expires | 27:50 | 15:37 | 15:37 | 23:46ac |
| Temple veil torn | 27:51a | 15:38 | | |
| Centurion confesses | 27:54 | 15:39 | 15:39 | 23:47 |
| Women from Galilee | 27:55 | 15:40a, 41a | 15:40a, 41a | 23:49 |
| Mary, Mary, Salome | 27:56 | 15:40b | | |
| **Jesus' burial** | | | | |
| Joseph requests body | 27:57–58a | 15:42–43 | 15:42–43 | 23:50–52 |
| Pilate gives body | 27:58b | 15:45b | | |
| Jesus entombed | 27:59–60a | 15:46a | 15:46a | 23:53 |
| Stone over tomb | 27:60b | 15:46b | | |
| The women watch | 27:61 | 15:47 | 15:47 | 23:55 |
| **The empty tomb** | | | | |
| Women buy spices | | | 16:1 | 23:56a |
| Women go to tomb | 28:1 | 16:2 | 16:2 | 24:1 |
| Stone rolled away | 28:2b | 16:4a | 16:4a | 24:1 |
| They enter the tomb | | | 16:5a | 24:3a |
| Man/men in white | 28:3 | 16:5b | 16:5b | 24:4b |
| They are afraid | 28:4 | 16:5c | 16:5c | 24:5a |
| Do not fear | 28:5a | 16:6a | | |
| He is risen | 28:5b–6a | 16:6b | 16:6b | 24:5b–6a |
| See the place | 28:6b | 16:6c | | |
| See him in Galilee | 28:7 | 16:7 | | |
| They leave tomb | 28:8a | 16:8a | 16:8a | 24:9a |
| With fear | 28:8b | 16:8b | | |
| They tell the others | 28:8c | (16:8c) | (16:8c) | 24:9b |
| **Jesus' resurrection** | | | | |
| Mary sees Jesus | 28:9 | 16:9a | | |
| See me in Galilee | 28:10 | — | | |
| Names of women | | | cf. 16:9a | 24:10a |
| Report disbelieved | | | 16:10–11 | 24:10b–11 |

|  | Matthew (PMA) | Mark (PMA) | Mark (PMB) | Luke (PMB) |
|---|---|---|---|---|
| Appearance to two |  |  | 16:12–13 | 24:13–33, 35 |
| Eleven go to Galilee | 28:16 | — |  |  |
| Appearance to 11 | 28:17 | 16:14a | 16:14a | 24:36 |
| Charge to preach | 28:19a | 16:15 | 16:15 | 24:47 |
| Charge to baptize | 28:19b | 16:16 |  |  |
| Jesus taken up |  |  | 16:19 | 24:51 |

In Table 8.1, the two columns with the heading "PMA" show the contents of Proto-Mark A in Matthew and Mark respectively. The two columns titled "PMB" show the contents of Proto-Mark B in Mark and Luke respectively. Mark has two columns in this table because Mark shared Proto-Mark A with Matthew and Proto-Mark B with Luke.

We can classify the material in Table 8.1 using three categories: the Synoptic core, the A material, and the B material.

1. *The Synoptic core.* A substantial amount of material in Table 8.1 occurs in both Proto-Mark A and Proto-Mark B in the same order with much the same wording. I will call this material the "Synoptic core," because it constitutes the common core of material found in each of the Synoptic Gospels. For example, the Synoptic core includes a series of controversy stories (Mark 2:1–3:6 parr). These occur in all three Synoptics in the same order even though Matthew has other material between some of them. In our theory, the Synoptic core occurs in all three gospels in the same order because it occurred in that order in both Proto-Mark A and Proto-Mark B. Matthew received it in that order from Proto-Mark A, Luke received it in the same order from Proto-Mark B, while Mark knew it from both sources.

2. *The A material.* Some material in Table 8.1 occurs in Proto-Mark A but not in Proto-Mark B. That is, Mark and Matthew, but not Luke, have this material in the same order and in the same position relative to the Synoptic core. I have designated this as the "A" material. For example, Mark and Matthew share a series of stories between the feeding of the five thousand and Peter's confession (Mark 6:45–8:21 par). These stories do not occur in Luke, but Mark and Matthew have them in the same order. They also have them in the same position relative to the Synoptic core. That is, in both gospels they occur between the same two stories from the Synoptic core, the feeding of the five thousand and Peter's confession. In our theory, Mark and Matthew have this material in the same order and position because both found it in that order and position in their common source, Proto-Mark A.

3. *The B material.* Some material in Table 8.1 occurs in Proto-Mark B but not in Proto-Mark A. That is, Mark and Luke, but not Matthew, have this material in the same order and in the same position relative to the Synoptic core. I have designated this as the "B" material. For example, Mark and Luke share a series of miracle stories (Mark 4:35; 5:43 parr). Both have these in the same order. They also have them in the same position relative to the Synoptic core. That is, in both gospels these stories occur between the same two pericopes from the Synoptic core, "Jesus' true family" (Mark 3:31–35 parr) and "Opinions about Jesus" (Mark 6:14–16 parr). Matthew also has these miracle stories, but not where they occur in Mark and Luke. In Matthew they occur earlier, mixed in with the controversy stories from the Synoptic core. In our theory, Mark and Luke have these stories in the same order and position because both found them in that order and position in their common source, Proto-Mark B. Matthew did not know Proto-Mark B but did know these miracle stories (B material) and inserted them in his gospel independently.

In our theory, the Synoptic core represents the minimum content of Proto-Mark. The A material is material that an editor added to Proto-Mark to produce Proto-Mark A. The B material is material that another editor added to Proto-Mark to produce Proto-Mark B. We will examine each type of material in turn, beginning with Proto-Mark in the present chapter and continuing with A and B in the next two.

## The Contents of Proto-Mark

Our theory proposes that the Synoptic core stood in the same order in both Proto-Mark A and Proto-Mark B because both received it in that order from the same source, a source that we could call Proto-Mark. Thus, the Synoptic core ultimately came from Proto-Mark. It does not necessarily represent the whole of Proto-Mark, but only its assured minimum content. It represents that portion of Proto-Mark that came down into all three Synoptics in its original order.

It is likely that Proto-Mark also included other material that was omitted or moved from its original order at some stage of the process, whether in Proto-Mark A, Proto-Mark B, or one of the three Synoptics. Thus, to reconstruct the contents of Proto-Mark, we must begin with the Synoptic core and then add other material from the Synoptics when there is a compelling reason to think that it stood in Proto-Mark. Table 8.2 lists a number of items that do not belong to the Synoptic core but probably stood in Proto-Mark. The items in Table 8.2 do not belong to the Synoptic core either because they do not occur in each Synoptic or because they do not occur in the same order in each. Yet, prior to the stage of the Synoptic Gospels, these items probably did

Table 8.2
Proto-Mark material other than the Synoptic core

|  | Matthew | Mark | Luke |
|---|---|---|---|
| Preaching baptism | — | 1:4b | 3:3b |
| Written in Isaiah | 3:3a | →1:2a | 3:4a |
| Isaiah 40:3 | 3:3b | →1:3 | 3:4b |
| Preaching the kingdom | 4:17 | 1:14c–15 | — |
| Jesus calls fishermen | 4:18–22 | 1:16–20 | →5:2, 10–11 |
| Demon in synagogue | — | 1:23–27 | 4:33–36 |
| Report goes out | — | 1:28 | 4:37 |
| Prohibition to demons | — | 1:34d | 4:41c |
| Demons know him | — | 3:11 | →4:41b |
| Prohibition to demons | 12:16 | 3:12 | →4:41c |
| A mute demoniac | 12:22–23 | — | — |
| Beelzebul debate | 12:24–29 | 3:22–27 | — |
| Unforgivable sin | 12:31 | 3:28–29 | — |
| Jesus at hometown | 13:53b–58 | 6:1–6a | →4:16, 22, 24 |
| The 12 go forth | — | 6:12–13 | 9:6 |
| John's imprisonment | 14:3 | 6:17 | →3:19–20 |
| Great commandment | 22:35–40 | 12:28b–31 | — |
| No one dared | →22:46b | 12:34b | 20:40 |
| Anointing at Bethany | 26:6–13 | 14:3–9 | →7:36–38 |

stand in the same order and position in both Proto-Mark A and Proto-Mark B. In Chapters 4 and 5 I justified this judgment for all but the first item in the table, which will be discussed later. The present state of these items in the Synoptics resulted from one evangelist or another omitting or rearranging them from their original order. If these items originally stood in the same order and position in both Proto-Mark A and Proto-Mark B, then they must have come from Proto-Mark, the common source of those gospels. It is possible that other material in Mark/Matthew or Mark/Luke also came from Proto-Mark, but it may not be possible in every case to make that determination.

To reconstruct the contents of Proto-Mark, then, we start with the Synoptic core, which we can extract from Table 8.1, and add the items in Table 8.2. The result is given in Table 8.3.

Table 8.3
Contents of Proto-Mark

|  | Matthew | Mark | Luke |
|---|---|---|---|
| **John and Jesus** | | | |
| John in wilderness | (3:1b) | 1:4a | (3:2b) |
| Preaching baptism | — | 1:4b | 3:3b |
| Written in Isaiah | 3:3a | →1:2a | 3:4a |
| Isaiah 40:3 | 3:3b | →1:3 | 3:4b |
| One more powerful | (3:11) | 1:7–8 | (3:16) |
| Jesus' baptism | 3:13, 16b–17 | 1:9–11 | 3:21c–22 |
| Jesus' temptation | 4:1–2a | 1:12–13a | 4:1–2a |
| **Jesus in Galilee** | | | |
| To Galilee | 4:12b | 1:14b | 4:14a |
| Preaching the kingdom | 4:17 | 1:14c–15 | — |
| Jesus calls fishermen | 4:18–22 | 1:16–20 | →5:2, 10–11 |
| Jesus teaches | 5:2 | 1:21b | 4:31b |
| People astonished | 7:28–29a | 1:22 | 4:32 |
| Demon in synagogue | — | 1:23–27 | 4:33–36 |
| Report goes out | — | 1:28 | 4:37 |
| At Peter's house | 8:14–15 | 1:29–31 | 4:38–39 |
| Healing the ill | 8:16 | 1:32, 34a–c | 4:40–41a |
| Prohibition to demons | — | 1:34d | 4:41c |
| **Controversy stories** | | | |
| Lame man healed | 9:2–8 | 2:3–12 | 5:18–26 |
| Eating with sinners | 9:9–13 | 2:14–17 | 5:27–32 |
| About fasting | 9:14–15 | 2:18–20 | 5:33–35 |
| Old and new | 9:16–17 | 2:21–22 | 5:36–38 |
| Plucking grain | 12:1–4, 8 | 2:23–26, 28 | 6:1–5 |
| Withered hand | 12:9–10, 12b–14 | 3:1–6 | 6:6–11 |
| **Further ministry** | | | |
| Ministry to crowd | 12:15 | 3:7–10a | 6:17b–19 |
| Demons know him | — | 3:11 | →4:41b |
| Prohibition to demons | 12:16 | 3:12 | →4:41c |
| A mute demoniac | 12:22–23 | — | — |
| Beelzebul debate | 12:24–29 | 3:22–27 | — |
| Unforgivable sin | 12:31 | 3:28–29 | — |
| Jesus' true family | 12:46–50 | 3:31–35 | 8:19–21 |

|  | Matthew | Mark | Luke |
|---|---|---|---|
| Jesus at hometown | 13:53b–58 | 6:1–6a | →4:16, 22, 24 |
| The 12 go forth | — | 6:12–13 | 9:6 |
| Opinions about Jesus | 14:1–2 | 6:14–16 | 9:7–9 |
| John's imprisonment | 14:3 | 6:17 | →3:19–20 |
| The 12 return | 14:12b | 6:30 | 9:10a |
| To a deserted spot | 14:13a | 6:31a, 32 | 9:10b |
| A crowd follows | 14:13b | 6:33 | 9:11a |
| Ministry to crowd | 14:14b | 6:34c | 9:11b |
| Jesus feeds 5,000 | 14:15–21 | 6:35–44 | 9:12–17 |
| Peter's confession | 16:13–16, 20 | 8:27–30 | 9:18–21 |
| **Going to Jerusalem** |  |  |  |
| 1st passion prediction | 16:21 | 8:31 | 9:22 |
| Take up the cross | 16:24 | 8:34 | 9:23 |
| Lose life to find it | 16:25 | 8:35 | 9:24 |
| Gain world, lose life | 16:26a | 8:36 | 9:25 |
| Son of Man in glory | 16:27a | 8:38b | 9:26b |
| Some standing here | 16:28 | 9:1 | 9:27 |
| Transfiguration | 17:1–9 | 9:2–10 | 9:28–36 |
| Demonized boy | 17:14–18 | 9:14–27 | 9:37–42 |
| 2nd passion prediction | 17:22b–23 | 9:31 | 9:43b–44 |
| On greatness | 18:1, 4 | 9:33c–35 | 9:46, 48c |
| On little ones | 18:2, 5 | 9:36–37 | 9:47–48b |
| Ruling on divorce | 19:9 | 10:11–12 | 16:18 |
| Jesus and children | 19:13–14 | 10:13–14 | 18:15–16 |
| Rich young man | 19:16–22 | 10:17–22 | 18:18–23 |
| Riches and rewards | 19:23–29 | 10:23–30 | 18:24–30 |
| 3rd passion prediction | 20:17b–19 | 10:32e–34 | 18:31–33 |
| Blind man at Jericho | 20:29–34 | 10:46–52 | 18:35–43 |
| **In Jerusalem** |  |  |  |
| Triumphal entry | 21:1–3, 6–9 | 11:1–10 | 19:29–38 |
| Jesus cleanses Temple | 21:12–13 | 11:15b–17 | 19:45–46 |
| Question of authority | 21:23–27 | 11:27b–33 | 20:1–8 |
| Parable of tenants | 21:33–46a | 12:1–12a | 20:9–17, 19 |
| **Controversy stories** |  |  |  |
| Tribute to Caesar | 22:16–22a | 12:13–17 | 20:20–26 |
| On resurrection | 22:23–32 | 12:18–27a | 20:27–38 |
| Great commandment | 22:35–40 | 12:28b–31 | — |

|                          | Matthew           | Mark          | Luke           |
|--------------------------|-------------------|---------------|----------------|
| No one dared             | →22:46b           | 12:34b        | 20:40          |
| Christ and David         | 22:41–45          | 12:35–37a     | 20:41–44       |
| Against scribes          | 23:1, 6–7a, 14    | 12:37b–40     | 20:45–47       |
| **Eschatology**          |                   |               |                |
| Temple prediction        | 24:1–2            | 13:1–2        | 21:5–6         |
| Signs of the end         | 24:3–8            | 13:3–8        | 21:7–11        |
| On persecution           | 24:9, 13          | 13:9bc, 11–13 | 21:12–17, 19   |
| Desolating sacrilege     | 24:15–21          | 13:14–19      | 21:20–24       |
| Son of Man comes         | 24:29, 30b        | 13:24–26      | 21:25–27       |
| Within a generation      | 24:32–35          | 13:28–31      | 21:29–33       |
| **Passover**             |                   |               |                |
| Jewish leaders plot      | 26:2a, 3–5        | 14:1–2        | 22:1–2         |
| Anointing at Bethany     | 26:6–13           | 14:3–9        | →7:36–38       |
| Judas makes a deal       | 26:14–16          | 14:10–11      | 22:3–6         |
| Passover prepared        | 26:17–20          | 14:12–17      | 22:7–14        |
| Betrayal predicted       | 26:21–25          | 14:18–21      | 22:21–23       |
| Denial predicted         | 26:33–34          | 14:29–30      | 22:33–34       |
| To Gethsemane            | 26:36a            | 14:32a        | 22:40a         |
| Jesus prays              | 26:38b–41         | 14:35–38a     | 22:40b–46      |
| **Jesus' arrest**        |                   |               |                |
| Judas and crowd          | 26:47a            | 14:43a        | 22:47a         |
| Judas kisses Jesus       | 26:49             | 14:45         | 22:47b         |
| Slave's ear cut off      | 26:51             | 14:47         | 22:50          |
| As against a thief       | 26:55a            | 14:48         | 22:52          |
| I taught in Temple       | 26:55b            | 14:49a        | 22:53a         |
| **Peter's denial**       |                   |               |                |
| Led to high priest       | 26:57a            | 14:53a        | 22:54a         |
| Peter follows            | 26:58a            | 14:54a        | 22:54b         |
| Sitting with servants    | 26:58c            | 14:54c        | 22:55          |
| Peter denies Jesus       | 26:69–75          | 14:66–72      | 22:56–62       |
| **Before Pilate**        |                   |               |                |
| In the morning           | 27:1a             | 15:1a         | 22:66a         |
| Jesus led to Pilate      | 27:2b             | 15:1c         | 23:1b          |
| You King of Jews?        | 27:11b            | 15:2          | 23:3           |
| Jesus stays silent       | 27:12–14          | 15:3–5        | 23:9–10        |
| Barabbas or Jesus        | 27:15–16          | 15:6–7        | 23:[17], 19    |
| Barabbas or Jesus        | 27:21–23, 26      | 15:12–15      | 23:18–25       |

|  | Matthew | Mark | Luke |
|---|---|---|---|
| **Jesus' crucifixion** | | | |
| They lead him out | 27:31b | 15:20b | 23:26a |
| Simon carries cross | 27:32 | 15:21 | 23:26b |
| Arrival at Golgotha | 27:33 | 15:22 | 23:33a |
| They crucify him | 27:35a | 15:24a | 23:33b |
| Garments divided | 27:35b | 15:24b | 23:34b |
| Epigraph/charge | 27:37 | 15:26 | 23:38 |
| Darkness over land | 27:45 | 15:33 | 23:44 |
| Jesus expires | 27:50 | 15:37 | 23:46ac |
| Centurion confesses | 27:54 | 15:39 | 23:47 |
| Women from Galilee | 27:55 | 15:40a, 41a | 23:49 |
| **Jesus' burial** | | | |
| Joseph requests body | 27:57–58a | 15:42–43 | 23:50–52 |
| Jesus entombed | 27:59–60a | 15:46a | 23:53 |
| The women watch | 27:61 | 15:47 | 23:55 |
| **The empty tomb** | | | |
| Women go to tomb | 28:1 | 16:2 | 24:1 |
| Stone rolled away | 28:2b | 16:4a | 24:2 |
| Man/men in white | 28:3 | 16:5b | 24:4b |
| They are afraid | 28:4 | 16:5c | 24:5a |
| He is risen | 28:5b–6a | 16:6b | 24:5b–6a |
| They leave tomb | 28:8a | 16:8a | 24:9a |
| They tell the others | 28:8c | (16:8c) | 24:9b |
| **Jesus' resurrection** | | | |
| Appearance to 11 | 28:17 | 16:14a | 24:36 |
| Charge to preach | 28:19a | 16:15 | 24:47 |

# Historical Setting of Proto-Mark

Proto-Mark was the common ancestor of Proto-Mark A and Proto-Mark B, which in turn served as the main sources of the Synoptic Gospels. It accounts for the common core of material that occurs in the same order in all three Synoptics. While Proto-Mark was thus an early gospel, its editor did not compose completely *de novo*, but drew on earlier written sources. As we shall see in Chapter 11, one of those sources was the C material. This source focused on the preaching of the gospel, the message that the kingdom of God would soon arrive, and ended with the risen Jesus sending the disciples to preach this message to the Gentiles. It entered the Synoptic tradition at more than one stage, including the stage of Proto-Mark, whose editor took a number of items from it. I will discuss C in Chapter 11. Here I restrict my comments to the material in Proto-Mark that did not come from C. An examination of this material indicates that it reflects the perspective of Judaic Christians. At least some of it has a connection with Jerusalem. Though some of it dates from a fairly early period, the editor of Proto-Mark made it a part of his gospel sometime around 70 CE.

## Judaic Christian Character of Proto-Mark

The material in Proto-Mark has not merely a Jewish Christian, but a Judaic Christian character. I use the term "Jewish Christian" to refer to any Jew who believed in Jesus as some sort of savior figure. This would include Paul and other Jewish Christians who rejected the Jewish law as the means of justification. By the term "Judaic Christians," I mean a more limited group: Jews who acknowledged Jesus as the Messiah but continued to practice the religion of Judaism as the way to God. We encounter Judaic Christians in the letters of Paul (Galatians; Phil 3:2), in Acts (e.g., Acts 15:1, 5; 21:20–25), and in the writings of other early Christians (Ignatius, *Magnesians* 10:3; Justin, *Dialogue* 46–47; Irenaeus, *Against Heresies* 1.26.2). The surviving literature of Judaic Christianity includes the Synoptic sources known as Q and M, the Letter of James, the Didache, and the Pseudo-Clementine Recognitions 1.27–71. Since much of the Proto-Mark material shares the distinctive characteristics of this literature, this material too probably arose among Judaic Christians. In particular, it has a Judaic Christian perspective on the law and on Jesus.

1. Judaic Christians differed from other varieties of early Christianity primarily in the fact that they continued to rely on the Jewish law as the way to God. The Q community, for example, expected the law to remain in force as long as heaven and earth endured (Matt 5:18//Luke 16:17). Even more strongly than Q, the material in M affirms that the community had a continuing obligation to practice the Jewish law. Jesus did not come to abolish the law, but to fulfill it (Matt 5:17). Therefore, even the least commandment of the law had to be kept (Matt 5:19). Accordingly, the community continued to practice Jewish rites, such as sacrificing at the Temple (Matt 5:23–24) and performing the basic acts of Jewish piety: giving alms, praying, and fasting (Matt 6:1–18). The Didache, while recognizing that not all community members would practice the law perfectly, still instructed them to keep as much of it as they could (Didache 6:2–3). The Judaic Christians known to Justin also continued to observe the law, practicing circumcision, keeping the Sabbath

and other Jewish holy days, and observing the rules of ritual purity (*Dialogue* 46–47). The Judaic Christians that Irenaeus calls "Ebionites" practiced circumcision, observed the other customs enjoined by the law, and even adored Jerusalem as if it were the house of God (*Against Heresies* 1.26.2).

Certain Proto-Mark material shows a similar Judaic Christian attitude toward the law. The controversy stories in particular presuppose a group of Judaic Christians who kept the law while disputing its interpretation with other Jewish groups (Mark 2:3–3:6 par). In these stories Jesus does not deny that those who keep the law are "righteous" (Mark 2:17 par) but defends his own ministry to the unrighteous. He does not abolish the Jewish custom of fasting, but defends its non-observance during the period of his ministry (Mark 2:19–20 par). He does not abolish the Sabbath, but defends the right to perform certain actions on that day (Mark 2:23–28 par; 3:1–6 par). All of these stories assume that the practice of the law continues. Another story takes for granted that keeping the commandments of the law leads to eternal life, even though one must also join the group of Jesus' followers and give away one's wealth (Mark 10:17–19 par).

2. Unlike Paul, Judaic Christianity placed little emphasis on the death of Jesus as a saving event. For Paul, faith in the atoning power of Jesus' death had replaced the Jewish law as the means of salvation. Judaic Christians, however, rejected this view. Irenaeus's Ebionites went so far as to repudiate Paul, maintaining that he was an apostate from the law (*Against Heresies* 1.26.2). Because Judaic Christians still regarded the law as the way to God, they had no need to ascribe this role to the death of Jesus. In most of the surviving Judaic Christian literature, therefore, including Q, M, James, and the Didache, the death of Jesus receives little or no attention.

While the death of Jesus does receive attention in Proto-Mark, it is not presented as a saving event. Those Synoptic passages that interpret Jesus' death as vicarious atonement occur only in strands of the tradition subsequent to Proto-Mark. The saying in which Jesus gives his life as a "ransom" for others was apparently added by the editor of Proto-Mark A (Mark10:45//Matt 20:28). The Lord's Supper saying, in which Jesus pours out his blood "for many," was inserted into the Passover narrative by the editor of Proto-Mark A (Mark14:24//Matt 26:28) and independently by Luke (Luke 22:19–20), as shown in Chapter 9.

Proto-Mark focuses on the death of Jesus not to present it as a saving event, but to show that it was consistent with the claim that Jesus was the Messiah. The idea of a crucified messiah, as Paul put it, was "a scandal to the Jews and foolishness to the Gentiles" (1 Cor 1:23). Many Jews expected the Messiah to drive out the Romans; none expected him to be crucified by them. Such Jews therefore saw the death of Jesus as a major objection to the church's claim that he was the Messiah. Proto-Mark sought to answer this objection by defending the idea of a crucified Messiah. Three times Proto-Mark has Jesus announce his approaching death and resurrection (Mark 8:31 par; 9:30–32 par; 10:32–34 par). These passion predictions function in three ways to take the "sting" out of Jesus' death. First, they present the crucifixion as the result of a conscious choice on Jesus' part. Jesus, in control of the situation, knows in advance what will happen. He thus appears as the master of his fate rather than as a helpless victim of the Romans. Second, they present Jesus' death as necessary: he "must" suffer and die. While Proto-Mark does not explain the reason for the necessity, nothing in it suggests vicarious atonement as the reason. Instead, the parable of the tenants indicates that Jesus died, like previous prophets, because he had a message from God that the Jewish leadership rejected (Mark 12:1–12b par). This perspective links Proto-Mark to other strands of the tradition that depict prophets as inevitably suffering rejection and death (Mark 6:4 PMA; Luke 6:22–23 Q; 11:49–51 Q), typically in Jerusalem (Luke 13:33 L; 13:34 Q). Third, the passion predictions point forward to Jesus' resurrection as his vindication. Jesus did not remain dead but was resurrected and ascended to heaven to be enthroned as king at the right hand of God (Mark 14:62b par). Thus Proto-Mark views Jesus' death not as a saving event, but primarily as an embarrassment to the claim that he was the Messiah. It focuses on Jesus' death in order to present an apology or defense against this embarrassment.

3. With respect to Jesus' nature, Judaic Christians such as the Ebionites thought that Jesus was a normal human being, born in a normal manner to Joseph and Mary, and that his power came from the Spirit that descended on him after his baptism (Irenaeus, *Against Heresies* 1.26.2; cf. 1.26.1). Proto-Mark seems to reflect a similar view. Unlike John, Proto-Mark does not present Jesus as the incarnation of a preexistent divine being. It never calls Jesus "God" or claims that he existed before his life on earth. Unlike Matthew and Luke, Proto-Mark does not present Jesus as a demigod, the offspring of a virgin mother and a divine Father. As far as we know from Proto-Mark, Jesus was a normal human being with a birth like that of everyone else. Proto-Mark does present Jesus as the Son of God, but not necessarily in an ontological sense. Since Proto-Mark's Jesus is neither an incarnation nor a demigod, he is not a son of God in either of those senses. In Proto-Mark, Jesus is first designated as the Son of God at his baptism after he receives the Spirit (1:11). Apparently, then, it is the Spirit that empowers him and makes him the Son of God.

4. With respect to Jesus' function, Judaic Christianity identified him as the Messiah. However, just as Judaism in general had different conceptions of the Messiah, so did Judaic Christianity. One strand thought of him as the Davidic Messiah, the son of David (Matt 1:1; Didache 9:2). Another argued

that the Messiah was not the son of David but superior to David (Mark 12:35–37). Both strands thought of the Messiah primarily as an eschatological figure. Jesus' primary function as Messiah still lay in the future when he would return to execute judgment (Q and M passim; James 5:7–9; Didache 16:1–8). In speaking of Jesus as the future Messiah, both Q and M refer to him as "the Son of Man."

In Proto-Mark too, Jesus is the future Messiah. Jesus, as the Son of Man, would return with the clouds of the sky (Mark 13:26 par) within a generation of Jesus' death (Mark 9:1 par; 13:30 par). The question of whether or not the Messiah was also the son of David receives different answers in Proto-Mark. A blind man calls Jesus "son of David" (Mark 10:47 M 48 par), yet Jesus himself argues that the Christ is not the son of David (Mark 12:35 M 37a par).

### Links to Jerusalem

While the aforementioned features of Proto-Mark connect it with Judaic Christianity in general, at least some of its traditions seem to have a connection specifically with Jerusalem.

1. First, it gives preeminence to the "inner circle" of Jesus' disciples: Peter and the two sons of Zebedee, James and John. Several references to this trio occur in the Synoptic tradition, two of them in Proto-Mark (Mark 1:16 M 20 par; 9:2 par). In the story where Jesus calls some fishermen as disciples, Proto-Mark A includes Andrew with this trio. However, Luke's version (Luke 5:2, 10–11), which probably comes from Proto-Mark B, mentions only the three and may represent the more original reading of Proto-Mark. In the story of the transfiguration, Jesus takes the inner circle onto a mountain. This story gives a place of preeminence to these three disciples, since they alone witness Jesus' transformation into heavenly glory.

This preeminent role corresponds to what we know about the structure of leadership in the church at Jerusalem. In Galatians 2:1–10, Paul describes a visit that he made to see the three "pillars" of the church in Jerusalem, namely, James the brother of Jesus, Cephas (or Peter), and John, presumably the son of Zebedee. Here the "inner circle" consists of Peter, James, and John, though the James mentioned by Paul is not the son of Zebedee. If Acts 12:1–2 is correct, James the son of Zebedee was killed by Herod Agrippa I, who ruled over Judea from 41 to 44. It is likely that before this time the inner circle at Jerusalem consisted of Peter and the two sons of Zebedee. A story in Proto-Mark A suggests that the sons of Zebedee claimed a position of preeminence that was resented by other factions in the early church (Matt 20:20–24; Mark 10:35–41). After the death of James the son of Zebedee, James the brother of Jesus apparently took his place.

The role of the inner circle in Proto-Mark thus corresponds to the leadership of the Jerusalem church prior to the early forties. It is probable that the transfiguration account, where they put in an appearance, is not historical but symbolic, a retrojection of the early church's faith in the resurrection or ascension of Jesus. In retrojecting that faith, the composer of the story apparently also retrojected a form of leadership that was familiar from the church in Jerusalem. This link to Jerusalem suggests that this story had its origin in or near that city.

2. A related feature of Proto-Mark leads to the same conclusion. Proto-Mark casts less negative light on the leaders at Jerusalem than do its subsequent revisions. Peter is the first to recognize that Jesus is the Messiah (Mark 8:29 par). However, contrary to the later revision in Proto-Mark A (Mark 8:32–33//Matt 16:22–23), Jesus does not rebuke Peter subsequent to his confession. Proto-Mark thus leaves the portrayal of Peter on a positive note. Likewise, Proto-Mark casts no negative light on the sons of Zebedee. The story that criticizes their desire for preeminence also belongs to Proto-Mark A (Mark 10:35–41//Matt 20:20–24). As for Jesus' disciples in general, Proto-Mark does not present them as lacking in comprehension. Those passages that do belong either to Proto-Mark A (Mark 8:17a, 21//Matt 16:8, 11), Proto-Mark B (Mark 9:32//Luke 9:45), or to the final layer of Markan redaction (Mark 6:52; 8:17b–18). In two instances, however, Proto-Mark does give a more negative portrayal of Jesus' disciples. It criticizes the disciples for lack of faith when they are unable to cast out a demon (Mark 9:19 par) and it includes the story in which Peter denies Jesus.

While Proto-Mark presents the inner circle and the disciples generally in a positive light, it downplays the importance of Jesus' mother and brothers. In one story, they are left standing outside while Jesus recognizes those around him as his true family (Mark 3:31–35 par). The story may have had its original setting in a conflict over leadership. If so, it was apparently designed to negate the claims of Jesus' family to a position of preeminence. While it is impossible to know the exact details, such a conflict is consistent with the view that the story arose in Jerusalem when the inner circle consisted of Peter and the sons of Zebedee, prior to the time that James the brother of Jesus rose to power.

3. A third possible link to Jerusalem occurs in the story in which Jesus feeds five thousand (Mark 6:35–44 par). Of the two feeding stories in the Synoptic tradition, Proto-Mark included only this one. It depicts a large crowd from different towns and villages assembling outside to receive teaching from Jesus and to eat together. This story may depict Jesus' ministry in terms that were familiar to the composer from later practice at Jerusalem. Acts portrays the Jerusalem church meeting not only in small groups in var-

ious homes in the city (Acts 2:46; 12:12), but also as a whole in "Solomon's Portico," a covered colonnade to the east of the Temple (Acts 3:11; 5:12; cf. John 10:23). Once the early church fell out of favor with the Temple authorities, it would be unlikely for them to assemble there. We can imagine them instead assembling outside the city in the open air. We also have reason to believe that Christians from the neighboring towns and villages would come to join them (e.g., Acts 5:16). Especially during the Jewish festivals, when pilgrims came to Jerusalem from all over the world, many Jewish Christians would have visited Jerusalem to meet with the Christian community there. To accommodate the crowd, the community may have had to meet at some place outside the city in the open air.

The story in which Jesus feeds the five thousand presupposes a Jewish Christian gathering when it mentions the twelve baskets of leftovers, one for each of the twelve tribes of Israel. It also has a link to the Jerusalem church in numbering the crowd at five thousand men. Acts gives five thousand as the number of men in the early Jewish Christian movement at Jerusalem (Acts 4:4). While this number would be high for Jewish Christians living in Jerusalem, it might reflect the total number of Jewish Christians who would assemble at Jerusalem during a festival. In any case, whether the number reflects an actual count of population or not, it is a number associated in early Christian tradition with Jerusalem. It links the feeding story to Jerusalem, suggesting that the story had its provenance there.

### Date of Proto-Mark

Some of the material that we have discussed seems to reflect a time prior to the early forties when James the son of Zebedee was killed. Other material is much later, from the time of the Jewish War with Rome. Thus, while Proto-Mark drew on traditions from an earlier time, in its final form it must be dated around 70 CE.

The basis for dating Proto-Mark is the same as that which has traditionally been used to date the Gospel of Mark: i.e., the eschatological discourse. In this discourse, Jesus predicts the destruction of the Temple in Jerusalem (Mark 13:2 par). Thereupon follows an apocalyptic review of end-time events from the time of Jesus to the coming of the Son of Man. This discourse is the earliest known instance of a "revelatory discourse" attributed to Jesus, a genre that later became popular in Gnostic Christian literature for non-eschatological revelations. This type of discourse has its roots in earlier apocalypses in which a heavenly being brings revelation to a seer from the ancient past. In the revelatory discourse, Jesus takes the place of the heavenly being and the disciples take the place of the ancient seer.

If Proto-Mark's discourse follows the typical pattern found in other historical reviews in apocalyptic literature, it employs *vaticinium ex eventu*. That is, the revealing figure, in this case Jesus, reviews the past as if it were a prediction of the future. As long as the author is reviewing the past, his "predictions" are generally accurate historically. Once the review reaches his own time, however, the author typically predicts an imminent end of the age. Thus, the point at which the review shifts from actual history to unfulfilled apocalyptic prediction marks the time in which the author is writing. Proto-Mark's version of the review includes false Christs, rumors of war, earthquakes and famines, persecution of Christians, an "abomination of desolation," flight of Christians in Judea to the mountains, and a time of severe affliction. These may well be historical events of the author's past, which then lead to an unfulfilled prediction of the coming of the Son of Man amid celestial phenomena associated in the Hebrew Bible with the day of the Lord. The point of transition from history to prediction of the end indicates that the author lived in a time of severe affliction in which Jewish Christians in Judea had been forced to flee from their homes. This would have been the time of the Jewish War with Rome in 66–70. Since the review does not mention the destruction of the Temple, it may have been written shortly before 70, when that event occurred. The prediction that prefaces the review, however, does mention the destruction of the Temple (Mark 13:1–2 par). Scholars disagree on whether this prediction was made before or after the fact. In any case, the discourse must be dated around 70, whether shortly before or after. Proto-Mark itself, then, must be dated no earlier than around 70 CE.

If that is the case, the revisions of Proto-Mark, namely Proto-Mark A and Proto-Mark B, must have been made sometime after 70 and the Synoptic Gospels yet later. Let us allow five to fifteen years from Proto-Mark to Proto-Mark A and Proto-Mark B, and another five to fifteen years from Proto-Mark A and Proto-Mark B to the Synoptic Gospels. That would place Proto-Mark A and Proto-Mark B somewhere in the decade from 75 to 85 and the Synoptic Gospels between 80 and 100.

## The Language of Proto-Mark

I have assumed that Proto-Mark was written in Greek. Is it possible, alternatively, that it might have been written in Aramaic or Hebrew? Philippe Rolland, in a theory similar to mine, raises this possibility. Rolland posits a primitive Gospel C (similar to my Proto-Mark), which served as a source for AC (similar to my Proto-Mark A) and BC (similar to my Proto-Mark B). He regards the primitive gospel as a Semitic document, written in either Aramaic or, more likely, Hebrew. In his theory, the subsequent editions AC and BC were based on two different Greek translations of the Semitic C. While Matthew used AC and Luke used BC, Mark combined the two.[1]

Rolland finds support for the Semitic character of the primitive gospel in divergences in wording between Matthew and Luke, which he explains as translation variants. He has worked out this theory in detail with respect to the controversy story on fasting (Matt 9:14–17; Mark 2:18–22; Luke 5:33–39). While he recognizes that this pericope has undergone redaction in Matthew and Luke, he traces many of the differences between their versions to different translations of a Semitic original. For example, he sees Matthew's ἐφ᾽ ὅσον (Matt 9:15) and Luke's ἐν ᾧ (Luke 5:34) as variant translations of the same Hebrew expression. He gives the same explanation for Matthew's ἀγνάφου (Matt 9:16) and Luke's καινοῦ (Luke 5:36). He also explains the present tenses in Matthew 9:17 and the future tenses in Luke 5:37 as two different ways of translating the Hebrew imperfect.

These explanations for divergent readings seem reasonable when taken in isolation. However, to be acceptable, a theory must explain not only the divergences, but also the similarities between Matthew and Luke. At several places in this pericope Matthew and Luke have practically identical Greek wording, as Table 8.4 shows.

**Table 8.4**
**Identical wording in Matthew 9:14–17 and Luke 5:33–39**

| Matthew 9:14–17 | Luke 5:33–39 |
|---|---|
| μετ᾽ αὐτῶν ἐστιν ὁ νυμφίος | ὁ νυμφίος μετ᾽ αὐτῶν ἐστιν |
| ἐλεύσονται δὲ ἡμέραι ὅταν ἀπαρθῇ ἀπ᾽ αὐτῶν ὁ νυμφίος, . . . τότε νηστεύσουσιν. | ἐλεύσονται δὲ ἡμέραι . . . ὅταν ἀπαρθῇ ἀπ᾽ αὐτῶν ὁ νυμφίος, τότε νηστεύσουσιν |
| οὐδεὶς . . . ἐπιβάλλει ἐπίβλημα . . . ἐπὶ ἱματίῳ παλαιῷ | οὐδεὶς ἐπίβλημα . . . ἐπιβάλλει ἐπὶ ἱμάτιον παλαιόν |
| οἶνον νέον εἰς ἀσκοὺς παλαιούς· εἰ δὲ μή γε, | οἶνον νέον εἰς ἀσκοὺς παλαιούς· εἰ δὲ μή γε, |
| ἀλλὰ . . . οἶνον νέον εἰς ἀσκοὺς καινούς | ἀλλὰ οἶνον νέον εἰς ἀσκοὺς καινούς |

Such identical wording makes it unlikely that Matthew and Luke depended on variant translations of a Semitic original, for two reasons. 1) It is unlikely that two translators working independently would produce so much identical

1. On the language of Rolland's primitive gospel, see Rolland, "Les prédécesseurs de Marc"; idem, *Les premiers évangiles*, 147–48; idem, "L'arrière-fond sémitique des évangiles synoptiques."

Greek wording in their translations. 2) The identical wording occurs in the words attributed to Jesus rather than in the narrative framework. This phenomenon, in which the Synoptics agree more closely in the words of Jesus than in the accompanying narrative, occurs not infrequently in other pericopes in the Synoptic core (see for example the same phenomenon in the story about plucking grain on the Sabbath discussed in Chapter 12). This phenomenon is difficult to explain if Matthew and Luke were using different Greek translations of a Semitic original. In that case we would expect the amount of divergence between the translations to be just as great in the words of Jesus as in the narrative framework. The phenomenon is more easily explained if the evangelists were redacting material passed down from the same Greek original. As they redacted the material, they took greater liberty with the narrative than with the words of Jesus.

Rolland acknowledges that the Greek texts of Matthew and Luke are in places too similar to attribute to different Greek translations. As an example he cites Matthew 16:24–28 and Luke 9:23–27. Here the versions of Matthew and Luke agree too closely to be independent translations. Rolland explains this fact by theorizing that an old oral translation of the primitive gospel influenced the two written translations.[2] Such a theory, however, raises more questions than it solves. How was such an oral translation preserved? How did it happen that both translators knew it? How did it happen that both decided to use it at certain places in their work and not in others? It is simpler to suppose that Matthew and Luke knew material passed down from the same original written in Greek.

Other evidence suggesting that Proto-Mark was a Semitic document has been presented by William O. Walker Jr. Walker argues that the Aramaic term *rabbi* or *rabbouni* stood in either an earlier version of Mark or some type of Ur-Gospel. In the subsequent Synoptic Gospels, this term was sometimes transliterated and sometimes translated as κύριος (in Matthew and Luke) or as ἐπιστάτης (in Luke) or as διδάσκαλος (in Mark).[3] Walker makes a good case, and we need not dispute it. However, even if we accept his thesis, it does not lead to the conclusion that Proto-Mark was written in Aramaic. We could just as easily assume that the Aramaic term *rabbi/rabbouni* stood as a borrowed expression in a Proto-Mark written in Greek. This assumption has the advantage of being able to explain not only the divergences in the translation of *rabbi* but also the frequently identical Greek wording in the same context. Take, for example, Peter's words to Jesus at the transfiguration, shown in Table 8.5.

---

2. Rolland, *Les premiers évangiles*, 148n. 2.

3. William O. Walker Jr., "Κυριος and Επιστατης as Translations of "*Rabbi/Rabbouni*," *The Journal of Higher Criticism* 4, 1 (1997): 56–77.

### Table 8.5
### Mark 9:5 and parallels

| Matthew 17:4 | Mark 9:5 | Luke 9:33 |
|---|---|---|
| κύριε, | ῥαββί, | ἐπιστάτα, |
| καλόν ἐστιν ἡμᾶς ὧδε εἶναι | καλόν ἐστιν ἡμᾶς ὧδε εἶναι | καλόν ἐστιν ἡμᾶς ὧδε εἶναι |

Here the Greek wording is identical except for the title by which Peter addresses Jesus. To decide whether Proto-Mark was written in Greek or Aramaic, we must take account of this identical Greek wording as well as the divergent title of address. It seems necessary to conclude that Proto-Mark was written in Greek but included the Aramaic expression *rabbi* in transliteration. Mark has best preserved the original wording at this point, while Matthew and Luke have altered the title of address.

I do not wish to exclude the possibility that at some early stage of the Synoptic tradition a document or documents written in a Semitic language existed. However, if such a document existed, it was not Proto-Mark as I have delineated it. Without ignoring the presence of Semitic terms in Proto-Mark, I find it most likely that this gospel was written in Greek. Divergences in wording among the Synoptics in parallel material can be explained as variations produced by redaction of a Greek original. In our theory we must consider the redactional activity not only of the evangelists Matthew, Mark, and Luke, but also of the editors of Proto-Mark A and Proto-Mark B. The material in Proto-Mark passed through the hands of these editors before it ever reached the Synoptic evangelists. Given the number of editors who played a role in shaping the material, it should come as no surprise if the original Greek wording did not always survive the process.

# Chapter 9

# *The A Material*

As TABLE 8.1 SHOWED, some material in Proto-Mark A (common to Mark and Matthew) had no parallel in Proto-Mark B (common to Mark and Luke). Consequently, Mark and Matthew have this material in the same order and in the same position relative to the Synoptic core, while Luke does not. I have called this the "A" material. I exclude from A the passages of this type in Table 8.2, since we determined that these passages originally did have a parallel in Proto-Mark B. In our theory, an editor added the A material to Proto-Mark in order to produce Proto-Mark A. We can state this process as an equation: Proto-Mark + A = Proto-Mark A. Table 9.1 lists the A material as it occurred in Proto-Mark A, in the order common to Mark and Matthew.

Table 9.1
The A material in Proto-Mark A

|  | Matthew (A in PMA) | Mark (A in PMA) |
| --- | --- | --- |
| **John and Jesus** |  |  |
| All go to John | 3:5a | 1:5a |
| Baptism for sins | 3:6 | 1:5b |
| Jesus comes to John | 3:13a | 1:9a |
| Out of the water | 3:16b | 1:10a |
| Angels minister | 4:11b | 1:13c |
| **Jesus in Galilee** |  |  |
| John arrested | 4:12a | 1:14a |
| To his own town | 9:1b | 2:1a |
| With the Herodians | — | 3:6b |
| Jesus withdrew | 12:15a | 3:7a |
| **Parable discourse** |  |  |
| Ministry from a boat | 13:1–3a | 4:1–2 |
| Parable of sower | 13:3b–9 | 4:3–9 |
| Reason for parables | 13:10–11, 13 | 4:10–12 |

| | Matthew (A in PMA) | Mark (A in PMA) |
|---|---|---|
| Sower explained | 13:18–23 | 4:13–20 |
| Lamp on lampstand | — | 4:21 |
| The hidden revealed | — | 4:22 |
| How you hear | — | 4:24a |
| Have and have not | →13:12 | 4:25 |
| Man growing seed | — | 4:26–29 |
| The mustard seed | 13:31–32 | 4:30–32 |
| The leaven | 13:33 | — |
| Use of parables | 13:34–35 | 4:33–34 |
| Leaving the crowd | 13:36a | 4:36a |
| **Further ministry** | | |
| Death of John | 14:4–12a | 6:18–29 |
| Jesus walks on water | 14:22–33 | 6:45–52 |
| In Gennesaret | 14:34–36 | 6:53–56 |
| On hand washing | 15:1–20 | 7:1–23 |
| A Gentile woman | 15:21–28 | 7:24–30 |
| To Sea of Galilee | 15:29a | 7:31 |
| Various healings | 15:29b–30 | — |
| The crowd amazed | 15:31 | 7:37 |
| Jesus feeds 4,000 | 15:32–39 | 8:1–10 |
| Pharisees seek sign | 16:1, 4 | 8:11–13 |
| No bread | 16:5 | 8:14 |
| Leaven of Pharisees | 16:6 | 8:15 |
| No bread | 16:7–11a | 8:16–21 |
| **Going to Jerusalem** | | |
| Jesus rebukes Peter | 16:22–23 | 8:32–33 |
| The soul's worth | 16:26b | 8:37 |
| Coming of Elijah | 17:10–13 | 9:11–13 |
| On failed exorcisms | 17:19–20 | 9:28–29 |
| Going through Galilee | 17:22a | 9:30a |
| House in Capernaum | 17:24a, 25b | 9:33ab |
| Offensive member | 18:8–9 | 9:43–47 |
| **In Judea** | | |
| Jesus goes to Judea | 19:1b–2 | 10:1 |
| Teaching on divorce | 19:3–8 | 10:2–9 |
| Laying on hands | 19:15a | 10:16b |

|  | Matthew (A in PMA) | Mark (A in PMA) |
|---|---|---|
| Last shall be first | 19:30 | 10:31 |
| Up to Jerusalem | 20:17a | 10:32bc |
| Brothers seek honor | 20:20–24 | 10:35–41 |
| Ransom saying | 20:28 | 10:45 |
| **In Jerusalem** |  |  |
| Jesus enters Jerusalem | 21:10a | 11:15a |
| They leave Jesus | →22:22b | 12:12d |
| With the Herodians | 22:16b | 12:13b |
| **Eschatology** |  |  |
| Days shortened | 24:22 | 13:20 |
| Not here nor there | 24:23 | 13:21 |
| False Christs | 24:24–25 | 13:22–23 |
| The elect gathered | 24:31 | 13:27 |
| No one knows | 24:36 | 13:32 |
| Stay awake | 25:13 | 13:33 |
| Man on a journey | 25:14 | 13:34 |
| **Passover** |  |  |
| Anointing at Bethany | 26:6–13 | 14:3–9 |
| Lord's Supper sayings | 26:26–28 | 14:22–24 |
| Passover sayings | 26:29 | 14:25 |
| To Mount of Olives | 26:30 | 14:26 |
| All will scatter | 26:31 | 14:27 |
| I will go to Galilee | 26:32 | 14:28 |
| Fidelity affirmed | 26:35 | 14:31 |
| Jesus grieves | 26:36b–37 | 14:32b–33 |
| My soul disturbed | 26:38a | 14:34a |
| Let the hour pass | — | 14:35b |
| Jesus prays again | 26:42–45a | 14:39–41a |
| Hour of Son of Man | 26:45b | 14:41b |
| Get up, let's go | 26:46a | 14:42a |
| Betrayer has arrived | 26:46b | 14:42b |
| **Jesus' arrest** |  |  |
| Group with weapons | 26:47b | 14:43b |
| Kiss as signal | 26:48 | 14:44 |
| They seize Jesus | 26:50b | 14:46 |
| Scriptures fulfilled | 26:56a | 14:49b |

| | Matthew (A in PMA) | Mark (A in PMA) |
|---|---|---|
| The disciples flee | 26:56b | 14:50 |
| **Before Sanhedrin** | | |
| Council convenes | 26:57b | 14:53b |
| False witnesses | 26:59–63a | 14:55–61a |
| Sanhedrin's question | 26:63b–66 | 14:61c–64 |
| Jesus is mocked | 26:67–68 | 14:65 |
| **Before Pilate** | | |
| Council meets | 27:1b | 15:1b |
| They bind Jesus | 27:2a | 15:1c |
| They hand him over | 27:2b | 15:1d |
| Jesus and Barabbas | 27:17–18, 20 | 15:8–11 |
| Pilate flogs Jesus | 27:26b | 15:15c |
| Hail, King of Jews | 27:27–31a | 15:16–20a |
| **Jesus' crucifixion** | | |
| To crucify him | 27:31c | 15:20c |
| Wine with myrrh | 27:34 | 15:23 |
| Bandits crucified | 27:38 | 15:27 |
| Passersby mock | 27:39–40 | 15:29–30 |
| Rulers mock | 27:41–42 | 15:31–32a |
| Bandits mock | 27:44 | 15:32c |
| Jesus forsaken | 27:46–47 | 15:34–35 |
| Jesus given vinegar | 27:48 | 15:36a |
| Will Elijah come | 27:49 | 15:36b |
| Temple veil torn | 27:51a | 15:38 |
| Names of women | 27:56 | 15:40b |
| **Jesus' burial** | | |
| At evening | 27:57a | 15:42a |
| Disciple of Jesus | 27:57c | — |
| Pilate gives body | 27:58b | 15:45b |
| A new tomb | 27:60a | — |
| Stone over tomb | 27:60b | 15:46b |
| **The empty tomb** | | |
| After the Sabbath | 28:1a | 16:1a |
| At dawn | 28:1b | →16:2d |
| Two Marys | 28:1d | 16:1b |

|                          | Matthew (A in PMA) | Mark (A in PMA) |
|--------------------------|--------------------|-----------------|
| Messenger(s) seated      | 28:2c              | 16:5b           |
| Do not fear              | 28:5a              | 16:6a           |
| See the place            | 28:6b              | 16:6c           |
| See him in Galilee       | 28:7               | 16:7            |
| With fear                | 28:8b              | 16:8b           |
| Jesus' resurrection      |                    |                 |
| Mary sees Jesus          | 28:9a              | 16:9a           |
| They worship             | 28:9b              | —               |
| See me in Galilee        | 28:10              | —               |
| Eleven go to Galilee     | 28:16              | —               |
| Some doubt               | 28:17b             | 16:14b          |
| Charge to baptize        | 28:19b             | 16:16           |

The A material in Proto-Mark A apparently came from several distinct sources other than Proto-Mark. Some of these sources can be identified from the fact that the A material in Proto-Mark A overlaps with material in Luke. These overlaps arose as the editors of Luke and Proto-Mark A independently incorporated components of the A material into their respective works. This A material common to Proto-Mark A and Luke consists of a parable discourse, the words of institution of the Lord's Supper, a narrative of Jesus' trial before the Sanhedrin, and elements of a passion narrative. We previously identified these components in Luke in Chapter 5 (Table 5.2). There we saw that these items do not fit into the sequence of Proto-Mark B common to Mark and Luke, though Table 4.3 shows that they do fit into the sequence of Proto-Mark A common to Mark and Matthew. We inferred that these items once circulated independently as isolated traditions or collections of tradition. The editor of Proto-Mark A knew them, and they became part of the extra material (A) that he added to Proto-Mark to create Proto-Mark A. Luke also knew them and added them to his own gospel. Since these two editors worked independently, the material occurred in a different combination in Proto-Mark A (hence in Mark and Matthew) than in Luke.

## Parable Discourse

The first component of A common to Proto-Mark A and Luke is the parable discourse. Table 9.2 shows the contents of this discourse as it appears in Mark and its parallels.

Table 9.2
The parable discourse

|  | Matthew (A in PMA) | Mark (A in PMA + A) | Luke (A) |
|---|---|---|---|
| Ministry from a boat |  | 3:7b, 8e–9 | 5:1, 3 |
| Ministry from a boat | 13:1–3a | 4:1–2 |  |
| Parable of the sower | 13:3b–9 | 4:3–9 | 8:5–8 |
| Reason for parables | 13:10–11, 13 | 4:10–12 | 8:9–10 |
| The sower explained | 13:18-23 | 4:13–20 | 8:11–15 |
| Lamp on a lampstand |  | 4:21 | 8:16 |
| The hidden revealed |  | 4:22 | 8:17 |
| Ears to hear |  | 4:23 |  |
| How you hear |  | 4:24a | 8:18a |
| Measure for measure |  | 4:24b |  |
| Added to you |  | 4:24c |  |
| Have and have not | →13:12 | 4:25 | 8:18b |
| Man sowing seed |  | 4:26–29 |  |
| The mustard seed | 13:31–32 | 4:30–32 | 13:18–19 |
| The leaven | 13:33 |  | 13:20–21 |
| Use of parables | 13:34–35 | 4:33–34 |  |

Several features of this discourse call for comment.

1. The discourse material common to Mark and Matthew occurs in a single location, the same in each gospel, following the pericope about Jesus' true family. The discourse in Luke, however, is split into three parts, none of which occupies the same position in Luke as the corresponding material in Mark and Matthew. The introduction to the discourse, in which Jesus gets into a boat to teach, precedes the discourse proper by several chapters (Luke 5:1, 3). The main part of the discourse occurs before the pericope about Jesus' true family instead of after, as in Mark and Matthew (Luke 8:5–18). And the last two parables of the discourse occur several chapters later (Luke 13:18–21). The common position of the material in Mark and Matthew reflects their common dependence on Proto-Mark A, while the distinctive distribution of the material in Luke reflects Luke's independence of Proto-Mark A. Luke took the boat material at the beginning of the discourse and conflated it with two other stories relating to boats and fishermen, one in which Jesus shows Peter where to catch fish (Luke 5:4–9) and another in which Jesus calls fishermen as disciples (Luke 5:2, 10). He then inserted most of the discourse before the

pericope about Jesus' true family, which he found in Proto-Mark B. Finally, he added the last two parables several chapters later. Though these parables are often assigned to Q, it is unnecessary to assume that Luke found a second version of them in Q, especially since neither Matthew nor Luke includes a doublet of either.

2. Mark apparently knew two versions of the parable discourse: one from Proto-Mark A that he shared with Matthew and one that he, like Luke, found circulating independently of any larger source. The basis for this inference lies primarily in the fact that Mark includes two versions of the introductory scene in which Jesus ministers from a boat. While the other Synoptics have this narrative only once each, Mark has it twice. Table 9.3 illustrates this feature of the material.

Table 9.3
Markan doublets of ministry from a boat

| Matthew | Mark | Luke |
|---------|------|------|
|  |  | 5:1 As the crowd pressed upon him and heard the word of God, he was standing by the lake of Gennesaret . . . 3 Getting into one of the boats, that of Peter, he asked him to put out a little from the land. Sitting down, out of the boat he taught the crowds. |
|  | 3:7 . . . to the sea . . . 8 . . . A large multitude, hearing what he was doing, came to him. 9 And he told his disciples that a boat should be on hand for him because of the crowd, lest they crush him. |  |
| 13:1 . . . He sat by the sea. 2 And large crowds were gathered to him, so that he got into a boat to sit. 3 And he spoke to them . . . | 4:1 And again he began to teach by the sea. And a considerable crowd gathered to him, so that he got into a boat to sit in the sea. 2 And he taught them |  |

Mark did not usually create doublets, but generally conflated duplicate material. However, he does have doublets of this particular narrative. Since the second doublet (Mark 4:1) parallels that of Matthew (Matt 13:1–3), it can be traced to their common source, Proto-Mark A. The first doublet (Mark 3:7b, 8e–9) occurs in a story in which Jesus ministers to a crowd. It probably did not originally belong to this story, since it has no parallel in the corresponding material in Matthew or Luke. More likely, Mark added it from a second version of the parable discourse, which he, like Luke, found circulating separately. Mark, working independently of Luke, placed the boat material later in the narrative than did Luke.

3. Apart from the material common to all three Synoptics, it is difficult to be certain what material stood in the original discourse. Matthew lacks several short sayings found in Mark and Luke or in Mark alone (Mark 4:21–24). It is possible that Proto-Mark A lacked these, while Mark and Luke found them in the separate version of the discourse. Alternatively, it is possible that Proto-Mark A did include them but that Matthew omitted them because he found most of them in Q (Matt 5:15//Luke 11:33; Matt 10:26//Luke 12:2; Matt 11:15, 13:43//Luke 14:35; Matt 7:2b//Luke 6:38c; Matt 6:33b//Luke 12:31b). In that case, however, he failed to omit Matthew 13:12, which also has a parallel in Q (Matt 25:29//Luke 19:26). While Mark and Luke have this saying after the explanation of the parable of the sower, Matthew has it earlier in the discourse. Since in Matthew it interrupts the explanation of why Jesus speaks in parables, it is likely that Mark and Luke preserve the more original order while Matthew has moved this element from its original position. Matthew and Luke both lack the parable of the man sowing seed. This probably did stand in Proto-Mark A, from which Matthew omitted it in favor of the parable of the weeds that now occupies its place (Matt 13:24–30). It remains uncertain whether or not it also stood in the version of the discourse that Luke knew. Mark lacks the parable of the leaven. It may be that Mark omitted it because he felt that the idea of corruption associated with leaven made it a poor metaphor for the kingdom of God (cf. Mark 8:15 parr; 1 Cor 5:6–8; Gal 5:9). The statement concerning Jesus' use of parables (Mark 4:33–34 par), though lacking in Luke, may have constituted the original conclusion of the discourse. Luke would have omitted it when he separated the final parables from the rest of the discourse, since apart from the discourse it would lose its original function. Alternatively, it may have ended the discourse only in Proto-Mark A, while Luke's version did not have it.

# Lord's Supper Sayings

The second component of A common to Proto-Mark A and Luke consists of the words of institution of the Lord's Supper. Mark and Matthew have these in the sequence of Proto-Mark A (Mark 14:22–24; Matt 26:26–28). Luke's version (Luke 22:19–20), as Table 5.2 shows, does not fit into the sequence of either Proto-Mark B or the C material. It does, however, fit into the same column as the other A material common to Luke and Proto-Mark A.

Paul cites the words of institution as a tradition that he received and passed on through oral instruction to the church at Corinth (1 Cor 11:23–26). Most likely, these words were recited during the celebration of the Lord's Supper. It is quite possible therefore that they entered the Synoptic tradition not as part of a larger source but as an isolated formula familiar from the church's liturgical tradition. While Mark and Matthew have a non-Pauline formulation from Proto-Mark A, Luke's version resembles that of Proto-Mark A in some respects, but that of Paul in others (Table 9.4).

### Table 9.4
### Words of institution of the Lord's Supper

| Matthew 26:26–28 | Mark 14:22–24 | Luke 22:19–20 | 1 Cor 11:23–26 |
|---|---|---|---|
| 26 As they were eating, Jesus took bread and blessed it and broke it. And giving it to the disciples he said, "Take it, eat it. This is my body." 27 And taking a cup and giving thanks he gave it to them saying, "Drink from it, all of you. 28 For this is the blood of my covenant that is poured out for many for forgiveness of sins." | 22 And as they were eating, he took bread and blessed it and broke it. And he gave it to them and said, "Take it. This is my body. 23 And taking a cup and giving thanks he gave it to them and all of them drank from it. 24 And he said to them, "This is the blood of my covenant that is poured out for the sake of many." | 19 And taking bread *and giving thanks* he broke it and gave it to them saying, "This is my body *that is given for your sake. Do this in my memory." And the cup likewise after the dinner saying, "This cup is the new covenant in my blood* that is poured out for your sake." | 23 The Lord Jesus . . . took bread 24 *and giving thanks* he broke it and said, "This is my body *that is [given] for your sake. Do this in my memory."* 25 *Likewise the cup after the dinner saying, "This cup is the new covenant in my blood.* Do this, as often as you drink it, in my memory." |

In the table, words common to Proto-Mark A and Luke are underlined, while words common to Paul and Luke are in italics. This comparison suggests that Luke and the editor of Proto-Mark A found similar versions of the formula in circulation, but that Luke conflated this with Paul's version. Luke and the editor of Proto-Mark A independently combined this formula with other material relating to Jesus' last meal.

## Sanhedrin Trial Source

The third component of A common to Proto-Mark A and Luke is a narrative relating Jesus' trial before the Sanhedrin and his subsequent execution. Mark and Matthew have this in the sequence of Proto-Mark A. In Luke, as shown in Table 5.2, it does not fit into the sequence of either Proto-Mark B or the C material, but does fit into the same column as the other A material common to Luke and Proto-Mark A. A variant version of the narrative occurs in the trial of Stephen in Acts. Table 9.5 shows all these versions.

Table 9.5
Sanhedrin trial source

|  | Matthew (A in PMA) | Mark (A in PMA) | Luke (A) | Acts |
|---|---|---|---|---|
| Council convenes | 26:57b | 14:53b | 22:66bc | 6:12 |
| False witnesses | 26:59–61 | 14:55–59 | — | 6:13–14a |
| High priest asks | 26:62 | 14:60 |  | 7:1 |
| Jesus is silent | 26:63a | 14:61a |  |  |
| Are you Christ | 26:63b | 14:61b | 22:67a |  |
| If I told you | — | — | 22:67b–68 |  |
| At right hand | 26:64b | 14:62b | 22:69 | 7:55–56 |
| With clouds | 26:64c | 14:62c |  |  |
| Are you Son | →26:63c | →14:61c | 22:70a |  |
| You say that I am | →26:64a | →14:62a | 22:70b |  |
| Garments torn | 26:65a | 14:63a |  |  |
| No witnesses | 26:65b | 14:63a | 22:71 |  |
| Condemnation | 26:66 | 14:64 |  | 7:57 |
| Execution | (27:35a) | (15:24a) | (23:33b) | 7:58 |

|                  | Matthew (A in PMA) | Mark (A in PMA) | Luke (A) | Acts  |
|------------------|--------------------|-----------------|----------|-------|
| Passersby mock   | 27:39–40           | 15:29–30        | —        |       |
| Receive my spirit |                   |                 | 23:46b   | 7:59  |
| Father forgive   |                    |                 | [23:34a] | 7:60a |
| Death            | (27:50b)           | (15:37b)        | (23:46c) | 7:60b |

The trial source in Proto-Mark A relates Jesus' trial before the Sanhedrin. Apart from its present context in the Synoptics, nothing indicates that the trial occurs either during the Passover or at night. It begins with "false witnesses" who testify that Jesus threatened to tear down the Temple and build another in three days (Mark 14:55–61a; Matt 26:59–63a). Though the Gospel of Luke does not mention these witnesses, it seems to presuppose them later when the Sanhedrin asks, "What need do we have of further testimony?" (Luke 22:71). It seems likely therefore that the account of false witnesses stood in the trial source but was omitted by Luke. Another Lukan omission from this source may be the scene in Proto-Mark A where passersby mock Jesus as he hangs on the cross (Matt 27:39–40; Mark 15:29–30). In this scene the people mock Jesus as one who claimed that he would tear down the Temple and rebuild it in three days. Since this is the same accusation leveled against Jesus by the false witnesses earlier in the trial source, we can assume that this mocking came from the same source.

This account of Jesus' trial and execution by the Sanhedrin bears a striking resemblance to the narrative of Stephen's trial in Acts 6:8–7:1; 7:55–57, as shown in Table 9.5. In both the Synoptics and Acts, the trial takes place before the Sanhedrin in Jerusalem. "False witnesses" testify that the accused threatened to destroy the Temple, and the high priest asks the accused to reply to the charges. In the Proto-Mark A version, Jesus declines to answer (missing from Luke), while in Acts, Stephen gives a lengthy speech. At the end of the interrogation in both the Synoptics and Acts, the accused makes a statement about seeing the Son of Man at the right hand of God, and the statement provokes the condemnation of the tribunal. In Luke's version as in Acts, the accused dies committing his spirit to God. The most common explanation for these parallels has been that Luke modeled Stephen's trial on that of Jesus.[1] However, if our theory is correct, a trial source containing these elements

---

1. E.g., M. Sabbe, "The Son of Man Saying in Acts 7,56," in *Les Actes des Apôtres: Traditions, rédaction, théologie* (ed. J. Kremer; BETL 48; Gembloux: Duculot; Leuven: Leuven University Press, 1979), 241–79.

once existed independently of the rest of the Synoptic passion tradition. If so, it seems likely that this trial source formed the basis for the two Synoptic accounts of Jesus' trial before the Sanhedrin (i.e., in Proto-Mark A and Luke) and for the similar account of Stephen's trial in Acts.

Interestingly, in the Sanhedrin trial source the Romans play no part. The Sanhedrin carries out both the trial and the execution. This absence of the Romans makes sense in the Stephen version and is consistent with Stephen's death by stoning, a method of execution practiced by Jews. The absence of Romans from the Jesus version is more striking, especially given that Jesus dies by crucifixion, a Roman method of execution. The inconsistency suggests that the Stephen version in this respect stands closer to the original story, with both a Jewish judgment and a Jewish method of execution. Crucifixion would have been substituted later, either independently in Proto-Mark A and Luke or even earlier in their common source, to conform the story to other traditions about Jesus' death.

There remains the question of whether the story originally referred to Stephen or Jesus. Even if the story originally narrated a Jewish method of execution, it might still have referred to Jesus, like the tradition about Jesus' death in the Babylonian Talmud.

> It has been taught (in a Baraitha): On the eve of Passover they hanged Yeshu. And an announcer went out, in front of him, for forty days (saying): "He is going to be stoned, because he practiced sorcery and enticed and led Israel astray. Anyone who knows anything in his favor, let him come and plead in his behalf." But, not having found anything in his favor, they hanged him on the eve of Passover. (bSanhedrin 43a)

This Baraitha, like the Sanhedrin trial source, ascribes no role to the Romans in Jesus' death. The accusation that "he practiced sorcery and led Israel astray" is a charge that would have been tried only in a Jewish court, and the reference to stoning implies a Jewish method of execution. The further reference to hanging may or may not represent a different tradition, but it need not refer to crucifixion. This Baraitha may have no relation to the Sanhedrin trial source, but it does show that even in a Jewish context the death of Jesus could be considered a purely Jewish affair, accomplished with a Jewish method of execution. The Sanhedrin trial source, whether it originally referred to Jesus or Stephen, reflects such a tradition.

# Elements of a Passion Narrative

The fourth component of A shared by Proto-Mark A and Luke consists of elements of a passion narrative (Table 9.6).

Table 9.6
Elements of a passion narrative

|                    | Matthew (PMA) | Mark (PMA) | Luke      |
|--------------------|---------------|------------|-----------|
| Up to Jerusalem    | 20:17a        | 10:32ab    | 19:28     |
| Passover sayings   | 26:29         | 14:25      | 22:15–18  |
| To Mount of Olives | 26:30         | 14:26      | 22:39a    |
| Jesus is mocked    | 26:67–68      | 14:65      | 22:63–65  |
| Bandits crucified  | 27:38         | 15:27      | 23:33c    |
| People watch       |               |            | 23:35a    |
| The rulers mock    | 27:41–42a     | 15:31–32a  | 23:35b    |
| The soldiers mock  |               |            | 23:36–37  |
| The bandits mock   | 27:44         | 15:32c     | 23:39     |
| Darkness over land | 27:45         | 15:33      | 23:45a    |
| Temple veil torn   | 27:51a        | 15:38      | 23:45b    |

This passion material fits into the sequence of Proto-Mark A common to Mark and Matthew. It occurs in the same order in Luke, but does not fit into the sequence of Proto-Mark B common to Mark and Luke. We infer therefore that it did not come from Proto-Mark, the common source of Proto-Mark A and Proto-Mark B. Instead, the editor of Proto-Mark A inserted it into Proto-Mark, while Luke independently inserted it into Proto-Mark B. For that reason, Luke has it in a different position than Proto-Mark A with respect to the Synoptic core. In Table 5.2, I assigned this passion narrative to C, a source that entered the Synoptic tradition at more than one stage. I will consider this possibility more fully in Chapter 11.

# Other A Material

When we take the A material in Table 9.1 and subtract the material that also occurs in Luke, a substantial amount of material remains. While some of this material has no parallel elsewhere, some has a parallel in the Fourth Gospel and some has a parallel in Q. To discuss this material fully therefore would require an examination of the Q material and the sources of the Fourth

Gospel. Such an examination exceeds the scope of the present study. I will therefore simply discuss some of the characteristics of the A material with no parallel in Luke.

1. The feeding of the four thousand, a story unique to A, may have some connection with the Jerusalem Hellenists. While Proto-Mark included only the feeding of the five thousand, the A material included the feeding of the four thousand and possibly also the feeding of five thousand. These two narratives must have circulated originally as two different versions of the same story. The most significant difference between them is the number of baskets of leftovers: twelve in the feeding of the five thousand and seven in the feeding of the four thousand. In our discussion of Proto-Mark, we saw reason to believe that the feeding of the five thousand originated in Jerusalem, where the number twelve signified the claim of that community to reconstitute the twelve tribes of Israel, represented by and embodied in the twelve apostles. If the feeding of the four thousand is a variant version of the story, then its substitution of seven for twelve implies that it arose in a community that did not attribute to the twelve the same degree of preeminence. But why the number seven? It is tempting to associate that number with the seven leaders of the "Hellenists" in Jerusalem (Acts 6:1–6). Though Acts describes them merely as distributors of food, some scholars have felt that they actually occupied a more significant role, constituting a council of leadership comparable to the Twelve among the "Hebrews."[2] In any case, the Hellenists apparently associated the number seven with the "daily distribution" of food in their community. Thus the feeding of the four thousand, which connects the distribution of bread with the number seven, may represent a version of the story that the Hellenists in Jerusalem adapted to reflect such distribution in their own community.

2. Another possible connection to the Hellenists is provided by another story unique to A, the story in which the sons of Zebedee seek positions of preeminence (Matt 20:20–24; Mark 10:35–41). In certain stories in the Synoptic tradition, the sons of Zebedee along with Peter constitute an inner circle among Jesus' disciples. As we saw in our discussion of Proto-Mark, such a threesome probably corresponded to the leadership of the Jerusalem church prior to the death of James the son of Zebedee in the early forties. The story in question portrays the sons of Zebedee in a bad light, presenting them as negative examples of desire for exaltation. Such criticism suggests that the

---

2. E.g., Martin Hengel, *Between Jesus and Paul: Studies in the Earliest History of Christianity* (London: SCM, 1983), 13.

story arose among a group that challenged the authority of the Jerusalem inner circle. While we cannot say with certainty that this was the group gathered around the Hellenists of Jerusalem, such a conclusion would at least be plausible. Criticism of the sons of Zebedee may reflect the attitude of the Hellenists toward the leaders of the Hebrews as tensions arose between those two groups.

3. Some of the material unique to A probably originated in Galilee. This seems a safe conclusion to draw from the fact that it locates the resurrection appearance of Jesus to the eleven in Galilee (Table 9.7).

Table 9.7
A Galilean resurrection narrative

|                          | Matthew (A) | Mark (A) |
|--------------------------|-------------|----------|
| I will go to Galilee     | 26:31–32    | 14:27–28 |
| See him in Galilee       | 28:6c–7     | 16:6d–7  |
| See me in Galilee        | 28:9b–10    | —        |
| The eleven go to Galilee | 28:16       | —        |

No other Synoptic source places this appearance in Galilee. Proto-Mark included the appearance to the eleven, apparently without specifying a location. Proto-Mark B, followed by Luke, set the resurrection appearances in Jerusalem and its environs, and the same setting is at least implied in the longer ending of Mark (Luke 24:36–43; Mark 16:14). The A material, however, announces three times that Jesus will see the disciples in Galilee after the resurrection, and the eleven subsequently go there to see him. Whether the editor of Proto-Mark A found this account or created it, it constituted the resurrection narrative of Proto-Mark A. From there it passed into Matthew and partially into Mark.

4. The material unique to A also includes redactional elements that could not have stood alone, but presuppose the Proto-Markan material to which they relate. Since these elements occur in both Mark and Matthew but not Luke, they probably represent redactional additions made to Proto-Mark by the editor of Proto-Mark A. One of the significant features of this redaction is its revision of the eschatological timetable. If our theory is correct, Proto-Mark A was a revision of Proto-Mark, which dates from sometime around 70. Proto-Mark A must therefore be later than this, though how much later is uncertain. The later perspective of Proto-Mark A can be seen in the fact that it revises Proto-Mark's eschatological timetable. The eschatological discourse

in Proto-Mark described a period of tribulation beginning with the "abomination of desolation" to which Daniel referred (Matt 24:15–21; Mark 13:14–19; Luke 21:20–24). In Daniel this tribulation lasts "a time, two times, and half a time," i.e., three and a half years, alternately reckoned as 1290 days or 1335 days (Dan 12:7, 11–12). The description of this event in Proto-Mark makes it clear that the author identified it with the siege of Jerusalem by the Romans, and that view was probably followed by the editor of Proto-Mark A. We do not know how this editor reckoned the years of the siege, but apparently he found that it did not last the prescribed length of time. To account for this discrepancy, the editor of Proto-Mark A added an explanation to the description of the tribulation in Proto-Mark: "And if the Lord had not shortened the days, no flesh would be saved. But because of the elect whom he chose he shortened the days" (Mark 13:20; cf. Matt 24:22). This revision of the timetable, written after the fact, thus serves to explain why the event did not last as long as expected.

5. A second revision to the timetable concerns the time of Jesus' return. The eschatological discourse in Proto-Mark, written around 70, had Jesus predict confidently that the end would come within a generation of his own time (Matt 24:34–35; Mark 13:30–31; Luke 21:32–33). It affirmed that Jesus, the Son of Man, would return immediately after the crisis of the Jewish War. This promise apparently created a problem as soon as it became clear that Jesus had not returned at the expected time. In revising the eschatological discourse, the editor of Proto-Mark A dealt with the problem in a creative manner. He did not omit Jesus' prediction but added a sort of disclaimer directly after it: "But about that day or hour no one knows, neither the angels in heaven, nor the Son, but only the Father" (Mark 13:32; Matt 24:36). This denial that Jesus himself knew the time of the end explained why the prediction that Jesus had just made did not come to pass.

6. The redaction of Proto-Mark by the editor of Proto-Mark A also featured a different view of Jesus' death. While Proto-Mark saw his death as that of a prophet, the editor of Proto-Mark A added two passages that interpret it as vicarious. We have already discussed one of these, the words of institution of the Lord's Supper. In the saying over the cup, Jesus' blood is "poured out for many" (Mark 14:24//Matt 26:28). The editor of Proto-Mark A added this, probably from the liturgical tradition of the church, to the account of Jesus' final Passover meal from another source. Likewise, this editor is probably responsible for the ransom saying, in which Jesus' purpose is "to give his life as a ransom for many" (Mark10:45//Matt 20:28). Only Mark and Matthew have this saying, though Luke has a variant version of the pericope in which it occurs (Luke 22:24–27). Apparently Luke preserves the more original form of the pericope without the ransom saying, while the form with it, preserved

in Mark and Matthew, originated with the editor of Proto-Mark A. The same editor also probably added the scene in which Jesus rebukes Peter after Jesus first predicts his passion (Matt 16:22–23; Mark 8:32–33). This rebuke of Peter for failing to understand the necessity of Jesus' crucifixion may reflect the editor's polemic against more Judaic understandings of Jesus' death, which did not view it as necessary for the salvation of others.

These features of the material unique to A distinguish it from Proto-Mark. Whereas Proto-Mark has links to Judaic Christianity in Jerusalem, the material unique to A has links to the Hellenists and Galilee. Whereas Proto-Mark continues to regard the law as the way to God, the material unique to A looks to the blood of Jesus. Whereas Proto-Mark expresses an unqualified hope for the imminent return of Jesus, the material unique to A reflects the disappointment of that hope.

## Conclusion

We have identified several distinct components within the A material. All of these components were incorporated into Proto-Mark A, four of them independently into Luke, and one into Mark. The following diagram shows this distribution of the A material.

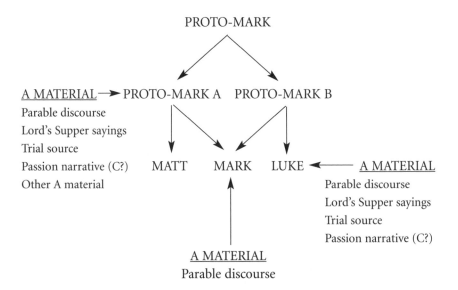

An editor combined the A material with Proto-Mark to produce Proto-Mark A, which served as a source for Mark and Matthew. Luke combined some of the A material with Proto-Mark B to produce his own gospel. Since he worked independently, he inserted this A material at different positions in the sequence of Proto-Mark than did the editor of Proto-Mark A. Mark knew the A material from Proto-Mark A and also knew a separate version of the parable discourse. He included the introduction to the discourse from both sources, thus creating a doublet in his gospel.

The results of this chapter show further reason for rejecting the theory of Markan priority. In the theory of Markan priority, the material common to Mark and Matthew that Luke has in a different position is explained solely as material from Mark that Luke rearranged. While it is likely that Luke did rearrange his sources to some degree, this theory takes no account of the fact that some of the supposedly rearranged material includes major units of tradition such as the parable discourse and the Sanhedrin trial narrative. It is more plausible to assume that these circulated as separate sources and that Luke incorporated them independently of the source shared by Mark and Matthew.

# CHAPTER 10

# *The B Material*

IN TWO PREVIOUS TABLES, we have encountered material from a source that I have designated as "B."

1. As Table 8.1 showed, some material in Proto-Mark B (the source common to Mark and Luke) had no parallel in Proto-Mark A (the source common to Mark and Matthew).[1] Because this material occurs in the "B" version of Proto-Mark, but not the "A" version, I have called it the "B" material. In our theory an editor added the B material to Proto-Mark in order to produce Proto-Mark B. We can state this process as an equation: Proto-Mark + B = Proto-Mark B. Because Mark and Luke both knew Proto-Mark B, they both have the B material in the sequence of Proto-Mark B.

2. Matthew too knew at least some of the B material. In the fourth column of Table 4.3 we found a sequence of material in Matthew that did not fall into the sequence of Proto-Mark A, but formed its own distinct sequence. I did not explain at the time why I designated this material with the letter "B," but the reason should now be clear. It is parallel to part of the B material known to Mark and Luke. Mark and Luke have this material in the same order and in the same position relative to the Synoptic core because both drew it from the same source, Proto-Mark B. Matthew did not know Proto-Mark B, but did know some of the B material, apparently in a document by itself. Since Matthew incorporated this material without knowledge of Proto-Mark B, it occurs in Matthew in a different position relative to the Synoptic core.

Table 10.1 lists the most significant passages of the B material. The editor who combined Proto-Mark with B also probably made redactional changes and additions to these sources. What I have designated as B would therefore include redactional additions to Proto-Markan pericopes in Mark and Luke. However, I have not included these in Table 10.1.

---

1. I exclude the passages of this type in Table 8.2, since we determined that these passages originally did have a parallel in Proto-Mark A.

## Table 10.1
## The B material

|  | Matthew | Mark | Luke |
|---|---|---|---|
| To Capernaum | 4:13b | 1:21a | 4:31a |
| A preaching tour |  | 1:35–39 | 4:42–44 |
| Jesus heals a leper | 8:2–4 | 1:40–45 | 5:12–16 |
| Certain women healed |  | — | 8:2a |
| Mary's seven demons |  | →16:9b | 8:2b |
| And many others |  | →15:41b | 8:3 |
| Jesus calms a storm | 8:18, 23–27 | 4:35a, 36b–41 | 8:22–25 |
| Gerasene demoniac | 8:28–34 | 5:1–17 | 8:26–37a |
| Jesus gets in boat | 9:1a | 5:18a | 8:37b |
| Would-be follower |  | 5:18b–20 | 8:38–39 |
| Jesus crosses sea | 9:1a | 5:21a | 8:40a |
| A crowd gathers |  | 5:21b | 8:40b |
| Jairus's daughter | 9:18–26 | 5:22–43 | 8:41–56 |
| He summons the 12 | 10:1a | 6:7a | 9:1a |
| Power over spirits | 10:1b | 6:7c | 9:1b |
| What not to take | 10:9–10a | 6:8–9 | 9:3 |
| Stay in one house | 10:11 | 6:10 | 9:4 |
| If not received | 10:14 | 6:11 | 9:5 |
| Who denies me |  | 8:38a | 9:26a |
| Unknown exorcist |  | 9:38–39 | 9:49–50a |
| With or against |  | 9:40 | 9:50b |
| Spoiled salt |  | 9:50a | 14:34 |
| Receive as a child | 18:3 | 10:15 | 18:17 |
| Priests and scribes |  | 11:18 | 19:47–48 |
| Widow's offering |  | 12:41–44 | 21:1–4 |
| The women report |  | 16:10–11 | 24:10–11 |
| Appearance to two |  | 16:12–13 | 24:13–33, 35 |
| Jesus taken up |  | 16:19 | 24:51 |

The B material in Matthew consists of a series of miracle stories and a set of mission instructions. These occur in the same order in Matthew as the parallels in Mark and Luke (i.e., Proto-Mark B), but in different positions relative to the Synoptic core. The common order, that is, miracle stories before mission instructions, suggests that both Matthew and the editor of Proto-

Mark B found this material already joined in this order in a common source. Since they used this miracle/mission source independently, they incorporated it in different positions with respect to their respective versions of the Proto-Markan material. Mark and Luke found the miracle/mission material already incorporated into Proto-Mark B. However, evidence presented below suggests that they probably also knew a separate version of the miracle/mission source like that used by Matthew, which they conflated with the version from Proto-Mark B.

## Miracle Stories in B

The first part of the B material in Table 10.1 consists of a series of miracle stories. Here I will focus on those that Matthew shares with Mark and Luke: Jesus heals a leper, calms a storm, casts out a demon, heals a woman with a hemorrhage, and raises Jairus's daughter.

Mark apparently knew two versions of these miracle stories, one incorporated into Proto-Mark B (known also to Luke) and one from the earlier miracle/mission source (known also to Matthew). Evidence for this conclusion comes from the conflated character of these stories in Mark's gospel. Several times in each story, Luke gives the Proto-Mark B version, Matthew gives a different version, while Mark combines the two (Table 10.2).

### Table 10.2
### Conflation in Mark's miracle stories

| Matthew (B) | Mark (PMB+B) | Luke (PMB) |
| --- | --- | --- |
|  | 1:42 the leprosy left him | 5:13 the leprosy left him |
| 8:3 his leprosy was cleansed | and it was cleansed |  |

| Matthew (B) | Mark (PMB+B) | Luke (PMB) |
| --- | --- | --- |
| 8:24 a great tremor | 8:37 a great |  |
|  | storm of wind | 8:23 a storm of wind |

| Matthew (B) | Mark (PMB+B) | Luke (PMB) |
| --- | --- | --- |
| 8:24 the boat was covered by the waves | 8:37 the waves came over into the boat |  |
|  | so that the boat was already filled | 8:23 and they were filling up |

| Matthew (B) | Mark (PMB+B) | Luke (PMB) |
| --- | --- | --- |
| 8:28 from the tombs | 5:2 from the tombs |  |
|  | 5:3 in the tombs | 8:27 in the tombs |

| Matthew (B) | Mark (PMB+B) | Luke (PMB) |
|---|---|---|
| 8:31 send us into the herd of pigs | 5:12 Send us into the pigs, | |
| | so that we may go into them. | 8:32 that he allow them to go into them |

| Matthew (B) | Mark (PMB+B) | Luke (PMB) |
|---|---|---|
| 9:21 For she said to herself, "If I just touch his garment, I will be healed." | 5:28 For she said, "If I touch even his garments, I will be healed." | |
| | 5:29 And immediately the fount of her blood dried up. | 8:44 And at once the flow of her blood stopped. |

| Matthew (B) | Mark (PMB+B) | Luke (PMB) |
|---|---|---|
| 9:22 Jesus turned around | 5:30 Turning around in the crowd, | |
| | he said, "Who touched my garments?" | 8:45 And Jesus said, "Who is it that touched me?" |

| Matthew (B) | Mark (PMB+B) | Luke (PMB) |
|---|---|---|
| | 5:34 Go in peace, | 8:48 Go in peace. |
| 9:22 And the woman was healed from that hour. | and be healed of your affliction. | |

| Matthew (B) | Mark (PMB+B) | Luke (PMB) |
|---|---|---|
| 9:23 and seeing the flutists and the crowd in an uproar | 5:38 And he sees an uproar | |
| | and people weeping and grieving greatly | 8:52 All were weeping and mourning her. |

| Matthew (B) | Mark (PMB+B) | Luke (PMB) |
|---|---|---|
| | 5:37 And he did not let anyone follow with him except Peter, James, and John the brother of James. . . . | 8:51 he did not let anyone enter with him except Peter, John, and James, |
| 9:25 When he had thrown out the crowd . . . | 5:40 Throwing everyone out, | |
| | he took along the father and mother of the child. | and the father and mother of the child. |

Table 10.2 illustrates the "duality" that scholars have long recognized as a characteristic of Mark. As proponents of the Griesbach hypothesis have correctly seen, this duality results from the approach that Mark commonly took when he combined more than one source. The Griesbach hypothesis erred, however, in identifying these sources as Matthew and Luke. In the present instance, Mark was combining two different versions of these miracle stories, one from Proto-Mark B that he shared with Luke, and one from a miracle/mission source like that used by Matthew.

Other features of the material suggest that Luke too knew both versions of the miracle stories. The evidence is greatest in the calming of the storm. Here Mark and Luke have a number of agreements against Matthew, as we would expect if they both knew the story from Proto-Mark B. In addition, however, Luke has significant agreements with Matthew against Mark (Table 10.3 = Table 2.1).

### Table 10.3
### Matthew/Luke agreements in Mark 4:35–41 parr

| Matthew | Mark | Luke |
|---|---|---|
| — | 4:35 when evening came | — |
| 8:23 he got into the boat | 4:36 they took him along as he was in the boat. | 8:22 he got into the boat |
| — | 4:36 and other boats were with him | — |
| 8:23 his disciples followed him | | 8:22 along with his disciples |
| 8:24 in the sea | | 8:23 into the lake |
| — | 4:38 and he was in the stern on the pillow | — |
| 8:25 they approached him | | 8:24 they approached him |
| 8:25 saying | 4:38 and say to him | 8:24 saying |
| — | 4:38 do you not care that | — |
| — | 4:39 "Quiet, be still." | — |
| — | 4:39 the wind | — |
| — | 4:41 a great fear | — |
| 8:27 the men were amazed | | 8:25 they were amazed |

We previously saw that these agreements pose a problem for the theory of Markan priority (Table 2.1). In our theory, these agreements against Mark could be places where Matthew and Luke preserve a more original form of the story that Mark changed in his redaction. However, since Mark did not generally revise his sources so heavily, most of the agreements are probably places where Luke, like Matthew, drew from the miracle/mission source that circulated separately, while Mark followed the Proto-Mark B version. Thus Luke's agreements with Mark against Matthew indicate that Luke knew the Proto-Mark B version, while Luke's agreements with Matthew against Mark indicate that Luke also knew the separate version.

## Mission Instructions in B

The second part of the B material consists of a set of mission instructions. If Mark and Luke knew the miracle stories of B from two sources, and if these miracle stories were followed by mission instructions in each source, then we might expect to find evidence that Mark and Luke also knew two versions of the mission instructions. We do find such evidence, at least in Luke. Luke preserves two distinct sets of mission instructions, the first parallel to Mark in the sequence of Proto-Mark B (Luke 9:1–5), the second from Q (Luke 10:1–16). The first of these has a few agreements of Luke and Mark against Matthew, as we would expect if both evangelists drew it from Proto-Mark B. However, the introduction to the instructions also has what we would not expect, namely, significant agreements between Luke and Matthew, as shown in Table 10.4.

Table 10.4
Introduction to mission instructions

| Matthew | Mark | Luke |
|---|---|---|
| 1 And summoning his Twelve disciples, | 7 And he summoned the Twelve, | 1 Summoning the Twelve, |
| | and he began to send them out two by two, | |
| he gave them authority over unclean spirits so as to cast them out | and he gave them authority over the unclean spirits | he gave them power and authority over all the demons |
| and to heal every disease and every illness . . . | | and to heal diseases. |
| 5 Jesus sent these Twelve . . . | | 2 And he sent them |
| 7 "As you go, preach and say that the kingdom of heaven has drawn near. Heal the sick . . ." | | to preach the kingdom of God and cure [the sick]. |

Here Matthew and Luke have several significant agreements—of order, inclusion, and omission—against Mark. As we pointed out earlier, at Table 2.2, these cannot be explained plausibly by the two-document hypothesis. It appears that Mark followed one version of the material, while Matthew and Luke followed another. But the version followed by Matthew and Luke was not Q, since Luke keeps the Q version separate in Luke 10:1–16. Instead, in our theory, Matthew and Luke followed the miracle/mission source, which constituted part of the B material. While Mark took the introduction from Proto-Mark B, Luke, though he knew Proto-Mark B, took the introduction from the miracle/mission source that he shared with Matthew.

## B Material Absent from Matthew

Except for the miracle stories and the mission instructions, the rest of the B material in Table 10.1 occurs, for the most part, only in Mark and Luke. Either Matthew omitted this material from the miracle/mission source that he knew, or, more likely, it did not stand in that source. The editor responsible for creating Proto-Mark B presumably gathered this material from undetermined sources along with the miracle/mission source and added it to Proto-Mark to create Proto-Mark B.

Three sayings in this material also occur in Q. These are shown in Table 10.5.

Table 10.5
Overlap of B and Q

|  | Mark (B in PMB) | Luke (B in PMB) | Luke (Q) | Matthew (Q) |
|---|---|---|---|---|
| Who confesses me |  |  | 12:8 | 10:32 |
| Who denies me | 8:38a | 9:26a | 12:9 | 10:33 |
| With or against | 9:40 | 9:50b | 11:23 | 12:30 |
| Spoiled salt | 9:50a | 14:34 | 14:34–35a | →5:13 |

In these passages, Mark knew the B version from Proto-Mark B, Matthew knew the Q version, while Luke knew both. In the first two instances, Luke included both versions, thus creating doublets in his gospel. In the third instance, Luke conflated the B version with the Q version.

Other B material not listed in Table 10.1 consists of redaction added to pericopes in Proto-Mark made by the editor of Proto-Mark B. In the pericopes of Proto-Mark B that have a parallel in Matthew, Mark and Luke frequently share elements that are lacking in the parallel in Matthew. In some cases these may represent original elements of the pericope that Matthew omitted. In other cases, they probably represent additions to the pericope made by the editor of Proto-Mark B. Such elements are numerous, but I have not found any that give a clear impression of the tendencies or historical setting of the editor.

## Relation of Proto-Mark and Proto-Mark B

We have theorized that two distinct editors added material to Proto-Mark: one added the A material, the other added the B material. Overall, the B material is far less extensive than the A material. With respect to the amount of material, therefore, Proto-Mark B stood closer to Proto-Mark than did Proto-Mark A. Would it be possible then to regard Proto-Mark B not as a revision of Proto-Mark, but as basically identical with Proto-Mark? Such a possibility would have affinities with Koester's theory, previously described in Chapter 7, in which Luke used Proto-Mark, while Matthew used an expansion of Proto-Mark.

The answer to this question depends on our evaluation of the B material. If what I have called Proto-Mark B were identical with Proto-Mark, then the B material must originally have stood in Proto-Mark. It would be material in Proto-Mark that was retained in the version of that source used by Mark and Luke, but that was either omitted or rearranged as the editor of Proto-Mark A revised Proto-Mark or as Matthew subsequently revised Proto-Mark A. As we have seen, the B material consists of two primary types: 1) pericopes absent from Matthew that occur in Mark and Luke in the sequence of Proto-Mark B; and 2) miracle stories and mission instructions that occur in Mark and Luke in the sequence of Proto-Mark B, but in a different position in Matthew. It would certainly be possible to explain the first type as material from Proto-Mark that was omitted in the line of transmission that led to Matthew. It would be more difficult, however, to explain the second type as material from Proto-Mark. The considerations adduced above suggest that this material came from a miracle/mission source that entered the Synoptic tradition at various points subsequent to the creation of Proto-Mark. The fact that Matthew has this material in a different position than Mark and Luke indicates that Matthew and the editor of Proto-Mark B incorporated it independently into their respective versions of Proto-Mark. It thus apparently never stood in Proto-Mark or Proto-Mark A, but was first combined with the Proto-Markan tradition in Proto-Mark B.

If these conclusions are correct, then Proto-Mark B included some material—the miracle/mission material at least—that did not occur in Proto-Mark. If so, then we must regard Proto-Mark B not as identical to Proto-Mark, but as a revision of Proto-Mark that incorporated additional material.

## Conclusion

In our theory, the editor of Proto-Mark B combined the B material with Proto-Mark, and in this combination it passed down to Mark and Luke. Part of the B material, a miracle/mission source, was also known separately to each of the Synoptic evangelists. The following diagram shows this distribution of the B material.

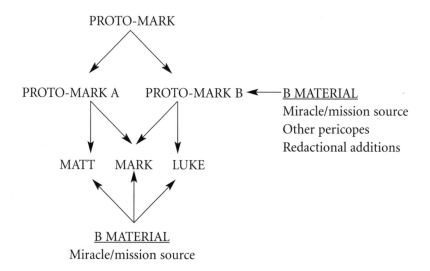

# CHAPTER 11

# *The C Material*

THE C MATERIAL came from a source used independently by each of the Synoptic evangelists. Prior to the Synoptics, some C material had already been incorporated into Proto-Mark and other C material into Proto-Mark A. The Synoptic evangelists thus knew the material both as it had been incorporated into the Proto-Markan gospels and as a separate document. This overlap in their sources led Matthew and Luke occasionally to include doublets of the material, while Mark consistently conflated the different versions of it that he knew. The C source was apparently a passion gospel that focused on "preaching the gospel," the announcement that the kingdom of God was at hand. It circulated prior to the composition of Proto-Mark in 70 CE among a group of Christians who embraced missionary activity toward both Jews and Gentiles.

## C in the Synoptics

We first encountered this source when we found a sequence of material common to Mark and Matthew that did not fit into either Proto-Mark A or the B material (Table 4.3). Subsequently we found a similar sequence common to Mark and Luke that did not fit into either Proto-Mark B or the A material (Table 5.2). For convenience, I reproduce both sequences here as Table 11.1.

Table 11.1

The C material

| | Matthew (C) | Mark (C) | Luke (C) |
|---|---|---|---|
| **John the Baptist** | | | |
| Beginning of gospel | | 1:1 | |
| I send my messenger | | 1:2b | |
| John in wilderness | 3:1b | 1:4a | |

|                        | Matthew (C) | Mark (C)   | Luke (C) |
|------------------------|-------------|------------|----------|
| Kingdom at hand        | 3:2         |            |          |
| John's lifestyle       | 3:4         | 1:6        |          |
| **Ministry in Galilee** |             |            |          |
| To Galilee             | 4:23a       | 1:14b      |          |
| Teaching in synagogues | 4:23b       |            | 4:15a    |
| Preaching the kingdom  | 4:23c       | 1:14c–15   |          |
| Report goes out        | 4:24a       | 1:28       | 4:14b    |
| They bring the ill     | 4:24b       | 1:32       |          |
| Jesus heals many       | 4:24c       | 1:34a      |          |
| A crowd follows        | 4:25a       | 3:7c       | (5:17b)  |
| From Galilee           | 4:25b       | 3:7d       | 5:17c    |
| Judea and Jerusalem    | 4:25c       | 3:7e–8a    | 5:17d    |
| Across the Jordan      | 4:25d       | 3:8c       |          |
| Jesus heals many       |             | 3:10a      | 5:17e    |
| **Jesus chooses 12**   |             |            |          |
| On the mount           | 5:1b        | 3:13a      | 6:12a    |
| Jesus chooses 12       | →10:1–4     | 3:13b–19   | 6:13–16  |
| Down the mount         | 8:1a        |            | 6:17a    |
| A crowd gathers        | 8:1b        | 3:20b      | 6:17b    |
| **Beelzebul debate**   |             |            |          |
| A mute demoniac        | 9:32–33     |            |          |
| By Beelzebul           | 9:34        | 3:22       |          |
| **Further ministry**   |             |            |          |
| Cities and villages    | 9:35        | 6:6b       | 8:1      |
| Jesus' compassion      | 9:36        | 6:34a      |          |
| **Up to Jerusalem**    |             | 10:32ab    | 19:28    |
| **The fig tree**       |             |            |          |
| Jesus enters Jerusalem |             | 11:11a     |          |
| Out to Bethany         | 21:17       | 11:11b     |          |
| Jesus curses fig tree  | 21:18–19a   | 11:12–14   |          |
| Fig tree withers       | 21:19b–20   | 11:20–21   |          |
| Moving mountains       | 21:21–22    | 11:22–24   |          |
| To be forgiven         | →6:14–15    | 11:25[–26] |          |
| **Eschatology**        |             |            |          |
| First the gospel       | 24:14       | 13:10      |          |
| Stay awake             | 24:42       | 13:35a     |          |

|  | Matthew (C) | Mark (C) | Luke (C) |
|---|---|---|---|
| **Passion narrative** |  |  |  |
| Passover sayings |  | 14:25 | 22:15–18 |
| To Mount of Olives |  | 14:26 | 22:39a |
| Jesus is mocked |  | 14:65 | 22:63–65 |
| Bandits crucified |  | 15:27 | 23:33c |
| People watch |  |  | 23:35a |
| The rulers mock |  | 15:31–32a | 23:35b |
| The soldiers mock |  |  | 23:36–37 |
| The bandits mock |  | 15:32c | 23:39 |
| Darkness over land |  | 15:33 | 23:45a |
| Temple veil torn |  | 15:38 | 23:45b |

No two Synoptic Gospels have this material in the same position with respect to any other source. This fact suggests that each Synoptic evangelist used this source independently, each inserting elements from it at different places with respect to their other shared sources.

## C in Proto-Mark A and Proto-Mark B

The C material was known not only by each of the Synoptic evangelists, but probably also at an earlier stage by the editors of the Proto-Markan gospels. This conclusion is based on the fact that in Matthew several doublets occur between the C material and Proto-Mark A, while in Luke several doublets occur between the C material and Proto-Mark B. Table 11.2 shows such doublets in Matthew, and Table 11.3 shows such doublets in Luke.

Table 11.2
Doublets in Matthew between C and PMA

| Matthew (C) | Matthew (C in PMA) |
|---|---|
| 4:23a he went about in the whole of Galilee | 4:12b he withdrew to Galilee |
| 4:23c preaching the gospel of the kingdom | 4:17 Jesus began to preach and say, "Repent, for the kingdom of heaven has drawn near." |
| 4:24 they brought to him all who were ill . . . and who had demons . . . and he healed them | 8:16 they brought to him many who had demons . . . and all the ill he healed |

| Matthew (C) | Matthew (C in PMA) |
|---|---|
| 4:25 and many crowds followed him | 12:15b and many crowds followed him |
| 9:32 . . . behold, they brought him a mute demonized man. 33 And when the demon had been cast out, the mute spoke. And the crowds were amazed, saying, "Such was never seen before in Israel." 34 But the Pharisees said, "He casts out the demons by the ruler of the demons." | 12:22 Then a blind and mute demoniac was brought to him. And he healed him, so that the mute spoke and saw. 23 And all the crowds were astonished and said, "This is not the Son of David, is it?" 24 When the Pharisees heard, they said, "He does not cast out the demons except by Beelzebul the ruler of the demons." |
| 9:36a seeing the crowds he had compassion for them | 14:14a he saw a large crowd and he had compassion on them |

Table 11.3
Doublets in Luke between C and PMB

| Luke (C) | Luke (C in PMB) |
|---|---|
| 4:14b And news went out through the whole region about him. | 4:37 And talk about him went out into every place of the region. |
| 5:17 . . . Pharisees and teachers of the Law who had come from every village of Galilee and Judea and Jerusalem. And there was power of the Lord for him to heal. | 6:17 . . . and a large multitude of the people from all Judea and Jerusalem . . . 19 . . . because power came from him and healed all. |

In both Matthew and Luke, the doublets occur in the same order in both C and the Proto-Markan material. What explanation would account for this overlap? It appears that prior to the creation of the Synoptic Gospels, elements of C already stood in Proto-Mark A and Proto-Mark B. The C material in these gospels was then passed down from Proto-Mark A to Mark and Matthew, and from Proto-Mark B to Mark and Luke. Meanwhile, the C material continued to circulate, and each of the Synoptic evangelists knew a copy. Matthew thus knew two versions of the material, one from Proto-Mark A and one from C, and he sometimes included both to produce doublets. Likewise, Luke knew two versions of the material, one from Proto-Mark B and one from C, and he sometimes included both to produce doublets. Mark knew three versions of the material—from Proto-Mark A, Proto-Mark B, and C. The fact that he knew all three sources but does not include doublets where they overlapped indicates that he either chose one version of the overlapping material or else conflated it into a single more detailed version.

This explanation would also account for another feature of the C material. Some material that falls into the sequence of C in Luke falls into the sequence of Proto-Mark A in Mark and Matthew. This is true for the passion narrative in Table 11.1, along with the earlier element "Up to Jerusalem." We can theorize then that Proto-Mark A took this passion material from C. Mark and Matthew took it from Proto-Mark A, while Luke drew it directly from C. Consequently, Mark and Matthew have this material in the sequence of Proto-Mark A, while Luke has it in the sequence of C.

One could appropriately call C the "Evangelion source" because it favors the term εὐαγγέλιον ("gospel"), particularly in the expression "preaching the gospel." This expression occurs in three passages of C in Table 11.1 (Mark 1:14–15 par; 6:6b parr; 13:10 par). Similarly, the term εὐαγγέλιον without the verb "preaching" occurs in the first verse of Mark: "The beginning of the gospel (εὐαγγέλιον) . . ." (Mark 1:1). It is likely therefore that this verse represents the first sentence of C. Matthew and Luke would have omitted it since they began their gospels two chapters earlier with birth narratives. The term εὐαγγέλιον as the object of the verb "preach" also occurs in two passages in the Proto-Markan tradition: Jesus' anointing at Bethany (Mark 14:9; Matt 26:13) and the saying in which the risen Jesus commissions his disciples to preach (Mark 16:15; cf. Matt 28:19a; Luke 24:47). Therefore, these passages as well probably represent C material that stood in the Proto-Markan gospels.

Taking the C material in Proto-Mark A and Proto-Mark B and adding it to the C material previously identified in Table 11.1, we can make a more comprehensive list of material taken from C. This is given in Table 11.4.

### Table 11.4
### More comprehensive list of C

|  | Matthew (C) | Matthew (C in PMA) | Mark | Luke (C in PMB) | Luke (C) |
|---|---|---|---|---|---|
| **John the Baptist** |  |  |  |  |  |
| Beginning of gospel |  |  | 1:1 |  |  |
| I send my messenger |  |  | 1:2b |  |  |
| John in wilderness | 3:1b |  | 1:4a |  |  |
| Kingdom at hand | 3:2 |  |  |  |  |
| John's lifestyle | 3:4 |  | 1:6 |  |  |
| **Ministry in Galilee** |  |  |  |  |  |
| To Galilee | 4:23a | 4:12b | 1:14b | 4:14a |  |
| Teaching | 4:23b |  |  |  | 4:15a |

|  | Matthew (C) | Matthew (C in PMA) | Mark | Luke (C in PMB) | Luke (C) |
|---|---|---|---|---|---|
| Preaching kingdom | 4:23c | 4:17 | 1:14c–15 | | |
| Report goes out | 4:24a | | 1:28 | 4:37 | 4:14b |
| At evening/sunset | | 8:16a | 1:32ab | 4:40a | |
| They bring the ill | 4:24b | 8:16b | 1:32c | 4:40b | |
| And the demonized | 4:24c | 8:16c | 1:32d | | |
| Jesus heals many | 4:24d | 8:16e | 1:34a | 4:40c | |
| Demons cast out | | 8:16d | 1:34b | 4:41a | |
| Demons silenced | | | 1:34c | 4:41c | |
| Jesus with disciples | | | 3:7a | 6:17b | |
| Jesus withdraws | | 12:15a | 3:7a | | |
| A crowd follows | 4:25a | 12:15b | 3:7c | 6:17c | (5:17b) |
| From Galilee | 4:25b | | 3:7d | | 5:17c |
| Judea and Jerusalem | 4:25c | | 3:7e–8a | 6:17d | 5:17d |
| Across the Jordan | 4:25d | | 3:8c | | |
| Tyre and Sidon | | | 3:8d | 6:17e | |
| Hearing, they come | | | 3:8e | 6:18a | |
| Jesus heals many | | 12:15c | 3:10a | 6:19b | 5:17e |
| They touch him | | | 3:10b | 6:19a | |
| Demons know him | | | 3:11 | →4:41b | |
| Demons silenced | | 12:16 | 3:12 | →4:41c | |
| **Jesus chooses 12** | | | | | |
| On the mount | 5:1b | | 3:13a | | 6:12a |
| Jesus chooses 12 | →10:2–4 | | 3:13b–19 | | 6:13–16 |
| Down the mount | 8:1a | | | | 6:17a |
| A crowd | 8:1b | | 3:20b | | 6:17b |
| **Beelzebul debate** | | | | | |
| A mute demoniac | 9:32–33 | 12:22–23 | | | |
| By Beelzebul | 9:34 | 12:24 | 3:22 | | |
| **Further ministry** | | | | | |
| Cities and villages | 9:35 | | 6:6b | | 8:1 |
| Jesus' compassion | 9:36 | 14:14a | 6:34a | | |
| **Up to Jerusalem** | | 20:17a | 10:32ab | | 19:28 |

| | Matthew (C) | Matthew (C in PMA) | Mark | Luke (C in PMB) | Luke (C) |
|---|---|---|---|---|---|
| **The fig tree** | | | | | |
| Into Jerusalem | | | 11:11a | | |
| Out to Bethany | 21:17 | | 11:11b | | |
| Jesus curses fig tree | 21:18–19a | | 11:12–14 | | |
| Fig tree withers | 21:19b–20 | | 11:20–21 | | |
| Moving mountains | 21:21–22 | | 11:22–24 | | |
| To be forgiven | →6:14–15 | | 11:25[–26] | | |
| **Eschatology** | | | | | |
| First the gospel | 24:14 | | 13:10 | | |
| Stay awake | 24:42 | | 13:35a | | |
| **Passion narrative** | | | | | |
| Jesus anointed | | 26:6–13 | 14:3–9 | →7:36–38 | |
| Passover sayings | | 26:29 | 14:25 | | 22:15–18 |
| To Mount of Olives | | 26:30 | 14:26 | | 22:39a |
| Jesus is mocked | | 26:67–68 | 14:65 | | 22:63–65 |
| Bandits crucified | | 27:38 | 15:27 | | 23:33c |
| People watch | | | | | 23:35a |
| The rulers mock | | 27:41–42a | 15:31–32a | | 23:35b |
| The soldiers mock | | | | | 23:36–37 |
| The bandits mock | | 27:44 | 15:32c | | 23:39 |
| Darkness over land | | 27:45 | 15:33 | | 23:45a |
| Temple veil torn | | 27:51a | 15:38 | | 23:45b |
| **Resurrection** | | | | | |
| Preach the gospel | | 28:19a | 16:15 | 24:47 | |

In Table 11.4, the first Matthean column shows C material that Matthew drew directly from the C source, while the second shows C material that he found in Proto-Mark A. Occasionally these overlap to form doublets. Similarly, the first Lukan column shows C material that Luke found in Proto-Mark B, while the second shows C material that he drew directly from the C source. These too occasionally overlap to form doublets. Mark knew the C material in Proto-Mark A and Proto-Mark B as well as that in the C source. Yet he did not create doublets from the overlapping material, but chose one version or another or conflated them. Mark's C material can therefore be presented in a single column.

# History of the C Tradition

As we have seen, doublets of the C material occur in Matthew and Luke in the sequences of Proto-Mark A and Proto-Mark B, respectively. Such doublets indicate that elements of the C source were known to Proto-Mark A and Proto-Mark B prior to the creation of the Synoptics. Starting with Proto-Mark, we can identify three stages at which material from C entered the Synoptic tradition.

1. In the first stage, the editor of Proto-Mark knew C and incorporated parts of it into his proto-gospel. Table 11.5 shows the C material that occurs in the same position in both Proto-Mark A and Proto-Mark B. We can infer that this material stood in their common source, Proto-Mark.

Table 11.5
C in Proto-Mark

|  | Matthew (PMA) | Mark (PMA+PMB) | Luke (PMB) |
|---|---|---|---|
| **Ministry in Galilee** |  |  |  |
| To Galilee | 4:12b | 1:14b | 4:14a |
| Preaching the kingdom | 4:17 | 1:14c–15 | — |
| Report goes out | — | 1:28 | 4:37 |
| Healing κακῶς ἔχοντας | 8:16 | 1:32, 34a–c | 4:40–41a |
| A crowd follows | 12:15b | 3:7c–8d | 6:17c |
| Jesus heals many | 12:15c | 3:10a | 6:18c |
| At evening/sunset | 8:16a | 1:32ab | 4:40a |
| They bring the ill | 8:16b | 1:32c | 4:40b |
| And the demonized | 8:16c | 1:32d | — |
| Jesus heals many | 8:16e | 1:34a | 4:40c |
| Demons cast out | 8:16d | 1:34b | 4:41a |
| Prohibition to demons | — | 1:34c | 4:41c |
| A crowd follows | 12:15b | 3:7c | 6:17c |
| From Judea and Jerusalem | — | 3:7e–8a | 6:17d |
| Jesus heals many | 12:15c | 3:10a | 6:19b |
| Demons know him | — | 3:11 | →4:41b |
| Prohibition to demons | 12:16 | 3:12 | →4:41c |
| **Beelzebul debate** |  |  |  |
| A mute demoniac | 12:22–23 | — | — |
| By Beelzebul | 12:24 | 3:22 | — |

| | Matthew (PMA) | Mark (PMA+PMB) | Luke (PMB) |
|---|---|---|---|
| **Resurrection** | | | |
| Charge to preach | 28:19a | 16:15 | 24:47 |

The first section in this table, "Ministry in Galilee," corresponds to the C material in Matthew 4:23–25, a passage which shows that this part of C stood as a connected whole before it was incorporated into Proto-Mark. The editor of Proto-Mark inserted other material between the elements of this passage, thus separating them and breaking up their original unity.

2. In the second stage, the editors of Proto-Mark A and Proto-Mark B took over Proto-Mark, which already included some of C. The editor of Proto-Mark A also knew C and added other C material. To the feeding of the five thousand from Proto-Mark, he added "Jesus' compassion" from C (Mark 6:34ab; Matt 14:14a). He also added "Up to Jerusalem" (Mark 10:32ab; Matt 20:17a) and the passion narrative of C. Table 11.6 shows this material.

Table 11.6
C in Proto-Mark A

| | Matthew (C in PMA) | Mark (C in PMA) |
|---|---|---|
| Jesus' compassion | 14:14a | 6:34ab |
| Up to Jerusalem | 20:17a | 10:32ab |
| Anointing at Bethany | 26:6–13 | 14:3–9 |
| Passover sayings | 26:29 | 14:25 |
| To Mount of Olives | 26:30 | 14:26 |
| Jesus is mocked | 26:67–68 | 14:65 |
| Bandits crucified | 27:38 | 15:27 |
| The rulers mock | 27:41–42a | 15:31–32a |
| The bandits mock | 27:44 | 15:32c |
| Darkness over land | 27:45 | 15:33 |
| Temple veil torn | 27:51a | 15:38 |

3. In the final stage, the Synoptic evangelists independently added other material from C to their respective versions of Proto-Mark A and Proto-Mark B. Matthew added the material in the second column of Table 11.4 to Proto-Mark A. In doing so, he created a number of doublets (Table 11.2) between this additional C material and the C material already incorporated into Proto-Mark A. Luke added the material in the sixth column of Table 11.4 to

Proto-Mark B. In doing so, he created a few doublets (Table 11.3) between this additional C material and the C material already incorporated into Proto-Mark B. Mark also added material from C to that which he found in Proto-Mark A and Proto-Mark B, but since he conflated his sources, a closer examination of the material is required to distinguish them.

## Survey of C Material

Since the C source is not lengthy, we can examine its contents in more detail. We will follow the order of the material as it is presented in Table 11.4.

*John the Baptist*

Table 11.7 shows the beginning of the C source as we have reconstructed it. Elements from this pericope were used by Matthew and Mark but not by Luke.

Table 11.7
Beginning of C

| Matthew (C) | Mark (C) |
|---|---|
| | 1:1 The beginning of the *gospel* of Jesus Christ [the Son of God]. |
| | 1:2b Behold I send my messenger before your face who will prepare your way. |
| 3:1b John the Baptist came preaching in the wilderness of Judea | 1:4a John the Baptizer appeared in the wilderness |
| 3:2 and saying, "Repent, for the kingdom of heaven has drawn near." | |
| 3:4 He, John, had his clothes from camel hair and a leather belt around his waist, and his food was locusts and wild honey. | 1:6 John was clothed in camel hair and a leather belt around his waist and was eating locusts and wild honey. |

Three elements in this pericope occur in only one gospel or the other, but nevertheless probably came from C. Mark 1:1 has no parallel in Matthew, but since it contains the word εὐαγγέλιον ("gospel"), a key term for C, it most likely represents the first sentence of C. Since Matthew had already begun his gospel two chapters before, he did not need a new beginning here and so omitted it. The next sentence, Mark 1:2b, also has no parallel in Matthew. This sentence cites Malachi 3:1 (cf. Exod 23:20), the promise of a messenger to come, whom Malachi apparently identified as Elijah (Mal 4:5). This quotation introduces John the Baptist (Matt 3:1b//Mark 1:4a). Since the final sentence of the pericope (Matt 3:4// Mark 1:6) describes John as dressed in clothing similar to that of Elijah the prophet (2 Kgs 1:8), it is likely that the allusion to Elijah in Mark 1:2b also came from C. Matthew 3:2, which has no parallel in Mark, depicts John as announcing the imminence of the kingdom. Later the C source will depict Jesus preaching the same message that John preaches here: "Repent for the kingdom of God has drawn near" (Matt 4:17; Mark 1:14b–15). It is likely therefore that Matthew 3:2 also came from C.

It appears then that the beginning of the C source showed John preaching the gospel of the imminent kingdom and implicitly identified him as Elijah. Since this material does not fit into the sequence of Proto-Mark A, we can infer that Mark and Matthew drew it independently from C and inserted it at different positions with respect to the Proto-Mark A material.

### Ministry in Galilee

If C included a section on Jesus' baptism by John, we cannot reconstruct it. The next recoverable section of C gives a summary of Jesus' ministry in Galilee. Matthew has preserved this summary intact in Matthew 4:23–25:

> 23 And he went about in the whole of Galilee, teaching in their synagogues and preaching the gospel of the kingdom [and healing every sickness and every disease among the people]. 24 And the report about him went out into the whole of Syria. And they brought to him all who were ill with various diseases [and afflicted with pains] and demonized [and the lunatics and the paralyzed], and he healed them. 25 And many crowds followed him from Galilee [and Decapolis] and Jerusalem and Judea and across the Jordan.

The bracketed items occur only in Matthew and may be Matthean redaction. The rest of the summary was known to all three Synoptic evangelists, both from C and from its incorporation into Proto-Mark, as shown in Table 11.8.

Table 11.8
Ministry in Galilee

| Matthew (C) | Matthew (C in PMA) | Mark | Luke (C in PMB) | Luke (C) |
|---|---|---|---|---|
| 4:23a And he went about in the whole of Galilee, | 4:12b he withdrew to Galilee | 1:14b Jesus came into Galilee | 4:14a And Jesus returned . . . to Galilee | |

| Matthew (C) | Matthew (C in PMA) | Mark | Luke (C in PMB) | Luke (C) |
|---|---|---|---|---|
| 4:23b teaching in their synagogues | | | | 4:15a And he was teaching in their synagogues . . . |
| 4:23c and **preaching the gospel** of the kingdom . . . | 4:17 Jesus began to **preach** and say, "Repent, for the kingdom of heaven has drawn near." | 1:14c **preaching the gospel** of God 15 and saying, "The time is fulfilled and the kingdom of God has drawn near. Repent and believe in the **gospel**." | — | |
| 4:24a And the report about him went out into the whole of Syria. | | 1:28 And the report about him went out immediately everywhere into the whole region of Galilee. | 4:37 And talk about him went out into every place of the region. | 4:14b And news went out through the whole region him |
| | 8:16a When evening came | 1:32a When evening came, when the sun set, | 4:40a The sun having set, | |
| 4:24b And they brought to him all who were ill with various diseases . . . | 8:16b they brought to him | 1:32c they were bringing to him all who were ill | 4:40b all who had sick with various diseases, they brought them to him | |
| 4:24c and demonized . . . | 8:16c many demonized | 1:32d and the demonized | | |
| 4:24d and he healed them. | 8:16e and all who were ill he healed. | 1:34a And he healed many who were ill with various diseases | 4:40c and . . . he healed them. | |

| Matthew (C) | Matthew (C in PMA) | Mark | Luke (C in PMB) | Luke (C) |
|---|---|---|---|---|
| | 8:16d And he cast out the spirits with a word, | 1:34b and cast out many demons. | 4:41a And demons too came out of many . . . | |
| | | 1:34c And he did not let the demons speak, because they knew him. | 4:41c he did not permit them to speak because they knew that he was the Christ. | |
| | 12:15a When he found out, Jesus withdrew from there. | 3:7a And Jesus with his disciples withdrew . . . | 6:17b . . . and a large crowd of his disciples, | |
| 4:25a And many crowds followed him | 12:15b And many crowds followed him, | 3:7c And a large multitude | 6:17c and a large multitude of the people | 5:17b Pharisees and teachers of the law who had come |
| 4:25b from Galilee . . . | | 3:7d from Galilee followed | | 5:17c from every village of Galilee |
| 4:25c and Jerusalem and Judea | | 3:7e and from Judea 8a and from Jerusalem . . . | 6:17d from all Judea and Jerusalem | 5:17d and Judea and Jerusalem. |
| 4:25d and across the Jordan. | | 3:8c and across the Jordan | | |
| | | 3:8d and around Tyre and Sidon. | 6:17e and the coast of Tyre and Sidon | |
| | | 3:8e A large multitude, hearing what he was doing, came to him. | 6:18a who came to hear him . . . | |

| Matthew (C) | Matthew (C in PMA) | Mark | Luke (C in PMB) | Luke (C) |
|---|---|---|---|---|
| | 12:15c and he healed them all. | 3:10a For he healed many, | 6:19b because power was going out from him and curing all. | 5:17e And there was power of the Lord for him to cure. |
| | | 3:10b so that all who had afflictions fell on him to touch | 6:19a And all the crowd was seeking to touch him, | |
| | | 3:11 And the unclean spirits, when they saw him, fell before him and cried out, saying, "You are the Son of God." | →4:41b . . . crying out and saying, "You are the Son of God." | |
| | 12:16 And he warned them not to make him known. | 3:12 And he warned them repeatedly not to make him known. | →4:41c And warning . . . | |

The first two columns show the two versions of this material in Matthew, the one cited above (Matt 4:23–25) directly from C and a doublet integrated into the sequence of Proto-Mark A. Likewise, the last two columns show the two versions of this material in Luke, one from C and one from the parallel material in Proto-Mark B, with the two versions occasionally overlapping to form doublets. All of the elements of this section originally stood together as a connected whole in C, as seen in Matthew 4:23–25. When the editor of Proto-Mark took it over, however, he not only expanded the summary, but also inserted other pericopes between the elements, breaking up the original unity. Therefore, the elements of this material that the Synoptics have included from the Proto-Markan gospels are spread out over several chapters. Luke followed a similar procedure, so that the summary that he took from C now appears in two different contexts (Luke 4:14b–15a and 5:17). Only Matthew 4:23–25 preserves the original unity of the summary.

While both Matthew and Luke have doublets of this summary, i.e., two versions in different contexts, Mark has duplications within the same context as a result of conflating C, Proto-Mark A, and Proto-Mark B. 1) Where Proto-Mark A read "When evening came" (Matt 8:16a), and Proto-Mark B read

"The sun having set" (Luke 4:40a), Mark conflated the two: "When evening came, when the sun set" (Mark 1:32a). 2) The C source had the wording "they brought to him all who were ill" (Matt 4:24b), while the parallel in Proto-Mark A read "all who were ill he healed" (Matt 8:16d). Mark included both in the same context: "they were bringing to him all who were ill. . . . And he healed many who were ill" (Mark 1:32c, 34a). 3) In C, crowds followed Jesus from "across the Jordan" (Matt 4:25d), while Proto-Mark B changed this to "the coast of Tyre and Sidon" (Luke 6:17e). Mark included both geographical references from his sources: "and across the Jordan and around Tyre and Sidon" (Mark 3:8cd). Thus Mark, rather than creating doublets, combined the material into a single version, sometimes duplicating the same material from the different sources. As a result of such conflation, Mark's version became fuller and more detailed than that of his sources.

## Jesus Chooses Twelve

Table 11.9 shows the next segment of C material.

### Table 11.9
### Jesus chooses Twelve

|  | Matthew | Mark | Luke |
|---|---|---|---|
| On the mount | 5:1 | 3:13a | 6:12b |
| Names of the 12 | →10:1–4 | 3:13b–19 | 6:13–16 |
| Down the mount | 8:1a | — | 6:17a |
| A crowd | 8:1b | 3:20b | 6:17b |

No two Synoptics have this material in exactly the same position with respect to Proto-Mark. Matthew has placed it prior to the controversy stories. Since Matthew's version immediately follows the summary of Jesus' ministry in Galilee from C (Matt 4:23–25), it is probably the immediate continuation of the C source. Mark and Luke both have the material after the controversy stories, but while Luke has it before Jesus' ministry to a crowd, Mark has it after. The different placements suggest that all three evangelists drew this material directly from C and independently combined it with their respective versions of Proto-Mark.

Within this material, both Mark and Luke agree on placing Jesus' choice of the Twelve immediately after his ascent to the mount. This agreement makes it likely that they both preserve the original order of C: Jesus ascended the mount, chose the Twelve, then descended and encountered a crowd. Matthew rearranged this material by transferring the names of the Twelve to his missionary discourse in Matthew 10. He also inserted a lengthy collection of teaching material between Jesus' ascent to the mount and his descent from it. Thus, in Matthew's redaction, the mountain serves as the platform for the Sermon on the Mount rather than for the selection of the Twelve.

It is likely that Mark and Luke knew two lists of the Twelve: one from C and one from another source that they independently conflated with the list from C. This conclusion can be inferred from a comparison of the four extant lists of the Twelve (Table 11.10).

Table 11.10
### Lists of the Twelve

| Matthew 10:2–4 | Mark 3:16–19 | Luke 6:14–16 | Acts 1:13 |
|---|---|---|---|
| Simon Peter | Simon Peter | Simon Peter | Peter |
| Andrew his brother | | Andrew his brother | |
| James | James | James | John |
| the son of Zebedee | the son of Zebedee | | |
| John his brother | John his brother | John | James |
| | Andrew | | Andrew |
| Philip | Philip | Philip | Philip |
| | | | Thomas |
| Bartholomew | Bartholomew | Bartholomew | Bartholomew |
| | Matthew | Matthew | Matthew |
| Thomas | Thomas | Thomas | |
| Matthew | | | |
| James of Alphaeus | James of Alphaeus | James of Alphaeus | James of Alphaeus |
| Thaddeus | Thaddeus | | |
| Simon of Cana | Simon of Cana | Simon the Zealot | Simon the Zealot |
| | | Judah of James | Judah of James |
| Judas Iscariot | Judas Iscariot | Judas Iscariot | |

The variations between the four lists can be explained most simply as developments from two original lists. The list from C has been best preserved by Matthew. It listed Andrew second after Peter, used the explanatory terms "his brother" and "the son of Zebedee," and included Thaddeus as one of the Twelve. The other list has been best preserved in Acts. This list put the "inner circle" of Peter, James, and John together before Andrew, did not include the expansions "his brother" or "the son of Zebedee," and included Judah of James rather than Thaddeus as one of the Twelve. The list on which Acts drew probably mentioned James before John. Luke, who elsewhere in Acts pairs

Peter and John (Acts 3:1; 8:14; etc.), probably inverted the order of James and John in order to pair John with Peter here too. The original list may also have had Thomas after Matthew.

While Matthew and Acts represent one list or the other, Mark and Luke have independently conflated the two, preserving distinctive features of each. Mark, on the one hand, has listed the inner circle before Andrew like Acts, but included Thaddeus like Matthew. Luke, on the other hand, has taken the reverse approach: like Matthew, he has listed Andrew second, but like Acts, he has included Judah of James instead of Thaddeus.

Thus, the best explanation for the evidence seems to be that all three Synoptics knew a version of the list like that in Matthew from C. In addition, Mark and Luke knew another version of the list, similar to that in Acts, which they independently conflated with the list from C. It is not clear from what source Mark and Luke obtained this second list. It is possible that it came from their common source, Proto-Mark B, or that it came to them as a separate document, not integrated into any larger source.

### Beelzebul Debate

The next observable pericope of C consisted of the Beelzebul debate (Table 11.11).

Table 11.11

The Beelzebul debate

|                       | Matthew (C) | Matthew (C in PMA) | Mark    | Luke (C in PMB) |
|-----------------------|-------------|--------------------|---------|------------------|
| A mute demoniac       | 9:32–33     | 12:22–23           | —       | —                |
| By Beelzebul          | 9:34        | 12:24              | 3:22    | —                |
| Satan divided         |             | 12:25–26           | 3:23–26 | —                |
| Binding the strong    |             | 12:29              | 3:27    | —                |
| Unforgivable sin      |             | 12:31              | 3:28–29 | —                |
| Because they said     |             |                    | 3:30    | →11:18b          |

It is unclear how much of the Beelzebul debate stood in C. Only Matthew gives the C version by itself, in Matthew 9:32–34, and there only the first two elements of the debate appear (i.e., "A mute demoniac" and "By Beelzebul"). Mark and Matthew knew a more extensive version from their common source, Proto-Mark A. Mark and Luke probably found a parallel version in Proto-Mark B, but Luke omitted most of this in favor of a Q version (not shown in Table 11.11), retaining only the element "Because they said," which he moved to conflate with the Q version. Since the pericope stood in Proto-Mark A and probably in Proto-Mark B, it must have stood in their common source, Proto-Mark.

*Further Ministry*

After the Beelzebul debate—immediately after, according to Matthew—C included a second summary of Jesus' ministry. This second summary (Matt 9:35 parr) is quite similar to the first (Matt 4:23 parr).

> And he went about in the whole of Galilee, teaching in their synagogues and preaching the gospel of the kingdom. . . . (Matt 4:23)

> And Jesus went about in all the cities and villages, teaching in their synagogues and preaching the gospel of the kingdom. . . . (Matt 9:35)

The second summary occurs in some form in all three Synoptics (Table 11.12).

Table 11.12<br>Mark 6:6b and parallels

| Matthew 9:35 (C) | Mark 6:6b (C) | Luke 8:1 (C) |
|---|---|---|
| And Jesus went about in all the cities and villages | And he went about in the surrounding villages | and he was traveling through each city and village |
| teaching in their synagogues | teaching | |
| and *preaching the gospel* of the kingdom | | *preaching and proclaiming the gospel* of the kingdom of God |

While all three evangelists included this summary, each inserted it in a different position with respect to the Proto-Mark material. Matthew has it in the middle of the controversy stories. Luke has it later, after the controversy stories but before the pericope "Jesus' true family." Mark has it still later, after that pericope. Matthew preserved the key C expression "preaching the *evangelion*," while Luke changed *evangelion* to the verb form of the word. Mark included neither, apparently feeling that it sufficed to mention Jesus' teaching, one of Mark's favorite themes (see Table 2.11).

This summary in C continued immediately, as it does in Matthew 9:36, with a description of Jesus' compassion (Table 11.13).

Table 11.13

Jesus' compassion

| Matthew (C) | Matthew (C in PMA) | Mark (C in PMA) |
|---|---|---|
| 9:36 Seeing the crowds, he felt compassion for them | 14:14a And getting out, he saw a large crowd and felt compassion for them. | 6:34a And getting out, he saw a large crowd and felt compassion for them |
| because they were harassed and worn down like sheep without a shepherd. | | 6:34b because they were like sheep without a shepherd. |

Matthew 9:36 preserved the original sequence of this C material following the summary of Jesus' ministry in Matthew 9:35. The editor of Proto-Mark A excerpted this material from C and integrated it into the feeding of the five thousand from Proto-Mark (Matt 14:14a//Mark 6:34a). Thus Matthew has doublets of this description, one in the sequence of C (Matt 9:36) and one in the sequence of Proto-Mark A (Matt 14:14a), while Mark has it in the sequence of Proto-Mark A (Mark 6:34ab). It is unclear whether the second half of the sentence in Mark (Mark 6:34b) occurred in Proto-Mark A and was omitted in Matthew 14:14, or whether Mark found it in his copy of C (cf. Matt 9:36b) and added it to a truncated version in Proto-Mark A.

## Up to Jerusalem

C continued with a statement that Jesus went up to Jerusalem. The editor of Proto-Mark A inserted this statement before the third passion prediction in Proto-Mark, and Mark and Matthew followed Proto-Mark A (Mark 10:32ab; Matt 20:17a). Luke drew the statement independently from C and placed it later in the narrative, immediately before the triumphal entry (Luke 19:28). Table 11.14 gives both versions.

Table 11.14

Going up to Jerusalem

| Matt 20:17a (C in PMA) | Mark 10:32ab (C in PMA) | Luke 19:28 (C) |
|---|---|---|
| And as Jesus was going up to Jerusalem . . . | They were on the way, going up to Jerusalem, and Jesus was preceding them . . . | And having said these things, he went in front going up to Jerusalem. |

*The Fig Tree*

Once Jesus arrived in Jerusalem, he went to Bethany, near which he cursed a fig tree. If this story came from C, as I have assumed, it is part of C that neither the Proto-Markan gospels nor Luke utilized. Mark and Matthew drew this material directly from C, and each inserted it into a different position with respect to Proto-Mark A (Table 11.15).

Table 11.15

The fig tree

|  | Matthew (C) | Matthew (PMA) | Mark (PMA) | Mark (C) |
|---|---|---|---|---|
| Going to Jerusalem |  | 20:17a | 10:32ab |  |
| Triumphal entry |  | 21:1–9 | 11:1–10 |  |
| Jesus enters Jerusalem |  |  |  | 11:11a |
| Out to Bethany |  |  |  | 11:11b |
| Jesus curses fig tree |  |  |  | 11:12–14 |
| Jesus enters Jerusalem | — | 21:10a | 11:15a |  |
| Jesus cleanses Temple |  | 21:12–13 | 11:15b–17 |  |
| Out to Bethany | 21:17 |  |  |  |
| Jesus curses fig tree | 21:18–19a |  |  |  |
| Fig tree withers | 21:19b–20 |  |  | 11:20–21 |
| Moving mountains | 21:21–22 |  |  | 11:22–24 |
| To be forgiven | →6:14–15 |  |  | 11:25[–26] |

In Table 11.15, the inner columns show the sequence of Proto-Mark A common to Matthew and Mark, respectively. The outer columns show how they have placed the fig tree material differently with respect to this common sequence. Mark split the story in two, placing part of it (Mark 11:11–14) before the cleansing of the Temple and part after (Mark 11:20–25). Matthew, on the other hand, kept the story together (Matt 21:17–22), placing it after the cleansing of the Temple. Matthew also apparently moved the last saying in the fig tree material to his Sermon on the Mount (Matt 6:14–15).

*Eschatology*

The next C material that we find consists of two sayings with an eschatological cast (Table 11.16). The first saying refers to preaching the *evangelion,*

## Table 11.16
## Eschatological sayings

| Matthew (C) | Mark (C) |
|---|---|
| 24:14 And this *gospel* of the kingdom will be *preached* in the whole world as a testimony to all the nations, and then will come the end. | 13:10 And to all the nations the *gospel* must first be *preached*. |
| 24:42 Stay awake, then, because you do not know on what day your Lord is coming. | 13:35a Stay awake then. For you do not know when the Lord of the house is coming . . . |

a theme that we have found characteristic of C. The two sayings appear in the eschatological discourse in both Matthew and Mark, but at different positions in each gospel with respect to Proto-Mark A. We can infer therefore that Matthew and Mark drew them directly from C and independently added them to the Proto-Markan eschatological discourse.

### Anointing at Bethany

The story of Jesus' anointing occurs in Proto-Mark A, in Luke 7:36–50, and in John 12:1–8. The Proto-Mark A version appears to be conflated from two distinct versions, one like that in John and one without a parallel elsewhere. Table 11.17 shows the words of Jesus in these two versions.

## Table 11.17
## Anointing at Bethany

| Mark 14:6–9 (Matt 26:10–13) C in PMA | Mark 14:6–9 (Matt 26:10–13) PM in PMA | John 12:7–8 |
|---|---|---|
|  | 6a Leave her alone. | 7 Leave her alone, |
|  | 8b She acted beforehand to anoint my body for entombment. | so that she may keep it for the day of my entombment. |
| 6b Why do you trouble her? She did a good deed to me. |  |  |
|  | 7 For you always have the poor with you and when you wish you can do good to them, but you do not always have me. | 8 For you always have the poor with you, but you do not always have me. |

| Mark 14:6–9<br>(Matt 26:10–13)<br>C in PMA | Mark 14:6–9<br>(Matt 26:10–13)<br>PM in PMA | John 12:7–8 |
|---|---|---|
| 8a What she had she did. | | |
| 9 Amen I say to you, wherever **the gospel is preached** in the whole world, what she did will also be told in her memory. | | |

The second Proto-Mark A column has a parallel in John, while the first does not. We previously saw that this story probably stood in Proto-Mark. The second column probably came from that source. The first column apparently came from C, since it contains C's typical theme of preaching the gospel: "wherever **the gospel is preached** in the whole world" (Mark 14:9; Matt 26:13). The editor of Proto-Mark A conflated the version from Proto-Mark with the version from C, and this conflated version passed into both Mark and Matthew. Luke presumably knew the Proto-Mark version from Proto-Mark B, but retained only part, which he conflated with an earlier story (Luke 7:36–38).

### Passion Narrative

Did the C source have a passion narrative? A number of elements in Luke's passion narrative do not fit into the sequence of Proto-Mark B, but could fit in the sequence of C (Table 5.2). The same elements appear in Mark and Matthew in the sequence of Proto-Mark A. Table 11.18 shows these elements. We could account for these elements in more than one way. 1) They could be elements of Proto-Mark's passion narrative that either Luke or the editor of Proto-Mark A rearranged. 2) They could be elements from an otherwise unknown passion source that Luke and the editor of Proto-Mark A independently combined with Proto-Mark. 3) They could be elements of a passion narrative in C that Luke and the editor of Proto-Mark A independently combined with Proto-Mark. One consideration supports the third option. Material that probably belongs to C has Jesus going to Jerusalem and cursing a fig tree nearby (Table 11.15 above). This transition from Galilee to Jerusalem seems to prepare the way for a passion narrative. I will tentatively assume therefore that the elements in Table 11.18 came from a passion narrative in C and were taken over from C by Proto-Mark A. Mark and Matthew drew them from Proto-Mark A and thus have them in the same position with respect to Proto-Mark's passion narrative. Luke, on the other hand, drew them directly from C and inserted them at different places in the sequence of Proto-Mark than did the editor of Proto-Mark A.

## Table 11.18
### Possible passion material from C

|  | Matthew (C in PMA) | Mark (C in PMA) | Luke (C) |
|---|---|---|---|
| Passover sayings | 26:29 | 14:25 | 22:15–18 |
| To Mount of Olives | 26:30 | 14:26 | 22:39a |
| Jesus is mocked | 26:67–68 | 14:65 | 22:63–65 |
| Bandits crucified | 27:38 | 15:27 | 23:33c |
| People watch |  |  | 23:35a |
| The rulers mock | 27:41–42a | 15:31–32a | 23:35b |
| The soldiers mock |  |  | 23:36–37 |
| The bandits mock | 27:44 | 15:32c | 23:39 |
| Darkness over land | 27:45 | 15:33 | 23:44 |
| Temple veil torn | 27:51a | 15:38 | 23:45 |

If this material came from C, then Mark and Matthew would have known two versions of it, one from Proto-Mark A and one directly from C (shared with Luke). We do find a little evidence that Mark knew two versions of this, which, in agreement with his usual practice, he conflated (Table 11.19).

## Table 11.19
### Conflation of C's passion material in Mark

| Matthew (C in PMA) | Mark (C in PMA + C) | Luke (C) |
|---|---|---|
|  | 15:32 the Christ | 23:35 the Christ of God |
| 27:42 king of Israel | the king of Israel |  |

This passion material begins with a set of sayings relating to a Passover meal. Since these immediately follow Jesus' anointing at Bethany in the sequence of C, we can assume that C presented Jesus' meal at Bethany as a Passover meal. This meal at Bethany is Jesus' Last Supper. The Passover sayings spoken at this meal in C have been preserved more fully in Luke than in Proto-Mark A, as Table 11.20 shows. In this tradition, Jesus pronounced sayings concerning the Passover meal (Luke 22:15–16) and the Passover cup (Luke 22:17–18). This meal presumably consisted of the traditional Passover lamb and the items associated with it. It is followed by a cup of wine. The sayings concerning the meal and cup do not interpret them as metaphors for Jesus' body and blood, but as anticipations of the coming kingdom of God. The meal and the ideas associated with it are thus predominantly Jewish, with little that is distinctively Christian about them.

Table 11.20

Passover meal and cup

| Mark 14:23, 25 (C in PMA) cf. Matt 26:27, 29 | Luke 22:15–18 (C) |
|---|---|
| [omitted] | 15 And he said to them, "With desire I have desired to eat this Passover with you before I suffer. 16 For I say to you that I will not eat it until it is fulfilled in the kingdom of God." |
| 23 And taking a cup and giving thanks, he gave it to them and all drank from it . . . | 17 And taking a cup and giving thanks, he said, "Take this and distribute it among yourselves. |
| 25 "Amen I say to you that I will not again drink of the fruit of the vine until that day when I drink it anew in the kingdom of God." | 18 For I say to you that I will not drink of the fruit of the vine from now until the kingdom of God comes." |

To this tradition of the Last Supper as a Passover meal, both Proto-Mark A and Luke added other A material: the words of institution of the Christian meal that Paul called "the Lord's Supper" (1 Cor 11:20). We discussed these previously at Table 9.4. Two considerations point to the conclusion that Proto-Mark A and Luke independently combined the Lord's Supper tradition with the Passover tradition. First, the words of institution of the Lord's Supper appear in Paul independent of the Passover tradition (1 Cor 11:23–26). This fact suggests that the two traditions had different origins and originally circulated independently. Second, the two traditions are combined differently in Luke than in Mark and Matthew. This fact suggests that Luke combined the two traditions independently of Proto-Mark A, the common source of Mark and Matthew.

Luke combined the two traditions by placing them consecutively: first the Passover tradition (Luke 22:15–18), then the Lord's Supper tradition (Luke 22:19–20). As a consequence of including all of both, Luke's version has two meals and two cups: a Passover meal followed by a cup, then the bread of the Lord's Supper followed by a second cup. The manuscripts of Luke at this point show a number of variant readings, all of which can be understood as attempts to reduce Luke's two cups to one, in accordance with the church's usual practice of the Lord's Supper. The editor of Proto-Mark A avoided this problem from the beginning by combining the two meal traditions into a single meal and cup. His procedure can be seen by placing his single meal in parallel with Luke's two meals, as in Table 11.21. The first two columns of

Table 11.21
Conflation of supper sayings in PMA

| Luke 22:15–18 Passover | Luke 22:19–20 Lord's Supper | Mark 14:22–25 par (PMA) Passover + Lord's Supper |
|---|---|---|
| | 19 And taking bread and giving thanks, he broke it and gave it to them saying, "This is my body given for you. Do this in memory of me." | 22 And as they were eating, taking bread and blessing it, he broke it and gave it to them and said, "Take it. This is my body." |
| 15 And he said to them, "With desire I have desired to eat this Passover with you before I suffer. 16 For I say to you that I will not eat it until it is fulfilled in the kingdom of God." | | [omitted] |
| 17 And taking a cup and giving thanks, he said, "Take this and distribute it among yourselves. | 20 And the cup likewise after supper, | 23 And taking a cup and giving thanks, he gave it to them and all drank from it. |
| | saying, "This cup is the new covenant in my blood, which is poured out for you." | 24 And he said to them, "This is the blood of my covenant that is poured out for many. |
| 18 For I say to you that I will not drink of the fruit of the vine from now until the kingdom of God comes." | | 25 Amen I say to you that I will not again drink of the fruit of the vine until that day when I drink it anew in the kingdom of God." |

Table 11.21 gives Luke's Passover tradition and Lord's Supper tradition, respectively. The last column shows the corresponding material in Proto-Mark A. As this column indicates, Proto-Mark A did not place the traditions one after the other as Luke did, but took elements from each, combining them into an account of a single meal followed by a single cup. For the meal, Proto-

Mark A used only the Lord's Supper tradition, but for the cup, combined both traditions.

It is quite possible that the words of institution of the Lord's Supper entered the Synoptic tradition not as part of a larger source but as an isolated formula familiar from the church's liturgical tradition. It is less likely that the Passover meal tradition circulated apart from a larger source. It seems probable therefore that the Passover meal tradition belonged to C, while the words of institution came from oral tradition. We can thus summarize the development of the Last Supper pericope. 1) C's passion narrative, known to both Proto-Mark A and Luke, described the Last Supper as a Jewish Passover meal followed by a cup of wine. 2) Proto-Mark A revised this Passover account by conflating it with the Lord's Supper formula familiar from the church's liturgical tradition. The conflated account in Proto-Mark A had a single meal followed by a single cup. Both Mark and Matthew followed Proto-Mark A. 3) Luke also revised the Passover account by adding the Lord's Supper formula. However, he did not mix the traditions like Proto-Mark A, but placed the Lord's Supper tradition after the Passover tradition.

After the Passover sayings in C comes a transition to the Mount of Olives, placed in Proto-Mark A before Jesus predicts his denial, but afterward in Luke. Presumably C then related Jesus' arrest and some sort of judgment. What is preserved includes a scene in which those who arrest Jesus mock him. Proto-Mark A has this after Jesus' trial by the Sanhedrin but before Peter's denial. Just the reverse is true for Luke, where the mocking occurs after Peter's denial but before the trial. The remaining elements from C relate to Jesus' crucifixion. All of these too occur in a different place in Luke than in Proto-Mark A. Elements of C that can be identified emphasize groups that mocked Jesus during his crucifixion. The crucifixion was accompanied by portents as the sky darkened and the Temple veil was torn. Presumably the narrative concluded with Jesus' death and burial. As this summary indicates, all of these elements occur in the same sequence in Luke as in Proto-Mark A, yet all occur in different positions with respect to Proto-Mark's passion narrative. Most plausibly, therefore, they came from a source (presumably C) that Luke and the editor of Proto-Mark A independently combined with their other sources.

The material listed for this passion narrative in Table 11.18 probably does not exhaust the full extent of the source. It shows only those elements of C that were preserved by Mark/Matthew and Luke. It is possible that some elements were preserved only by Mark/Matthew or only by Luke. Hence, some of the passion material that occurs in one of these traditions but not the other may have come from this source. It is also possible that some of the source was not preserved in either tradition, especially if the editors used it merely to supplement Proto-Mark's passion narrative.

*Resurrection*

The last element of C that we can identify is Jesus' final mission charge to his disciples. If we count the long ending of Mark, some form of this occurs in each of the Synoptic Gospels (Table 11.22).

Table 11.22
Charge to preach

| Matt 28:19a | Mark 16:15 | Luke 24:47 |
|---|---|---|
| "Going then make disciples of all the nations . . ." | And he said to them, "Going into all the world, *preach the gospel* to all the creation." | ". . . and that repentance for forgiveness of sins should be *preached* in my name to all the nations." |

Mark's expression "preach the gospel," a typical expression of C, appears to belong to the most original form of the saying. The corresponding phrase in Matthew is probably Matthean redaction, since only Matthew uses the word "make disciples" (μαθητεύειν). Likewise, Luke's interest in the theme of repentance suggests that his "preach repentance" is less original than Mark's "preach the gospel." I am inclined to think, then, that a saying similar to Mark 16:15 concluded C. If we assume that this saying followed the passion narrative as it does now, C must also have included some mention of Jesus' resurrection, though it may not be possible to reconstruct it.

# Conclusion

We first encountered the C material in a comparison of Mark and Matthew. It showed up as a sequence of material common to these gospels that did not fit into the sequence of Proto-Mark A. In a comparison of Mark and Luke, it showed up again as a similar sequence of material common to these gospels that did not fit into the sequence of Proto-Mark B. We inferred that all three Synoptic evangelists used this source independently, incorporating it at different positions in their respective versions of Proto-Mark. At the same time, we saw that doublets of this material occur in the Proto-Markan gospels. These doublets led to the conclusion that the source was transmitted to the Synoptic evangelists through more than one channel. We theorized that part of this source was incorporated into Proto-Mark. At the next stage, the editors of Proto-Mark A and Proto-Mark B adopted the C material from Proto-Mark, and the editor of Proto-Mark A also added other elements from it to his gospel. At the final stage, the Synoptic evangelists knew the material both as it had been incorporated into the Proto-Markan gospels and as a separate document. This overlap in their sources led Matthew and Luke occasionally to include doublets of the material, while Mark consistently conflated the different versions of it that he knew. The following diagram shows this distribution of the C material.

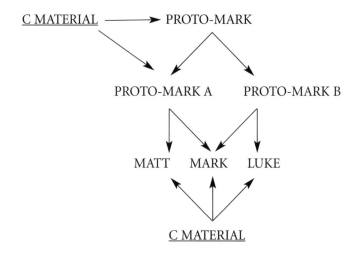

The ubiquity of C among the evangelists indicates that it was a well-known collection of material at the time. Already before Proto-Mark it apparently demonstrated the typical kerygmatic form of a passion gospel: a narrative that began with John the Baptist, related the ministry of Jesus, and concluded with his passion and resurrection.

The C source had a fairly unified focus on "preaching the gospel." The first sentence introduced this theme in the words "The beginning of the gospel" (Mark 1:1). Subsequently, the narrative portrayed both John the Baptist and Jesus preaching the gospel, the message that the kingdom of God was at hand. John, who is implicitly identified as Elijah the forerunner, first proclaimed this message (Matt 3:2). Jesus then took it up in Galilee as he taught in synagogues, preached to crowds, and healed their ill (Mark 1:14c–15 parr; cf. Mark 6:6b parr). On a mountain, Jesus chose the twelve apostles, presumably to help him in preaching. Once he arrived in Jerusalem, he predicted that the gospel would be preached to all the nations before the end (Mark 13:10 par). As he ate his last meal at Bethany, he predicted concerning a woman who anointed him that what she had done would be remembered wherever the gospel was preached in all the world (Mark 14:9 par). Following an account of Jesus' death and presumably his resurrection, the source ended as Jesus commissioned his disciples to preach the gospel to all the nations (Mark 16:15 parr).

Since C predated Proto-Mark, it must have been composed prior to 70 CE, the approximate date that we have set for the composition of Proto-Mark. Its focus on preaching to all the nations shows that it originated within a group of early Christians who embraced missionary activity toward both Jews and Gentiles. A more detailed study of C might lead to further clues concerning the type of Christianity that it represented.

## CHAPTER 12

# *The Making of Mark*

PREVIOUS CHAPTERS have identified all the sources that Mark would have used in creating his gospel. To discuss in detail Mark's use of these sources would require a separate book. Previous chapters have given some examples. This chapter presents a few more, showing how the new theory accounts for the material in selected portions of Mark.

## Mark's Sources

In our theory, Mark combined five sources that he shared with Matthew and/or Luke. He also included several items of tradition known only to himself, and he added a layer of redaction to the whole.

Mark shared the following sources with Matthew and/or Luke:

- Proto-Mark A (PMA): shared with Matthew
- Proto-Mark B (PMB): shared with Luke
- C: shared with Matthew and Luke
- a miracle/mission source: shared with Matthew and Luke
- a parable discourse: shared with Luke

This general picture is complicated by the fact that several of these sources overlapped.

- Proto-Mark A and Proto-Mark B overlapped in the material that both drew from Proto-Mark.
- Elements of C were incorporated into Proto-Mark A and Proto-Mark B. These elements of C in the Proto-Markan gospels overlapped with the separate copy of C used by Mark.
- The miracle/mission source that Mark shared with Matthew and Luke overlapped with the version of this source that was incorporated into Proto-Mark B.

- The parable discourse that Mark shared with Luke overlapped with the version of this source that was incorporated into Proto-Mark A.

Mark combined these sources, generally following the order of the sources. Where they overlapped, he generally conflated them, drawing elements from each, to produce a single more detailed version of the material.

In addition to these sources that Mark shared with Matthew and/or Luke, Mark also knew several units of tradition that have no parallel in Matthew or Luke, and he added these to the mix. These include:

- a story in which Jesus praises a scribe's insight (Mark 12:32–34a);
- a story in which a young man flees the scene of Jesus' arrest (Mark 14:51–52);
- various sayings (Mark 2:27 and possibly 4:23, 24b, 24c; 9:48, 49, 50b);
- various miracle stories, including the healing of a deaf man (Mark 7:32–36), the healing of a blind man (Mark 8:22–26), and Version B of an exorcism story (Mark 9:14–27) that Mark conflated with Version A from the Proto-Markan gospels (Table 2.14).

To top it off, Mark left a layer of redactional additions and revisions from his own hand. I have previously discussed a number of these in Chapter 2. In the diagram of my theory at the end of Chapter 7, I use the letter "K" to include both the traditions and the redaction that Mark added to his sources.

The rest of this chapter provides examples of how Mark used these sources. I do not present these examples as arguments for my theory. The arguments have been made in previous chapters. In these examples I presuppose the theory and illustrate how it works in practice. At the same time, if my theory can plausibly account for features of the tradition that others cannot, then that might at least create a presumption in its favor.

## The Beginning of Mark (Mark 1:1–8)

Mark commences with an account of John the Baptist (Mark 1:1–8). The delineation of sources here is complicated somewhat by the presence of Q material in the parallels in Matthew and Luke. The Q material probably consisted of Luke 3:2b; Luke 3:3//Matt 3:5b; Luke 3:7–9//Matt 3:7–10; and Luke 3:16–17//Matt 3:11–12. Mark compiled his own account from three sources: C, Proto-Mark A, and Proto-Mark B.

Mark began by combining material from C and the Proto-Markan gospels (Table 12.1).

Table 12.1
Mark 1:1–3

| Mark (C) | Mark (PMA/PMB) |
|---|---|
| 1:1 The beginning of the gospel of Jesus Christ [the Son of God]. | |
| | 1:2a As it is written in Isaiah the prophet, |
| 1:2b Behold I send my messenger before your face who will prepare your way. | |
| | 1:3 "The voice of one crying in the wilderness: Prepare the way of the Lord, make straight his paths." |

The beginning of C, in speaking of "the beginning of the gospel," was appropriate for Mark to use here, since it was in fact the beginning of his gospel. Not surprisingly, neither Matthew nor Luke used it, since each had begun his respective gospel several chapters earlier. C continued with a quotation of scripture, a combination of Malachi 3:1 and Exodus 23:20. When Mark turned to the Proto-Markan gospels, he found another scripture quotation, this one from Isaiah 40:3, following the mention of John's appearance in the wilderness. He took the Proto-Markan quotation out of its original order to combine it with the quotation from C. Unfortunately, he kept the reference to Isaiah in the Proto-Markan quote (Mark 1:2a), thus incorrectly attributing both quotations to Isaiah. Though we see the error, Mark apparently did not. Matthew and Luke got it right, not because they corrected Mark, but because they knew the pre-blunder version of the material and neither tried to combine the two quotes.

Mark then returned to the mention of John's appearance in his Proto-Markan sources (Mark 1:4) that he had skipped over to retrieve the quotation from Isaiah. Each of the Synoptic sources in use here (Proto-Markan, C, and Q) mentioned John's appearance in the wilderness, and each of the Synoptic evangelists made a different use of the sources (Table 12.2).

Table 12.2
John in the wilderness (Mark 1:4)

| Matthew | Mark | Luke |
|---|---|---|
| 3:1b (C) John the Baptist comes preaching in the wilderness of Judea | 1:4a (PMA/PMB) John the Baptizer appeared in the wilderness | 3:2b (Q) . . . the word of God came upon John the son of Zachariah in the wilderness |

| Matthew | Mark | Luke |
|---|---|---|
| 3:2 (C) and saying, "Repent, for the kingdom of heaven has drawn near." | | |
| 3:5b (Q) . . . and all the region of the Jordan . . . | | 3:3a (Q) and he came into all the region of the Jordan |
| | 1:4b (PMA/PMB) preaching a baptism of repentance for forgiveness of sins. | 3:3b (PMB) preaching a baptism of repentance for forgiveness of sins. |

While Matthew drew this material primarily from C with one element added from Q, Luke drew it primarily from Q with one element added from Proto-Mark B. Mark stuck to the Proto-Markan tradition that he found in Proto-Mark A and Proto-Mark B.

Table 12.3 shows the next two items in Mark.

Table 12.3
Mark 1:5–6

| Matthew | Mark |
|---|---|
| 3:4 (C) He, John, had his clothing from camel hair and a leather belt around his waist, and his food was locusts and wild honey. | |
| 3:5 (PMA) Then Jerusalem and all Judea went out to him . . . 6 and were baptized in the Jordan River by him as they confessed their sins. | 1:5 (PMA) And all the Judean countryside and all the Jerusalemites went out to him and were baptized by him in the Jordan River as they confessed their sins. |
| | 1:6 (C) John was clothed in camel hair and a leather belt around his waist and was eating locusts and wild honey. |

While Mark 1:5 came from Proto-Mark A, Mark 1:6 came from C. As the table shows, both Mark and Matthew included these two items, but in reverse order. While Matthew inserted the C material before that from Proto-Mark A, Mark inserted it after.

In the concluding verses of this pericope, John announces the one more powerful than himself (Mark 1:7–8). Mark probably found this announcement in both Proto-Mark A and Proto-Mark B, where Matthew and Luke, respectively, would have found it as well. Matthew and Luke, however, substituted an overlapping tradition from Q (Matt 3:11; Luke 3:16).

## Healing the Ill (Mark 1:32–34)

The pericope "Healing the ill" (Mark 1:32–34) provides a good illustration of our theory. This summary of Jesus' healing ministry was part of C (Matt 4:24). From there it was incorporated into Proto-Mark, from which it passed into both Proto-Mark A (Matt 8:16) and Proto-Mark B (Luke 4:40–41). Mark thus knew three versions of this summary: two from the Proto-Markan gospels and one directly from C. He took elements from each in composing his own version. Table 12.4 shows Mark's version in comparison with his sources as these were incorporated into Matthew and Luke.

Table 12.4
Mark 1:32–34 and parallels

| Mark 1:32–34 | Matthew 4:24 (C) | Matthew 8:16 (C in PMA) | Luke 4:40–41 (C in PMB) |
|---|---|---|---|
| 1:32 When evening came, | | 8:16a When evening came, | |
| when the sun set, | | | 4:40a The sun having set, |
| they were bringing to him | 4:24b And they brought to him | 16b they brought to him | 40d they led them to him |
| all the ill | 24c all the ill | | 40b all who had sick |
| and the demonized. | 24f and demonized . . . | 16c many demonized. | |
| 33 And the whole city was gathered at the door. | | | |
| 34 And he healed many ill | 24h . . . and he healed them. | 16e And he healed all the ill. | 40f . . . he was healing them |
| with various diseases. | 24d with various diseases . . . | | 40c with various diseases |
| And he cast out many demons. | | 16d And he cast out the spirits with a word. | 41a And demons came out of many . . . |

| Mark 1:32–34 | Matthew 4:24 (C) | Matthew 8:16 (C in PMA) | Luke 4:40–41 (C in PMB) |
|---|---|---|---|
| And he did not allow the demons to speak, because they knew him. | | | 41c And . . . he did not let them speak, because they knew that he was the Christ. |

As the table shows, Proto-Mark A (seen in Matt 8:16) and Proto-Mark B (seen in Luke 4:40–41) both began the passage with similar temporal expressions: "when evening came" and "the sun having set" respectively. Mark included both, thus duplicating the Proto-Markan material.

Mark has two references to the ill (κακῶς ἔχοντας), the first as the object of "they were bringing" (Mark 1:32) and the second as the object of "he healed" (Mark 1:34). The former came from C (seen in Matt 4:24bc), the latter from Proto-Mark A (seen in Matt 8:16e). The same two sources provided Mark with the phrase "and the demonized" (Matt 4:24f; 8:16c).

Only Mark has the sentence "And the whole city was gathered at the door" (Mark 1:33). This sentence did not occur in any of his sources, but was added by Mark. As we saw in Table 1.9, this sentence expresses a typical motif in Mark, the theme of Jesus' popularity. It is one of seven thematically and stylistically related passages in Mark, none of which occur in Matthew or Luke. It thus belongs to the layer of Mark's redaction.

At Mark 1:34, all of Mark's sources pictured Jesus healing. The phrase "with various diseases" occurred in both C (cf. Matt 4:24d) and Proto-Mark B (cf. Luke 4:40c). The next statement, "And he cast out many demons," has both Proto-Mark A and Proto-Mark B as sources. The final element, in which the demons recognize Jesus, came from Proto-Mark B and probably Proto-Mark A as well, though Matthew lacks the Proto-Mark A version that would confirm this. Here and elsewhere, Matthew probably omitted the demons' recognition of Jesus lest Jesus appear to be in league with them.

In this way our theory explains why Mark has affinities in language with three parallel passages, two in Matthew and one in Luke. While Matthew knew two versions of the summary, keeping them separate, and Luke knew a third version, Mark knew all three and melded them into a single more comprehensive version, adding one of his own typical motifs to the mix.

## Plucking Grain on the Sabbath
## (Mark 2:23–28)

The controversy stories in Mark 2:1–3:6 belong to the Synoptic core, which in our theory ultimately came from Proto-Mark. Mark knew these stories from both Proto-Mark A (shared with Matthew) and Proto-Mark B (shared with Luke). Here I will discuss only one story, that in which Jesus' disciples pluck grain on the Sabbath (Mark 2:23–28).

The material common to all three Synoptics relates the same basic story. The Pharisees ask Jesus why his disciples, who are plucking grain, do what is not permitted on the Sabbath (Mark 2:23–24). Jesus replies that David also did what was not permitted: he took the consecrated bread from the house of God when he and his followers needed food (Mark 2:25–26). Jesus then adds, "The son of man is Lord of the Sabbath" (Mark 2:28). This basic story is complete in itself. Jesus' response implies that hunger may override the normal requirement of the Sabbath law and that, like David, the son of man (whether this refers to Jesus or the human being in general) has the right to make such a decision.

In relating this core story, Mark uses a number of the same words as Matthew and Luke:

2:23 σαββα- -πορευ- διὰ σπορίμων οἱ μαθηταὶ αὐτοῦ -τιλλ-στάχυας 24 Φαρισαι- ποι- σαββα- ὃ οὐκ ἔξεστιν 25 οὐ- ἀνέγνωτε ἐποίησεν Δαυὶδ ὅτε ἐπείνασεν καὶ οἱ μετ᾽ αὐτοῦ 26 -ως εἰσῆλθεν εἰς τὸν οἶκον τοῦ θεοῦ καὶ τοὺς ἄρτους τῆς προθέσεως ἔφαγ- ο-οὐκ ἐξ- φαγεῖν εἰ μὴ τ- ἱερ- τοῖς αὐτ- 27 ... 28 κύριός ἐστιν ὁ υἱὸς τοῦ ἀνθρώπου τοῦ σαββάτου

Except for those underlined, these words occur in the same order in all three Synoptics. In our theory, these are words from Proto-Mark that survived every stage of the redaction process. They passed unchanged from Proto-Mark into both Proto-Mark A and Proto-Mark B and from there passed unchanged into the three Synoptic Gospels. The words attributed to Jesus in 1:25–26, 28 underwent less change than the accompanying narrative in 1:23–24.

Mark has a number of agreements with Luke against Matthew in this story (Table 12.5).

### Table 12.5
#### Mark/Luke agreements in Mark 2:23–28

| Matthew | Mark | Luke |
|---|---|---|
| ἐν ἐκείνῳ τῷ καιρῷ | καὶ ἐγένετο | ἐγένετο δέ |
| | ἐν | ἐν |
| ἐπορεύθη ὁ Ἰησοῦς | αὐτὸν παραπορεύεσθαι | διαπορεύεσθαι αὐτόν |
| δέ | καί | καί |
| στάχυας | τοὺς στάχυας | τοὺς στάχυας |

| Matthew | Mark | Luke |
|---|---|---|
| | τί | τί |
| ἐν σαββάτῳ | τοῖς σάββασιν | τοῖς σάββασιν |
| οὐκ | οὐδε- | οὐδε |
| | αὐτός | αὐτός |
| ἔφαγον | ἔφαγεν | ἔφαγεν |
| ὃ οὐκ ἐξὸν ἦν αὐτῷ | οὓς οὐκ ἔξεστιν | οὓς οὐκ ἔξεστιν |
| τοῖς ἱερεῦσιν | τοὺς ἱερεῖς | τοὺς ἱερεῖς |
| οὐδέ | καὶ ἔδωκεν | καὶ ἔδωκεν |
| | καὶ ἔλεγεν αὐτοῖς | καὶ ἔλεγεν αὐτοῖς |

These agreements of Mark and Luke indicate the reading of Proto-Mark B. They may or may not preserve the reading of Proto-Mark. Matthew's minority reading may come from either Proto-Mark A or from Matthean redaction.

Likewise, Mark has a number of agreements with Matthew against Luke (Table 12.6).

### Table 12.6
### Mark/Matthew agreements in Mark 2:23–28

| Matthew | Mark | Luke |
|---|---|---|
| τοῖς σάββασιν | τοῖς σάββασιν | σαββάτῳ |
| τῶν σπορίμων | τῶν σπορίμων | σπορίμων |
| ἤρξαντο | ἤρξαντο | |
| οἱ δὲ Φαρισαῖοι | καὶ οἱ Φαρισαῖοι | τινὲς δὲ τῶν Φαρισαίων |
| αὐτῷ | αὐτῷ | |
| ἰδού | ἴδε | |
| ποιοῦσιν | ποιοῦσιν | ποιεῖτε |
| αὐτοῖς | αὐτοῖς | πρὸς αὐτούς |
| τί | τί | ὃ |
| πῶς | πῶς | (ὡς) |

These agreements of Mark and Matthew indicate the reading of Proto-Mark A. They may or may not preserve the reading of Proto-Mark. Luke's minority reading may come from either Proto-Mark B or Lukan redaction.

Matthew and Luke also have several positive agreements against Mark (Table 12.7).

Table 12.7
Matthew/Luke agreements in Mark 2:23–28

| Matthew | Mark | Luke |
|---|---|---|
| καὶ ἐσθίειν | | καὶ ἤσθιον |
| δέ | καί | δέ |
| εἶπαν | ἔλεγον | εἶπαν |
| εἶπεν | λέγει | εἶπεν |
| μόνοις | | μόνους |
| μετ᾽ αὐτοῦ | σὺν αὐτῷ | μετ᾽ αὐτοῦ |
| τοῦ σαββάτου ὁ υἱὸς τοῦ ἀνθρώπου | ὁ υἱὸς τοῦ ἀνθρώπου καὶ τοῦ σαββάτου | τοῦ σαββάτου ὁ υἱὸς τοῦ ἀνθρώπου |

In most of these instances, it is likely that Matthew and Luke preserved the original reading, from Proto-Mark A and from Proto-Mark B respectively, while Mark changed it. We cannot rule out the possibility, however, that in a few instances, Mark preserved the original reading, while Matthew and Luke independently made the same changes. In particular, it is not impossible that Matthew and Luke both changed καί to δέ, ἔλεγον to εἶπαν, or λέγει to εἶπεν.

In addition to these agreements, each gospel has some material unique to that gospel. In most cases such unique wording probably represents the redaction of the evangelist who includes it. The longest instance of unique wording occurs in Matthew: the example of the priests who work in the Temple on the Sabbath (Matt 12:5–7). Proto-Mark's story gave the example of David to justify the Sabbath conduct of the early Jewish Christian church. Matthew added the example of the priests to serve as a further justification.

The most notorious example of unique wording in this story occurs in Mark 2:27, the statement "The Sabbath was made for man and not man for the Sabbath." This saying was a free-floating logion that has an independent parallel in Jewish tradition: "The Sabbath is delivered to you, and you are not delivered to the Sabbath" (*Mekilta* on Exod 31:14). Proponents of Markan priority have had difficulty explaining why Matthew and Luke, supposedly following Mark, do not include this saying. According to one common suggestion, Matthew and Luke omitted Mark 2:27 in reaction against the Sabbath freedom expressed in the verse.[1] Hultgren, for example, thinks that Mark 2:27

---

1. E.g., Francis Wright Beare, "The Sabbath Was Made for Man?" *JBL* 79 (1960), 130–36, esp. 134; Arland J. Hultgren, *Jesus and His Adversaries: The Form and Function of the Conflict Stories in the Synoptic Tradition* (Minneapolis: Augsburg, 1979), 112; J. A. Fitzmyer, *The Gospel According to Luke* (2 vols.; Garden City, NY: Doubleday, 1981–85), 1:606; James D. G. Dunn, "Mark 2.1–3.6: A Bridge Between Jesus and Paul on the Question of the Law," *NTS* 30 (1984): 395–415, esp. 408.

may have been too extreme for Matthew, since his Jewish Christian community may have observed the Sabbath. While this explanation might work for Matthew, it would not explain why Luke, writing for non-Jews, would omit the saying. It would fit right in with other criticism of the Sabbath in Gentile Christianity.[2] Even for Matthew, the explanation is dubious, since other Jews who observed the Sabbath knew the parallel to Mark 2:27 that was cited above (*Mekilta* on Exod 31:14) and did not consider it too extreme. Hay believes that Matthew and Luke omitted the verse because its generic "man" made it impossible for them to interpret "Son of Man" in the following verse as a title of Jesus.[3] Yet innumerable commentators throughout Christian history have interpreted "Son of Man" in 2:28 as a title in spite of the generic "man" in 2:27. Matthew and Luke probably would not have found it any more difficult to do the same. In reviewing other proposed explanations, Ulrich Luz concludes: "The most difficult question [given the priority of Mark] is why Matthew and Luke did not transmit Mark 2:27. There are several possible explanations, none of which is entirely satisfactory. . . . There simply is no satisfying explanation."[4] Unlike the theory of Markan priority, our theory has no such problem. Mark probably found this saying circulating in Jewish Christian circles and added it to the story that he received from Proto-Mark A and Proto-Mark B. Matthew and Luke lack it because they did not know it. It did not occur in the sources that they shared with Mark. Mark added this saying for the same reason that Matthew added the example of the priests in Matthew 12:5–7. The story in Proto-Mark provided a justification for the church's Sabbath conduct. Since the church tended to want more arguments for its position, not fewer, the evangelists added other justifications in the process of transmission, one in Matthew 12:5–7 and one in Mark 2:27.

A third example of unique wording in this story is more difficult to assess. Only Mark includes the phrase "when Abiathar was high priest" (Mark 2:26), an erroneous dating of the time when David ate the sanctified bread. Proponents of Markan priority assume that Matthew and Luke omitted the phrase from Mark precisely because it is erroneous. Given the theory of Markan priority, that explanation is possible but not as obvious as it might seem. I might not have realized that the phrase is erroneous if I had not read it in a commentary on Mark. This fact makes me wonder if Matthew and Luke knew the story in 1 Samuel 21–22 so well that they both would have recognized that Ahimelech was high priest at the time rather than his son Abiathar. That is possible, but somewhat remarkable. In our theory, some-

---

2. Helmut Koester points to Col 2:16; Ignatius, *Magn.*; *Barn.* 15 ("History and Development," 40n. 17).

3. Lewis S. Hay, "The Son of Man in Mark 2:10 and 2:28," *JBL* 89 (1970): 69–75, esp. 75.

4. Ulrich Luz, *Matthew 8–20* (Hermeneia; Minneapolis: Fortress, 2001), 179–80.

thing of the same sort is possible. The phrase may have entered the tradition prior to Mark—in Proto-Mark or Proto-Mark A or Proto-Mark B—and while Matthew and/or Luke recognized the error and omitted it, Mark did not and retained it. It is also possible that the phrase originated with Mark, perhaps through some hazy memory of the story that he did not have the means or the inclination to check.

## Ministry to a Crowd (Mark 3:7–12)

I previously gave Mark 3:7–12 as an example of a passage where Mark conflated several different sources (Table 6.3). We can now discuss Mark's procedure more fully. Table 12.8 sets out this passage with the relevant parallels.

Table 12.8
Mark 3:7–12 and parallels

| Mark 3:7–12 | Matthew 4:25 (C) | Luke 5:17 (C) | Matthew 12:15–16 (PMA) | Luke 6:17–19; 4:41b (PMB) | Luke 5:1, 3 (Par) |
|---|---|---|---|---|---|
| 7 And Jesus | | | 15 When Jesus found out | | |
| with his disciples | | | | 17 and a large crowd of his disciples | |
| withdrew | | | he withdrew from there. | | |
| to the sea. | | | | | 1b he was standing by the Lake of Gennesaret . . . |
| And a large crowd followed | And large crowds followed him | Pharisees and teachers of the law who had come | And large crowds followed him. | and a large multitude of the people | |
| from Galilee | from Galilee . . . | from every village of Galilee | | | |

| Mark 3:7–12 | Matthew 4:25 (C) | Luke 5:17 (C) | Matthew 12:15–16 (PMA) | Luke 6:17–19; 4:41b (PMB) | Luke 5:1, 3 (Par) |
|---|---|---|---|---|---|
| and from Judea 8 and from Jerusalem | and Jerusalem and Judea | and Judea and Jerusalem | | from all of Judea and Jerusalem | |
| and from Idumea | | | | | |
| and across the Jordan | and across the Jordan. | | | | |
| and around Tyre and Sidon. | | | | and the coast of Tyre and Sidon | |
| A large crowd, hearing what he was doing, came to him. | | | | 18 who came to hear from him and to be healed of their diseases. | 1a when the crowd pressed against him to hear the word of God |
| 9 And he told his disciples that a boat should wait for him because of the crowd, lest they crush him. | | | | | 3 Getting in one of the boats, which was Simon's, he asked him to stand off a little from the land. |
| 10 For he healed many, | | and there was power of the Lord for him to cure. | And he healed them all. | And those oppressed by unclean spirits were healed. | |
| with the result that those who had afflictions would fall upon him that they | | | | 19 And the whole crowd was seeking to touch him because power went forth from him and healed all. | |

| Mark 3:7–12 | Matthew 4:25 (C) | Luke 5:17 (C) | Matthew 12:15–16 (PMA) | Luke 6:17–19; 4:41b (PMB) | Luke 5:1, 3 (Par) |
|---|---|---|---|---|---|
| might touch him. | | | | | |
| 11 And the unclean spirits when they saw him, fell before him | | | — | — | |
| and cried out saying, "You are the Son of God." | | | — | →4:41b . . . crying and saying, "You are the Son of God." | |
| 12 And he ordered them repeatedly not to make him known. | | | 16 And he ordered them not to make him known. | →4:41c And ordering them . . . | |

Though the table has two columns for C, these represent only one source that Mark would have used. Thus the table indicates that Mark combined material from four sources here: C, Proto-Mark A, Proto-Mark B, and the parable discourse (Par). As far as I am aware, this is the only place in Mark where four of his sources come together in the same passage.

To understand the genesis of this Markan passage we must begin with C, which all three of the Synoptic evangelists used independently. It included a summary statement concerning a crowd that followed Jesus. Matthew has preserved this with some alterations (Matt 4:25 in the second column), as has Luke (Luke 5:17 in the third column). By comparing the two versions with each other and with the other parallels, we can identify with a good degree of certainty the changes that each evangelist made. Luke changed the crowd to Pharisees and teachers of the law, dropped "and across the Jordan," and added a reference to the power of the Lord. Matthew reversed the order of Judea and Jerusalem and dropped the reference to healing. We can thus arrive at a fairly close reconstruction of the original: "And large crowds (or 'a large crowd') followed him from Galilee and Judea and Jerusalem and across the Jordan, and he healed them." Mark knew something similar to this reconstruction from his copy of C.

A similar summary occurs in the Synoptic core in both Matthew and Luke: Matthew 12:15–16 from Proto-Mark A (column 4) and Luke 6:17–19 from Proto-Mark B (column 5). To explain this fact, it appears necessary to assume that the summary from C was incorporated into Proto-Mark. From there it passed through Proto-Mark A into Matthew and through Proto-Mark B into Luke. This theory explains why Matthew and Luke each have two versions of the summary—one directly from C at different places in their respective gospels and one from Proto-Mark at the same place in each gospel.

When we compare the Proto-Markan versions of the summary (columns 4 and 5) with each other and with the parallels, it is again fairly easy to see the changes that have been made. Since Mark shows awareness of most of these changes, they must have been made for the most part by the editors of the Proto-Markan tradition rather than by Matthew and Luke. To the C summary, the editor of Proto-Mark added the ending in which the unclean spirits recognize Jesus and he prohibits them from speaking (Mark 3:11–12 parr). Only Mark has retained this fully. Matthew retained the prohibition, but he omitted the demons' testimony to Jesus, apparently because it might give credence to the charge that Jesus was in league with them. As a result, in Matthew the prohibition is addressed to the crowd. This result makes for a strange narrative, since if Jesus is already being followed by large crowds, it seems a little late to ask them not to make him known—much like closing the barn door after the cows have already escaped. Luke apparently knew the material on unclean spirits, but transferred it to another story with a similar motif (→Luke 4:41bc).

After the Proto-Mark version passed into Proto-Mark A, the editor of the latter prefaced the story with a statement that Jesus "withdrew." Either Proto-Mark A or Matthew also dropped the list of locations from which the crowd came. In the other line of transmission, the editor of Proto-Mark B prefaced the summary with a reference to Jesus' disciples, dropped Galilee but kept Judea and Jerusalem, substituted "the coast of Tyre and Sidon" for "across the Jordan," and expanded the simple statement that Jesus healed the crowd into a fuller description. It was probably Luke who added a reference to the "power" of God (Luke 6:19), as he did in revising the C version (Luke 5:17).

Mark combined three versions of this summary, from C, Proto-Mark A, and Proto-Mark B, respectively. By comparing his conflated version with the parallels, we can usually see what source he drew from in each case. In the first sentence, Jesus' "disciples" came from Proto-Mark B (shared with Luke), the term "withdrew" from Proto-Mark A (shared with Matthew). In the second sentence, the statement "And a large crowd followed" has a parallel in all the versions, but probably comes close to the original wording of C, as do the phrases "from Galilee" and "from Judea and from Jerusalem." The phrase "from Idumea," which has no parallel in any other version, probably came from Mark himself. Its addition is in line with Mark's tendency to portray Jesus as popular and besieged from all quarters. The phrase "across the Jordan" came from C, and Mark also took the phrase that Proto-Mark B had substituted for it, "the coast of Tyre and Sidon." In verse 10, the statement

"And he healed many" probably comes close to the original version of C, except that the word "many" probably came from Mark (see Table 2.3). Following this, the description of people falling on Jesus to touch him was at least inspired by the parallel in Proto-Mark B. At the end of the pericope, Mark drew the material on unclean spirits from Proto-Mark A (partially omitted by Matthew) and Proto-Mark B (moved elsewhere by Luke).

Once we have identified all of the different versions of the summary that originated with C and all the elements of Mark that came from these versions, we are still left with other material in Mark's pericope. This material introduces a setting by the sea and a boat that is prepared for Jesus lest he be crushed by the crowd. The sea and the boat have a parallel in Luke (5:1, 3, in column 6) in material that we previously identified as the introduction to the parable discourse (see Chapters 5 and 9). Thus, it appears that to round off his story, Mark added material from this source. This additional material has affinities with the summary that we saw above in Proto-Mark B. Just as Proto-Mark B describes the crowd seeking to touch Jesus, the parable discourse describes a crowd pressing upon Jesus. It may have been this link between the stories that led Mark to see them as appropriate for conflating into one larger description of Jesus' ministry to a crowd.

## Ministry to Another Crowd (Mark 6:30–34)

Immediately preceding the feeding of the five thousand in the Synoptic core, another episode occurs in which Jesus ministers to a crowd (Mark 6:30–34). Since this material also belongs to the Synoptic core, it came ultimately from Proto-Mark. Matthew received it from Proto-Mark A, Luke from Proto-Mark B, while Mark combined Proto-Mark A and Proto-Mark B. To facilitate the discussion, I have divided the episode into two parts. Table 12.9 sets out the parallels for the first part (Mark 6:30–32).

Table 12.9
Mark 6:30–32 and parallels

| Mark 6:30–32 (PMA+PMB) | Matthew 14:12b–13a (PMA) | Luke 9:10 (PMB) |
|---|---|---|
| 30 And the apostles gather to Jesus. And they reported to him all the things they had done | 12 and coming they reported it to Jesus. | 10 And returning, the apostles related to him the things they had done. |
| and the things they had taught. | | |

| Mark 6:30–32 (PMA+PMB) | Matthew 14:12b–13a (PMA) | Luke 9:10 (PMB) |
|---|---|---|
| 31 And he says to them, "Come, you privately, to a deserted spot | | And taking them along, he withdrew privately to a city called Bethsaida. |
| and rest a little." For there were many coming and going, and they did not have time even to eat. | | |
| | 13 When Jesus heard, | |
| 32 And they went away in the boat to a deserted spot privately. | he withdrew from there in a boat to a deserted spot privately. | |

By excerpting from Table 12.9 the material common to Mark and Luke, we can reconstruct in general what stood in Proto-Mark B, as follows:

| Mark (PMB) | Luke (PMB) |
|---|---|
| 30 And the apostles gather to Jesus. And they reported to him all the things they had done | 10 And returning, the apostles related to him the things they had done. |
| 31 And he says to them, "Come, you privately, to a deserted spot | And taking them along, he withdrew privately to a city called Bethsaida. |

Jesus previously sent out the apostles to preach (Mark 6:12–13; Luke 9:6). They now return to Jesus and make a report on their activities. Jesus and they then withdraw privately to a deserted spot. For whatever reason, Luke changed "a deserted spot" to "a city called Bethsaida," a change that created an inconsistency with the following feeding story, which is still set in "a deserted spot" (Mark 6:35; Luke 9:12). While Luke relates the group's departure in third-person narrative, Mark has Jesus speak to the apostles in direct discourse, inviting them to leave. Since the narrative presentation in Luke's version is supported by Proto-Mark A, which we will examine below, the direct discourse must be Markan redaction. Mark had two accounts of the departure, both of which he included, but to avoid saying exactly the same thing twice he changed the first instance into an invitation to depart. This is interesting, because it shows that the historical present "he says" in Mark 6:31 reflects Mark's own style. We cannot draw sweeping conclusions from one instance, but we can say that the historical present, a pervasive stylistic feature in Mark, in this instance and probably in others reflects Mark's redaction rather than the prior tradition.

Similarly, by excerpting from Table 12.9 the material common to Mark and Matthew, we can reconstruct in general what stood in Proto-Mark A, as follows:

| Mark (PMA) | Matthew (PMA) |
| --- | --- |
| 30 And the apostles gather to Jesus. And they reported to him all the things they had done | 12 and coming they reported it to Jesus. |
| 32 And they went away in the boat to a deserted spot privately. | he withdrew from there in a boat to a deserted spot privately. |

This Proto-Mark A version has Jesus and his disciples leave in a boat, whereas Proto-Mark B did not mention a boat. Judgments may differ here as to whether the boat belonged to the original story in Proto-Mark or not. Mark preserves a more original form of the story than Matthew in having the apostles report on their mission. Matthew, who previously omitted the apostles' preaching mission, has them tell Jesus about the death of John rather than about their missionary activities.

While Matthew and Luke have included one version of Jesus' departure or the other, Mark has included both: the Proto-Mark B version without the boat, followed by the Proto-Mark A version with it. In addition, Mark has some material with no parallel in either Matthew or Luke. In Mark 6:30, the apostles relate to Jesus not only the things they had done, but also "the things they had taught." Given Mark's redactional interest in the teaching mission of Jesus and his disciples (Table 2.11), we can safely identify this phrase as Markan redaction. The same is true for the end of Mark 6:31: "'. . . and rest a little.' For there were many coming and going, and they did not have time even to eat." This reflects the Markan theme of Jesus' popularity and consequent lack of privacy (Table 2.12).

The second part of the passage (Mark 6:33–34) is set out in Table 12.10.

### Table 12.10
### Mark 6:33–34 and parallels

| Mark 6:33–34 (PMA+PMB) | Matthew 14:13b–14 (PMA) | Luke 9:11 (PMB) |
| --- | --- | --- |
| 33 And they saw them going | And when they heard, | |
| and many found out. | | 11 And finding out, |
| | the crowds followed him | the crowds followed him. |

| Mark 6:33–34 (PMA+PMB) | Matthew 14:13b–14 (PMA) | Luke 9:11 (PMB) |
|---|---|---|
| And on foot from all the cities | On foot from the cities. | |
| they ran together there and preceded them. | | |
| | | And receiving them, |
| 34 And getting out he saw a large crowd and felt compassion for them, | 14 And getting out he saw a large crowd and felt compassion for them. | |
| because they were like sheep without a shepherd. | | |
| And he began to teach them many things. | | he spoke to them about the kingdom of God. |
| | And he healed their sick. | And those having need of healing he cured. |

Here I will focus on three specific aspects of this passage. The first is an inconsistency that occurs in Matthew's version: the crowds are following Jesus, yet when he arrives they are already there. Did this inconsistency originate with Matthew, or did he inherit it from an earlier stage of the tradition? To answer this question, let us examine the two elements that stand in tension. The first, the statement that "the crowds followed him," occurs also in Luke. It is likely then that this statement stood in Proto-Mark, Matthew receiving it from Proto-Mark A and Luke from Proto-Mark B. The second, the statement "getting out he saw a large crowd and felt compassion for them," does not occur in Luke, but occurs here in Mark (from Proto-Mark A) and elsewhere in Matthew as a doublet from C (Matt 9:36a). It appears then that this second statement did not originally belong to the story in Proto-Mark, but came from another summary relating to crowds in C. It was incorporated into Proto-Mark A, known to Mark and Matthew but not to Luke. The inconsistency in question thus arose in Proto-Mark A when the editor of that gospel added a statement from C that stood in tension with the previous statement from Proto-Mark. Since the inconsistency did not occur in Proto-Mark B, it was unknown to Luke, while Mark and Matthew both knew it from Proto-Mark A. Matthew simply retained it from that source. Mark, on the other hand, found a way to resolve the tension. While preserving both elements of the tension from Proto-Mark A, he inserted an explanatory note between them: "they (the crowd) ran there together and arrived before them (Jesus and his disciples)." Here Mark's explanation is that the crowd started out following Jesus, but because they ran they were able to get ahead of him, and thus be there when he arrived. This short note includes a feature of

Mark's style: the use of τρέχω in a compound (Table 2.13B). That and the absence of the note from Matthew and Luke indicate that it is from Mark's own hand. Thus, Mark's redaction illustrates his way of resolving the tension in Proto-Mark A that Matthew preserved.

A second aspect of the passage relates to Mark 6:34a and 34b, a reference to Jesus' compassion followed by a reference to sheep with no shepherd. The C source contained both elements (Matt 9:36). The first element stood in Proto-Mark A (Matt 14:14a), but it is not clear whether the second did as well. If it did, Matthew omitted it. If it did not, Mark added it from C (Mark 6:34b).

The final aspect of the passage is Mark's conclusion: "And he began to teach them many things." Luke has a parallel to the idea—"he spoke to them about the kingdom of God"—so the idea may have come from their common source, Proto-Mark B. However, Mark's wording is pure Markan redaction, both ἤρξατο διδάσκειν αὐτούς (Table 2.11) and πολλά (Table 2.3). With this redactional statement, Mark chose to conclude the episode. Matthew and Luke, however, agree that the original ending had Jesus healing the crowd. Exactly why Mark chose to omit this is not certain, but the result was to put the emphasis on one of Mark's redactional themes, his depiction of Jesus as a teacher (Table 2.11). In at least one other instance as well, it appears that Mark has substituted this theme for a reference to Jesus' healing: where Matthew has "he healed" (Matt 19:2), Mark has "he taught" (Mark 10:1).

## No Bread (Mark 8:14–21)

The pericope "No bread" provides an excellent example of how the meaning of a story could change through the process of transmission. In the form in which we find it, it occupies the same position in Mark as in Matthew (Mark 8:14–21//Matt 16:5–12). According to our theory, these evangelists drew it from Proto-Mark A. By noticing what their two versions have in common, we can reconstruct approximately what must have stood in Proto-Mark A (Table 12.11).

Table 12.11
No bread (PMA)

| Matthew 16:5–12 | Mark 8:14–21 |
|---|---|
| 5 And . . . they forgot to take loaves. | 14 And they forgot to take loaves. |
| 6 Jesus said to them, "Watch out and keep away from the leaven of the Pharisees and Sadducees." | 15 And he warned them, saying, "Watch out, look out for the leaven of the Pharisees and the leaven of Herod." |

| Matthew 16:5–12 | Mark 8:14–21 |
|---|---|
| 7 And they were discussing among themselves, saying, "We brought no loaves." | 16 And they were discussing with one another that they had no loaves. |
| 8 When Jesus found out, he said, "Why are you discussing among yourselves, you of little faith, that you have no loaves? | 17 And finding out, he says to them, "Why are you discussing that you have no loaves? |
| 9 Do you not yet understand and do you not remember the five loaves of the five thousand and how many baskets you took up? | Do you not yet understand . . . 18 . . . and do you not remember? 19 When I broke the five loaves for the five thousand, how many baskets full of fragments did you pick up? . . . |
| 10 Or the seven loaves of the four thousand and how many baskets you took up? | 20 When (I broke) the seven loaves for the four thousand, how many baskets full of fragments did you pick up? . . . |
| 11 How can you not understand?" | 21 And he said to them, "Do you not yet comprehend?" |

This version of the story in Proto-Mark A is still not the most original form of the story that we can reconstruct. Scholars have long suspected that the warning against the leaven of the Pharisees (Matt 16:6; Mark 8:15) is an interpolation, because it breaks up the continuity of thought in the pericope and appears as an isolated saying in Q (Luke 12:1). At some stage prior to Proto-Mark A, therefore, the story lacked the warning against leaven. Without this warning, the original meaning of the story becomes clear. The disciples are worried about what they will eat, since they have no bread. Jesus has to remind them of how he fed the five thousand and the four thousand, since the disciples have not yet understood that Jesus can provide for their needs.

It may have been the editor of Proto-Mark A who inserted the warning against the leaven of the Pharisees into the bread story. He thus introduced an element that stood in tension with the original meaning of the story. When Matthew inherited the story from Proto-Mark A, it was this intrusive element concerning the leaven of the Pharisees that determined the meaning of the story for him. The disciples' failure to understand that Jesus could provide for them now became a failure to understand his warning against the leaven of the Pharisees. Matthew made this interpretation explicit by adding to the original ending, "How can you not understand," a further explication: "'that I did not speak to you about loaves? Keep away from the leaven of the Pharisees and Sadducees.' Then they comprehended that he said to keep away not from the leaven of the loaves, but from the teaching of the Pharisees and the Sadducees" (Matt 16:11b–12). In Matthew's interpretation, the disciples' lack of understanding consisted of taking Jesus' reference to leaven literally instead of as a symbol for teaching. Thus Matthew developed the story further away from its original meaning in the direction that was initiated by the editor of Proto-Mark A.

Mark also inherited the interpolated version of the story from Proto-Mark A, but he would give yet another interpretation of the disciples' failure to understand. In the bread story itself, Mark did not make his interpretation explicit as Matthew did. Instead, he emphasized the disciples' lack of understanding. What in the original story was a mild rebuke—"Do you not yet understand?"—becomes in Mark a virtual denunciation: "Do you not yet understand nor comprehend? Do you have your hearts hardened? Having eyes do you not see and having ears do you not hear?" (Mark 8:17b–18a). Here Mark really gets on the disciples' case for not understanding something about the feeding miracles, and not only here. Earlier in the story Mark has related the feeding of the five thousand (Mark 6:35–44) followed by Jesus' walk on the sea (Mark 6:45–51). At the end of the latter story, Mark adds a note to explain why the disciples were astonished: "For they did not comprehend about the loaves, but their hearts were hardened" (Mark 6:52).

Clearly Mark thinks that the disciples should have understood something from the feeding miracles, and he berates their lack of understanding—first after the feeding of the five thousand and then again in the bread story after the feeding of the four thousand. But what should they have understood? Mark gives the answer in the two pericopes that immediately follow the bread story: the healing of a blind man from an undetermined source (Mark 8:22–26) and Peter's confession from Proto-Mark (Mark 8:27–30). The progression of these three stories makes their significance apparent: Jesus berates the disciples for being blind, he heals a blind man, and then the disciples realize that Jesus is the Christ. At last the disciples understand Jesus' identity, which according to Mark they should have understood from the feeding miracles, but it is not until Jesus symbolically heals their blindness that they are able to see it. The story of the blind man, unique to Mark, is thus essential to Mark's redactional purpose in this section. The story itself is unique as a healing story in that it takes Jesus two attempts to heal the blind man. The significance of this becomes clear when we realize that Mark uses the blind man to symbolize the disciples. Just as Jesus has to make two attempts to heal the blind man, so he had to perform two feeding miracles before the disciples could see who Jesus was.

Mark's redaction in this section thus presents a third interpretation of the pericope "No bread." In the original story, the disciples failed to understand that Jesus could meet their needs. Matthew reinterpreted the story in light of the interpolation added in Proto-Mark A: now the disciples failed to understand the symbolic meaning of Jesus' warning against leaven. Mark gave the story yet a third meaning, reinterpreting it christologically: now the disciples failed to understand that Jesus was the Christ. We find here then an example of how Mark and Matthew each interpreted the earlier tradition differently and modified it accordingly.

## The Gentile Mission in Mark

As we saw in Chapter 8, most of the material in Proto-Mark originated in the context of Judaic Christianity, within a Jewish Christian community that had not broken with the law. To this material, the editor of Proto-Mark added from C a mission charge that promoted evangelization of the Gentiles (Matt 28:19a; Mark 16:15; Luke 24:47). This interest in the Gentile mission was taken a step further by the editor of Mark. In at least three instances, he over-laid Judaic Christian traditions from his sources with redaction that shows an interest in Gentile Christianity.

1. Mark's Gentile perspective shows up most clearly in Mark 7:2–4, an addition to a controversy story from Proto-Mark A (Matt 15:1–20; Mark 7:1–23). The story addresses the question of whether it was necessary to wash one's hands before eating, a custom apparently practiced by the Pharisees to avoid ritual impurity. At the beginning of the story, Mark explains this cus-tom, presumably to Gentile readers who would not be familiar with it. In so doing he speaks as one outside the Jewish tradition, referring to "the Pharisees and all the Jews" in the third person, as "they." While it is perhaps conceivable that a Jewish Christian might have distanced himself from non-Christian Jews in this way, it seem more likely that the language reflects a Gentile per-spective.

The explanatory note in Mark does not occur in Matthew's version of the story. In this respect, Matthew preserves the more original form of the story. Since this story concerns a controversy that would only have been relevant among Jewish Christians, it must have had its origin in that context, where no explanatory note would have been necessary. The addition would have become necessary when the story came to be used among Gentiles. This development of the story from Matthew's version to Mark's thus matches the historical development of Christianity, which originated in a Jewish context but then spread into the larger Gentile world. The theory of Markan priority has never had a particularly convincing explanation for Mark's note, since it must affirm the reverse process, i.e., that the Gentile perspective in Mark is prior to the Jewish perspective in Matthew.

2. In the same story, we see a second element of Markan redaction that reflects a concern of early Christianity as it began to include Gentiles. The story originally addressed the question of whether or not one had to wash one's hands before eating to avoid transmitting impurity from the hands to

the mouth. The saying attributed to Jesus, that impurity comes not from what goes in but from what comes out of the mouth, originally served as a justification for not washing the hands. But Mark saw a further implication in it, which he expressed by adding the phrase "cleansing all foods" (Mark 7:19). He thus turned the saying into an argument against the law's requirement to avoid certain foods as ritually impure. Since no other reference to this issue occurs in the story, and since Mark's phrase has only a loose grammatical relationship to the rest of the sentence, it is clear that Mark added the phrase. Matthew's version without the addition again represents the more original form of the story.

Mark thus modified the story to address an issue that must have been of concern in his own situation. As long as the Jesus movement remained within the fold of Judaism, the question of whether or not one had to keep the Jewish law would not have arisen. It arose in earnest once the movement spread to Gentiles who had no inclination to adopt either circumcision or the law's dietary restrictions. Mark found an argument against the latter in a saying that originally served a different purpose, and he made that argument clear in his redactional addition. Mark's perspective here shows that he was either a Gentile Christian or a Jewish Christian who took the same point of view as Paul in denying the need to keep the dietary restrictions of the law. He must have belonged to a form of Christianity that included Gentiles and that had begun to break its ties with the earlier Jewish context of the movement.

3. The next story in Mark includes a third element of Markan redaction that points in the same direction. In this story, also from Proto-Mark A, Jesus reluctantly agrees to cast a demon out of a Gentile woman's daughter. At first he refuses, with the saying, "It is not good to take the children's bread and throw it to the dogs" (Matt 15:26; Mark 7:27). In light of this absolute distinction—Jesus' ministry is for Jews, not Gentiles—his subsequent agreement to heal the daughter comes across as the exception rather than the rule. Mark, however, prefaces Jesus' sharp saying with another remark that dulls its edge: "Let the children be fed first." Since "first" implies a "second," the idea here is not that Jews receive while Gentiles do not, but that Jews receive first, after which Gentiles receive. This remark appears to be Mark's version of Paul's principle, "to the Jew first, and then to the Greek" (Rom 1:16). In light of Paul's principle, which refers to "the Greek," it may be significant that Mark identifies the woman as Greek, unlike Matthew, who identifies her as Canaanite. In any case, rather than excluding Gentiles, Mark's redactional remark includes them in their proper order.

This additional remark is absent from Matthew's version of the story. I find it easier to believe that Mark added it than that Matthew omitted it. Matthew, who approved of the Gentile mission that developed after Jesus' death (Matt 28:19), would have had no reason to quarrel with it had he found it in Proto-Mark A. Mark, on the other hand, did have a reason to add it, since it muted the implication that Gentiles should receive only the crumbs and not the bread itself. Here again it appears that Matthew has the more original Judaic Christian version that Mark redacted from the perspective of Gentile Christianity.

In formulating the principle "Let the children be fed (χορτασθῆναι) first," Mark may well have had in mind the two feeding stories that stand on either side of it, especially since they both use the same word for "fed" (Mark 6:42; 8:8). Proto-Mark A included both the feeding of the five thousand and the feeding of the four thousand. Mark may have seen some significance in the presence of two such stories in the material that he inherited, and his redactional addition may reveal what that was: just as Jesus first fed the five thousand and then the four thousand, so the Jews were to be fed first and then the Gentiles.

In these three instances from Proto-Mark A material, we see the same pattern. In each case, Mark has a short phrase or brief explanation that appears to be a secondary addition to the story. In each case, Matthew has a version of the story without the secondary addition. In each case, the effect of the addition is the same: to modify a Judaic Christian perspective in light of a perspective that is more favorable or more accessible to Gentile Christianity. Thus the direction of the modification matches the development of Christianity from a Jewish context to a Gentile context. I think that my theory provides a reasonable explanation for these features of the tradition. Proto-Mark A included material that originated in Judaic Christianity. In drawing this material from Proto-Mark A, Matthew, at least in these three instances, preserved its Judaic Christian character, while Mark modified it in light of a perspective more favorable to Gentile Christianity.

## The Passion Narrative in Mark

For the passion narrative, Mark had three sources: Proto-Mark A (shared with Matthew), Proto-Mark B (shared with Luke), and the C source (shared in the passion narrative primarily with Luke). Table 12.12 shows these sources.

Table 12.12
Sources of Mark's passion narrative

|                               | Mark     | Matthew (PMA) | Luke (PMB) | Luke (C) |
|-------------------------------|----------|---------------|------------|----------|
| Up to Jerusalem               | 10:32ab  | 20:17a        |            | 19:28    |
| 3rd passion prediction        | 10:32d–34| 20:17b–19     | 18:31–34   |          |
| Etc.                          | Etc.     | Etc.          | Etc.       |          |

|  | Mark | Matthew (PMA) | Luke (PMB) | Luke (C) |
|---|---|---|---|---|
| **Passover** |  |  |  |  |
| Jewish leaders plot | 14:1–2 | 26:2a, 4–5 | 22:1–2 |  |
| Anointing at Bethany | 14:3–9 | 26:6–13 | →7:36–38 | — |
| Judas makes a deal | 14:10–11 | 26:14–16 | 22:3–6 |  |
| Passover prepared | 14:12–17 | 26:17–20 | 22:7–14 |  |
| Betrayal predicted | 14:18–21 | 26:21–25 | 22:21–23 |  |
| Lord's Supper sayings | 14:22–24 | 26:26–28 |  |  |
| Passover sayings | 14:25 | 26:29 |  | 22:15–18 |
| **Mount of Olives** |  |  |  |  |
| To Mount of Olives | 14:26 | 26:30 |  | 22:39a |
| All will scatter | 14:27 | 26:31 |  |  |
| I will go to Galilee | 14:28 | 26:32 |  |  |
| Denial predicted | 14:29–30 | 26:33–34 | 22:33–34 |  |
| Fidelity affirmed | 14:31 | 26:35 |  |  |
| To Gethsemane | 14:32a | 26:36a | 22:40a |  |
| Jesus grieves | 14:32b–34a | 26:36b–38a |  |  |
| Jesus prays | 14:34b–38 | 26:39–41a | 22:40b–46 |  |
| Jesus prays again | 14:39–41a | 26:42–45a |  |  |
| The hour arrives | 14:41b–42 | 26:45b–46 |  |  |
| **Jesus arrested** |  |  |  |  |
| Judas and crowd | 14:43a | 26:47a | 22:47a |  |
| Group with weapons | 14:43b | 26:47b |  |  |
| Kiss as signal | 14:44 | 26:48 |  |  |
| Judas kisses Jesus | 14:45 | 26:49 | 22:47b |  |
| They seize Jesus | 14:46 | 26:50b |  |  |
| Slave's ear cut off | 14:47 | 26:51 | 22:50 |  |
| As against a thief | 14:48 | 26:55a | 22:52 |  |
| I taught in Temple | 14:49a | 26:55b | 22:53a |  |
| Scriptures fulfilled | 14:49b | 26:56a |  |  |
| The disciples flee | 14:50 | 26:56b |  |  |
| Youth flees naked | 14:51–52 |  |  |  |
| **Denial and trial** |  |  |  |  |
| Led to high priest | 14:53a | 26:57a | 22:54a |  |
| Council convenes | 14:53b | 26:57b |  |  |
| Peter follows | 14:54a | 26:58a | 22:54b |  |
| To priest's courtyard | 14:54b | 26:58b |  |  |
| Sitting with servants | 14:54c | 26:58c | 22:55 |  |

|  | Mark | Matthew (PMA) | Luke (PMB) | Luke (C) |
|---|---|---|---|---|
| False witnesses | 14:55–61a | 26:59–63a |  |  |
| Sanhedrin's question | 14:61b–64 | 26:63b–65 |  |  |
| Jesus is mocked | 14:65 | 26:67–68 |  | 22:63–65 |
| Peter denies Jesus | 14:66–72 | 26:69–75 | 22:56–62 |  |
| **Before Pilate** |  |  |  |  |
| In the morning | 15:1a | 27:1a | 22:66a |  |
| Council decides | 15:1b | 27:1b |  |  |
| They bind Jesus | 15:1c | 27:2a |  |  |
| Jesus led to Pilate | 15:1c | 27:2b | 23:1b |  |
| You King of Jews? | 15:2 | 27:11b | 23:3 |  |
| Jesus stays silent | 15:3–5 | 27:12–14 | 23:9–10 |  |
| Barabbas or Jesus | 15:6–7 | 27:15–16 | 23:[17], 19 |  |
| Barabbas or Jesus | 15:8–11 | 27:17–18, 20 |  |  |
| Barabbas or Jesus | 15:12–15 | 27:21–23, 26 | 23:18–25 |  |
| Pilate flogs Jesus | 15:15c | 27:26b |  |  |
| Hail, King of Jews | 15:16–20a | 27:27–31a |  |  |
| **Jesus' crucifixion** |  |  |  |  |
| They lead him out | 15:20b | 27:31b | 23:26a |  |
| To crucify him | 15:20c | 27:31c |  |  |
| Simon carries cross | 15:21 | 27:32 | 23:26b |  |
| Arrival at Golgotha | 15:22 | 27:33 | 23:33a |  |
| Wine with myrrh | 15:23 | 27:34 |  |  |
| They crucify him | 15:24a | 27:35a | 23:33b |  |
| Garments divided | 15:24b | 27:35b | 23:34b |  |
| At third hour | 15:25 |  |  |  |
| Epigraph/charge | 15:26 | 27:37 | 23:38 |  |
| Bandits crucified | 15:27 | 27:38 |  | 23:33c |
| People watch |  |  |  | 23:35a |
| Passersby mock | 15:29–30 | 27:39–40 |  |  |
| The rulers mock | 15:31–32a | 27:41–42a |  | 23:35b |
| Let him come down | 15:32b | 27:42b |  |  |
| The soldiers mock |  |  |  | 23:36–37 |
| The bandits mock | 15:32c | 27:44 |  | 23:39 |
| Darkness over land | 15:33 | 27:45 | 23:44 | 23:45a |
| Jesus forsaken | 15:34–35 | 27:46–47 |  |  |
| Jesus given vinegar | 15:36a | 27:48 |  |  |
| Will Elijah come | 15:36b | 27:49 |  |  |

|  | Mark | Matthew (PMA) | Luke (PMB) | Luke (C) |
|---|---|---|---|---|
| With a loud voice | 15:37a | 27:50a | 23:46a | |
| Jesus expires | 15:37b | 27:50b | 23:46c | |
| Temple veil torn | 15:38 | 27:51a | | 23:45b |
| Centurion confesses | 15:39 | 27:54 | 23:47 | |
| Women from Galilee | 15:40a, 41a | 27:55 | 23:49 | |
| Mary, Mary, Salome | 15:40b | 27:56 | | |
| And many others | 15:41b | | from 8:3 | |
| **Jesus' burial** | | | | |
| Joseph requests body | 15:42–43 | 27:57–58a | 23:50–52 | |
| Pilate inquires | 15:44–45a | | | |
| Pilate gives body | 15:45b | 27:58b | | |
| Jesus entombed | 15:46a | 27:59–60a | 23:53 | |
| Stone over tomb | 15:46b | 27:60b | | |
| Day of preparation | →15:42b | 23:54a | | |
| The women watch | 15:47 | 27:61 | 23:55 | |

The first two columns of Table 12.12 set out Mark's passion narrative. The last three show his sources, as these have been preserved in Matthew, Luke, and Luke, respectively.

Proto-Mark A provided Mark's most extensive source for the passion narrative. This account combined the passion narrative of Proto-Mark, the words of institution of the Lord's Supper, the Sanhedrin trial source, the passion narrative of C, and other passion material in A. Mark shared Proto-Mark A with Matthew, and both generally followed it in the passion narrative. Consequently, Mark and Matthew have very much the same passion material, and this shared material never diverges in order.

Proto-Mark B provided Mark with a less extensive passion account, since it included only the passion narrative of Proto-Mark. Mark shared Proto-Mark B with Luke and used this source to supplement the overlapping material in Proto-Mark A. We find evidence for this conclusion in the frequent instances where Luke has one element of a sentence, Matthew has another, and Mark has both. The instances given in Table 12.13 illustrate this feature of the material.

Mark's third source, the passion narrative of C, had already been incorporated into Proto-Mark A but was also known separately to each of the Synoptic evangelists. Matthew used only the passion material of C that had been inserted in Proto-Mark A. Luke, since he did not know Proto-Mark A, used the separate version of C, inserting it independently into the passion narrative of Proto-Mark B. Mark for the most part used the C material in

### Table 12.13
### Mark's conflation of PMA and PMB

| Matthew (PMA) | Mark (PMA+PMB) | Luke (PMB) |
|---|---|---|
|  | 14:1 Unleavened Bread | 22:1 the feast of Unleavened Bread |
| 26:2 after two days | after two days |  |

| Matthew (PMA) | Mark (PMA+PMB) | Luke (PMB) |
|---|---|---|
| 26:17 On the first | 14:12 On the first |  |
|  | day | 22:7 The day came |

| Matthew (PMA) | Mark (PMA+PMB) | Luke (PMB) |
|---|---|---|
|  | 14:30 today | 22:34 today |
| 26:34 in this night | in this night |  |

| Matthew (PMA) | Mark (PMA+PMB) | Luke (PMB) |
|---|---|---|
|  | 14:37 You sleep? | 22:46 Why do you sleep? |
| 26:40 Could you not stay awake with me one hour? | Could you not stay awake one hour? |  |

| Matthew (PMA) | Mark (PMA+PMB) | Luke (PMB) |
|---|---|---|
| 26:58 with the servants | 14:54 with the servants |  |
|  | before the fire | 22:56 before the fire |

| Matthew (PMA) | Mark (PMA+PMB) | Luke (PMB) |
|---|---|---|
| 26:74 the man | 14:71 this man |  |
|  | whom you speak about | 22:60 what you speak about |

| Matthew (PMA) | Mark (PMA+PMB) | Luke (PMB) |
|---|---|---|
|  | 15:26 the epigraph | 23:38 the epigraph |
| 27:37 the charge | the charge |  |

Proto-Mark A, but a few pieces of evidence suggest that he occasionally drew on the separate version of C as well. Such evidence is provided by two places where Mark shares elements of C with Luke that do not occur in Matthew (Table 12.14).

Mark's third source, the passion narrative of C, had already been incorporated into Proto-Mark A but was also known separately to each of the Synoptic evangelists. Matthew used only the passion material of C that had been inserted in Proto-Mark A. Luke, since he did not know Proto-Mark A, used the separate version of C, inserting it independently into the passion narrative of Proto-Mark B. Mark for the most part used the C material in Proto-Mark A, but a few pieces of evidence suggest that he occasionally drew on the separate version of C as well. Such evidence is provided by two places where Mark shares elements of C with Luke that do not occur in Matthew (Table 12.14).

Table 12.14
C material shared by Mark and Luke but not Matthew

| Matthew | Mark | Luke |
|---------|------|------|
| 20:17— | 10:32 and Jesus was preceding them | 19:28 he went in front |

| | Mark | Luke |
|---------|------|------|
| | 15:32 the Christ | 23:35 the Christ of God |
| 27:42 king of Israel | the king of Israel | |

In the first instance, Mark could be drawing directly from C like Luke in a place where Proto-Mark A, followed by Matthew, did not include the relevant material from C. An alternative explanation, however, might be that Mark included C material from Proto-Mark A, while Matthew omitted it. In the second instance, Mark is probably conflating parallel expressions from the two different versions of C: "king of Israel" from the Proto-Mark A version shared with Matthew and "the Christ" directly from the C source shared with Luke.

The C passion material contains one of the most notorious minor agreements of Matthew and Luke against Mark, the question addressed to Jesus by his mockers: τίς ἐστιν ὁ παίσας σε (Matt 26:68; Luke 22:64). It may be well then to see how our theory accounts for it. In this theory, the C source included a story in which Jesus' tormentors covered his eyes, hit him, and then asked him to prophetically reveal who hit him. This story was taken into Proto-Mark A but not Proto-Mark B. Luke knew it directly from C, while Mark and Matthew drew it from their common source, Proto-Mark A. Luke best preserved the essence of the story by retaining all the significant elements. Matthew and Mark did less well. Matthew omitted the covering of the eyes and Mark omitted the question τίς ἐστιν ὁ παίσας σε. It was this omission by Mark that created the agreement of Matthew and Luke against Mark.

## The Ending of Mark

In 1952, Vincent Taylor referred to "the almost universally held conclusion" that the longer ending of Mark (Mark 16:9–20) is not an original part of Mark. According to Taylor, "Both the external and the internal evidence are decisive."[5] Today one would have to make a more nuanced statement of these claims. It is still true that most scholars reject the longer ending as part of

---

5. Taylor, *St. Mark*, 610.

Mark, though dissenting voices have been raised.[6] However, the basis for this view has shifted almost completely from external evidence (i.e., the manuscript tradition) to internal (e.g., considerations of Mark's style). The best illustration of this shift is seen in the discussion of the longer ending given by Bruce Metzger on behalf of the editorial committee of the United Bible Societies' *The Greek New Testament*. The UBS committee did not regard the longer ending as part of Mark and gave their decision an "A" ranking, indicating their highest level of certainty. It is instructive to see the reasons that Metzger gives for their decision.[7] After setting out the testimony of the manuscripts, Metzger writes that the longer ending must be judged secondary "by internal evidence." Conspicuously absent is any claim that the manuscript tradition in itself is decisive, as Taylor thought. Almost the full weight of the argument rests on internal considerations, which prevail even though the longer ending is "current in a variety of witnesses, some of them ancient." The manuscript evidence in itself then does not settle the question. Instead, as Kenneth Clark noted, the witnesses both for and against the genuineness of the longer ending are "early and impressive," and "we should consider the question still open."[8]

If the external evidence is not decisive, then is the internal evidence? The UBS committee apparently thought so. Metzger gives two types of internal evidence to support the committee's decision. One is that the connection between Mark 16:8 and 16:9 is awkward in three ways. First, "the subject of ver. 8 is the women, whereas Jesus is the presumed subject in ver. 9." It is true that awkwardness results from the omission of Jesus' name in 16:9. However, this type of awkwardness could be used instead as an argument for Mark's authorship of the longer ending, since Mark often omits Jesus' name after shifting from another subject. This happens in Mark 1:21 and 1:29–30, but Mark sets the record between Mark 3:7 and 5:6 by omitting Jesus' name completely through several shifts of subject.[9]

Second, "in ver. 9 Mary Magdalene is identified even though she has been mentioned only a few lines before (15.47 and 16.1); the other women of verses 1–8 are now forgotten." This feature of Mark 16:9, even if awkward, need not count against Mark's authorship of the longer ending. It is likely that in Proto-Mark A, Jesus appeared to Mary Magdalene alone in a story distinct

---

6. Eta Linnemann, "Der (wiedergefundene) Markusschluss," *ZTK* 66 (1969): 255–87 (Mark 16:15–20 was the original ending of Mark); William R. Farmer, *The Last Twelve Verses of Mark* (SNTSMS 25; Cambridge: Cambridge University Press, 1974).

7. Bruce M. Metzger, *A Textual Commentary on the Greek New Testament* (2nd ed.; Stuttgart: Deutsche Bibelgesellschaft, 1994), 102–7.

8. Kenneth W. Clark, "The Theological Relevance of Textual Variation in Current Criticism of the Greek New Testament," *JBL* 85 (1966): 1–16, esp. 10.

9. I owe this observation to Farmer, *Last Twelve Verses*, 83–84.

from the empty tomb story (see below). Thus, Mark may simply have been following one of his sources, Proto-Mark A, in mentioning Mary Magdalene alone in 16:9.

Third, "the use of ἀναστὰς δέ and the position of πρῶτον are appropriate at the beginning of a comprehensive narrative, but they are ill-suited in a continuation of verses 1–8." This observation contains an element of truth: Mark 16:9 does constitute a new beginning in the narrative. It begins a section that enumerates the resurrection appearances of Jesus. However, that fact need not imply that Mark did not write it as a sequel to 16:1–8. Since most manuscripts of Mark include the longer ending, someone in the early church thought that 16:9–20 served as an appropriate continuation of 16:1–8. That someone may well have been Mark himself. Even if we think he could have done better, we can see his plan of organization. Mark 16:8 ends one story, the story of the empty tomb. That story leaves us with the expectation of something more to come. At this point we have only the word of some man in the tomb that Jesus was raised and no statement from the author to confirm the fact. Mark 16:9 begins a new section that gives the verification. The first words, ἀναστὰς δέ, provide the author's confirmation that the man in the tomb was right. The author then proceeds to relate three appearances of Jesus. He enumerates these with appropriate introductory words: πρῶτον for the first (16:9), μετὰ δὲ ταῦτα for the second (16:12), and ὕστερον for the last (16:14). Mark 16:9–20 thus constitutes one way of continuing 16:1–8, even if not the only way, and there is no reason from a literary perspective to think that it was not Mark's way. Whatever awkwardness occurs in the connection between 16:8 and 16:9, it is no greater than what we can attribute to Mark himself.

In addition to the awkwardness of the connection, Metzger cites another type of internal evidence: the vocabulary and style of the longer ending are "non-Markan." As examples, he lists nine words or phrases that occur here but nowhere else in Mark, and two that occur nowhere else in the New Testament. The arguments of the UBS committee are not new of course, and this one in particular has received emphasis previously.[10] The problem with this argument is that those who use it never make explicit their presuppositions about what constitutes "Markan" and "non-Markan" style. Implicitly they presuppose that Mark's style is coterminous with the style of Mark 1:1–16:8. Implicitly they presuppose that Mark was an author who composed all of this material, not an editor who compiled most of it from earlier sources. Thus implicitly they presuppose Markan priority, and more specifi-

10. E.g., Taylor, *Mark*, 610–14; J. K. Elliott, "The Text and Language of the Endings to Mark's Gospel," in idem, *The Language and Style of the Gospel of Mark* (Leiden: Brill, 1993), 203–11. For an examination that reaches the opposite conclusion, see Farmer, *Last Twelve Verses*, 79–103.

cally one particular interpretation of Markan priority that makes Mark a composer rather than a compiler. Since they presuppose that Mark composed 1:1–16:8, they assume that all of this material reflects Mark's style and further that Mark's style is fully reflected in this material. Therefore, if the style of Mark 16:9–20 differs from that of 1:1–16:8, Mark could not have written it.

Given the theory of Markan priority, all of these presuppositions could be correct, though they need not be. Even if the Gospel of Mark served as the source for Matthew and Luke, it might still be based on earlier sources, such that it reflects not the style of Mark, but the style of pre-Markan sources. In that case, if the longer ending reflects a different style, it might well be the style of Mark himself. Given other theories besides Markan priority, the presuppositions of the UBS committee and others are almost certainly not correct. It is no coincidence that William Farmer, prime exponent of the Griesbach hypothesis, also wrote a monograph defending the authenticity of the longer ending of Mark. From the Griesbach perspective, Mark did not compose *de novo*, but drew material from Matthew and Luke. Mark 1:1–16:8 therefore does not always reflect his own style. If a different style appears in Mark 16:9–20, it could be Mark's own style coming to the fore, in which case the longer ending would be the original ending of Mark.

The stylistic argument against the longer ending thus stands or falls with the theory of Markan priority; in fact, with one particular view of Markan priority. If Markan priority falls, so does the stylistic argument against the longer ending. It may be premature to say that the theory of Markan priority has fallen, but at least in this study I have tried to give it a good shove. It would be well therefore to take another look at the style of the longer ending. In my theory, the style of Mark the evangelist is not readily available in Mark 1:1–16:8. Elements of style common to Mark and Matthew come from their common sources, and the same goes for elements of style common to Mark and Luke. Elements of style common to all three Synoptics go back to Proto-Mark. That does not leave a great deal of room for Mark's own style. The primary way to uncover this is to look in the cracks between the material, so to speak—to identify redactional elements that are unique to Mark. That is what I tried to do in Chapter 2. The elements of Mark's style identified there are not extensive, but they may suffice to draw some tentative conclusions about the longer ending.

When we examine the vocabulary and style of the longer ending, we find five of the features of Markan style identified in Chapter 2 (all from Table 2.17): ἀναστάς (16:9), πρωΐ (16:9), κηρύσσειν + δαιμόνια ἐκβάλλειν (16:15–17), ἄρρωστοι (16:18), and -χου as adverbial ending (16:20). We might also consider σκληροκαρδία (16:14) as a sixth feature. Three times Mark introduces the theme of "hardness of heart" with the words πωρόω and πώρωσις (Mark 3:5; 6:52; 8:17), but he also uses σκληροκαρδία in the A material (Mark 10:5; Matt 19:8). Thus, the theme is Markan, while the wording is not un-Markan. These six features suggest that Mark's hand is visible in the longer ending. Other words and phrases in the longer ending do not occur in the list of Markan stylistic features identified in Chapter 2. However, since our list is so limited, we have no basis for labeling these words and phrases in the longer ending as non-Markan. What evidence we have points in the direction of a common editor for Mark 1:1–16:8 and 16:9–20.

More telling than these vocabulary items is the editorial procedure visible in the longer ending. The editor combines material found in Matthew's resurrection narrative with material found in Luke's resurrection narrative, adding several redactional elements. None of the resurrection stories unique to John appears. The one point of contact between the longer ending and John is the appearance to Mary Magdalene, and this could be simply a variation of Matthew's account, in which Jesus appears to Mary Magdalene and another Mary. Thus, if the editor was not Mark but a later scribe, then he drew from the resurrection narratives of Matthew and Luke to create the longer ending. However, if we substitute Proto-Mark A for Matthew and Proto-Mark B for Luke, then we have exactly the same editorial procedure as that of Mark. As we have seen, Mark's procedure was to conflate his sources, usually Proto-Mark A shared with Matthew and Proto-Mark B shared with Luke, occasionally adding material from other sources or his own redaction. Exactly the same procedure appears in the longer ending. It would be somewhat of a coincidence if a later editor eschewed John and adopted toward Matthew and Luke precisely the same method that Mark adopted with respect to Proto-Mark A and Proto-Mark B. In this case, if it looks like a duck, it probably is a duck. Since the editor looks like Mark, he probably was Mark.

Given our theory, both the stylistic features of the longer ending and the editorial procedure used in it suggest that it came from the same person who edited Mark 1:1–16:8, i.e., the evangelist Mark. If Mark did create the longer ending, then it would be the original ending of the gospel. In that case, we still need an explanation for the absence of Mark 16:9–20 in part of the manuscript tradition and an explanation for the shorter ending. With our theory, it is possible to provide a plausible explanation for both. By starting with Proto-Mark, we can trace the development of the Synoptic resurrection narratives down to their later stages.

Let us begin therefore by reconstructing the ending of Proto-Mark. We do this by identifying those elements that occur in all three Synoptic resurrection narratives. These are given in Table 12.15. At the end of the empty tomb story, Matthew and Luke agree that the women reported the empty tomb to the disciples. This is a significant agreement against Mark, who has the women say nothing. Matthew and Luke in their agreement show that in Proto-Mark the women reported the news. Matthew preserved this element from Proto-Mark A; Luke from Proto-Mark B. Later we will discuss why Mark changed it. After the women's report, only two more items stand in all

Table 12.15

Overlap of the Synoptic resurrection narratives

| Matthew (PMA) | Mark (Longer ending) | Luke (PMB) |
|---|---|---|
| 28:8c they ran to tell his disciples. | 16:8c And they said nothing to anyone, for they were afraid. | 24:9b they told all these things to the eleven and to all the rest. |
| 28:17 And when they saw him, they worshipped . . . | 16:14a Finally he appeared to the eleven . . . | 24:36 As they were saying these things he stood in their midst . . . |
| 28:18 Jesus spoke to them saying, ". . . 19a So go and make disciples of all the nations . . ." | 16:15 And he said to them, "Go into all the world and preach the gospel to all creation." | 24:46 And he said to them, ". . . 47 . . . that repentance for forgiveness of sins should be preached in his name to all the nations . . ." |

three accounts: Jesus appears to the disciples and he charges them to preach to all the nations. These three items then constitute the minimum assured content of the ending of Proto-Mark.

It is significant, then, that precisely these three items, no more and no less, make up the shorter ending of Mark (Table 12.16).

Table 12.16

Ending of Proto-Mark and the shorter ending of Mark

| Ending of Proto-Mark | Shorter ending of Mark |
|---|---|
| Report of the women | All that had been commanded they made known briefly to those about Peter. |
| Appearance to disciples | After this Jesus himself appeared to them. |
| Charge to preach | And from the east even to the west he sent out through them the sacred and imperishable proclamation of eternal salvation. |

The shorter ending consists of precisely those items that on other grounds we have identified as the ending of Proto-Mark. Is the shorter ending then the original ending of Proto-Mark? While it does preserve the content of Proto-Mark that we have reconstructed, for two reasons it appears that it does not preserve the actual wording of Proto-Mark. First, in a few instances we can reconstruct the wording of Proto-Mark from agreements between Matthew and Luke, and the wording of the shorter ending differs. In the report of the women, Matthew and Luke use the same verb (ἀπαγγεῖλαι, ἀπήγγειλαν), while the shorter ending has ἐξήγγειλαν. In the charge to preach, Matthew and Luke agree on the phrase πάντα τὰ ἔθνη, but the shorter ending lacks this. Second, in the shorter ending, the phrase τὸ ἱερὸν καὶ ἄφθαρτον κήρυγμα τῆς αἰωνίου σωτηρίας seems to reflect a more ornate style than the simple prose of Proto-Mark.

How then do we explain why the shorter ending matches the ending of Proto-Mark in content but not in wording? In one of two ways, I think. Both presume that a scribe created the shorter ending for a copy of Mark from which the original ending (Mark 16:9–20) had been removed. 1) The scribe may have proceeded exactly as I have done: comparing the resurrection accounts of Matthew and Luke to find the common elements. He would then have rewritten these in his own words and added them to his truncated copy of Mark to provide an ending. 2) Alternatively, the scribe may have had a copy of Proto-Mark. He took the ending from Proto-Mark, rewrote it in his own words, and added it to his truncated copy of Mark. In the first scenario, the scribe in effect reconstructed the ending of Proto-Mark without realizing it. In the second scenario, he knew the ending of Proto-Mark. I think that the second is far more likely. The shorter ending then is probably the ending of Proto-Mark rewritten by a later hand to serve as an ending for Mark 16:1–8.

The ending of Proto-Mark was brief and apparently did not specify whether Jesus appeared to the disciples in Jerusalem or Galilee. Proto-Mark A expanded this ending into a Galilean resurrection narrative, while Proto-Mark B expanded it into a Jerusalem resurrection narrative. Matthew followed Proto-Mark A, Luke followed Proto-Mark B, while Mark as usual conflated the two. Table 12.17 puts in parallel the elements of Proto-Mark A in Matthew's account, the elements of Proto-Mark B in Luke's account, and Mark's conflated account.

## Table 12.17
### Mark 16:8c–20 with parallels

| Matthew (PMA) | Mark 16:8c–20 | Luke (PMB) |
| --- | --- | --- |
| 28:8c they ran to tell his disciples. | 16:8c And they said nothing to anyone, for they were afraid. | 24:9b they told all these things to the eleven and to all the rest. |
|  | 16:9a Now rising early on the first day of the week, |  |
| 28:9 And behold Jesus met them . . . | 9b he appeared first to Mary Magdalene, | cf. 24:10a |

| Matthew (PMA) | Mark 16:8c–20 | Luke (PMB) |
|---|---|---|
| | 9c from whom he had cast out seven demons. | 8:2 from whom seven demons had come out |
| 28:10 Then Jesus said to them, "Don't be afraid. Go tell my brothers to go to Galilee and they will see me there." | — | |
| | 10a She went and told those who had been with him | 24:10b They told these things to the apostles. |
| | 10b as they were mourning and crying. | |
| | 11 But they, when they heard that he was alive and had been seen by her, disbelieved. | 11 But these words appeared to be nonsense to them and they disbelieved the women. |
| | 12 After this he appeared in a different form to two of them as they were walking and going to the country. | 13 And behold two of them were going to a village . . . And Jesus coming near went with them, but their eyes were kept from recognizing him . . . 30 As he dined with them, taking the bread he blessed it and breaking it he distributed it to them, 31 and their eyes were opened and they recognized him . . . |
| | 13a And they went and told the rest. | 33 And getting up in that hour they returned to Jerusalem and found the eleven and those with them . . . 35 And they related what had happened on the way . . . |
| | 13b But they did not believe them either. | —? |

| Matthew (PMA) | Mark 16:8c–20 | Luke (PMB) |
|---|---|---|
| 16 The eleven disciples went to Galilee, to the mountain to which Jesus had directed them. | — | |
| 17 And when they saw him, they worshipped, | 14a Finally he appeared to the eleven | 36 As they were saying these things he stood in their midst . . . |
| | as they were dining | cf. 24:43–44 |
| though some doubted. | 14b and he rebuked their unbelief and hardness of heart because they had not believed those who had seen him risen. | —? |
| 18 Jesus spoke to them saying, ". . . 19a So go and make disciples of all the nations | 15 And he said to them, "Go into all the world and preach the gospel to all creation. | 46 And he said to them, ". . . 47 . . . that repentance for forgiveness of sins should be preached in his name to all the nations . . ." |
| 19b baptizing them . . ." | 16 He who believes and is baptized shall be saved, but he who disbelieves shall be condemned. | |
| | 17 These signs will follow those who believe: in my name they will cast out demons, they will speak with new tongues, 18 [and in their hands] they will pick up serpents, and if they drink anything poisonous it will not harm them, they will lay hands on the sick and they will get well." | |
| | 19 So the Lord Jesus after speaking to them was taken up into heaven | 24:51 And as he was blessing them, he parted from them and was carried up into heaven. |
| | and sat at the right hand of God. | |

| Matthew (PMA) | Mark 16:8c–20 | Luke (PMB) |
|---|---|---|
| | 20 And going forth they preached everywhere, the Lord working with them and confirming the word through the signs that followed. | |

From comparing Mark and Matthew in Table 12.17, we can reconstruct the ending of Proto-Mark A. This gospel ended with a Galilean resurrection narrative, partially preserved in Mark but more fully in Matthew. In this narrative, Jesus appeared first to one or more women. Mark limits this appearance to Mary Magdalene, while Matthew includes "the other Mary," whom he had earlier placed at the empty tomb. I suspect that Mark better preserves Proto-Mark A. The appearance to Mary Magdalene alone, also attested by the Fourth Gospel (John 20:14–18), in Proto-Mark A was probably distinct from the visit of the women to the tomb. Matthew connected these two events by having the appearance occur as the women returned from the tomb, a feature unique to Matthew. Connecting the two stories in this way made it necessary to have Jesus appear to all the women who were at the tomb, not just to Mary Magdalene. In the continuation of Proto-Mark A, Jesus had Mary tell his disciples to go to Galilee, they went and saw Jesus, and he charged them to preach to all the nations and baptize them.

From comparing Mark and Luke in Table 12.17, we can reconstruct the ending of Proto-Mark B. In this gospel, when the women report the message of the angel(s) at the tomb, the disciples disbelieve them. Apparently Jesus does not appear to Mary. The first appearance occurs to "two of them" as they are going to the country. Luke specifies the village of Emmaus, but since Mark lacks this, it may be Lukan redaction. Mark may have abbreviated the account of Proto-Mark B here, but Luke surely lengthened it with the typically Lukan theme of proof from prophecy. The two then return and tell the others. Again, Luke gives a specific location, Jerusalem, but its absence from Mark may indicate that it did not stand in Proto-Mark B. In Mark the disciples again respond with unbelief. Luke lacks this, but he may have omitted it from Proto-Mark B because he has mentioned at this point an appearance to Peter (Luke 24:34). The disciples in Luke could not very well respond with unbelief if they had already given credence to Peter's vision. Mark may therefore preserve Proto-Mark B at this point. Jesus then appears to the disciples as a group, perhaps at a meal. Mark has "as they were dining," while in Luke, Jesus asks for food and the disciples give him fish. In Mark but not Luke, Jesus then rebukes the disciples for unbelief. Some form of this may well have stood in Proto-Mark B if both instances of their unbelief also stood in it. Jesus then charges them to preach to all the nations, after which he is taken up to heaven.

Mark had the task of combining the resurrection accounts of Proto-Mark A and Proto-Mark B. The former placed Jesus' appearance to the disciples in Galilee. The latter, while it may not have mentioned Jerusalem specifically, at least never described the disciples going to Galilee. It implied, therefore, that Jesus appeared to them in their last known location, i.e., Jerusalem. Mark decided to go with the implicit Jerusalem appearance of Proto-Mark B, while including as much of Proto-Mark A's Galilean account as he could. Four passages in the Galilean account were particularly problematic for including in a Jerusalem resurrection narrative: 1) Jesus told the disciples at the Last Supper that he would precede them to Galilee after his resurrection (Matt 26:32; Mark 14:28); 2) the messenger at the tomb instructed the women to tell the disciples that Jesus would precede them to Galilee, where they would see him (Matt 28:7; Mark 16:7); 3) Jesus had Mary Magdalene give the same message to the disciples (Matt 28:10); and 4) the disciples went to Galilee to see Jesus (Matt 28:16). Mark solved the problem of the last two by omitting them. He kept the second, but nullified its effect by revising the ending of the empty tomb story. In Proto-Mark A, the messenger sent the message to go to Galilee through the women, and they delivered it to the disciples. Mark changed the story so that the disciples never got the message. The women did not deliver it because they were afraid. The disciples therefore had no reason to go to Galilee and thus were implicitly in Jerusalem when Jesus appeared to them. So far, so good, but what about the first problem passage, Jesus' words at the Last Supper? Why did Mark omit or nullify the last three but leave the first? Unfortunately, Mark is not telling, so we can only speculate. Perhaps at the point in the story where the first reference to Galilee occurs, Mark had not yet thought ahead to consider how he would deal with the resurrection narratives, and so included the reference from Proto-Mark A. When he came to the resurrection narratives and decided his strategy, he dealt with the last three references accordingly, but never went back to change the first.

While most of the material in Mark's account came from the resurrection narratives, the reference to Mary's seven demons came from an earlier passage in Proto-Mark B (Mark 16:9c//Luke 8:2). Other passages appear to be Markan redaction (Mark 16:9a, 10b, 17–18, 19b, 20). The most interesting of these relate to the "signs" that would follow believers (Mark 16:17–18, 20). These give us some insight into the perspective of Mark himself.

Now that we have identified the endings of the various documents involved, we can return to the manuscript tradition for the ending of Mark. If our theory is correct, Proto-Mark ended with something similar to the shorter ending; Proto-Mark A, followed by Matthew, ended with a Galilean resurrection narrative; Proto-Mark B, followed by Luke, ended with a Jerusalem resurrection narrative; and Mark ended with Mark 16:9–20, conflated from Proto-Mark A and Proto-Mark B. We must now explain the confusion in the manuscript tradition. The following reconstruction provides one plausible explanation. 1) A scribe omitted Mark 16:9–20. We cannot be certain why, but there are three main possibilities. First, the scribe may have known both Proto-Mark and Mark. Since Proto-Mark, a document that resembled Mark, lacked the longer ending, the scribe concluded that this material did not belong to the original ending of Mark and so omitted it. Second, the scribe may have noticed that Mark looks forward to a Galilean resurrection narrative (Mark 14:28; 16:7), which the longer ending does not provide. From that fact the scribe may have concluded that the longer ending was not the original ending of Mark and so omitted it. Third, the scribe may have omitted Mark's resurrection narrative because it did not agree with the Gospel of Matthew. Any one, two, or even all three of these reasons may have played a part in the scribe's decision not to include Mark 16:9–20. In any case, his omission created the reading preserved in ℵ and B and other manuscripts. 2) In a separate line of tradition, Mark 16:9–20 was never omitted. 3) Some scribes knew both traditions and reattached Mark 16:9–20—some with asterisks, obeli, or a critical note in the manuscript, and others without. 4) A scribe who knew the truncated version of Mark also had a copy of Proto-Mark. He took the short ending from Proto-Mark, rewrote it in his own words, and substituted it for Mark 16:8 to provide a more appropriate ending. This stage is preserved in the Old Italian manuscript k. 5) A scribe or scribes who knew one version of Mark with the shorter ending and another with the longer ending included them both in that order after Mark 16:8. Our theory thus provides a plausible explanation not only for the development of the resurrection tradition from Proto-Mark to Mark, but also for the subsequent manuscript tradition of Mark's ending.

## Final Considerations

The theory that I have presented in this study postulates the existence of several lost documents from which the extant gospels drew their material, just as the two-document hypothesis postulates the existence of a lost document, Q. Some scholars resist any appeal to such hypothetical documents on principle. After all, doesn't "Occam's razor" warn us not to multiply entities unnecessarily in formulating hypotheses?[11] The key word here, I believe, is "unnecessarily." Occam's razor does not imply that the correct solution will always be simple. It merely advises us to try the simpler theories first, until it becomes necessary to move on to the more complex. The simpler route has been taken by most New Testament scholarship over the last two hundred years. Occam's razor has been given its full due. But the simpler theories have been found wanting, and it is time to move on to the more complex. As we do

---

11. Goulder, *Luke*, 14; Goodacre, *Synoptic Problem*, 160.

so, we should keep in mind how easily documents from the past can be lost. The fortuitous discoveries at Qumran and Nag Hammadi illustrate how documents can be lost for centuries. It would be no wonder if other documents from that time have been lost for good.

Some theories of Synoptic relations have been criticized because the compositional procedure that they attribute to one evangelist or another seems implausible. In particular, the Farrer hypothesis is susceptible to the charge that it makes Luke proceed in an implausible manner, while the same is true of the Griesbach hypothesis with respect to Mark. Gerald Downing has argued that such charges are true not only from a contemporary perspective, but also from a first-century perspective.[12] It may be useful therefore to put our own theory to the test to determine whether or not it requires of Mark a procedure that would be implausible by ancient standards.

My theory affirms that Mark took two major sources and three minor sources and combined them into a larger whole, usually conflating them when they overlapped. The analogy closest in time to this procedure would be that of Tatian in the second century, who did pretty much the same thing with the four gospels. Mark would have had an easier time than Tatian, because none of his sources were as large as Tatian's smallest (i.e., the Gospel of Mark itself). Mark had only two sources of any length, Proto-Mark A and Proto-Mark B. The C source, miracle/mission source, and parable discourse were minor in comparison. The physical difficulty that Mark faced in comparing different scrolls (or codices) would thus have been less than that faced by Tatian.

Tatian also appears to provide a good analogy for Mark's aim. In the words of Downing, "If we can trust our available texts at all, Tatian's aim seems to be to include as much detail as possible from all of his sources." That would apply almost equally well to Mark in my theory. In this respect, my own theory differs from the Griesbach hypothesis, which has Mark conflating Matthew and Luke. That theory has to explain why Mark omitted all of the material generally designated as Q, M, and L. In my own theory, Mark's sources did not include that material. He did not omit it; he simply did not know it. Mark did make minor omissions from his sources, but for the most part it seems that he tried to include as much of his source material as possible.

For much of the material, Mark had only two sources, Proto-Mark A and Proto-Mark B. Mark's task of combining these sources was made easier by the fact that they were two different revisions of the same document (Proto-Mark). Where they had the same material, therefore, they almost always had

12. F. Gerald Downing, "Compositional Conventions and the Synoptic Problem," *JBL* 107 (1988): 69–85; idem, "A Paradigm Perplex: Luke, Matthew and Mark," *NTS* 38 (1992): 15–36.

it in the same order. Mark did not have to do much scrolling back and forth to find the same pericope in one as in the other. After Mark copied a pericope shared by both sources and moved on, he would sometimes find material in one that did not occur in the other. He would add this and then proceed to the next instance of shared material. In this way, he kept the order of the material that was unique to each source as well as the order of the material that they shared.

In passages where his sources overlapped, Mark conflated them. As far as I can tell, in only one instance did he conflate material from four of his sources in the same passage (Mark 3:7–12 above). We also find a few instances in which he conflated three of them in a single passage (e.g., Mark 1:32–34 above). Generally, however, the conflation involved only two sources at a time. Downing provides possible analogies for this procedure from Josephus and Plutarch.[13] Proponents of the two-document hypothesis will acknowledge that Matthew also furnishes an analogy when he conflates Mark and Q. In my own theory as well, conflation of two sources occurs in Matthew, though it is conflation of Q with Proto-Mark A rather than with Mark.

It appears then that the editorial procedure that I attribute to Mark is not implausible in light of analogies from near the same time. We can find other analogies that are further removed in time. Julius Wellhausen's documentary hypothesis concerning the Pentateuch comes to mind. In this theory, ancient scribes combined material from four different sources to create the Pentateuch. Though this view has been challenged, it has never been replaced by a more plausible theory. Whether or not Wellhausen's theory is correct in every particular, it is difficult to account for the features of the Pentateuch apart from some documentary source hypothesis. Whoever composed this work sometimes left doublets and even triplets of parallel traditions. For example, the story in which a patriarch pretends that his wife is his sister occurs three times (Gen 12:10–20; 20:1–18; 26:6–11). In other cases, the composer conflated parallel traditions, as in the flood narrative (Gen 6:9–9:17). Here two distinct flood accounts, generally assigned to J and P respectively, have been woven together into a single new version. The composer thus dealt with his sources in ways that are precisely analogous to those used by Mark and the other editors of the Synoptic tradition.

In more modern times, the same procedures can be observed in gospel "harmonies," in which latter-day Tatians have sought to make a single narrative from the four canonical gospels. It is this impulse toward harmonization that accounts for all of the editorial activities that I have mentioned, from the composer of the Pentateuch to Mark and from Tatian to the modern harmo-

---

13. F. Gerald Downing, "Redaction Criticism: Josephus' *Antiquities* and the Synoptic Problem, I, II," *JSNT* 8 (1980): 46–65; 9 (1980): 29–48; idem, "Compositional Conventions."

nizers. These editors had a desire for a single sacred narrative, whether of the sacred history of Israel or the sacred history of Jesus. Their interest lay not in noticing the differences in their sources as these reflected the differing perspectives of their authors, but in looking beyond the differences to see how their sources might be incorporated into a larger whole. There was only one history of Israel, and only one history of Jesus, so there should only be one narrative of the same. The form that this narrative took was determined by the uncritical attitude that the editors took toward their sources. They did not proceed, as a modern critical scholar might do in pursuit of the historical Jesus, by analyzing the sources critically, rejecting here and accepting there, and putting the conclusions together in a new, tentative reconstruction. Without necessarily accepting everything in their sources, they proceeded in general as if each of their sources contained a part of the truth and they could obtain a fuller truth by combining and conflating them.

If the conclusions of this study are correct, this practice of uncritical harmonization played a role from the beginning of the Synoptic tradition. Just as Matthew, Mark, and Luke combined and conflated earlier sources, so did the editors of Proto-Mark A and Proto-Mark B before them, as did the editor of Proto-Mark at an even earlier stage. The Synoptic Gospels attest to a complex prehistory in which a variety of documents and revisions of documents were combined and conflated. We may never reach the goal of understanding that prehistory completely. I can only hope that the present study makes some contribution toward that goal.

# APPENDIX

# *Dual Temporal and Local Expressions*

IN CHAPTER 6, I conduct a test of dual expressions in Mark. Here I explain why my approach differs from that taken by Christopher Tuckett in his examination of the dual expressions.[1]

For several reasons the list of dual expressions compiled by Tuckett does not serve my purpose. First, many of his examples occur in Markan material to which either Matthew or Luke has no parallel context. It is impossible in these instances to compare all three gospels, since one gospel does not have the relevant material. Tuckett argues that this procedure is justified in a study that aims to evaluate the Griesbach hypothesis, as his does: "In the cases of 'no parallel', it is immaterial whether there is no parallel to the phrase alone or to the whole context. In either case, Matthew/Luke cannot be the source of either half of Mark's duplicate expression."[2] This procedure may be justifiable in evaluating the Griesbach hypothesis, but it is misleading if, as I am suggesting, Mark drew not directly from Matthew and Luke, but from sources shared with Matthew and Luke, respectively. Mark may have drawn half of a duplicate expression from a passage in the source that he shared with Matthew (or Luke) even if Matthew (or Luke) omitted that passage. Since my purpose is not to evaluate the Griesbach hypothesis, but the theory of Markan priority, I need instances where all three gospels share the same material. Only with examples of this kind can we examine each author's usage. I will therefore eliminate from consideration all duplicate expressions in Mark that do not meet this criterion.

Secondly, Tuckett relied primarily on the lists provided by Neirynck, most of which I find inadequate for my purpose. The lists of Neirynck from which Tuckett drew most of his examples are the following: 10) "Double Statement: Temporal or Local"; 11) "Double Statement: General and Special"; 12) "Double Statement: Repetition of the Motif"; and 13) "Synonymous

---

1. Tuckett, *Revival of the Griesbach Hypothesis*, 16–21.
2. Ibid., 20.

Expression."[3] Except for the first, these categories are either too limited or too ill defined for our purpose. For example, Neirynck's category 11 consists of dual expressions where one is a special case of the other (e.g., Mark 1:5, all the Judean country/all the Jerusalemites). This category has only twenty-eight instances to begin with, and after we eliminate questionable instances,[4] temporal or local expressions that also belong to category 10,[5] and instances where either Matthew or Luke has no parallel to Mark,[6] only five remain,[7] too few to be useful for our purpose.

While category 11 is too limited, category 12 is too ill defined. Neirynck designates this category as "Double Statement: Repetition of the Motif." When he introduces it, he gives as an example Mark 3:14, 16: καὶ ἐποίησεν δώδεκα . . . καὶ ἐποίησεν τοὺς δώδεκα.[8] We might expect, then, instances where Mark makes the same statement twice. In fact, however, most of the instances cited by Neirynck do not fulfill this criterion. One that does not, for example, is Mark 1:7: ἔρχεται ὁ ἰσχυρότερός μου ὀπίσω μου . . . οὗ οὐκ εἰμὶ ἱκανὸς κύψας λῦσαι τὸν ἱμάντα τῶν ὑποδημάτων αὐτοῦ. Here the parallel is between the ideas "He is more powerful than me" and "I am not worthy to do X for him." It is no doubt a matter of judgment, but it seems to me that the second statement does not repeat the first but explicates it. Another example is Mark 1:17: καὶ ποιήσω ὑμᾶς . . . γενέσθαι (ἁλιεῖς ἀνθρώπων). Here again, no motif is repeated. These are not separate statements but parts of the same statement, with the second verb dependent on the first. Thus, the examples in this category are too disparate for our purpose.

The same is true for Neirynck's category 13, which he labels "Synonymous Expression." We might expect here instances where Mark says basically the same thing twice in different words, such as Mark 1:42: ἀπῆλθεν ἀπ᾽ αὐτοῦ ἡ λέπρα . . . καὶ ἐκαθαρίσθη. In fact, however, in many of the examples given, the expressions are not synonymous but simply parallel: e.g., Mark 1:24: Ἰησοῦ Ναζαρηνέ . . . ὁ ἅγιος τοῦ θεου. In others, the expressions are not even parallel: e.g., Mark 1:4: μετανοίας . . . εἰς ἄφεσιν ἁμαρτιῶν. The lack of a clear criterion for determining inclusion in this category makes it also too ill defined to be useful.

Of the four categories of Neirynck used by Tuckett, the only one that is sufficiently well-defined and sufficiently extensive for our purpose is

3. Neirynck, *Duality in Mark,* 94–106.

4. 14:63, 64; 15:35, 36.

5. 1:21; 2:1; 3:7, 8; 11:1; 13:35; 14:3.

6. 1:5; 1:5, 9; 1:40, 45; 4:13; 6:13; 7:3; 7:26; 7:37; 13:37; 14:29; 14:31; 14:50, 52; 14:55; 14:56–57; 15:1.

7. 5:3–4; 6:30; 10:29; 14:69–70; 15:40.

8. Neirynck, *Duality in Mark,* 35.

Neirynck's list 10, consisting of instances where Mark has two temporal or local expressions in the same context. Neirynck's list includes sixty-nine dual temporal or local expressions in Mark.[9] I have eliminated some of these and added others for various reasons. I eliminate one of Neirynck's examples by considering Mark 6:31–32 as a single instance rather than two (see below). I omit Mark 9:2, since only one of the expressions here is truly local.[10] I also omit Mark 11:1, since it contains a triple expression rather than a double.[11] We can add three examples that Neirynck puts in other categories: Mark 3:7c–8a (from Judea/and from Jerusalem); 5:12 (into the pigs/into them); and 13:35 (when/in the evening). We can also add others that Neirynck does not include: Mark 1:21b (immediately/on the Sabbath); 2:19bc (while/as long as); 3:7b, 8b (from Galilee/from Idumaea); 3:8cd (across the Jordan/and around Tyre and Sidon); 4:5 (on the rocky ground/where there was not much soil); 4:15ab (those beside the road/where the word is sowed); 4:15cd (when they hear/immediately); 4:16 (when they hear/immediately); 4:21 (under the bushel/under the bed); 5:13 (into the sea/in the sea); 5:21 (in the boat/back to the other side); 6:35 (a late hour/a late hour); 9:33–34 (on the way/on the way); 10:27 (with God/with God); 12:23 (at the resurrection/when they rise); and 16:1–2 (when the Sabbath had passed/on the first day of the week).

For my analysis, I need instances where we can compare all three gospels. The following are therefore inadequate for our purpose, since no sentence or clause parallel to Mark occurs in Matthew and/or Luke: Mark 1:35; 1:38; 1:45; 2:4; 2:4; 3:34; 5:5a; 5:5b; 5:19; 6:3; 6:6; 6:21; 6:25; 6:45; 6:51; 7:17; 7:21; 7:24; 7:33; 8:4; 9:28; 9:33; 9:33–34; 10:1; 11:4; 11:11; 11:11–12; 11:14; 11:27;[12] 13:3; 13:35; 14:3; 14:9; 14:66. That leaves fifty instances where we can compare the readings of all three gospels. These fall into the categories set out in Chapter 6 in Table 6.2.

In that table I list fourteen examples in my category 5a (Matthew and Luke have different halves of the dual expression). Several of the expressions in this category require further discussion, since my analysis of these differs from that of Tuckett.[13]

First, Tuckett cites Mark 1:12(–13) as an example of the category that I have designated 5b (Matthew and Luke both have the same half). I am not sure why, since here Mark has two local expressions, one that he shares with

---

9. Ibid., 94–96.

10. In contrast to "onto a mountain," the expressions "by themselves" and "alone" do not actually designate a place.

11. Likewise Mark 6:4, though this is not on Neirynck's list.

12. In Mark 11:27, the two halves of the dual expression occur in two different sentences. Though the second sentence has a parallel, the first does not.

13. Tuckett, *Revival of the Griesbach Hypothesis*, 20, with notes on 194.

Matthew (εἰς τὴν ἔρημον) and one that he shares with Luke (ἔν τῇ ἐρήμῳ). This then is an example of my category 5a.

Second, Tuckett analyzes the dual expression in Mark 1:28 as an instance of my category 8 (Matthew has neither half, while Luke has one). The reason, I suspect, is that, following Aland's synopsis, he has overlooked the parallel to Mark 1:28 in Matthew 4:24a. With that verse included, Mark has the expression attested by Matthew along with that attested by Luke. Again, rhis is an instance of my category 5a.

Third, Tuckett cites Mark 3:8 as an instance where Matthew has neither half while Luke has one. It is unclear to what dual expression in this verse Tuckett is referring. Mark 3:7–8 includes six expressions of place, the first four of which are the following:

| Matt 4:25 | Mark 3:7–8 | Luke 6:17 |
|---|---|---|
| ἀπὸ τῆς Γαλιλαίας | ἀπὸ τῆς Γαλιλαίας | |
| καὶ Ἱεροσολύμων | καὶ ἀπὸ τῆς Ἰουδαίας | ἀπὸ πάσης τῆς Ἰουδαίας |
| καὶ Ἰουδαίας | καὶ ἀπὸ Ἱεροσολύμων | καὶ Ἱερουσαλήμ |
| | καὶ ἀπὸ τῆς Ἰδουμαίας | |

Neirynck cites "from Judaea/from Jerusalem" as an instance of a dual expression in which one half is a special or more specific case of the other.[14] Since Matthew and Luke each have both halves, this is an instance of my category 1. Additionally, Mark designates a locale north of Judea ("from Galilee") and another south of Judea ("from Idumaea"). If we count these as another dual expression, it would belong to my category 6 (Matthew has one, Luke has neither). Finally, Mark has two other local expressions following these:

| πέραν τοῦ Ἰορδάνου | πέραν τοῦ Ἰορδάνου | |
|---|---|---|
| | περὶ Τύρον καὶ Σιδῶνα | τῆς παραλίου Τύρου καὶ Σιδῶνος |

Since Matthew and Luke each have one half, this dual expression belongs to my category 5a.

Fourth, Tuckett follows Neirynck in analyzing Mark 6:31 (κατ᾽ ἰδίαν / εἰς ἔρημον τόπον) separately from 6:32 (εἰς ἔρημον τόπον / κατ᾽ ἰδίαν). This procedure obscures the relation between the two verses. The former has a parallel only in Luke, while the latter has a parallel only in Matthew:

14. Neirynck, *Duality in Mark*, 96.

| Matt 14:13 | Mark 6:31–32 | Luke 9:10b |
|---|---|---|
| | 31 δεῦτε ὑμεῖς αὐτοὶ | παραλαβὼν αὐτοὺς … |
| | κατ᾽ ἰδίαν | κατ᾽ ἰδίαν |
| | εἰς ἔρημον τόπον | εἰς πόλιν καλουμένην Βηθσαϊδά |
| ἐν πλοίῳ | 32 ἐν τῷ πλοίῳ | |
| εἰς ἔρημον τόπον | εἰς ἔρημον τόπον | |
| κατ᾽ ἰδίαν | κατ᾽ ἰδίαν | |

On the one hand, Mark 6:31 parallels Luke 9:10b, though Luke has the expression "to a city called Bethsaida" for "to a deserted spot." On the other hand, Mark 6:32 parallels Matt 14:13. Thus, taking 6:31 and 6:32 together, we have an example of my category 5a: two instances of the local expression εἰς ἔρημον τόπον, one with a parallel in Matthew and one with a parallel in Luke. I do not count 6:31 or 6:32 separately, since the former has no parallel in Matthew and the latter has no parallel in Luke.

Fifth, Tuckett analyzes the dual expression in Mark 10:27 as an instance where Matthew and Luke have the same half (my category 5b). However, in this instance Mark has two different forms of the expression "with God" (παρὰ θεῷ, παρὰ τῷ θεῷ). The first matches that of Matthew (anarthrous and preceding δυνατά), while the second matches that of Luke (articular and following δυνατά). This example therefore is an instance of my category 5a.

Sixth and finally, Tuckett analyzes the dual expression in Mark 16:2 as an instance where Matthew and Luke each have the same half (my category 5b). The following comparison suggests otherwise:

| Matt 28:1 | Mark 16:2 | Luke 24:1 |
|---|---|---|
| | λίαν πρωΐ | ὄρθρου βαθέως |
| εἰς μίαν σαββάτων | τῇ μιᾷ τῶν σαββάτων | τῇ δὲ μιᾷ τῶν σαββάτων |
| τῇ ἐπιφωσκούσῃ | ἀνατείλαντος τοῦ ἡλίου | |

Here, all three gospels have the expression "on the first day of the week." Apart from this phrase common to all three gospels, none of the remaining expressions is exactly the same as any other. Yet Mark and Luke have temporal expressions that are parallel in meaning, indicating a time very early in the day. Likewise, Mark and Matthew have temporal expressions that are parallel in meaning, indicating first light or sunrise. Since Mark has two expressions for dawn, one paralleled in Matthew and the other in Luke, it appears that this is another example of my category 5a.

# Select Bibliography on the Synoptic Problem

Allen, Willougby C. *A Critical and Exegetical Commentary on the Gospel According to Matthew*. ICC. New York: Scribner's, 1907.

Bellinzoni, Arthur J., ed. *The Two-Source Hypothesis: A Critical Appraisal*. Macon, GA: Mercer University Press, 1985.

Benoit, Pierre, and M.-É. Boismard, ed. *Synopse des quatre Evangiles en français*. 3 vols. Paris: Editions du Cerf, 1965–77.

Black, David Alan, and David R. Beck. *Rethinking the Synoptic Problem*. Grand Rapids: Baker Academic, 2001.

Boismard, M.-É. "Réponse aux deux autres hypotheses." Pages 259–88 in *The Interrelations of the Gospels*. Edited by David L. Dungan. Leuven: Leuven University Press, 1990.

———. "The Two-Source Theory at an Impasse." *NTS* 26 (1979): 1–17.

Buchanan, George Wesley. "Has the Griesbach Hypothesis Been Falsified?" *JBL* 93 (1974): 550–72.

Burrows, Edward W. "The Use of Textual Theories to Explain Agreements of Matthew and Luke Against Mark." Pages 87–99 in *Studies in New Testament Language and Text*. Edited by J. K. Elliott. Leiden: Brill, 1976.

Butler, Basil Christopher. *The Originality of St Matthew: A Critique of the Two-Document Hypothesis*. Cambridge: Cambridge University Press, 1951.

Catchpole, David R. "Did Q Exist?" Pages 1–59 in *The Quest for Q*. Edited by David R. Catchpole. Edinburgh: T & T Clark, 1993.

Dewey, Joanna. "Order in the Synoptic Gospels: A Critique." *Second Century* 6 (1987/88): 68–82.

Dickerson, Patrick L. "The New Character Narrative in Luke-Acts and the Synoptic Problem." *JBL* 116 (1997): 291–312.

Downing, F. Gerald. "Compositional Conventions and the Synoptic Problem." *JBL* 107 (1988): 69–85. Repr. pages 152–73 in F. Gerald Downing, *Doing Things with Words in the First Christian Century*. JSNTSS 200. Sheffield: Sheffield Academic Press, 2000.

———. "A Paradigm Perplex: Luke, Matthew and Mark." *NTS* 38 (1992): 15–36. Repr. pages 174–97 in F. Gerald Downing, *Doing Things with Words in the First Christian Century*. JSNTSS 200. Sheffield: Sheffield Academic Press, 2000.

———. "Redaction Criticism: Josephus' Antiquities and the Synoptic Problem, I, II." *JSNT* 8 (1980): 46–65; 9 (1980): 29–48.

———. "Towards the Rehabilitation of Q." *NTS* 11 (1964/65): 169–81. Repr. pages 269–85 in *The Two-Source Hypothesis: A Critical Appraisal*. Edited by Arthur J. Bellinzoni. Macon, GA: Mercer University Press, 1985.

Dungan, David Laird. *A History of the Synoptic Problem: The Canon, the Text, the Composition, and the Interpretation of the Gospels*. New York: Doubleday, 1999.

———. "Two-Gospel Hypothesis." Pages 6:671–79 in *The Anchor Bible Dictionary*. 6 vols. Edited by David Noel Freedman. Garden City, NY: Doubleday, 1992.

———, ed. *The Interrelations of the Gospels*. BETL 95. Leuven: Leuven University Press, 1990

Elliott, J. K., ed. *The Language and Style of the Gospel of Mark: An Edition of C. H. Turner's "Notes on Marcan Usage" Together with Other Comparable Studies*. Leiden: Brill, 1993.

Ennulat, Andreas. *Die "Minor Agreements": Untersuchungen zu einer offenen Frage des synoptischen Problems*. WUNT 2.62. Tübingen: Mohr, 1994.

Farrer, A. M. "On Dispensing with Q." Pages 55–88 in *Studies in the Gospels: Essays in Memory of R. H. Lightfoot*. Edited by D. E. Nineham. Oxford: Blackwell, 1955. Repr. pages 321–56 in *The Two-Source Hypothesis: A Critical Appraisal*. Edited by Arthur J. Bellinzoni. Macon, GA: Mercer University Press, 1985.

Farmer, William R. *The Last Twelve Verses of Mark*. SNTSMS 25. Cambridge: Cambridge University Press, 1974.

———. "Modern Developments of Griesbach's Hypothesis." *NTS* 23 (1976/77): 275–95.

———. *The Synoptic Problem: A Critical Analysis*. New York: Macmillan, 1964. Repr. Dillsboro, NC: Western North Carolina Press, 1976.

———, ed. *New Synoptic Studies: The Cambridge Gospel Conference and Beyond*. Macon, GA: Mercer University Press, 1983.

Fitzmyer, Joseph A. "The Priority of Mark and the 'Q' Source in Luke." Pages 1:131–70 in *Jesus and Man's Hope*. Edited by D. G. Miller. 2 vols. Pittsburgh: Pittsburgh Theological Seminary, 1970. Repr. pages 3–40 in Fitzmyer, *To Advance the Gospel: New Testament Studies*. New York: Crossroad, 1981.

Friedrichsen, Timothy A. "The Minor Agreements of Matthew and Luke Against Mark: Critical Observations on R. B. Vinson's Statistical Analysis." *ETL* 65 (1989): 395–408.

Frye, Roland Mushat. "The Synoptic Problems and Analogies in Other Literatures." Pages 261–302 in *The Relationships among the Gospels: An Interdisciplinary Dialogue*. Edited by William O. Walker Jr. San Antonio: Trinity University Press, 1978.

Fuchs, Albert. *Sprachliche Untersuchungen zu Matthäus und Lukas: ein Beitrag zur Quellenkritik*. Analecta Biblica 49. Rome: Biblical Institute Press, 1971.

Goodacre, Mark. "*Beyond the Q Impasse* or Down a Blind Alley?" *JSNT* 76 (1999): 33–52.

———. *The Case Against Q: Studies in Markan Priority and the Synoptic Problem*. Harrisburg, PA: Trinity Press International, 2002.

———. "Fatigue in the Synoptics." *NTS* 44 (1998): 45–58.

———. *Goulder and the Gospels: An Examination of a New Paradigm*. Sheffield: Sheffield Academic Press, 1996.

———. *The Synoptic Problem: A Way Through the Maze*. London/New York: Sheffield Academic Press, 2001.

Goulder, Michael D. "Is Q a Juggernaut?" *JBL* 115 (1996): 667–81.

———. *Luke: A New Paradigm*. 2 vols. JSNTSS 20. Sheffield: Sheffield Academic Press, 1989.

———. *Midrash and Lection in Matthew*. London: SPCK, 1974.

———. "On Putting Q to the Test." *NTS* 24 (1978): 218–34.

———. "The Order of a Crank." Pages 111–30 in *Synoptic Studies: The Ampleworth Conferences of 1982 and 1983*. Edited by C. M. Tuckett. JSNTSS 7. Sheffield: JSOT Press, 1984.

Gundry, Robert H. "Matthean Foreign Bodies in Agreements of Luke with Matthew Against Mark: Evidence that Luke Used Matthew." Pages 1466–95 in *The Four Gospels 1992*. Edited by F. van Segbroeck et al. 3 vols. BETL 100. Leuven: Leuven University Press, 1992.

———. *Matthew: A Commentary on His Literary and Theological Art*. Grand Rapids: Eerdmans, 1982.

———. "A Rejoinder on Matthean Foreign Bodies in Luke 10, 25–28." *ETL* 71 (1995): 139–50.

Hawkins, John C. *Horae Synopticae: Contributions to the Study of the Synoptic Problem*. 2nd ed. Oxford: Clarendon Press, 1909. Repr. Grand Rapids: Baker, 1968.

Head, Peter M. *Christology and the Synoptic Problem: An Argument for Markan Priority*. SNTSMS 94. Cambridge: Cambridge University Press, 1997.

Huggins, Ronald V. "Matthean Posteriority: A Preliminary Proposal." *NovT* 34 (1992): 1–22. Repr. pages 204–25 in *The Synoptic Problem and Q: Selected Studies from Novum Testamentum*. Edited by David E. Orton. Leiden: Brill, 1999.

Johnson, Sherman E. *The Griesbach Hypothesis and Redaction Criticism*. SBLMS 41. Atlanta: Scholars Press, 1991.

Koester, Helmut. "History and Development of Mark's Gospel (From Mark to Secret Mark and 'Canonical' Mark)." Pages 35–57 in *Colloquy on New Testament Studies: A Time for Reappraisal and Fresh Approaches*. Edited by Bruce Corley. Macon, GA: Mercer University Press, 1983.

Kümmel, Werner Georg. *Introduction to the New Testament*. Rev. ed. Nashville: Abingdon, 1975.

―――. *The New Testament: The History of the Investigation of Its Problems.* Nashville: Abingdon, 1972.

Lindsey, Robert L. "A Modified Two-Document Theory of the Synoptic Dependence and Interdependence." *NovT* 6 (1963): 239–63. Repr. pages 7–31 in *The Synoptic Problem and Q: Selected Studies from Novum Testamentum.* Edited by David E. Orton. Leiden: Brill, 1999.

―――. "A New Approach to the Synoptic Gospels." *Mishkan* 17–18 (1992–93): 87–106.

Linnemann, Eta. "Der (wiedergefundene) Markusschluss." ZTK 66 (1969): 255–87.

Lockton, William. "The Origin of the Gospels." *Church Quarterly Review* 94 (1922): 216–39.

Longstaff, Thomas R. W. *Evidence of Conflation in Mark? A Study in the Synoptic Problem.* Missoula, MT: Scholars Press, 1977.

Longstaff, Thomas R. W., and Page A. Thomas. *The Synoptic Problem: A Bibliography, 1716–1988.* New Gospel Studies 4. Macon, GA: Mercer University Press, 1988.

Luz, Ulrich. *Matthew 1–7: A Continental Commentary.* Minneapolis: Fortress, 1989.

McIver, Robert K., and Marie Carroll. "Experiments to Develop Criteria for Determining the Existence of Written Sources, and Their Potential Implications for the Synoptic Problem." *JBL* 121 (2002): 667–87.

McLoughlin, S. "Les accords mineurs Mt-Lc contre Mc et le problème synoptique." Pages 17–40 in *De Jésus aux évangiles: tradition et rédaction dans les évangiles synoptiques.* Edited by I. de la Potterie. Gembloux: Duculot, 1967.

McNicol, Allan J., ed., with David L. Dungan and David B. Peabody. *Beyond the Q Impasse—Luke's Use of Matthew: A Demonstration by the Research Team of the International Institute for Gospel Studies.* Preface by William R. Farmer. Valley Forge, PA: Trinity Press International, 1996.

Meijboom, Hajo Uden. *A History and Critique of the Origin of the Marcan Hypothesis 1835–1866: A Contemporary Report Rediscovered.* Translated and edited by John J. Kiwiet. New Gospel Studies 8. Macon, GA: Mercer University Press, 1993.

Metzger, Bruce M. *A Textual Commentary on the Greek New Testament.* 2nd ed. Stuttgart: Deutsche Bibelgesellschaft, 1994.

Neirynck, Frans. *Duality in Mark: Contribution to the Study of the Markan Redaction.* 2nd ed. BETL 31. Leuven: Leuven University Press, 1988.

―――. "Luke 10:25–28: A Foreign Body in Luke?" Pages 149–65 in *Crossing the Boundaries: Essays in Biblical Interpretation in Honour of Michael D. Goulder.* Edited by S. E. Porter et al. Biblical Interpretation Series 8. Leiden, 1994.

————. "Synoptic Problem." Pages 845a–48b in *The Interpreter's Dictionary of the Bible, Supplement.* Edited by Keith Krim. Nashville: Abingdon, 1976. Repr. pages 85–93 in *The Two-Source Hypothesis: A Critical Appraisal.* Edited by Arthur J. Bellinzoni Jr. Macon, GA: Mercer University Press, 1985.

————. "ΤΙΣ ΕΣΤΙΝ Ο ΠΑΙΣΑΣ ΣΕ: Mt 26,68 / Lk 22,64 (diff. Mk 14,65)." *ETL* 63 (1987): 5–47. Repr. pages 95–138 in Neirynck, *Evangelica II: 1982–1991: Collected Essays.* Edited by F. Van Segbroeck. BETL 99. Leuven: Leuven University Press, 1991.

————, with T. Hansen and F. Van Segbroeck. *The Minor Agreements of Matthew and Luke Against Mark with a Cumulative List.* BETL 37. Leuven: Leuven University Press, 1974.

Neville, David J. *Arguments from Order in Synoptic Source Criticism: A History and Critique.* Macon, GA: Mercer University Press, 1994.

Orchard, Bernard. *Matthew, Luke & Mark.* 2nd ed. Manchester: Koinonia Press, 1977.

Orton, David E., ed. *The Synoptic Problem and Q: Selected Studies from Novum Testamentum.* Leiden: Brill, 1999.

Parker, Pierson. "The Posteriority of Mark." Pages 67–142 in *New Synoptic Studies: The Cambridge Gospel Conference and Beyond.* Edited by William R. Farmer. Macon, GA: Mercer University Press, 1983.

Peabody, David Barrett. *Mark as Composer.* New Gospel Studies 1. Macon, GA: Mercer University Press, 1987.

Peabody, David B., ed., with Lamar Cope and Allan J. McNicol. *One Gospel from Two: Mark's Use of Matthew and Luke: A Demonstration by the Research Team of the International Institute for Renewal of Gospel Studies.* Harrisburg, PA: Trinity Press International, 2002.

Price, Ron. "A Three Source Theory for the Synoptic Problem." *Journal of Biblical Studies* 1:4 (2001). Online: http://journalofbiblicalstudies.org.

Rolland, Philippe. "L'arrière-fond sémitique des évangiles synoptiques." *ETL* 60 (1984): 358–62.

————. "Les évangiles des premières communautés chrétiennes." *RB* 90 (1983):161–201.

————. "Jésus connaissait leurs pensées." *ETL* 62 (1986): 118–21.

————. "Marc, première harmonie évangélique?" *RB* 90 (1983): 23–79.

————. "A New Look at the Synoptic Question." *EuroJTh* 8 (1999): 133–44.

————. "Les prédécesseurs de Marc: les sources présynoptiques de Mc, II, 18–22 et parallèles." *RB* 89 (1982): 370–405.

————. *Les premiers évangiles: un nouveau regard sur le problème synoptique.* Lectio Divina 116. Paris: Cerf, 1984.

————. "La question synoptique demande-t-elle une réponse compliquée?" *Biblica* 70 (1989): 217–23.

―――. "Synoptique, Question." Pages 1227–31 in *Dictionnaire encyclopédique de la Bible*. Maredsous, 1987.

Rollston, Christopher A., ed. *The Gospels According to Michael Goulder: A North American Response*. Harrisburg, PA: Trinity Press International, 2002.

Sanders, E. P. "The Argument from Order and the Relationship Between Matthew and Luke." *NTS* 15 (1968/69): 249–61. Repr. pages 409–25 in *The Two-Source Hypothesis: A Critical Appraisal*. Edited by Arthur J. Bellinzoni. Macon, GA: Mercer University Press, 1985.

―――. "The Overlaps of Mark and Q and the Synoptic Problem." *NTS* 19 (1972/73): 453–65.

Sanders, E. P., and Margaret Davies. *Studying the Synoptic Gospels*. Philadelphia: Trinity Press International, 1989.

Stein, Robert H. *Studying the Synoptic Gospels: Origin and Interpretation*. 2nd ed. Grand Rapids: Baker, 2001.

Stoldt, Hans-Herbert. *History and Criticism of the Marcan Hypothesis*. Translated and edited by Donald L. Niewyk. Introduction by William R. Farmer. Macon, GA: Mercer University Press, 1980.

Strecker, Georg, ed. *Minor Agreements: Symposium Göttingen 1991*. Göttingen: Vandenhoeck & Ruprecht, 1993.

Streeter, Burnett Hillman. *The Four Gospels: A Study of Origins*. Rev. ed. London: Macmillan, 1930.

Styler, G. M. "The Priority of Mark." Pages 285–316 in C. F. D. Moule, *The Birth of the New Testament*. 3rd ed. San Francisco: Harper & Row, 1982.

Talbert, Charles H., and Edgar V. McKnight. "Can the Griesbach Hypothesis Be Falsified?" *JBL* 91 (1972): 338–68.

Taylor, Vincent. *The Gospel According to St. Mark*. London: Macmillan, 1952.

Tevis, Dennis Gordon. "An Analysis of Words and Phrases Characteristic of the Gospel of Matthew." Ph.D. diss., Southern Methodist University, 1983.

Tuckett, Christopher M. "The Argument from Order and the Synoptic Problem." *TZ* 36 (1980): 338–54.

―――. "Arguments from Order: Definition and Evaluation." Pages 197–219 in *Synoptic Studies: The Ampleforth Conferences of 1982 and 1983*. Edited by Christopher M. Tuckett. JSNTSS 7. Sheffield: JSOT Press, 1984.

―――. "The Existence of Q." Pages 19–47 in *The Gospel Behind the Gospels: Current Studies in Q*. Edited by Ronald A. Piper. Leiden: Brill, 1995.

―――. "The Griesbach Hypothesis in the 19th Century." *JSNT* 3 (1979): 29–60.

―――. "On the Relationship Between Matthew and Luke." *NTS* 30 (1984): 130–42.

―――. *The Revival of the Griesbach Hypothesis: An Analysis and Appraisal*. SNTSMS 44. Cambridge/New York: Cambridge University Press, 1983.

————. "Synoptic Problem." Pages 6:263–70 in *The Anchor Bible Dictionary*. Edited by David Noel Freedman. New York: Doubleday, 1992.

————, ed. *Synoptic Studies: The Ampleforth Conferences of 1982 and 1983*. JSNTSS 7. Sheffield: JSOT Press, 1984.

Vinson, Richard Bolling. "The Significance of the Minor Agreements as an Argument Against the Two-Document Hypothesis." Ph.D. diss., Duke University, 1984.

Walker, William O. Jr. "Order in the Synoptic Gospels: A Critique." *Second Century* 6 (1987/88): 83–97.

————. "The State of the Synoptic Question: Some Reflections on the Work of Tuckett and McNicol." *Perkins Journal* 40 (1987): 14–21.

————, ed. *The Relationships among the Gospels: An Interdisciplinary Dialogue*. San Antonio: Trinity University Press, 1978.

Wenham, John. *Redating Matthew, Mark & Luke: A Fresh Assault on the Synoptic Problem*. London: Hodder & Stoughton, 1991; Downers Grove, IL: InterVarsity Press, 1992.

# Index of Ancient Sources

Mark (cont.)

| | |
|---|---|
| 1:23-28 | 63, 84 |
| 1:24 | 230 |
| 1:24-25 | 28n. 31 |
| 1:25 | 230 |
| 1:25-26 | 230 |
| 1:26 | 230 |
| 1:27 | 26, 26n. 29, 230 |
| 1:28 | 39, 230, 270 |
| 1:29-30 | 253 |
| 1:29-31 | 86, 102, 120 |
| 1:32 | 122, 209, 229 |
| 1:32-34 | 102, 120, 228, 265 |
| 1:33 | 27, 229 |
| 1:34 | 28n. 31, 84, 209, 229 |
| 1:35 | 269 |
| 1:35-39 | 63 |
| 1:37 | 39 |
| 1:38 | 39, 269 |
| 1:39 | 87n. 11 |
| 1:40 | 268n. 6 |
| 1:40-42 | 63, 64 |
| 1:40-45 | 64, 86 |
| 1:42 | 268 |
| 1:43-44 | 63, 64, 74 |
| 1:43-45 | 28n. 31 |
| 1:44 | 63, 64 |
| 1:45 | 28, 63, 64, 74, 268n. 6, 269 |
| 2:1 | 268n. 5 |
| 2:1-3:6 | 229, 232n. 1 |
| 2:1-22 | 63, 90 |
| 2:2 | 27-28 |
| 2:3-3:6 | 159 |
| 2:4 | 269 |
| 2:7 | 39 |
| 2:8 | 39 |
| 2:10 | 233n. 3 |
| 2:12 | 39 |
| 2:13 | 26n. 29 |
| 2:13-22 | 63 |
| 2:16 | 39 |
| 2:17 | 159 |
| 2:18-22 | 165 |
| 2:19 | 269 |
| 2:19-20 | 159 |
| 2:20 | 44 |
| 2:23-3:6 | 63 |

| | |
|---|---|
| 2:23-24 | 230 |
| 2:23-28 | 159, 229-30 |
| 2:25-26 | 230 |
| 2:26 | 233 |
| 2:27 | 225, 232-33 |
| 2:28 | 230, 233, 233n. 2 |
| 3:1-6 | 63, 120, 159 |
| 3:4 | 40 |
| 3:5 | 25, 39, 255 |
| 3:7 | 40, 49, 175, 253, 268n. 5, 269 |
| 3:7-8 | 269-70 |
| 3:7-11 | 129n. 14 |
| 3:7-12 | 102, 119, 129, 129n. 14, 234, 265 |
| 3:8 | 130, 209, 268n. 5, 269-70 |
| 3:8-9 | 175 |
| 3:10 | 39, 130 |
| 3:10-12 | 28n. 31 |
| 3:11 | 39, 84 |
| 3:11-12 | 102, 237 |
| 3:12 | 102, 129n. 14 |
| 3:13 | 75, 88 |
| 3:13-19 | 75 |
| 3:14 | 268 |
| 3:16 | 268 |
| 3:20 | 28, 75 |
| 3:22-30 | 102, 113 |
| 3:27 | 44 |
| 3:27-29 | 113 |
| 3:30 | 102 |
| 3:31 | 40 |
| 3:31-35 | 152, 162 |
| 3:32 | 25, 39 |
| 3:34 | 25, 269 |
| 4:1 | 40, 175 |
| 4:1-2 | 26n. 29 |
| 4:1-34 | 86, 117 |
| 4:5 | 269 |
| 4:10 | 25 |
| 4:10-12 | 28n. 31 |
| 4:13 | 268n. 6 |
| 4:15 | 269 |
| 4:16 | 269 |
| 4:21 | 269 |
| 4:22 | 28n. 31 |
| 4:23 | 225 |

Acts (cont.)

| | |
|---|---|
| 3:11 | 163 |
| 4:4 | 163 |
| 4:36 | 39 |
| 5:12 | 163 |
| 5:16 | 163 |
| 6:1-6 | 181 |
| 6:8-7:1 | 178 |
| 6:9 | 48 |
| 6:12-7:1 | 114 |
| 6:13-14 | 115 |
| 7:55-57 | 178 |
| 7:55-60 | 114 |
| 8:14 | 211 |
| 8:29 | 47n. 2 |
| 8:30 | 30 |
| 9:1 | 47n. 2 |
| 9:4 | 40 |
| 10:28 | 47n. 2 |
| 12:1-2 | 161 |
| 12:12 | 163 |
| 13:8 | 39 |
| 15:1 | 158 |
| 15:5 | 158 |
| 18:2 | 47n. 2 |
| 18:7 | 51 |
| 18:27 | 16 |
| 21:20-25 | 158 |
| 22:24 | 39 |
| 22:26 | 47n. 2 |
| 23:14 | 47n. 2 |

Romans

| | |
|---|---|
| 1:16 | 246 |
| 16:6 | 16 |
| 16:12 | 16 |

1 Corinthians

| | |
|---|---|
| 1:23 | 159 |
| 5:6-8 | 86, 175 |
| 11:20 | 218 |

| | |
|---|---|
| 11:23-26 | 176, 218 |
| 16:12 | 16 |
| 16:19 | 16 |

2 Corinthians

| | |
|---|---|
| 8:4 | 16 |

Galatians, 158

| | |
|---|---|
| 2:1-10 | 161 |
| 5:9 | 86, 175 |

Colossians

| | |
|---|---|
| 2:16 | 233n. 2 |

1 Timothy

| | |
|---|---|
| 6:3 | 47n. 2 |

Hebrews

| | |
|---|---|
| 4:16 | 47n. 2 |
| 7:25 | 47n. 2 |
| 11:6 | 47n. 2 |
| 12:9 | 16 |
| 12:18 | 47n. 2 |
| 12:22 | 47n. 2 |
| 12:25 | 16 |

James

| | |
|---|---|
| 3:2 | 16 |
| 5:7-9 | 161 |
| 5:16 | 16 |

Revelation

| | |
|---|---|
| 5:4 | 16 |

## APOSTOLIC FATHERS

*Didache*

| | |
|---|---|
| 6:2-3 | 158 |
| 9:2 | 160 |
| 16:1-8 | 161 |

# Index of Modern Authors

McNicol, Allan J., 4n. 14, 36n. 37, 40n. 39, 47, 53-54
Meijboom, Hajo Uden, 1n. 1
Metzger, Bruce, 253-54, 253n. 7
Moule, C. F. D., 2n. 3

Neirynck, Frans, 2n. 3, 2n. 5, 8, 8n. 3, 8n. 5, 122-23, 122n. 8, 122n. 10, 136n. 4, 267-70, 268n. 3, 268n. 8, 269n. 11, 270n. 14
Neville, David J., 60n. 2
Nineham, D. E., 31n. 35

Orchard, Bernard, 4n. 14

Parker, Pierson, 119n. 1, 122n. 8
Peabody, David B., 4n. 14, 17, 17n. 22, 36n. 37, 40, 40nn. 38-39
Price, Ron, 2, 2n. 6

Riley, Harold, 31n. 36
Rolland, Philippe, 122n. 8, 138-41, 138nn. 8-9, 139nn. 10-12, 164-66, 165n. 1, 166n. 2
Rollston, Christopher A., 3n. 10

Sabbe, M., 178n. 1
Sanders, E. P., 9, 9n. 10, 119, 119n. 2, 138, 138nn. 8-9

Sandevoir, P., 138n. 8
Schweizer, Eduard, 31n. 35
Stein, Robert H., 2n. 3, 13n. 16, 14nn. 18-19
Stoldt, Hans-Herbert, 1n. 1
Streeter, Burnett Hillman, 1, 1n. 2, 8n. 1, 8n. 5, 8n. 9, 9n. 7, 13, 13n. 14, 13n. 17, 14, 30, 62, 62n. 4
Styler, G. M., 2n. 3

Talbert, Charles H., 4n. 15
Taylor, Vincent, 31n. 35, 252-53, 252n. 5, 254n. 10
Tevis, Dennis Gordon, 56n. 5
Tuckett, Christopher M., 2n. 3, 3n. 10, 4n. 15, 8n. 5, 13n. 16, 60n. 2, 64-65, 64n. 10, 121-23, 121n. 5, 122n. 11, 122nn. 8-9, 267-71, 267n. 1, 269n. 13
Turner, C. H., 23

van Segbroeck, Frans, 8n. 3
Vinson, Richard Bolling, 9, 9n. 11

Walker, William O., Jr., 121, 121n. 7, 166, 166n. 3
Weiss, Johannes, 31n. 36
Wellhausen, Julius, 265
Wenham, John, 3n. 12